DATE DUE			

Philosophical
Theology

IN TWO VOLUMES

VOLUME I

Philosophical Theology

by

F. R. TENNANT, D.D., B.Sc.

*Fellow of Trinity College & Lecturer
in the University of
Cambridge*

VOLUME I

THE SOUL

&

ITS FACULTIES

CAMBRIDGE
AT THE UNIVERSITY PRESS
1928
REPRINTED
1968

Published by the Syndics of the Cambridge University Press
Bentley House, 200 Euston Road, London, N.W. 1
American Branch: 32 East 57th Street, New York, N.Y. 10022

PUBLISHER'S NOTE

Cambridge University Press Library Editions are re-issues of out-
of-print standard works from the Cambridge catalogue. The texts
are unrevised and, apart from minor corrections, reproduce the
latest published edition.

Standard Book Number: 521 07431 2
Library of Congress Catalogue Card Number: 29-3316

First published 1928
Reprinted 1968

First printed in Great Britain at the University Press, Cambridge
Reprinted in Great Britain by John Dickens & Co. Ltd, Northampton

PREFACE

This work is intended primarily for students of philosophical theology, or of those tracts of philosophy which have bearing on the cognitive basis of religion: the field that is usually and less aptly called philosophy of religion. But it covers so much of the fields of psychology and epistemology, that it is hoped to prove not without use to such as read those subjects without paramount interest in their theological bearing.

It is through knowledge about the self, mankind and the world that developed belief in God is mediated; and it is in relation to such knowledge, its nature, presuppositions, scope and validity, that the intellectual status of theology, and the reasonableness of theistic conviction, are to be estimated. The present volume accordingly deals with the human self, and with the mental functions of the social individual that are involved in scientific and theological thought. It will be succeeded by another volume in which the theistic interpretation of the world will be discussed, in the light of the prolegomena here set forth and with the aid of the conclusions to which the propaedeutic studies, here pursued, are taken to point.

The student of theology, in the comprehensive sense that has been indicated, needs to know what is known, and to be acquainted with the main types of theory, concerning the self as knower, its capacities and faculties, and concerning the world and our science thereof, in so far as such knowledge bears upon his own quest. He must therefore be equipped with learning in psychology and theory of knowledge; he must have some acquaintance with the facts and theories, with the methods and the limitations, of the natural sciences: and he must be familiar with the outstanding systems of metaphysic. Happily, there is much in these vast fields which it does not behove even the complete theologian to study. At the outset of his course, however, the student is not in a position always to discern what portions of them he can afford to neglect, as having no indirect relevance; to estimate the relative importance of topics that seem relevant; or to associate scattered items between which riper learning would see connexion. It is with a view to affording temporarily acceptable guidance, by doing this selective work for him, and in consequence of petitions to proffer to others help of this sort that some believe they have received in my lecture-room, that this treatise has been undertaken.

Seeing that the work, as a whole, does not set forth an assumed theological world-view, it does not pursue, as a mode of exposition, the *ordo essendi*. It does not set out from the achieved result of theistic thought, and, starting from God as *terminus a quo*, proceed in deductive fashion from the source of being to derivative existents, the world and man: theistic interpretation is only its final task. The first volume is not theological but philosophical. Concerned with studies requisite for serious discussion of the knowability of God, and for estimation of the intellectual grounds on which theology rests, it sets out from our presumptive fact-knowledge. After analysis and examination thereof, it advances from what presumably is best, as well as first, known to what, though logically prior and metaphysically ulterior, is in order of time last known. The *ordo cognoscendi* is deliberately chosen. It is only because this method is not commonly adopted in manuals on philosophy, that I have ventured to address my book to the student with interests not centring in theological issues, as possibly possessing sufficient of individuality, among the large number of cognate treatises, to offer him material on which to whet his critical faculty.

As it is part of the function of Vol. 1 to supply what is normally sought in several kinds of text-book, some portion of it necessarily consists of reproduction of facts, of analyses thereof and conclusions therefrom, already furnished by professed psychologists, logicians, etc. Such matter, though derived from standard authorities, has not been assumed to be the only doctrine in the field, or to be always beyond question. Impartiality has prescribed frequent reference to views emanating from other schools. Many books and articles have thus been drawn upon; but in outstanding degree, the *Psychological Principles* of the late Prof. J. Ward. It would have been simpler, in some of my earlier chapters, merely to refer to his pages; but, to do so, would defeat one of my purposes, viz. that of providing a concise compendium of fact and analysis, selected and arranged with relevance to the special needs of the reader that I chiefly contemplate. I can therefore only acknowedge the magnitude of my borrowing, which is greater than the explicit citations and references indicate. When these transcribed data are turned to account for construction of philosophy, the responsibility generally rests with myself, unless there is statement to the contrary.

Should a theological student, into whose hands this volume may fall, command sufficient leisure to prosecute psychological studies with more thoroughness than is provided in my selective compendium, he should turn to the fountain-head that I have mentioned. At a later stage of his psychological education, he may profitably study literature supplied by other schools of thought. But at the beginning, when he is relatively at the mercy of his teacher, I would venture to advise resort to portions of Ward's formidable work. Not because I myself regard it as the greatest single work, of any age, on the human mind; but on account of several specific characteristics of its masterliness, that make it pre-eminently suitable for the purpose now in view. Like the *Origin of Species*, it lets the facts which it marshals tell their own tale, and displays a sagacity in comparison with which, cleverness is a thing of naught. It may be read from cover to cover without the reader being able to guess from it, what are its author's metaphysical convictions: it is disinterested *science*, if abounding in the tentative theorising of a pioneer. Again, its sustained and unswerving adherence to the strictly psychological point of view, in which also it is perhaps unique, and which alone suffices to make it a classic, is another grace for which the beginner will follow on to become thankful.

In the constructive and the critical efforts put forth in the present volume, I have made plain the conclusions, as to many controversial issues, to which the collected facts or data have led me. That procedure does not of itself make impartiality, in the stating and examining of alternative views, impossible; while it may somewhat relieve tediousness by putting up a fight for the reader. But one's own partialities are generally beyond the range of one's own unaided introspection. Some of those that may lurk in my chapters, as well as defects in learning, diction, and perhaps judgement on minor matters, might have been obviated, had I submitted my proofs to others for scrutiny. But those of my friends, whose aid I most should value in revising the chapters that would most abundantly be improved by external help, are themselves engaged in more important work; so I have shrunk from seeking from them this service. I mainly regret that my loss will extend to my readers.

It will be observed that, besides positive statements that may safely be taken as assertions of established and accepted fact, others abound in this book, that rather express conclusions and opinions on disputable questions. Constant reiteration of phrases such as 'it seems', or 'I think that', is wearisome; while throwing a statement into question-form is but a transparent device. I have therefore often adopted the dogmatic method, also a device, leaving the reader to supply the writer's 'I think', as if outside algebraic brackets enclosing all that may be accounted his thought.

F. R. TENNANT

1927

CONTENTS

Chap. XII. Religious Experience . . . *pages* 306–332

CHAPTER I

Data and Method in Psychology and Philosophy

There is but one way of inquiring into the nature of the self, whether as knower or as object known, that can lead to science, and so provide a basis for trustworthy philosophy of human personality and human knowledge. It is to set out from the observable facts concerning mentality, as these are constituted at the level of experience-organisation involved in the presumptive knowledge that we employ in the conduct of life; or rather, as they are analysed and reduced to system in the science of psychology. These facts are by no means pure data, but they are our only data. Our minds have fashioned forms of thought and a body of 'knowledge', of which they cannot now wholly divest themselves, even when engaged in thinking these acquisitions away or conceiving them as transcended. What is given to our minds, at this status, is the facts on which psychology reflects: not the elements into which they may be analysed, nor the concepts which the conceptions of these elements may logically presuppose, nor the metaphysical entities of which observed actualities may be appearances, nor the simpler complexes that preceded them at earlier stages of our mental life. We can now no more begin inquiry otherwise than from fact-data, at the stage of elaboration and with that degree of compositeness and turbidity with which, as experience-units, they are actually received, than a bricklayer can start house-building with other units than bricks; though our data are capable of being resolved into constituents, just as bricks may be broken to fragments, ground to dust, or analysed into chemical elements. In the order of knowing, as distinguished from both the temporal order of the becoming of things known and the timeless order of logical presupposition, the analytica are attainable only after, and by means of, the analysanda: the antecedents are reached only through examination of the data. This is a consequence of the fact that we have elaborated, through stages of which we are obliviscent, our present system of experience-synthesis: a system that has grown up with us and is constitutive of what we call knowledge. The earliest, the simplest, the logically prior, the metaphysically ultimate, may be goals: none of them can be datum or starting-point.

Whether as common-sense people we simply accept our fact-data and, asking no question about them for conscience' sake, proceed to build with them; or whether as philosophers we first undertake the critical regress, scrutinising their construction and the logical presuppositions and processes involved therein: in either case we can *start* from no other 'origin', or point of departure, without our work being groundless. Of course our *prima facie* fact-knowledge is itself open to sifting examination. It involves prehistoric metaphysics; and man's language and modes of thought, formed with a view to practical needs, may fall short of the precision and subtilty required for exact science and philosophy. Indeed, the presuppositions involved in its pretension to be knowledge have been ascertained. But psychology is, in this respect, in no different case from that of other empirical sciences. If our foundation, epistemologically regarded, be thus provisional and unstable, so is that of all so-called knowledge of actuality that we deem worth having. Moreover, the indemonstrable beliefs that are unavoidably assumed in it, such as the trustworthiness of memory as immediate intuition of the past, the existence of other selves, the principles on which induction rests, can be explicitly confessed and allowed for: we can at least replace presumptive knowledge by learned ignorance. And if as philosophers we need eventually to choose other co-ordinates, so to speak, than those of common sense, as psychologists we can still retain our equations bodily; for, their truth not being affected by change of co-ordinates, they will be some version of the ultimate statements by which we hope to replace them. In terms of another analogy, common-sense knowledge is the original, or rather the only extant version of the original, of which metaphysics should be a translation; philosophy, as here conceived, is not free composition.[1] To drop metaphor: if any portion of the received facts or of the accepted analysis of them be disputed, it will still be

---

[1] Philosophy differs from science, at least to some extent, in both subject-matter and method. But it is not, on that account, talk too vague to be worthy of the name of science, nor eclectic opining, nor baseless speculation. It differs from science chiefly in what may be called direction of departure from the self-same data. It should be strenuous exploration of presuppositions and problems which it is not the business of any special science to investigate. Metaphysics, or, speaking more generally,

unavoidable that we make use of other portions of the same body of fact-knowledge, and of the same experience-organisation, in order to allege or to correct error in any part. Consequently this body of presumptive knowledge is not only our sole collective datum; it is also an indispensable instrument for intellectual operating, and, at the first stage at any rate, an irreplaceable vehicle for comprehensible expression of destructive criticism of its own contents. It will not be assumed that every generally received analysis is beyond question: forthcoming criticism shall be weighed. But at this stage it is insisted that the presumptive knowledge, taken over in the crude from common sense by analytical psychology, is the only starting-point for a science, and therefore for philosophy (other than vain deceit), of actual experience. When the data have been described without suppression or mutilation, without gratuitous interpretation in terms of supposititious theory framed according to predilection: then, and only then, can we reasonably proceed to consider what implications they contain, and what metaphysical interpretation they may suggest or require.

Psychology indeed not only may, but should, be expounded without influence of foregone metaphysical conclusions: that is to say, without assumptions of that sort, other than such as are involved in the very grammar of speech and in any supposition of there being knowledge of an actual world. That, at the outset, is our irreducible residuum of the metaphysical. Nevertheless, it may quite well count but for an ultimately supersedible tool or vehicle. The metaphysic of Mind, in so far as it is a theoretical end and not a provisional practical means, can only follow upon the empirical science of minds. To start from metaphysic, especially such as is constructed apart from exegesis of fact, is idle; to mate it with fact, is but to engender monstrosities and confusion. Fortunately, description and analysis can be prosecuted in psychology, as in physics, with indifference or unsectarian neutrality as to explicit metaphysics transcending experience. But too often exposition has been guided by dogmatic preconceptions—pure sensations and sensibles, neutral stuff, derivability of the psychical from the physical, etc.: and then the facts for which observation

philosophy, differs from physics, not in transcending perceptual experience, but in raising questions which physics takes as granted in consequence of its origination in, and continuity with, relatively unreflective common sense.

vouches, have been ignored, distorted, or used as a repertory whence, by advocate's selectiveness, instances have been producible in support of cunningly devised fables. These vicious tendencies, subversive of science and rendering philosophy fatuous, can be escaped if we study mental processes without prejudice as to the superiority of dualism or monism, realism or idealism, and renounce speculative gnosticism as to the unknowable. Facts must precede theory: science comes before philosophy; empiric knowledge, before science. To whatever definition and theory of knowledge in general, and to whatever doctrine of the self, we may be led, such theory must justify itself by its capacity to account for the *prima facie* facts *being what they are*. The one fact which every school of philosophy can accept as common ground, is the existence of so-called knowledge of so-called actuality by so-called persons: whatever knowledge, actuality and persons may turn out on examination to be. Our so-called knowledge may be assumptional, inadequate, a provisional makeshift; but its forthcomingness is fact with which our analyses and our refined interpretations must be compatible. It furnishes, so to say, equations which the values to be assigned to our as yet unknown quantities must satisfy. There is no escape from what these *prima facie* facts dictate, translate them how we may. Without them, as foundation, all building is in the air. They are the *sole* external control; there is nothing else whereby to distinguish opinion and speculation, baseless however ingenious and self-consistent, from knowledge and genuine philosophy of our world and what is therein. Commonsense knowledge, then, shall here be used as datum and as touchstone: the forthcomingness of it, however much it calls for scrutiny and restatement or translation, is the only broad fact that commands unanimous acceptance and can control speculation. At the outset, at least, private prepossessions such as are self-evident to this, but not to that, philosopher, will thus be avoided.

Our common ground, be it noted, does not assume that the *ratio essendi* is known, as does all procedure according to the *ordo essendi*, adopted by common sense and science. That sense-data are the *ratio cognoscendi* of the physical world, *i.e.* the conceptual world of science and common sense, is undoubted and indubitable; while that physical objects are the *ratio essendi* of sensation, is but opinion. Indeed, if the physical be not the ontal, but phenomenon thereof made by our minds as well as by ultimate reality, the physical cannot be the *ratio essendi* of the psychical. Hence it is that psychology cannot safely and finally, or otherwise than provisionally, be expounded from the standpoint of psychophysics. Such a method, based on such an assumption, involves some confusion of the phenomenal of science with the ontal of metaphysics; it assumes, as closed, a question that for psychology is open, and as to which psychological investigation may afford evidence. If dreams subsist at all through their reproductive imagery being for the time beyond correction by appeal to the impressional, our waking life in the conceptual world of common sense and science may be another sort of dream, subsisting only in virtue of the constructions of our creative and interpretative imagination being uncorrected by appeal to the ontal hidden from the mind's eye.

Whether or not we come to regard our presumptive knowledge as a dream-product of this kind, it is our sole datum whence more ultimate knowledge may possibly be derived; and it assuredly is some 'function' of such knowledge. It contains our explicandum, though it may be a faulty explication thereof. Knowledge, in the comprehensive sense of a structure of facts and generalisations, with analytica and logical presuppositions beneath, and philosophical interpretations above, may be compared with a house of several storeys, whose only entrance is on the ground-floor. Having gained access to the interior by the one door, we may proceed to explore from cellar to roof. But otherwise to seek knowledge of the house, involves either destructive violence or else recourse to the use of imagination. The latter method can be pursued perfectly well, if perfectly vainly, outside the building: the former substitutes another structure for the one to be investigated, and that on a scale which our analogy altogether fails to suggest. If to set out from fact, and to keep in touch with fact, be called empiricism, then, whatever else be found necessary, the empirical method is a *sine qua non* for knowledge of actuality of any sort.

The comparison of science and philosophy with a house, lends itself to illustrate a further important truth. For there is one respect, so far as the process of building is concerned, in which the house and the edifice of philosophical knowledge differ entirely. In house-building we first lay foundations: they are both the preconditions and the beginning of the house. But in philosophy we cannot so begin. The foundation is laid already; and no other can be laid than that has been laid. Existing structure, of empiric fact and obscure concepts, occupies the site. Philosophy cannot begin at the logical beginning, simply because the logically prior is only knowable from the logically posterior. Philosophy of the actual cannot begin otherwise than it did with Thales, *in mediis rebus*. That it has tried to do so, or to appear to do so, has sometimes persuaded itself that it has done so, we well know: likewise we know that it has then convinced but few of its own devotees as to its success. To make a purely *a priori* start, has always proved to set out, not only from arbitrary assumptions, but also from concealed brute facts. The ideal or pure science of mathematics was taken by Plato to be the ideal or paradigm of knowledge of actuality. And this, it must be affirmed, was philosophy's catastrophic fall from pristine innocence: its original sin which infected modern philosophy also from its birth. A method was thus prescribed to philosophy that is inapplicable within its sphere. Mathematics indeed lays its foundations, because it creates its entities by definition, postulates its indefinables, and has no place for 'real' categories such as those of substance and cause, which are indispensable for knowledge based on sense. But a science founded on non-actual entities such as the line without breadth, however exact, certain, and logically consistent with itself, has not necessarily any applicability to the actual world with which philosophy professes to deal.[1] Pure mathematics, and metaphysic that would fain be wholly *a priori* or pure, are free to lay any number of diverse foundations and then to construct an indefinite tale of possible worlds at their pleasure; but no such system will necessarily tell anything, worth knowing, about the one world in which we are interested. The application of a pure science to the actual world,[2] is wholly tentative and problematical.

[1] Though Euclid is used as illustration here, it is not a pure science; it presupposes knowledge of solid bodies. Definitions like that of the circle, moreover, are not creations out of nothing; the circle is partly an abstraction, partly an idealisation, constructed from the perceptual.

[2] By 'actual' is here meant whatever is known in the first instance through sense-perception. The word is preferable to the hopelessly ambiguous term 'real', but is itself not univocal because, as will be seen later, the perceptual objects of individual experience—actuality in its primary sense—are not identical with the so-called 'perceptual' of *common* sense and science, which is what 'actuality' usually denotes.

Moreover, it can never yield adequate or exhaustive knowledge of the world. When mathematics becomes applied science, it loses the precision and certainty, in virtue of which it was selected as the exemplar of knowledge. There is no "thought which pierces this dim universe like light". Our world owes its determinateness not wholly unto us; knowledge about it can be had only by attending to what is thrust upon us in the experience we happen to have. Instead of creating our foundations by fiat we have to discover them. Our logically prior concepts can only be attained through the *a posteriori*. Philosophy can proceed only by accepting obscure ideas, shaped by mankind for practical purposes, and refining them tentatively into tools suitable for theoretical ends. To the pure mathematician, the existence of our world is a superfluity. On the other hand, his 'possible' worlds are no affair to the philosopher. For him, laws of thought, unless laws of thought about things, have no significance; and logical constructions are irrelevances unless possessing applicability. There are doubtless *a priori* conditions of our thought, *i.e.* conditions independent of sense-data and their reception—according to one of the meanings of 'independence'; there are no such conditions of experience, and none as to our thought being the sole possible kind of thought, or as to our thought according with actuality— which experience alone can decide. Thus mathematics or any pure science, just because ideal in the sense of being concerned directly with ideas alone, is so far from being the ideal, in the sense of the paradigm, of knowledge about actualities, that it does not necessarily possess indirect relevance thereto: its method is out of place where a willy-nilly core or an element of 'brutality' in the data is determinative.

Enough has been said as to the mischievousness of an ancient prejudice, to account for avoidance, in this work, of the *a priori* method; perhaps enough to suggest that there is but one truth concerning actuality, that pure apriorism can reach: viz. that any other wholly *a priori* knowledge of actuality is *a priori* impossible. The case is the same with the metaphysically ultimate as with the logically prior; for if the ontal reveals itself only in the phenomenal, it can only be known by means of the phenomenal.

If philosophy is to be more than a pastime, it would seem that the only procedure open to it is to set out from the 'knowledge' that we have, the facts which *prima facie* are best known. Our one unimpugnable fact, at the level at which we must first use that word, is the existence of so-called knowledge of actuality. Of course, no philosopher has ever but set out from this collective datum, however he may have camouflaged his method when giving exposition to his system. In *ordine cognoscendi—i.e.* not the order of logical priority but of actual knowledge-process—the first things of Plato or Spinoza are last things. If this truth was first brought home to rationalists by Hume, his trumpet-blast, that roused Kant from rationalistic slumber, was one of the most momentous events in the history of philosophy. Kant, unfortunately, was but half aroused. He continued to assume that in Newtonian physics he possessed a pure science of Nature, separate indeed from mathematics, yet grounded on necessary principles and concepts; and he wasted his invaluable time in trying to discover its preconditions. The impurity of his pure science, *i.e.* its clandestine resort to brute fact, is now patent. The necessity of reliance on the empirical may be said to have become at last self-evident.[1]

The analysandum from which philosophy must needs set out having been indicated, it remains to justify the method of dealing with it that it is proposed to follow. Hitherto it has merely been urged that no analysis can stand, that is incompatible with the existence of any part of the analysandum itself; no theory of knowledge can be approved that involves the impossibility of the data being forthcoming. These statements may read as harmless platitudes: they will turn out to be engines of destruction for which much work lies to hand.[2]

There are two ways of proceeding from presumptive knowledge to philosophy. One of these, sometimes conventionally called the 'epistemological', seeks to ascertain the logical pre-

---

[1] In so far as Plato regarded mathematics as the paradigm of knowledge, it must be submitted that he was the Adam of the race of *a priori* philosophers, and his the *peccatum originans*. Perhaps some day a genius of like stature, a second philosophic Adam, will arise to pursue the *ordo cognoscendi* and work out the first completed system of genuinely empirical type. As yet but partial enterprises of this kind have been undertaken, beginning in Aristotle's incomplete break with Platonism.

[2] Common-sense knowledge is often said, truly enough, not to be knowledge in what may be called the perfectionist's sense, either in respect of adequacy and purity or in respect of rigid logical certainty: it has accordingly been here designated 'presumptive'. It is not so commonly stated, nor even borne in mind, that whatever ultimate reality and genuine knowledge be, they must have compatibility with the emergence and existence of the product called (of courtesy) knowledge, whatever its

conditions of knowledge and of its possibility.[1] It concerns itself with thinking and knowing, only as perfected arts; with knowledge, as an actually or ideally finished product; with reason, as a developed faculty, sometimes as abstracted from reasoners and hypostatised into a quasi-existent absolute. It deems insignificant the possibility that the nature of our reason is contingent on mankind's evolution, conditioned by relations with environment or by the fact that human selves are embodied. It is indifferent to genetic studies, and more than indifferent to the individual experiences by which common or universal knowledge is actually determined. Such matters are regarded as irrelevant. Psychological conditionings, it is said, have nothing to do with logical presuppositions; nor does the truth of a proposition depend on how it came to be believed. It is assumed, however, that there is a body of knowledge, properly so called, and a *ratio essendi* that is known, if but in part.

This method cannot be adopted here as all-sufficient. With the history of science behind us, it behoves us to be chary of supposing that we understand the nature, scope, or significance of anything—even knowledge—until we have learned how it came to be what it is.[2] It shall not be assumed that our kind of scientific thinking has the same preconditions as any other possible kind. Our thought shall not be identified with Thought, nor our reason with universal Reason. Nor shall it be presupposed that the world is through and through rational, and our reason adequate to the reading of its rationality. Such questions shall not be foreclosed; for it waits to be seen whether the office of our reason has not sometimes been magnified, and its aristocratic nature accredited, through ignorance as to its plebeian descent and connexions.

nature, constitution and status. To seek what is consistent with the forthcomingness of so-called fact-knowledge, despite its need of overhauling, is a profitable quest. The same cannot be assumed as to the quest for the presuppositions of 'necessary knowledge' of actuality, which may turn out to be a chimaera of our own making.

[1] As thus used, *e.g.* by Ward, 'epistemological' inclines towards the meaning of 'logical' and away from that of 'psychological', but also suggests connexion with the common or 'universal' (science), and transcendence of the private nature of individual experience. In later chapters we shall encounter another conventional use of 'epistemological', or rather of 'epistemic', adopted by Mr Johnson, where the opposite emphasis is intended, and the psychological, rather than the logical, aspect of the subject-matter is indicated.

[2] So taught Aristotle: we must know the generative principle, if we would understand the essence, of a thing.

As to truth being independent of the manner in which beliefs are reached, the dictum seems as insignificant as it is inexpugnable. It ignores the difference between truth recognised as such, and 'truth' independent of our recognition—which is rather 'fact' than correspondence of thought with fact. So long as a 'truth' remains unrecognised, its subsistence and its non-subsistence are alike nothing to us: it is little use there being true propositions, unless we *know* they are true. But, in order to know a proposition concerning actuality to be true, we do generally need to have ascertained how it was arrived at. And we need also to bear in mind that our most important convictions, in science, philosophy and theology alike, are partly due to causes other than logical grounds; that they rest on notions that are but postulated, and such postulation enters at so low a stage as the judgement of perception.

Again, although the logical implications of propositions, and the logical connexions of ideas, are independent of origin and developement, it is not self-evident that the range of their significance, and the scope of their *knowable* applicability, are other than coextensive with the experience-contexts within which they were evoked. When this consideration has been disregarded, as *e.g.* when concepts that are over-individual have been assumed to be also over-social, as to their origination and relevance, and then treated as absolute, perhaps grave errors have been made, whether in epistemology, natural philosophy, or ethics.

On these grounds the 'epistemological' method will here be made subsidiary to another. If we are to know actuality, and to know that we know about it and are not merely conjecturing as to it, we shall need to inquire, what knowledge of actuality is, and what it is not.[1] This involves recourse to analytic and genetic psychology.[2] At the worst such a resort would be a harmless

---

[1] It is sometimes said that it is as foolish to ask how knowing can know, as to inquire how being was made. But how knowers came to know, and what their knowing consists in, are questions for the answering of which positive fact-data lie to hand for exposition and analysis.

[2] By genetic psychology is not meant the attempt to shew that there is nothing, in the highly developed mind, that was not in the primitive mind; nor concentration of attention solely on the beginnings of experience, to the neglect of any characteristics of the complex final product that were absent from incipient stages of the process. All actual developement is epigenesis, growth out of something into something else; and it is the continuity of this growth through all its stages that genetic science studies. The dangers of the genetic method are avoided when it is coupled with the analytic. There

superfluity; if the foregoing contentions be granted, it becomes a *sine qua non*. Some account of the origin and context of philosophical concepts shall therefore be thrust upon the reader, in the hope that thereby a warning may be imparted against the hypostatising of abstractions, which leads but to metaphysic devoid of relevance in spheres beneath the supercelestial. The genesis of our knowledge shall be set forth at length, because any philosophy that ignores it, is here regarded as vain; and any definition of knowledge that does not reckon with it, may turn out to lack denotation. All concepts are derived ultimately from percepts: no sense-impressions, no science; no individual experience, no universal knowledge. If, then, we would learn what actuality and knowledge *are*, we must study *actual* sources and preconditions. It is only by tracing the developement of the knowledge-process that we can ascertain the nature, scope and limitations of the product. So the facts established by psychology concerning individual experience, must be the first quest. No less is meant than that the *ordo cognoscendi* is the sole route that possibly may lead to a *known ordo essendi*: that psychology is the fundamental science, the first propaedeutic to philosophy, rather than a science to be placed somewhere between chemistry and history. Perhaps the overlooking of this possibility is chiefly responsible for the resultlessness of so large a measure of philosophical endeavour. Even other kinds of empiricism than that which has just been propounded, are here excluded as either dogmatism or disguised rationalism: as setting forth from arbitrary concepts rather than from determinative data.

The reader, who happens to be at the beginning of his study of philosophy, should be cautioned that the opinion just expressed, viz. that critical investigation of knowledge cannot be effectively pursued by the 'epistemological'—the *a priori* or the logical—

is then little risk of overlooking the peculiarities and the complexity of the product or analysandum. To take the analysandum as a sacrosanct infallibility—which, in some respects, is what the method here conventionally designated 'the epistemological' does—and to proceed, without further ado, to analyse it and ascertain its logical preconditions, is dogmatism dangerous as is 'the naturalist's fallacy' just now referred to. The analytical-genetic method, it must be submitted, is the only safeguard against either error. Use of this method will be found to reveal metaphysical assumptions lurking unsuspected in what are taken for data; to detect the mediacy of many supposed immediacies, the acquiredness of much that has passed for innate or *a priori*; and to shew that part of what has been ascribed to our nature, is but second nature.

method alone, is accounted heresy by most philosophers whose judgement commands respect. If one be not mistaken, it is generally agreed that the difference, perhaps disparateness, between the two methods, and the irrelevance of the psychological to the 'epistemological', constitute one of the permanent lessons taught us by Kant. Nevertheless, it may be urged that certain shortcomings of Kant's great accomplishment are due to his too complete neglect of data which empirical investigation might have supplied, and to his too hasty assumption of their irrelevance, had he found them. Moreover, the Kantian epistemology is by no means independent of the faulty psychology that he inherited; and it must be submitted, in the light of Kant's instructive defects, that epistemology is not, and cannot be, a science *sui generis*, sitting loose to facts about the nature and conditioning of cognitive psychoses, a *tertium quid* between psychology and logic, but is a compound of the two. When apriorism takes the intellectual product in abstraction from its psychological and biological setting, and (neglecting its history, aim and function) conceives how it *can* be put together out of 'analytica' invented *ad hoc*, it becomes mythology of the fancy-bred, and has little connexion with science of the factual. However, if the view here adopted be heresy, Dr Schiller long ago proclaimed it; and the heresiarch is Locke. Indicating a change of application by italicising one word, I would quote from him the following sentence, as expressing my standpoint: "I thought that the *first* step towards satisfying several inquiries the mind of man is very apt to run into was to take a survey of our own understandings, examine our powers, and see to what things they are adapted".[1] And with this citation may be coupled another from Reid:

A creative imagination disdains the mean offices of digging for a foundation, of removing rubbish, and carrying materials; leaving these servile employments to the drudges in science, it plans a design, and raises a fabric. Invention supplies materials where they are wanting, and fancy adds colouring and every befitting ornament. The work pleases the eye, and wants nothing but solidity and a good foundation. It seems even to vie with the works of nature, till some succeeding architect blows it into rubbish, and builds as goodly a fabric of his own in its place.[2]

[1] *Essay concerning the Human Understanding*, I. i. 7.
[2] *An Inquiry into the Human Mind*, ch. I. § 3.

CHAPTER II

Consciousness: *Its Subject and Subjective Elements*

1. 'SELF-CONSCIOUSNESS' AS DATUM.

The primary crude datum of psychology is the fact that there are selves aware of their own existence and mentality. This, of course, has never been doubted at the level of experience-organisation involved in common sense. Whatever selves may be found to be, and into whatever analytica they and their minds may be resolvable, the analysanda simply are. And they are the only touchstone by which analytical theories can be tried.

The ground of belief of a self in its own existence is stated in *cogito ergo sum*; and as that dictum is wont to be regarded as a foundation-stone of modern philosophy, it may fittingly be taken as our starting-point. To Descartes it seemed to assert indubitable truth, because doubting it only reinstates the impugned fact. *Cogitatio*, even when *dubitatio de cogitatione*, is an actual occurrence involving a *res cogitans*. It is a further question *what* this *res* is, but it cannot be non-existent. To be conscious is to be: in the fact *ego cogitans sum*, being and thinking meet.

The point first to be noted as to the statement of Descartes, is that the *cogitatio*, that it asserts, is not consciousness such as the sentience of which we are aware, but awareness of it. If the dictum is to possess the significance it had for its author, *cogito* must not be equivalent to *sentio*, but rather to *scio (me) sentire*. The worm presumably feels: presumably it does not know that it exists. It is, then, awareness of consciousness, technically called self-consciousness, such as is generally believed to be explicit only in human beings, that Descartes laid down as foundation-fact, and that common sense offers as knowledge-datum. This datum, however, presupposes consciousness. Here we encounter an ultimate concept: the concept which is called for to indicate the whole class of actual occurrences that furnish the unique field of psychology, as distinguished from physical sciences. The actuality also is ultimate for us, because, as to the becoming of consciousness out of something else, we have no knowledge. Logically and actually, consciousness is prior to self-consciousness. Orderly procedure from what happens to be our prime datum, obliges us at once to turn from it to this first result of analysis.

2. CONSCIOUSNESS.

The word 'consciousness' has borne many meanings: indeed, a dozen or more have been counted. It was used as synonymous with awareness of consciousness, by Descartes and Locke; and as inclusive of self-consciousness, by Hamilton and Mill. Nowadays it is often restricted to awareness of objects, or to experience of the cognitive type, exclusive of feeling and conation. With some psychologists, the word then replaces 'subject', standing for the being or *res* that is conscious or has consciousness. With others, it denotes the 'contents' of consciousness, *i.e.* the objects, such as a noise, of which there is consciousness. Often it stands for states of consciousness, such as the mental act of hearing: and, whether as useful abbreviations or as fraught with psychologically iconoclastic intent, the somewhat barbarous phrases 'conscious process', 'conscious states', occur in the vocabulary of unfastidious writers. To call attention to the equivocality of this word, will convey the premonitory hint that slovenliness of speech, one source of confusion in thought, may account for some paradoxical views concerning consciousness that are rife: may it serve the further purpose of indicating that one of the requisites of thinking, is to ascertain, at the outset of any particular investigation, the several meanings which leading terms have borne, so that one may be saved from falling a victim to the commonest and often subtlest form of fallacy—the using of an ambiguous term as if it were univocal: which may reduce argumentation to a kind of punning, and substitute verbal legerdemain for logic.

For the much abused, and now hopelessly indefinite, word 'consciousness', it has been suggested that 'experience' be substituted. But, unfortunately, this term has acquired similar ambiguity. 'Experience' is preferable, in that it does not refer exclusively to the cognitive functioning of the mind, which 'consciousness', in keeping with etymology, is apt to suggest. Certainly some comprehensive term is needed to indicate the class of acts and states, inclusive of others besides awareness, which we are wont to regard as *sui generis*, disparate from physical or vital occurrences, and distinct even from many called mental. It is immaterial which term we retain for this specific purpose, provided we at once assign to it by convention this one definite denotation. Selecting 'consciousness', we may observe that it is not possible to define its connotation[1]: simply because consciousness is ultimate or indescribable in terms other than synonyms for itself. We may indicate what we propose to mean by it, though we but substitute for it another indefinable, when we say that a state of consciousness is one in which change not only takes place, but is 'felt', or accompanied by 'feeling'. So we point the difference between it and the impact which a stone receives, but of which it has no sensation; or between it and the response of a dead frog's nerve to stimulation, in which we observe a case of irritability, but not of sentience. However, though we cannot, without tautology, describe the connotation of 'consciousness', we are familiar with the various kinds of event which it denotes. Sensation, perceiving, enjoying, thinking, etc., possess in common a *quale* in virtue of which, in spite of their differences, they may be put into one class and cannot be qualitatively compared with anything outside that class: even with processes that are otherwise *erlebt* or lived through, as is the pulse. This *quale*, like that of red, can only be ostensively defined: we can but point to instances of it. So defined, 'consciousness' has wider denotation than 'awareness'. On the other hand, it is narrower than the 'mental' or 'psychic', if these terms include the memory-trace and all else of the subconscious or unconscious that psychology may postulate, in order to make coherent its account of mental processes. Whether consciousness is coextensive with life, is not known: whether with mentality, is a question for later discussion. That it is not coextensive with self-consciousness, is highly probable: certainly we can conceive anoetic experience, or mere sentience, unaccompanied by awareness of it, and can distinguish between, *e.g.*, tasting and awareness of tasting. Yet without the peculiar kind of *erlebnis*[2] which is the basis of cognition, there can be no knowledge of being, as distinct from being.

---

[1] Waiving subtleties here irrelevant, the connotation of a term may be said to comprise the attributes which make up its meaning, while its denotation is the sphere of its application. Thus 'metal' connotes a group of properties, and denotes iron, gold, etc.

[2] The useful term *erleben* will recur. It denotes not knowledge, even the simpler kind called acquaintance, but being that is prior to knowing. Whether we know a

Further consideration of self-consciousness, from which we have already been diverted, is deferred until the presuppositions of that advanced kind of experience have been investigated. The first of these is the existence of what is here denoted by 'consciousness', or the occurrence of events having the unique *quale* just now alleged. The allegation has been questioned; and therewith the very existence of psychology, as a science *sui generis*.

Denial of particular modes of consciousness is commoner than the semblance of repudiation of it *in toto*. All stages in attempted elimination of feeling, desire, imagination and sensatio,[1] respectively, are represented in recent literature, and may be dealt with as each of these kinds of mental process comes under consideration; but here we are concerned only with the cancelling of all difference between perception of events and occurrence of them. To take this issue seriously, may seem to the reader a supererogatory act of tolerance, and to suggest that psychology is a science deficient in self-respect. But he can be promised that discussion of apparent absurdity, in this instance, will conduce to recognition of certain characteristics of psychology, as a science distinct from all others: he may therefore be exhorted to suffer gladly. As the recent outcrop of the doctrine known as presentationism provides materialism with the substitute for psychology which it has needed, the student may also begin to fulfil his worthy wish to leave no system unexplored. He is referred to the Appendix, Note A, where types of such theory receive notice, and reasons are presented for believing that, instead of the first principle of psychology—that there is a unique kind of *erleben* which simply is and "shines by its own light"[2]—having been discredited, it is presupposed in the sophistry by which it is explained away.

---

mental *erlebnis* immediately or mediately, is not of vital importance; but the view adopted here is that a mental state such as longing is, like colour, directly apprehended, not inferred, by self-conscious subjects.

[1] We have unfortunately but one word, 'sensation', to denote both object 'sensed' and act of 'sensing' it. To avoid confusion, this word will here be replaced by 'sensum' or 'sensatio', as the one or the other is called for. If dog-Latin need apology, the inadequacy of the English tongue for philosophical purposes, is sufficient excuse; dog-English is the only other alternative by which to make up for our deficiency of inflexion.

[2] Double inverted commas, throughout this book, indicate quotation. Single commas have other signification.

3. THE EXISTENCE OF THE SUBJECT OF CONSCIOUSNESS.

The second fundamental proposition of psychology, received or rejected, is that consciousness involves a subject. *What* the subject is, is a remoter question; at this stage we are to be concerned solely with the assertion *that* it is. And, not to let assertion outstrip evidence, let us suppose that the alleged continuous self, of common-sense belief, involves assumptions; that it may be found possible to regard the enduring experience of an apparently enduring self, identical at different times, as resolvable into discrete events of short duration, each of which may be called an experience; that the thinker and the doubter of Descartes are two, and not one subject. For the present, it suffices to insist that whenever there is such an occurrence as an instance of consciousness, be it a passing sensatio or a mental βίος, that experience involves an experient. Perhaps this has never been disputed, save when 'there is awareness of red' and 'red exists' have been taken to be identical propositions. But it has been hushed up by psychologists who analyse a cognition into object and act of awareness, but shyly refrain from confessing that acts involve agents and are not themselves agents. A state which is not a state of some being or *res*, an act which is not an act of an agent, a relation which is not a relation between terms: these may be convenient logical counters, but they are not actualities. Indeed, consciousness once admitted to be unique *erleben*, it is but to assert an analytical proposition, when we go on to say: consciousness involves a subject. 'Awareness' is a meaningless term, a mere nonsense-word denoting nonentity, unless it be an elliptical expression for 'awareness of something by something'. So, although the distinction between subject and object may not 'exist for'—*i.e.* be known to—the subject, as is probably the case for many experients, it nevertheless always exists.[1] 'Consciousness' is an abstract noun; and it is always well to translate abstract propositions into concrete form, before

---

[1] The confusion between 'exist' and 'exist for', in the sense of 'be known to', is an instance of 'the psychologist's fallacy', of which behaviourism and kindred theories seem to be but tedious elaborations, and is perpetuated by writers who are not professed behaviourists or presentationists. Surely any sensitivity, even that of the amoeba, must be sensitivity *of* some being *to* some being. The former of these beings is subject, though it have no awareness of being so. Tasting is possible without awareness of tasting: it is non-existent unless there be (1) taster, (2) the tasted.

N.B. 'Behaviourism' shall here be used to denote only extremer forms of a tendency.

assuming them to be significant. When the abstraction is hypostatised, it does but reaffirm, while it superficially conceals, the concrete conscious subject which it is often used to suppress. To say 'consciousness feels', is simply to speak untruth. It follows that expressions such as 'conscious states', as used by writers to whom the concept of subject is obnoxious, are strictly nonsensical; and that unless by 'content of consciousness' we denote an object apprehended by a subject, the phrase means nothing. Such figurative phrases may be harmless, however uncouth, if mere abbreviations; to take them seriously, is to extract science out of solecisms. No one ever has really dispensed with the subject of consciousness, whatever terms he may have used to hush up its existence. No one ever will dispense with it, because to do so involves intrinsic impossibility. The subject is a logical substance or substantive, involved in affirming the existence of an experience, whether an experience be described as a state or as a relation. A subjectless experience is not merely an absurdity: a contradiction in meanings, it should be a contradiction in terms. If "the thoughts are the thinkers", *they* are subjects; if objects "play the rôle" of subjects, that is but to say they *are* subjects. And since we cannot by any means extract from the proposition 'objects exist', the proposition 'objects appear', the existence of the subject, as distinct from what appears to it, is incapable of gainsaying.

Nevertheless, the impossible has been attempted. And it will not be fruitless to examine the conditions that predisposed to the endeavour, and the mistakes on which 'psychology without a subject' has been founded.

Presentationism, as this theory is also called, has the merit of offering a foil against which empirical psychology may be expounded, and of supplying an object-lesson as to what scientific method in psychology is not.

One source of tendency to disparage the concept of the subject, is metaphysical prepossession, which scientific procedure avoids. It has been taught that subject and object arise out of undifferentiated "pure" experience or feeling. That they have arisen, should suffice the psychologist: for further back than actual experience, which is from the first a duality, we can only go by futile speculation as to the unknowable. "Pure *experience*" is thus the most complete misnomer that could be devised for the fiction in question, as is "radical *empiricism*" for the rationalistic method by which it was obtained. How such pure experience, by hypothesis structureless, initiates its own differentiation from within, and how it is to be distinguished from indeterminate being or from nothingness, are the first puzzles. James, among others, taught this doctrine that experience has no inner duplicity: the separation of it into consciousness and content comes, he said, "not by way of subtraction, but by way of addition". In order to "play the part of a knower, of a state of mind, of consciousness", all that is needed is that a given portion of 'experience' "be taken in one context of associates". There could hardly be a plainer admission that before "pure experience" can undergo its requisite fission, it needs an actual experient or subject to "take" it in its two contexts. All metaphysical speculation is out of place at the threshold of a science; but this particular dogma plays the rôle of Balaam in spontaneously indicating that the familiar analytica of actual experience cannot be dispensed with. Psychology is not a pure science like non-Euclidean geometry; but James, Bradley, and other expounders of pure experience, sometimes seem to have treated it as such. Nor is its method of explanation that of *obscurum per obscurius*. Genetic psychology, that is not based on analytical psychology, is on a par with the mythical cosmogonies that preceded science.

Another metaphysical assumption involved in attempts to dispense with the subject, is that of the pure sensum. Reasons will be given, in the next chapter, for the assertion that there is no such actuality. Experience has never stumbled on one; and the dogma that what thought can distinguish, is *ipso facto* a separable existent, is neither self-evident, nor demonstrable, nor suggested by our knowledge of how ideation is mediated. But if discrete pure sensa did exist, we could not derive from them alone "a special complex presentation which assumes the rôle of subject". For sensationism, a complex presentation can only be an aggregate of sensa; and that, after all, is but sensa in aggregation. From mind-dust, and *a fortiori* from unconscious dust, there is no more a way to experience with its intrinsic duality, than from mind-stuff, neutral stuff, or matter. From anything other than experience there is no deduction of it, no derivation that is not a *generatio aequivoca*. "Endless genealogies" belong to mythology: they are out of place in science that would set out from facts and abide by them. If consciousness is unique, we can now add that it is from first to last a duality in unity.

The second kind of motivation to 'psychology without a subject', is the desire to "simplify" the science by identifying its standpoint with that of physics. Science abstracts from the individual experient: let psychology adopt the same method, and not only may it then hope for the progress that physics has enjoyed, but it will find the so-called subject to be a product arising out of the interaction of pure objects. Some of the fallacies underlying this hope were pointed out by Prof. Ward[1] in the time of its infancy. Application and supplementation of points in his refutation of the theory of knowledge on which the presentationist hope is grounded, will put in clear light characteristics that mark off psychology from the physical sciences, assimilation to which has been zealously sought on its behalf.

It is true that science abstracts from the individual subject. But to leave him out, is not to deny that he is there. The data of science are not any individual's percepts, but things common to many experients. However, there could be no knowledge of, say, the moon, as a thing independent of this or that person's perceiving, and as thought to have a far side which has never been sensorily apprehended by anyone, unless individuals had first been presented, each with his numerically and qualitatively different object. The data of science, as knowledge-units, thus presuppose individual subjects; and the contents of our sciences are what they are, because the experiences we individually have, happen to be what they are. The conceptualised Object of 'universal' experience is a very different entity from the object immediately and sensorily apprehended by an individual.[2] In the

---

[1] Besides his *Psychol. Principles* see *Mind*, N.S. vol. ii. No. 5. Ward's criticisms seem to have escaped notice and not to have been met by more recent presentationists. Attention to them would perhaps have spared us a large outcrop of pseudo-science.

[2] Perhaps no instance of the bearing, by one word, of several senses, has been more productive of paralogism and confused discussion than this, of 'object' and its derivative 'objective'. When these terms denote what is over against, other than, presented to, an individual subject, or are used in their psychological sense, they shall here be printed with small initial letters; spelt with a capital, they will refer to what is common to the many, the conceptual, more or less abstract thought-constructions of 'universal' experience; *i.e.* they will be used in their 'epistemological' sense. The same device shall be used to distinguish the reality, encountered in the objective of individual

latter kind of object, we are one by one brought into touch with 'reality', in the psychologically fundamental sense of that word; were we not, there could be no ground for attributing Reality, in any derived sense, to the Object of universal experience. This we do when, looking at a distant coin, we say the elliptical shape actually seen, is the appearance of a circular Real coin which we do not see (in the same sense) but *think* is there, in spite of sense-evidence to the contrary. The derived Object is usually regarded as not only existing independently of all percipients, but as causing their diverse objects; and these are sometimes even called 'subjective'. It is obvious that, in so talking, we have exchanged the *ratio cognoscendi* for the *ratio essendi*. There need be no contradiction involved, for the *rationes* are different. But whatever Realities there be with which, in individual experience, we are in *rapport*, it is indisputable that objects presented to individual subjects are the precondition of *knowledge* as to them; and that any disparagement of the reality-status of individual experience involves disparagement of the body of knowledge, on the strength of which the disparaging remark is made.

If there cannot be scientific knowledge unless there be individual subjects, the hope that science can encourage psychology to cancel the subject, seems forlorn. The hope arose through confounding objects with Objects. It became robust through paralogistic usage of another ambiguous word—'phenomenon'. In the primitive sense of what shines forth or appears, in which no contrast of appearance with reality is insinuated, this word is only applicable to objects presented to a subject; and such objects are phenomena in this primitive sense alone. The objective, the real, the phenomenal, in their primary significations, are identical; and, for purely individual (unsocialised) experience, are indistinguishable. But 'phenomenon', as a technical term of science or of philosophy, does not bear this primary sense; it is applied to Objects and it points antithesis with the Real, of which the

experience, from the Reality ascribed to the conceptual and common. Yet a third class of entities is denoted by the terms in question: the noumenal or ultimate realities behind the phenomenal Objects (such as the sun) of common sense. The words then have a metaphysical sense. Lastly, the student of Descartes will meet with what is historically the original meaning of 'objective', by which term the schoolmen connoted existence in a mind. This usage, the inverse of the more modern, is now obsolete.

Object is appearance. Thirdly, common sense and science have been pleased to apply the word to what is neither presented to the individual subject (a percept proper) nor is, like the moon, a thought-construction or an Object known by conception as well as sense (a percept so called), but is altogether unpresentable to sense: *e.g.* the electron. Hence, in common parlance, 'phenomenon' has come to be used in what Dr Moore would call a Pickwickian sense, and to denote the thing *per se*, the antithesis of what the word means in its second sense. As a colloquialism within the sphere of physics, this self-contradictory usage (phenomenon *per se*) is harmless: science knows better than to take its own slang seriously. But when presentationism exploits such a terminological inexactitude for the demolition of psychology, the matter becomes grave. This theory calls objects 'phenomena', not in the primitive sense in which they can be so called; that would analytically involve the subject as correlate: but in the Pickwickian sense. To "moralise two meanings in one word", is no uncommon error: it is a less common blunder, to use one of several meanings precisely where another is required. And this is not all. Science is not concerned to make an epistemological excursus of its own; and, while minding its own business, is nonchalant as to whether its implicit epistemology be good or bad. It hazards no assertion as to whether its Objects (*i.e.* so-called phenomena, or phenomena in the second and third senses above distinguished) are independent of experients; but as a rule of its game, or as instrumental to its departmental procedure, it deliberately regards them *as if* they were. On the strength of this irrelevant fact, presentationism declares that the properly so called phenomena of individual experience, phenomena in the first sense, *are* thus independent. It is therefore by a double confusion that it has come to think that the subject, which science may for its own purpose ignore, can be dismissed as a nonentity by psychology. This is exactly what psychology cannot do, without ceasing to exist. It is to discard the one feature in which the 'content of consciousness' is fact at all, for psychological consideration. The object is only object for a subject, content for a *continens*: if the *continens* be suppressed, the content vanishes also. The standpoint of science, we have seen, presupposes that of psychology; though, while concerned with the conceptual and common, science needs must ignore the individual. It may now be added that, when returning from conceptual theory, it seeks concrete verification, science reinstates the subject-object duality of individual experience in all its pristine fundamentality. For verification of theory is always, in the last resort, the tallying, for this and that observer singly, of one object of private experience with another: *e.g.* a cross-wire in an eye-piece with a mark on a scale, as these objects are called when 'communised'. That in its procedure intermediate between start and finish, when the individual subject is irrelevant, science can overlook him, is thus no sign of ability to sanction the paradoxical notion of 'psychology without a subject'. This turns out to be "psychology which ignores the subject that it everywhere implies".

On the other hand, psychology cannot set out from the standpoint of physical science, because she has one of her own which conceptual science presupposes.[1] Dazzled by the prestige of science, the presentationist has been deprived of discrimination between things that differ. He seems to have been hypnotised into meek imitativeness, where that is singularly out of place.

What is to be regarded as a passing wind of doctrine has here received detailed notice, partly because any charge of instability as to the facts, and their first analysis-products, on which the assertion of a soul in man is ultimately based, needs to be taken seriously; and partly because examination of some of the fallacies on which behaviourism and kindred theories are built, will have served to make clear one or two points of fundamental importance. One of these is that the objective in individual and minimally conceptual experience, is the basis or the source of all common knowledge, scientific or philosophical, concrete or abstract, such as in its self-exposition pursues the *ordo essendi*. From the standpoint adopted here, that order awaits establishing, otherwise than as a construction of uncritical common sense; and if it is to be a

---

[1] We begin to see here the ground for the assertion that, from the comprehensive outlook of philosophy, psychology is the propaedeutic to theory of knowledge. To expound psychology from the epistemological standpoint *assumed* by any other science, and in terms of its findings, is not merely to invert the due order, but to expound something other than psychology proper. Psychophysics takes for granted a theory of knowledge which psychology cannot take for granted, save provisionally, just because it is psychology's business to examine the process, in virtue of which the theory came to be selectively adopted, and trusted.

known order, the knowledge of it can only be derived from the original data of individual experience. That 'universal' experience has established such an order with finality, cannot be assumed, save provisionally, at this stage. Thus the experience of the individual subject, which is the primary sphere of psychology and the starting-point for theory of knowledge, called for vindication, as against denials of its subject-object duality.

It has already been hinted that the plausibility, such as it is, of psychology that would dispense with the subject, is gained for it by its claim to have reduced consciousness to the one and only kind, awareness. How it has tried to dispose of that, we have seen.[1] It is necessary, in order to expel the theory from its last stronghold, to shew that, as a matter of fact, there are other factors in consciousness: states and acts of a determinate subject, over and above an abstract unity and continuity of a 'mind'. This will involve no deviation from the natural order of exposition of the first principles of psychology.

4. THE SUBJECTIVE ELEMENTS IN CONSCIOUSNESS.

(a) *Feeling*

A few pages back there was occasion to use 'feeling' colloquially, as an indicative synonym for 'consciousness'. Henceforth the word is to bear the restricted and technical denotation nowadays assigned to it in psychology, viz. the affective states of pleasure and displeasure (pain) which in some degree accompany perception of objects. Partly because 'pain' has been used also for organic sensum and sensatio, and partly because the affective states enter into emotions which are wont to be called both affective states and also feelings, the distinctness of feeling proper long escaped recognition.[2] But, from about the time of Kant, it has been regarded as an established fact, that pleasure and displeasure are unique and irreducible modes of consciousness, and cannot be other than states of the subject.

The facts, on which this doctrine is based, may be briefly stated.

---

[1] See Appendix, Note A.

[2] The usage of 'pleasure' is further confused by such expressions as 'higher and lower pleasures', denoting pleasurable presentations. Pleasure proper has no differences of quality.

They suffice to shew the arbitrariness of attempts to resolve feeling into sensatio, and feelings into sensa or 'feelables'.

Feelings cannot be localised like tastes nor, like colours, be projected into things. Disparate sensa, *e.g.* hardness and colour, coexist in one percept without losing their identity; whereas feelings of different 'sign' do not coexist side by side as accompaniments of a simple perception, but blend into an affective state neither purely pleasant nor purely unpleasant.[1] We never experience a sour colour or a blue flavour, as we do a pleasant taste or an unpleasing colour. The same person feels differently toward 'the same' percept at different times; and, in different persons, different feelings are evoked at the same time by the same stimulus. Again, physiology has discovered special nerves or centres for sensationes; none for feelings. Our fact-data shew that feelings cannot be differentiated into parts, nor associated and 'reproduced', in the same way as the sensa that evoke them. They do not follow the same laws as do the objective factors of experience. What has been called the feeling-tone of a percept, is therefore not to be regarded as a constituent of the percept or as a quality of a thing, but as a state evoked in the embodied percipient. Again, the kind and the intensity of feeling evoked, are conditioned by his mental dispositions and phase at the moment, while his sensory experience generally is not. Feeling, then, cannot be regarded as other than a subjective state consequent on apprehension of objects, without violence to fact. Were feelings sensa or sensationes, our fact-data could not be what they are.

That feeling is evoked, must be affirmed, because its emergence makes no alteration in the object cognised, whereas change of object does occasion change in feeling. How a subject is originally affected by the sensory, whether external or internal to his body, can depend only on that subject's determinate nature. Otherwise, there should ultimately be accounting for tastes, and one man's meat should not be another's poison. This is of importance in connexion with the question of self-determination. How feeling influences subsequent attention, and, as the subject's fundamental capacity, is involved in his individuality, appreciation of value, volition, morality, etc., will be treated in subsequent chapters.

[1] Stout, *A Manual of Psychology*, 1913, p. 114.

(b) *Conation*

The second kind of subjective functioning, conation, is as fundamental and irreducible, in mental life once begun, as feeling and awareness. It presupposes both, but is distinct from both. Broadly speaking, conation, as distinguished from conative action, is the mode of consciousness identifiable as the *erleben* of want— whether of continuance, or of change, of objects: it is unrest, whether it issue in desire or aversion. As it is thus directed towards the future, the active, as distinguished from the more receptive, side of experience is especially connected with it. It tends to bring about its own fulfilment. Movement such as has been found by chance or trial to lessen pain or displeasure, receives more concentrated attention; and action, thus prompted by feeling, takes the form of appropriation of the pleasing, and elimination of the unpleasing. At the earliest stage of mental developement, such action is determined by percepts; at a later stage, by ideas. The conative side of experience indeed advances in complexity *pari passu* with the cognitive, as will be described when the theory of value is dealt with. Feeling and conation may be regarded, respectively, as the passive and the active side of interest: *i.e.* of the fact that the subject's states have a difference made to them by its interaction with objects. Such interest will be found to prompt and direct cognition, at all stages after approximately bare sensatio, and to become increasingly evident as cognition advances to the intellectual level.

These few statements about conation suffice for our present purpose, viz. the analysis of experience into its ultimate kinds of elements, diversity between which cannot be resolved. Some of them have been cited from Prof. Stout, to supplement others taken from Prof. Ward. That striving or seeking, over and above purely cognitive apprehension, is an essential element in desire, etc., has been emphasised by Prof. Stout.[1] Prof. Ward also insists that conation, in so far as it is motivation to action, is *sui generis*. And when he describes conative action as "attention" to motor presentations, differing from non-voluntary attention only in being consequent on feeling, he is not to be understood to imply that desire or longing is but cognitive attention to objects that are

[1] See his *Manual of Psychology*.

pleasurably affecting; for 'attention', with this writer, is used as equivalent to 'activity' and as inclusive of conation as well as of cognition.[1]

Conation is no more reducible to feeling than to pure cognition. Perhaps the most serious attempt to obliterate the distinction between conation and feeling, and to revert to the ancient dichotomy from the Kantian (or earlier) trichotomous analysis of the psychosis, is that of the influential teacher, Brentano. But as Stout shews,[2] the argument that feeling and conation pass, the one into the other, by insensible gradations, would equally serve to abolish distinction between blue and green; while Brentano overlooks the fact that, in longing for a pleasurable object, the want, so far from being a pleasure-feeling, is cause of displeasure. A bolder attempt is that of behaviourism, which follows up its fact-repudiating account of feeling, by denying desire, etc., to be subjective attitudes. Desire is said to be a convenient fiction, like force in physics, read into the facts for the purpose of economically describing them. Introspection and its findings are supposed to have been already ruled out; so that "the facts" are only those constituting a person's outward behaviour, as witnessed by another observer. Romeo's restless motions are thus the only data for an account of his state. His passion is no felt longing, but a fiction invented by Benvolio and others, to spare themselves verbosity when discussing his sighs and postures, and which Romeo himself comes to know about only by the book. His desiring is his desideratum; and his desideratum is not anything wanted by him, but only what other people find wanting to complete his behaviour-cycle. As thus understood, Romeo, in attributing to himself *erlebt* desire, presents a case, the converse of that of *Punch's* deceased Christian-science patient, who "thinks he is dead". Behaviourism allows Romeo the faculty to make fictions; but even this concession only lasts so long as it is obviously indispensable for expositional purposes, and is withdrawn when thinking is identified with the "word-habit". How the fiction of felt desire, which most people

---

[1] The relation of conation to attention is treated in Stout's *Analytic Psychology* where, however, 'attention' is used in a sense different from that which the word bears with Ward. The same applies to the terms 'object' and 'presentation'. The meaning of many technical terms in psychology is unfixed, which imposes on the learner burdens that he might have been spared.

[2] *Analytic Psychology*, 1902, I. 116 ff.

are as sure they 'live through' as they are sure of anything, got coined, for the description of muscular movements, by organisms destitute of acquaintance with felt desire; and how that of force came to occur to beings whose sole activity consists in fiction-making, await, if one be not mistaken, behaviouristic explanation. Granted conative states, first lived through or 'enjoyed', and then contemplated, we can understand the poet's talk of the loves of plants; but, given only the clinging of ivy to oak, it is hard to account for the superfluous word 'love'. Sceptics as to the subject and its states, from Hume onwards, have been fortunate in finding to hand facts, ideas and words, which, were their own negative theories true, had never been forthcoming. They have not scrupled to use these conveniences, as they confess them to be. Hence the plausibility of their conclusions to themselves and to uncritical readers. When at last sceptics shall begin to dispense with these "conveniences", in the exposition of their negations, and to dismiss conation as non-actual, without invoking impulse and unrest while doing so, it will be time to take them seriously.

(c) *Attention and its Activity*

There is a third function of the subject, presupposed by feeling and conation, viz. that which is the source of all cognition: the primary interaction between subject and object, which constitutes awareness or direct, involuntary acquaintance. This has been called presentation of object, and, in the converse direction, attention of subject. In so far as 'attention' is a synonym for 'aware-ness' or 'consciousness of', it bears a technical sense, inclusive of what in ordinary speech would often be called inattention. The term, as technical, is due to Prof. Ward; but it is here used in a more restricted sense than that in which he employs it, when he understands by it the subject's "one faculty", comprising the whole range of cognitive processes, and apparently conative action also. If we are to credit the subject with but one faculty, we shall find it necessary to include distinguishable sub-species within it, over and above reception of impression. This last is the only function denoted by the word 'attention' in the present context.

In this analytically distinguishable, but actually inseparable, factor in the simplest perceptual experience, we encounter at its maximum the element of receptivity in cognition. It is the more in evidence, the more nearly perception approximates to pure sensibility, an ideal limit never reached in actual experience. Receptivity is not pure passivity. In sensatio there must be so much of subjective re*action* as is required for receiving an impression. And that is not nil. Just as, in the analogue of 'passive' reception by wax of the impress of a seal, something must be credited to the wax in that it undergoes what, in the same circumstances, iron or water does not; so in sensatio. The word 'activity', as applied to the subject, is a bugbear to many psychologists; but as another name for functioning by which something is done or determined, it should be tolerated, whether liked or not.

Further, this activity must be *erlebt* as process, different in kind from 'unconscious' vital processes such as normal heart-beat, whether it be apprehended directly or indirectly. Without the fact, the origin of this 'fiction' is inconceivable. "We are, being active". Consciousness is wider than cognition thereof, and is presupposed by it; hence it is idle to attempt to explain away the activity of certain subjective functionings, on the ground that it is not a 'content' known with explicitness. To deny activity in cognition, on the strength of the fact that it is not presented along with the object cognised, seems like denying our seeing, when we see things but do not see our seeing of them. It must be maintained, then, that activity is a characteristic of attention, as experienc*ing*. It is no metaphysical fiction imported into facts that contain it not, in order to rationalise or to interpret them. It is no dispensable hypothesis, a better than which may perchance be found. The explaining of activity away, always presupposes its actuality. This is as manifest in Bradley's criticism as in that of James, Münsterberg, and avowed presentationists. All these writers predicate activity, by implication, of that by which they would replace the active subject. And when the higher stages of the knowledge-process are studied analytically and genetically, or even 'epistemologically' as by Kant, it becomes evident that knowledge cannot be accounted for, save in terms of selective and synthetic *operation*. Psychologically regarded, experience is *rapport*, not timeless or static logical relation, between subject and objects; experience is not only change, but also interaction. Unless self-initiated change, different essentially from the "self-initiated changes" we may ascribe to physical systems, and exhibited in attention and conation, were *erlebt*, we could not have obtained the notion of activity in us or in things. It cannot be inferred; it cannot be extracted by passive experience from elements that are simply given. Unless the supposed activity be actual, our actual knowledge could not be forthcoming. Although Kant on occasion could treat activity as if it were a pure judging-concept like causality, his theory of knowledge essentially involves, and insists on, the activity of the subject.

The concept of activity, however, has often been disallowed. We have already seen that presentationism surreptitiously reinstates it, in openly renouncing it; also that activity is no projection into ourselves of the transeunt causality which we attribute to things, for that notion is certainly derived from our own activity, real or supposed. But other objections are forthcoming.

One of these is based on the fact that activity cannot be explained. But if it be ultimate and underivable, it is not surprising that it is inexplicable, or incapable of description in terms of anything else. Something must be ultimate for us. Bodily movements precede knowledge as to how they are performed, and are presupposed in such knowledge. We might as well deny our capacity to move before understanding how we do it, as deny our agency in cognition because we cannot supply a rationale of how we are active.[1] It does not follow, from the inexplicability of activity, that the concept thereof is a "superstition" or a "scandal", or anything but a necessary presupposition. Bradley's resolution of this particular piece of reality into appearance, besides confusing driving-power with machine, involves play on the different senses of such words as 'rational', 'intelligible'. What is unintelligible, in the sense of incapable of manipulation by the law of excluded middle—*e.g.* change—is not necessarily unintelligible, in the sense of nonsensical.

Sometimes, however, activity is dismissed on the ground that it *is* "analysable"; and then it is insinuated that orthodoxy is only

[1] The logistic philosopher would induce in us a hypnotic inactivity like that (to borrow a quotation used in this connexion by others) of the centipede who was asked by the toad   "in fun,
Which leg goes after which?
She lay distracted in a ditch
Considering how to run."

able to believe in activity, because too idle or too stupid to undertake the analysis. But the assertion that activity is analysable, turns out merely to mean that the concept of it is complex, involving prior concepts and relations. That is true, but irrelevant. What the statement 'activity is analysable' should mean, if it is to militate against the doctrine here maintained, is that alleged actual activity can be resolved into actual separate processes observable in isolation, and is known to arise out of their amalgamation. But this is not at all the case. Activity cannot undergo analysis, *i.e.* partition such as the chemist performs; nor even that, of very different kind, which is pursued in analytical psychology, where conceived constituents are distinguished, but separable parts are not actually isolated.[1]

Another short way with activity, is to relegate it to the realm of appearance or illusion. But, just as ideas presuppose percepts, so fictions presuppose facts. Knowledge of illusion is correlative with knowledge of real counterpart of some kind. Moreover, illusion is out of place when talk is of immediate experience: at that level, all that happens simply is, and illusion is an *ex post facto* condemnation of certain happenings, because in some respects they are unlike others. Lastly, if activity be illusion, the illusion involves as much activity as does reception of sense-impression.

Perhaps the ground on which activity is most often impugned, is that we have no immediate apprehension or presentation of it; that all we find, when we examine experiences alleged to evince it, is muscular sensationes. Two questionable implications are here involved. Firstly, attention is not to be identified with the adaptive motor activities that are a means for making it more effective, for these are not in all cases essential; while, instead of being prior to attention, movements are determined by previous attention to objects. Secondly, while the assertion, that we have no acquaintance-knowledge of subjective functionings, is disputable, it is fact that we claim scientific knowledge as to things with which no one has had acquaintance. By reflection on experience of change, we arrive at knowledge concerning temporal and spatial relations: it is, therefore, not inconceivable that reflection on experience may yield knowledge that activity is a precondition of knowledge. But further inquiry as to introspection can better

---

[1] See Appendix, Note B, on Analysis.

be prosecuted after study of the simpler stages of cognition of objects, a topic to which the next two chapters are devoted. To report progress up to the present: our *prima facie* facts, our data, could not be what they are, unless (1) there is a unique kind of *erleben*, viz. consciousness, which (2) involves an existent subject that (3) has determinate states and activities. Later it will be argued that the concept of subjective activity can be dispensed with, only if psychology renounce all claim to be an explanatory science of the Actual, and, dropping 'real' categories such as substance and cause, it become quasi-mathematically descriptive.

CHAPTER III

What is in the senses (In sensu) *and the Mind Itself* (Ipse intellectus)

The dictum *nihil est in intellectu quod non fuerit in sensu*, together with Leibniz's amendment *nisi ipse intellectus*, is appropriate to indicate the questions to be dealt with in this chapter. The sense-impression is the ultimate analyticum of experience on its objective side, and reception of it is the source in which perception and thought originate. The 'mind itself', used here to denote the apprehending subject and its functioning—usage differing from that of Leibniz—performs, from the first, more than passive reception of sensa; else perception and thought could not naturally arise. As Kant says,[1] "Although all our knowledge begins with experience [sensory], it does not follow that it arises from experience". To shew how psychology supports these conclusions, will be to describe the lowest stages of the knowledge-process.

I. THE OBJECTIVE FACTOR IN EXPERIENCE.

The psychological objects of individual, *i.e.* private, unshared or unsocialised, experience are actually presupposed, in the order of knowing, by the epistemological Objects of common sense. In pursuing that order, the endeavour shall be made to keep distinct, questions of priority in the different spheres of knowledge-process, temporal happening, logical presupposition, metaphysical ultimateness: which are easily confounded.

As to the objective in general, psychology knows no ground for supposing the whole being and nature of an object to be exhausted in the relation of presentation to a subject. For all that psychology can reveal, the entity which plays the rôle of object may, when not apprehended, exist just *as* the object apprehended, or otherwise, or not at all. It may have other rôles or it may have none.

As metaphysician, the psychologist may have his conviction on such matters; as psychologist, he can know nothing. But

---

[1] Introd. to 2nd ed. of his 1st *Critique*.

though psychology can furnish no direct knowledge of this sort, it does supply the only knowledge from which sober speculation on these questions must set out. Inquiries, of the kind just indicated, are not concerned with objects as such, and therefore not with objects at all. An object is what is immediately over-against a subject *in the act of apprehension*, not a real or supposed Object (for common and reflective thought) of which the object may be appearance. Of the psychological object in individual and non-conceptual experience, correlative with subject as left is with right, it can be said that its *esse* (its *objectum esse*) is *percipi*. That is simple fact, once our definition of object is clearly understood. To illustrate: blue, while seen, is an object; the blue abiding flower and the swarm of electrons it consists of, are kinds of Object. *Esse est percipi* is metaphysical and questionable, only when affirmed of Objects; or when it means that objects are subjective modes. But to appropriate Berkeley's dictum to objects (as other than modes) and to nothing else, is merely to enforce the fact that an individual's world is colourless, if he be blind: whatever the worlds of others or The World may be. It is but to assert that nothing is given that is not received; to say *quicquid recipitur, recipitur ad modum recipientis*; to deny that there are objects *per se*, though there may be Objects *per se*. The assertion, therefore, has nothing to do with idealism such as identifies the world, as known, with the world there is to know. Likewise, it avoids the converse assumption of realism, that there are 'reals' that are not perceived. There well may be; but plainly there cannot be acquaintance with them. To venture out of this ego-centric predicament, as it has been called, involves for the metaphysician, whether realist or idealist, a leap in the dark, a venture of faith, such as may or may not be justified by consequences. It is of first importance to distinguish between sensatio and sensum; but, as abstracted from one another, they are alike naught. To postulate 'sensibles', like sensa save in not being sensed, is to indulge in fiction which we have no means of distinguishing from falsity, even if it be fact. Such Objects are not objects.

Again, there is no psychological ground for the assumption that an object, such as a colour-sensum, is, like a feeling, a subjective state or a mode of the subject. Psychologically, sensa are objects presented. They are presented as objects and not as feelings, which, as already shewn, are subjective states consequent on presentation of objects. This is not to deny that feelings can be attended to, and so appear on the objective side of experience; it is merely to affirm that, before they can so appear or be cognised, they must be *erlebt* as subjective states. To be object, is to be over-against a subject: to be before the mind, but not necessarily to be in the mind, in the sense of state of mind or state of subject. Descartes bequeathed to Locke and Leibniz the assumption that sensa are changes in the subject, and so gave to early modern philosophy a bias towards idealism. It is now known that sensa have *qualia* and relations of their own, and that they are psychologically distinct from subjective modifications. If they were not, there should presumably be no Real world; experience would be 'absolute becoming'; and there should be no difference between percepts and images, such as we shall presently find to be forthcoming.

2. WHAT IS *IN SENSU*: SENSUM AND SENSATIO.

The objective is not coextensive with the sensory, nor with the explicitly discriminated. It is a genus of which sensa are species. Definitions of the sensum in terms of stimulus, commonly given in text-books, are psychophysical; they are of no deep significance for psychology, because stimulus contains and presupposes sensa. Sensa, collectively, are ultimate and inexplicable for psychology: and the fact is of importance. Psychology knows nothing of their origin, and should be chary of interpreting the unique and primordial subject-object relation as a case of the causal relation which subsists between objects, or rather Objects. Psychophysics, in asserting sensa to be caused by Objects, tacitly assumes a particular theory of knowledge and a *ratio essendi*; whereas psychology must suspend judgement and eschew assumption, as well as avoid metaphysics. She does not scorn psychophysics, however; she makes great use of its deliverances, as some 'function' of the truth that she herself seeks.

From the psychophysical, as distinguished from the purely psychological, point of view, sensa have been classified thus:

1. Those due to 'adequate' (*i.e.* appropriate) stimuli:
   (*a*) Sensa mediated by the special sense-organs, visual, auditory, etc.

(*b*) Organic sensa due to the body but not to sense-organs; *e.g.* aches, nausea, fatigue.

2. Those due to 'inadequate' stimuli: *e.g.* light seen when, in the dark, the head is bumped, or the optic nerve stimulated electrically.

3. So-called 'subjective sensations', *e.g.* the retina's own light, probably of cerebral conditioning.

4. Motor presentations. These differ from the preceding kinds, in that their order, being dependent on interest, is so far psychologically explicable.

It may be observed that 'sensory', usually meaning impressional or consisting of sensa, is also used as equivalent to sense-sustained, sensum-like, containing sensa, and is then applied to images, etc. as well as to sensa.

The denotation of 'sensum' has now been indicated. The only connotational statement that can be made from the standpoint of psychology, is that the sensum is that element in the objective which may be said first to break in upon the experient, because all other types of experience, that we can distinguish, are known to presuppose it. The point in this assertion is not that subjective states are consequent on sensatio, but that there is a species of objective presentation, the imaginal, which does not arise without previous attention to sensa, and which is derived from sensa when they are fused into a percept. It is in recognition of this important fact, that the sensum has been called 'primary presentation' and 'impression'. The presentation, order and nature of impressions, in so far as involuntary or non-selective attention is concerned, are thrust upon us willy-nilly: that is what renders the impressional psychologically ultimate and inexplicable. The analytically simple data of all knowledge as to our actual world, are thus posited for us, not by us: they constitute an irrational surd which pure thought cannot eliminate.

The next fact of philosophical significance about the impressional or what is 'in the senses', is that there are no such actualities as the pure sensa that have figured in philosophical, and have been foisted into psychological, literature. The pure sensum which is impression and nothing else, can no more be "caught" than Hume's "I". It is an analytically distinguishable element, a conceptual limit, like the line without breadth: if sensatio were pure or anoetic, perception and higher knowledge could never emerge from it. The patch of colour has been adduced as an instance of a pure sense-datum; but in order to be discriminated and described as a patch of colour, the pure sensum of colour must already be combined with sensory and motor presentations, and with re-presentations. It is then a relatively simple percept, not a pure sensum. Conversely, the pure sensum is a hypothetical simple, an artifact of conceptual and advanced intelligence; such a 'particular' is as much an abstraction from a percept as is a universal. If our sensa were pure, not fusions or complexes, and if sensatio were no more than passive reception, not a single step could be taken to explain a single psychological fact. This implies that at bottom, in experience once begun, there is no 'acquaintance' (*kennen*) without some slight tincture of 'knowledge about' (*wissen*), somewhat of assimilation and recognition; while there can be no acquaintance with universals, as explicit, because apprehension of them presupposes the intellectual comparison that bespeaks more advanced experience.

As the impression is the kernel of the developed percept, as there are no images not derived from percepts,[1] and as it is through images that ideas are mediated, we can now see the truth in the assertion that there is nothing in the understanding that was not previously in the senses; while in the fact that the only actuality that can be called sensatio, is germinal perception, richer than bare reception, we gain our first glimpse of the significance of the supplement: "save the mind itself". We have also made first acquaintance with the evidence for the fact that sense and understanding have a common root. The actual process commonly called sense, is from the first possessed of the promise and potency of thought.

There is, again, no ground known to empirical psychology for assuming sensa to be discrete, or that experience begins with separate, discriminated, presentations. When psychology was young, atomic theory dominated physics and was obsessive enough to induce resort, in mental science, to misleading and irrelevant analogies. Some of the suppositions thus engendered are now

---

[1] Percepts, *i.e.* of higher complexity than the very simplest, the sensum. We do not form an image of red or abstract redness, but only of an extended red something. Answering to the sensum or impression we have not an image, but a concept.

seen to be without basis in fact; and there is little room for doubt that the distinctness, which mature experience can attribute to its impressional elements, is due to acquired proficiency in differentiating what is first given as a continuum. Sensa will then be particular changes, parts rather than individuals, interfusing elements rather than parts. Indeed the ultimate actual and concrete bit of experience, prior to analysis by conceptual thought, is not a sensum or an aggregate of sensa, but a stretch of change, within which particular sensa come to be discriminated. It does not arise by combination of them; they arise as differentiations of it. To have always one and the same sensatio, would be tantamount to having none at all: it is the coming into, and the going out of, the field of consciousness or the focus of attention, by which, so to speak, the objective announces its objectivity, or otherness from its subject. It follows, by the way, that at the primary level of pristine, concrete, unanalysed experience, change is the fundamental reality: all being is becoming: flux is a condition of awareness. Ultimate analytica, then, are not to be mistaken for genetically first things: in order of knowing they come late.

Yet another error as to sensa, that has played mischief in philosophy, is the assumption that sensa are formless. If without form, they should be also void, and consequently unrecognisable. The prejudice was delectable to the rationalist: it secured to the mind the dignified function of imposing all form on the matter of perception. In this radical sense, the Kantian teaching expressed in the apparently non-Kantian terms that 'the mind makes Nature', is untenable. Sensa have form and character quite independent of our subjective activity.[1]

---

[1] From the standpoint of science, though not from that of the experient when engaged in unreflectively perceiving, sensa are complex. They have *quale* and intensity. Ward and other psychologists ascribe to them protensity (duration corresponding to that of stimulus, a precursor of the concept of time) and extensity (precursor in primitive individual or unsocialised experience of extension in common space). Those who, on the contrary, maintain that sensa have temporal duration and spatial extension, seem to be thinking of something different from what Ward discusses, viz. of percepts at a higher stage of elaboration, as they now are for us adults equipped with common knowledge or, at least, matured perception of the bodily self. As intensity, *e.g.* degree of loudness or brightness, varies with attention when stimulus is constant, it is in part subjectively determined: a fact which evidences the non-passivity of the barest actual sensatio, and renders futile all attempts to isolate a *pure* datum.

This complexity of the sensum does not argue separable constituents; it is not

The foregoing characterisation of sensa has exposed various errors, as to matter of fact, that have vitiated historically important philosophical systems.

Some of them are traceable to the rationalistic propensity to set out from abstract ideas, rather than facts of concrete experience. Sensationist psychology, though it arose in the school known as the empirical, is essentially a rationalistic theory in this respect. It still lives in the works of Mach, K. Pearson and neo-realists, where sensa are conceived as like atoms flying through space, now and again impinging on subjects, likewise conceived after analogy with the physicist's mass-particle, in that they are as destitute of 'insides', or intrinsic states and acts. Similarly rationalistic is the Platonic assumption that sense and thought are disparate, issuing from distinct sources. Before genetic sciences arose, this opinion was natural; it prevailed for centuries. Kant hinted at the possibility of a common root of sense and thought; but his disdain of empirical psychology, and his ingrained rationalistic leanings, prevented him from looking for the root. Taking from Locke and Hume, without question, the assumption that sensa are pure and atomic, and supposing thought to consist in forming, comparing and unifying them, he perpetuated the old dualistic view. Leibniz had vaguely anticipated Kant's suggestion of the common root, in supposing sense-perception to be obscure thought; but he was yet farther than Kant from the only kind of investigation that could establish their community of source. It will presently be found that 'thought is clarified sense' is nearer the truth than is 'sense is obscure thought'. But, of course, the common root is neither sense nor thought, in the differentiated form which we have come to know; it is the actual sensatio which, from the first, differs from 'pure' sensatio in consisting partly of, and being

expressible by $a+b+c$, but rather by abc, which $=0$ if $a=0$. If the intensity of a sensum be reduced to nil, the quality also vanishes. But, theoretically, sensa may be analysable into elements, homogeneous or heterogeneous, and be subconscious syntheses. If so, a limit is set to our power of discrimination. As to the different qualities of the sensa mediated by our several sense-organs, there is reason to believe that they have been differentiated out of one primordial kind.

Such intrinsic characteristics of sensa as have been mentioned, suffice to belie the assertion of their formlessness. There is form in Kant's matter, and also matter in his form; the supposed sharp antithesis between matter and form is another of the evil legacies of Greek philosophy.

accompanied by, operations that are already vague and implicit or germinal thinking. It may be that, in the present state of psychological science, the stages of the evolution are not all clearly and definitely traceable in detail: at any rate Prof. Stout has recently expressed his conviction that discontinuity is not over-come, in Ward's account of the developement of knowledge out of sense-knowledge, especially in the case of time-perception. But even supposing this expert doubt to be at present well grounded, the evidence for continuity is so strong and clear, almost all along the line, that belief in discontinuity, between sensatio and de-veloped thought, is now much more precarious than belief in their continuity. This evidence has yet to be submitted.

Several false assumptions have been exposed, on the strength of which assertions have been made concerning sensatio, that are inconsistent with fact. The science of psychology demands that a clean sweep be made of philosophical theories, however venerable, that are based on such assumptions. So far, we have found that this science enforces the conclusion that the only actualities that can be denoted by 'sensa', are germinal percepts, not pure im-pressions. Unless sensatio be something more than passive re-ception of impression, there could be no such thing as human mentality to discuss. To account for that mentality, we must proceed to study the primary stages of mental process, and the subjective activities over and above approximately passive or bare sensatio.

3. "THE MIND ITSELF."

The first of these activities is retention, the precursor of memory and mental dispositions. It is fact that sensa do not come and go, leaving the subject as if they had never been presented; and fact which sensationism and presentationism overlook. Sensa have after-effects. When the impression has vanished, a residuum is left, distinguishable from the impression itself. Neither persistence of the old, nor substitution of a new, sensum, as if each successive impression were for the time being our whole world, will account for the growing picture which we form, *e.g.* when examining a flower. At any moment, in the study of the flower, our total experience is the cumulative effect of impressions vanished and traces remaining. Retention involves change as well as persistence; and change that is not sudden substitution. It also involves the

activity and interest of the subject; for we do not retain all that
has been presented, but only what we select and assimilate. Again,
if sensa lapsed into complete oblivion, if the mind's only activity
were momentary awareness of fleeting impression, sensa could
never be signs of, or point to, others. All they could do, would
be but to occur and be done with. Each would be "a petty
absolute", with no reference beyond itself, no 'meaning'. But
sensa are not only sensed; they are also recognised: repetition
breeds familiarity, which can only be accounted for, it would
seem, by invoking subjective interest. Apart from retained elements, sensa could not even 'mean' themselves: they would have
no recognised individuality, and could not be identified. Primary
meaning, as it is called, thus only exists through relation to the
subject, as retainer.

Retention is much simpler than memory, and is not to be confounded with it. But, no retention, no recognition; and no recognition, no memory. Also, no comparison, no emergent knowledge
of relations. Thus, unless the germ of thought accompanied sensatio
from the first, thought could never arise, save by separate creation.
The purer we conceive our sensa to be, and the more passive
we suppose their reception, the further we remove the possibility
of a natural explanation of knowledge. At the conceptual limit
of absolute purity and passivity, that possibility vanishes altogether:
sensa become blind and dumb. In actual, as distinct from fictitious
or conceptual, sensatio, there is already the root of thought, the
germ of understanding. In the simplest recognition—in the fact
that a later sensatio of blue carries with it identification of the
sensum with a previous one, as resembling it, as 'blue again', or
a case of blue—there is implicit awareness of the universal in the
particular. Lastly, familiarity is not always, and therefore not
necessarily, the effect of repetition of impression, nor of the attention that alone would be involved in pure sensatio; it presupposes
the interest, affectiveness, selectiveness, of the subject whose
presentations at any moment are conditioned by the traces of the
presentations of previous moments. These facts will be found
significant, when we come to consider the attempt to describe the
continuity of a self's experience in terms of a series of momentary
subjects: it will then be argued that to banish the enduring
subject involves resort to supernaturalism.

Another primary functioning of 'the mind itself' is the assimilation or complication which fuses old presentations or their residua with new. This is the germ of all subjective synthesis. It is presupposed by the association of ideas, for, without it, there would be no ideas to associate. It had not been detected in the days of mental chemistry, when mechanical association was believed to render subjective synthesis a superfluous notion. As said before, in speaking of sensa, etc. as separate units for assimilation, it is not necessary to assume that experience begins with such. The relative individualness that sense-impressions have, is, genetically speaking, probably the result of differentiation of what is given to the experient as a continuum. Consciousness is not given in atoms; its smallest portion is a process, and its simplest portion is complex. Thus assimilation presupposes differentiation, discussion of which, were it not superfluous here, should have preceded that of retention.   It is enough merely to indicate this third primary function of the mind, and to observe that integration of the differentiated continuum developes *pari passu* with differentiation.

'Complication' must ensue on sensatio, if ever they were separate, before there can be presentation of images. For we never form an image of the simplest actual sensum, as such, any more than we form images without previous impressions; images are always of relatively complex presentations, assimilated sensa. Assimilation is also the precursor of developed perception; it is involved when we construct several different percepts out of the same aggregate of sensa (colours, sounds, etc.), and one percept out of sensa that are not presented together. Without this synthetic activity, there would be no explanation of the fact that sensa get combined otherwise than as they occur or are given. By means of it, we can account for the emergence of secondary or acquired meaning, as when we say that orange colour and spherical shape together mean juiciness; which, before tasting, is not given to sense. Here an aggregate of actual impressions suggests, stands for, means, something else.

The word 'attention', in the foregoing paragraphs, has borne a conventionally restricted meaning; and apology is due for adding one more to the uses to which an already overworked term has been put. But a name was temporarily wanted to distinguish barest reception of sense-impression, analytically isolated from the more obviously active functions with which, from the first, it is actually interfused, and at the same time to indicate that this relative passivity is itself by no means devoid of activity. The "one faculty" on which Dr Ward with equally conventional embracingness bestowed the same term, has already been seen to comprise a plurality of activities, which are none the less irreducibly different, for being refused the name of faculties. Naming is relatively an unimportant matter; discrimination of things that differ, is all-important. Retention, complication or fusion, and differentiation, are three primordial contributions of 'the mind itself'—which phrase is here borrowed as if equivalent to 'the subject'—in interaction with its objective continuum. The subject retains, fuses, etc.: it does not attend (in the restricted sense) to *retenta, complicata*, etc. Differentiation is partly an emergent from interaction: attention *makes* differences within the individual's field. There is thus ground in psychological fact for rejecting the epistemological theory, that all differences between distinguishable cognitive processes are entirely due to difference between objects attended to. Dr Ward speaks of the processes that so far have here been described, as "constituting what we may call the *plasticity*" of the presentational continuum; but he distinctly implies, in spite of appearance sometimes to the contrary, the diversity of subjective moulding of the plastic. Prof. Stout deals with these same processes in a chapter entitled "Primary laws of mental process". I have ventured more unambiguously to call them irreducible subjective activities.

If what a subject *is*, be largely a question of what it *does*, we are now well on the way to a science of its nature. We shall be carried further on our way by investigation, in the next chapter, of higher stages in the knowledge-process.

CHAPTER IV

Perception, Imagination, Memory, Ideation

I. PERCEPTION.

The sensum was stated in the preceding chapter to be a simple percept; and sensatio, the closest approximation to *pure* sensatio that can have occurred in incipient experience, to be germinal perception, already involving subjective activity and not consisting in reception of a bare impression or in simultaneous reception of several already distinct impressions. But the fluid term 'perception', even if restricted to the formation of what shall here be called the percept proper—*i.e.* the 'thing' constructed out of the subject's sensa by himself, without aid from communication with others, and before he has attained the common standpoint—is usually reserved for cognition involving further stages than have as yet been mentioned. To these we now turn. We find in them new synthetic operations; more of rudimentary conception than is implicit in simple recognition; and sometimes a supplementing of present impressions by the residual and the imaginal, or by what are called 'revived' presentations. Perception, when thus completed, includes localisation in the percipient's private space; also reification, in virtue of which sensa come to be regarded as qualities of 'things', though these are not to be identified with the 'things' of common or social experience. It should here be noted that the word 'perception' is used, both in ordinary parlance and in psychological literature, for cognition involving localisation in public or conceptual space, and reification in terms of explicated categories, such as are only forthcoming when individual perception has given place to conception dependent on intercourse. This so-called perception is nine-tenths conception, and will be examined at a later stage.

As for the difference between perception (what I have ventured to isolate as 'perception proper') and conception, it will have appeared already that no hard or absolute line can be drawn between them, or between perception and sensatio. We can distinguish between their ideal limits, which thought substitutes for indefinite actualities. We cannot allege, but can deny, the separateness of what we conceptually distinguish. Static concepts such as dominate the abstractive method, are indeed the only counters that formal logic can use. They are but makeshifts, if the actuality confronting us is fluid becoming.

Again, psychology must deny that philosophy can put its finger on any bit of actual experience, and say that there we are in touch with reality, in the sense of objectivity pure and subjectively undefiled. If it point to the pure sensum, there is no such thing. If it submit the developed percept, there is nothing perceptual that is not subjectively fused, and tinged with the incipiently or implicitly conceptual. The perceptually real contains more than temporally present datum; and the objective datum, in being received, is overlaid with subjective contribution—retention, integration, etc. It would be confounding the implicit with the explicit, to say that at this level of experience "all fact is already theory"; that speculation, in the current sense, already inheres in speculation in the obsolete sense.[1] But the objective is, from the first, somewhat humanised by interest, given meaning or reference to a beyond. It is to this extent—confessedly a slight extent—*interpreted*, if involuntarily and 'unconsciously' or 'instinctively'.[2] Full perception is thus a completion of the purest kind of sensatio that is actual, and is intermediate between sensing and ideation. It is in the percept alone, that we adults ever encounter the impressional; and there the non-impressional is already present. The neat distinctions, set up by abstractive thought, do not exist in actual experience. The percept, wont to be taken for bed-rock reality of which the conceptual is valid, has a foot in both worlds, the subjective and the objective. The very foundations of the *ratio essendi* are thus not real, in the sense that thoroughgoing realism would have them be—*i.e.* independent of subjectivity. In the percept, the datum of knowledge for adult experience, psychology can specify subjective elements.

[1] "There is no speculation in those eyes thou glar'st with."

[2] With a view to later developements let it be noted, for what it is worth, that already in the perceptio that is source of all 'knowledge', there is *some* reference to what is beyond temporally present sense-datum and *some* tincture of germinal interpretation. We shall increasingly find that if 'knowing' be so defined as to exclude interpreting and reading in, the definition may be pleasing, but nothing actually answers to it.

Yet another point, of philosophical import, emerges in the analytical study of perception. At the moment of perceiving a thing, we are unaware of performing synthetic activities: from the standpoint of our experience at that moment, the perception is immediate; and the percept has the unity, simplicity and instantaneousness of a flash-photograph. The whole act does not seem other than unanalysable, and unconditioned by previous experience. From the standpoint of the psychologist, however, whether another person or oneself, afterwards reflecting on that experience, the perception is neither simple nor immediate. These two standpoints, that of an experience and that of its exposition, have been named respectively the 'psychic' and the 'psychological'.[1] As this nomenclature is established, it is well to abide by it; though 'psychological', in this technical sense, is in danger of being confounded with the word as ordinarily used, and 'epistemological' would perhaps have been apter. 'Psychic' and its adverb shall in future be symbolised for brevity' sake by (ψ), and 'psychological' by (ps), when their introduction is necessary to avoid ambiguity. Digressing yet a little further from the topic which evoked mention of these two points of view, one may add here that recognition of the difference between them, is of importance such as can scarcely be exaggerated. To become obsessed by a fixed idea of it, is an invaluable asset for the accurate philosopher. It may be said to constitute the watershed that casts the streams of psychological method and theory in diverse directions. Behaviourism and kindred substitutes for psychology, seem to be founded on confusion of these standpoints, in which 'the psychologist's fallacy' consists. This fallacy is not confined to psychologists. It pervades epistemology, ethics, and various departments of theology; physicists who take artifacts, in virtue of their familiarity, for pure or (ps) immediate data, owe their scientific realism largely to it. Its fecundity in paralogistic offspring is hardly rivalled by ambiguity of philosophical terms.

To return: developed perception is a complex act, conditioned by previous experience and involving synthetic operations, of which, in the act of perceiving, the percipient is unaware. The facility with which we combine impressions with residua and images, has been acquired: we are told that a man born blind,

[1] See *Dict. of Philos. and Psychol.* ed. Baldwin; Art. "Psychic and Psychological."

but later becoming possessed of sight, needs to learn to perceive 'things' visually. We are also told that the capacity to form a complete percept lapses in certain diseases, when auditory or visual memory is lost, although the sense-organs remain sound: it can be destroyed. Nevertheless, the initial integration involved in the lower stages of perception, is normally so indissoluble that, in all definite imagery, what is said (unhappily) to be re-presented, is not separate sensa, but the relatively complex percept, with the fusion of its elements preserved intact.

As to localisation and projection of the percept into the per-cipient's private space, it is not necessary to go into detail. It suffices to know that reification into what, for the percipient, is one thing, occupying space and possessing materiality, is depen-dent on his bodily movement and effort resisted. But, however the spatial—and the temporal—relations of sense-data come to be known, it is important to observe, especially after emphasising the subjective activity involved in perception, that these rela-tions "are themselves in no way psychologically determined: they are primarily and in the main quite independent of the subject's interest or of any psychological principles of synthesis or associa-tion whatsoever".[1] Not only are impressions themselves psycho-logically inexplicable; our synthesis of them is largely compelled by the external control of their subjectively unalterable relations. Explicit apprehension of relations, is a stage of knowledge more advanced than that of perception or thing-intuition; we are at present only concerned to note its sensory grounding, and to observe that sensa—or qualities of things, as they become in developed perception—which hang together, cannot by us be actually disconnected, nor any of them be extruded from brute fact. The subjective activities involved in perceiving, no more make all the relations between sensa than they create the sensa themselves; though they are indispensable factors in knowledge. Their constitutiveness of object or thing perceived, is confined to the interest-determined choice that often decides which groups of conjoined qualities shall be regarded as one individual thing, or as constituting one process. In different creatures this selec-tiveness depends, perhaps, on reliance upon one sense, rather than another, as primary; and certainly on the creature's time-span and

[1] Ward, *Psychol. Principles*, 1918, p. 164.

natural *tempo*. An explosion, *e.g.* is one event for a man; though, for a tiny gnat, it may be a series of intermittent breezes: either a grain of sand or a sandhill may be one thing for us, as occasion and interest require. To a being with vastly greater time-span than ours, human history might seem as meaningless as the fall of sand in an hour-glass does to us. Possession of one natural *tempo* restricts us to one mode of viewing the course of Nature; just as choice of *largo* or *presto*, by a composer, conditions the meaning of a movement for its performer. The unity and fixity of a percept are thus far relative to *homo mensura*.[1] Taken more seriously than as conventions, contingently inevitable and pragmatically justified, the unity and fixity of 'things' have given rise to gratuitous logical puzzles, and provided exercise for the sophist. Sometimes it is temporally continuous disposition of ever-changing *disposita*, that constitutes one thing, as in the case of a river or of the body.

One's own body, it may here be noted, is psychologically by far the most important 'thing' one perceives.

Our body is both constant as a group, and a constant item in every other field of groups: and not only so, but it is, beyond all other things, an object of continual and peculiar interest, inasmuch as our earliest pleasures and pains depend solely on it and what affects it. The body becomes in fact...the first datum for our later conceptions of permanence and individuality. A permanence like that of the [bodily] self is then transferred to other bodies which resemble our own, so far as direct experience goes, in passing continuously from place to place and undergoing only partial and gradual changes of form and quality.... However permanent we suppose the conscious subject to be, it is hard to see how, without the continuous presentation to it of such a group as the bodily self, we should ever be prompted to convert the discontinuous presentations of external things into a continuity of existence.

[1] Cf. what is said about primary and secondary sensa in chap. XIII. *A propos* of time-span, *tempo*, and our having *become* incapable of scientifically describing phenomena otherwise than mainly in terms of the sensa that we have selected as primary, allusion may be made to the pleasing fancy of Prof. Royce, that natural things such as streams and stones are beings "who are, so to speak, not in our own social set, and who communicate to us, not their minds, but their presence" only; the diversity of time-span between them and us being such that we cannot hold communion with them, as with our fellows. "We have no right", he suggests, "to call the other tongues with which Nature speaks, barbarous, because, in our evolutionary isolation from the rest of Nature, we have forgotten what they mean" (*Studies of Good and Evil*, pp. 230, 232).

It is the bodily self that first gives us the right to pass from our fleeting and sporadic sensa to belief in permanent things and in other bodily selves.

Matured perception involves the distinction, essential to our logic, between the thing and its qualities, powers, etc. To resume quotation from Prof. Ward:[1]

Of all the constituents of things one only is universally present, that above described as physical solidity, which presents itself according to circumstances as impenetrability, resistance or weight. Things differing in temperature, colour, taste and smell, agree in resisting compression, in filling space. Because of this quality we regard the wind as a thing, though it has neither shape nor colour, while a shadow, though it has both but is non-resistent, is the very type of nothingness.... At the moment of contact an unvarying tactual magnitude is ascertained, while the other qualities and the visual magnitude reach a fixed maximum: then it becomes possible by effort to change or attempt to change the position and form of what we apprehend. This tangible plenum we thenceforth regard as seat and source of all the qualities we project into it. In other words, that which occupies space is psychologically the substantial.

This is the one sensum that is, for us men, a primary quality.[2] It is also *sui generis* in being "the only one that the subject gives to itself, or at any rate, gets for itself by its own activity".

Here we have an instance of the truth that knowledge presupposes *erleben*, and that the interpretative supplementation, by which alone we could pass from pure sensatio, had we ever experienced it, to perception of a thing, is subjectively originated and anthropically conditioned. Humanisation is involved in perception, or at the initial stage of transition from sense to understanding. Our first crude notions of permanence, unity and individuality, implicit in the synthesis of the complex percept, were derived from early experience of our bodily selves. So too is that of force or activity, which, through analogy with our effort exerted on things resisting our movements, we ascribe to such things. These interpretative notions are the precursors, the actual source, of the categories of substance, cause, etc. They implicitly contain what warrant there is for the corresponding later-explicated categories, whereby the experience-organisation which we call

[1] *Op. cit.* pp. 166–7.
[2] In canine metaphysics, doubtless the substantial is that which smells. Cf. chap. xiii.

knowledge of an external world, is effected. It is to the contingency that human beings are embodied in solid flesh, that
ultimately is due the particular form of the primary concepts
through which the world is 'known', and from which human
thought and reasoning are spun. Had we not been embodied,
may be we should not have possessed the categories we use: our
thought-synthesised experience, even if its sensory core had been
the same, would possibly not have been what it is. Thus the
logically *a priori* forms of *our* understanding and knowledge are
not necessarily those of the understanding and knowledge of other
intelligent beings, nor of Universal Understanding or Reason in
the abstract—whatever that may be. They are derived from life,
not from logic; they are regulative while they are constitutive;
they are both anthropic and mundane. Creations of the synthesising and interested subject, suggested by his body and
prompted, or at any rate suffered, by the sensory data into which
he reads them, they are tools for fashioning a phenomenal world
in some respects after his own likeness.

Possessed of this knowledge, we can see the foregone fruitless-
ness of attempts to account for the subject in terms of concepts
supposed to be read off from the external world, and to be involved
in any possible experience or in every conceivable kind of knowledge. Even at this early stage of our investigation, it may be
observed that genetic study of psychological facts shews up the
error of the apriorism, which seeks to transcend the actual context
in which our thought-forms were fashioned, and to which alone
they can be known to apply. The assertion of their absoluteness
or of their independence of sense, is scientifically unwarranted, and
therefore philosophically dogmatical. They are not innate as ready-
made mental furniture, without which *any* thinking would be
impossible; nor are they *a priori*, in the sense of originally independent of sensory experience, though they are not impressions.
They are 'of the mind', and are *a priori* only in the harmless sense
that they are regulative instruments, through use of which our
thought and 'knowledge' have come to be what they actually
are, as distinct from what, in other conditions, they might have
been.

One other ingredient in developed perception remains to be
noted. Such perception issues in the judgement that the percept

exists: reality or actuality is ascribed to a percept.[1] This actuality is not another sensum, over and above colour, etc. Nor is it a relation between sensa, such as that of substance and quality; for that is equally involved in the real and its image. It is not a separate item, but enters into all the items. Epistemologically expressed, as Ward says, it answers to the existential judgement 'it is', which developed perception involves. What is meant by this assertion of reality, turns then on the difference between the impressional and the imaginal. This is a very important question, calling the more for attention, because largely ignored in constructive philosophy. Hitherto, in our study of perception, we have only encountered imagination in the broad and loose sense of the word, inclusive of so-called re-presentation (which is *not* repetition), *i.e.* the traces or residua of past experience, falling short of memory proper, and, though something more than sensatio, something less than definite imaging.

2. FROM THE IMPRESSIONAL TO THE IMAGINAL: THE IMAGE.

The perceptual, it has been said, is credited with actuality that is refused to the imaginal; though both are objective, or real in the psychological sense, and both occur or exist. This bespeaks some difference between impression, or simple percept, and image, which only emerges when the two kinds of presentation are compared. The difference is further to seek than was supposed by

[1] On reality, actuality, existence, etc., see Note C, after reading to the end of this chapter. Judgement or belief, though genetically an emergent from perception, is a unique faculty, not identifiable with the earlier stages of perceiving, or with any kind of simple apprehension. Again we may see that it is an over-simplification to speak of our "one faculty of attention", unless we are to speak of sub-faculties.

To emphasise, as above, that the impressional core of all perception is, for psychology, the primary reality and the objective source of all knowledge as to the existent, is not to insinuate that all that exists is perceptual or even possibly perceptible: as if subjects, their states and their impressions, were all that is in heaven and earth. That would indeed be "parochial effrontery". It is but to affirm that no other analytic data are indubitably known to science. This will be disputed by the rationalist who believes in thought-given existents, and by the mystic such as claims to apprehend existents neither sensible nor intelligible.

It should be observed that when the individual judges that his percept exists, he cannot, before attaining through intercourse the common standpoint, have any explicit notion of its existing 'independently', *i.e.* out of the perception-relation: perception, so far as it is distinguishable from conception, is only of here and now.

Hume, who regarded it as consisting in the greater "liveliness" of the impression, and therefore as a matter of degree, rather than of kind. If 'liveliness' mean intensity, it is an insufficient criterion; for the image sometimes has greater vividness than the feeble impression. If it mean strikingness, we are confronted by the fact that even ideas may possess great impressiveness, for many minds eclipsing that of perceptual fact. Fortunately, the differences between impression and image, which escaped early psychologists, are observable. They have been carefully stated by Prof. Ward, from whose account the following facts are mostly taken.

(a) Impressions are psychologically independent of each other and, as to their character and order, are also independent of the impressions and images presented the moment before; whereas images are dependent on previous impressions. To receive an impression of blue, we do not require to have received already an impression of any sort; but it is a matter of fact that imaged blue is never presented, save after impressional blue: we cannot image what we have not previously sensed. Impressions are primary, images are secondary, presentations, conditioned as to existence and nature by the impressional, and an outgrowth therefrom. There is nothing in the complex image of a non-actual thing, such as a mermaid, that was not previously 'in the senses'.

(b) Images, in normal waking life, are usually in a state of flux or flickering; and this is so, even when we try to fix and retain them. In spite of our endeavour to call up the image of a familiar face, the portrait will often insist on passing through successive caricatures; and sometimes concentration of attention upon an image will result in its vanishing. There is no need, on the other hand, to make effort in order to retain an impression, *e.g.* to see the sky as blue. When the whole presentation-continuum is accessible to us, we are able, by appeal to percepts, to give the lie to the images which have just been presented in reverie or in sleep. And it is only when, as in sleep, contrast with the impressional continuum is precluded, that our imagery simulates the fixity characteristic of the impressional; or, when, as in hallucination, the presentation contains the impressional (*e.g.* organic sensa) as well as imaginal ingredients.

(c) We can form an image of a blue rose, but we can never see a red rose as at the same time blue. Such facts shew that, whatever be the connexion between the impressional and the imaginal, they are essentially different orders of the objective. The so-called revived impression is not impression at all.

(d) Images, like ideas derived from them, can be associated: the conditioning of their subsequent sequence and coexistence is psychological. But, apart from voluntary movement, the order and connexion of impressions is externally, not psychologically, controlled.

These facts, to which more could be added, are ever verifiable. It is not necessary, then, to deal with the tenets, "of violent birth but poor validity", of behaviourism such as denies the imaginal altogether or asserts images to be feeble motor-presentations, thus turning a blind eye on commonplace knowledge. It is more to the purpose to emphasise that the objective, the 'real' in the psychological and primary sense of the word, includes the imaginal; and that the developed percept often includes imaginal ingredients. The imaginal, we shall presently see, is the source of ideas.[1] So the thought-process by which we strain out the imaginal from what is Real for common knowledge, is offspring of unReality. The percept of individual experience, which is the presupposition of knowledge of the Objective, contains sometimes the unReal. Science and theory being obtained by clipping and manipulation of primary fact, it behoves us to watch the process by which the *ratio* and *ordo essendi* are set up, especially if they be taken for aught but provisional scaffolding.

It has been established that the imaginal, at least in its purest examples, and the impressional, are in some respects distinct and subject to different laws. Nevertheless, they can be subjectively fused in actual experience; and this is a psychologically ultimate fact, if an irresolvable mystery. But, distinct as they are, it is now to be shewn that there are links intermediate between them.

Starting from the impressional side, the first link is what is often called the after-image, but would more aptly be designated the after-sensation (sensum). Psychophysically regarded, this object is due either to persistence of excitation of a sense-organ after cessation of the physical stimulus—when it is but the original

---

[1] If images, metaphysically regarded, be due to *rapport* with the Real, then Being is cause, as well as occasion, of the source of ideas: while the cause of ideas, as distinct rom their image-sources, will be their own subjects solely.

impression in evanescence; or to nervous exhaustion or repair, consequent on the wear and tear of excitation—as in the familiar experience of seeing the colour complementary to that at which we have been gazing. In the latter case we receive a new, not an evanescing, impression—*e.g.* green instead of pink. These after-images, then, are not images at all. They are impressional and sense-sustained. Yet, like the imaginal and unlike the impressional, they do not lend themselves to synthesis into physical Objects: colloquial science would call them subjective. Those of the former class differ from the ordinary impression, in shewing a gradual waning; those of the latter class, when visual, may be seen when the eye is closed, lack the three-dimensional detail of the perceptual, and vary in size according to the area on which they are projected. Here, then, is a variety of the impressional sharing characteristics distinctive of the imaginal.

· Next, there is the 'recurrent sensation'. Things that have long been engaging attention will sometimes stand out, when no longer perceived. An artist may thus 'see' his picture, even in the dark, and long after physical stimuli have ceased and excitation-effects vanished. Such objects have marks of the percept which after-sensations lack. They are not hallucinations, because due neither to suggestion nor to any derangement. They are dependent, like images, on previous perception. Unlike percepts, they are not due to simultaneous stimulation. Psychologically on a par with the perceptual, they are separated from it by common sense and psychophysics. Again we may note, in passing, the selectiveness with which 'knowledge' proceeds. Not only is the imaginal rejected for the impressional, but some of the impressional is taken while other is left; or more accurately, any hybrid between impression and image is discarded, by application of an *ex post facto* criterion for distinguishing between deliverances having the same objectivity-vouch in individual experience. From the point of view of unsophisticated psychology, here is some arbitrariness calling for an epistemological *apologia*.

The last intermediary between impression and free image, is the sense-bound image. Its primitive form is Fechner's 'memory after-image' or the 'primary memory-image'. Perhaps 'after-percept', bespeaking retention rather than memory, would be an apter name for it. An instance of what is thus denoted, is the visual image that we may at any time see, on turning away from a thing at which we have been looking, and which we can often recover after it has lapsed. Another example is the persistent sound-image of the striking of a clock, which was not 'attended to' at the time. In such objects as these, we have what is not a residuum of an impression nor explicable by retention alone, though it is partly sense-sustained. It has the form of the percept, but is not localised in common space, nor accompanied by the feeling-tone and the motor adaptations incidental to the reception of impressions; it reproduces the *quale* and the fusion, but not the proportionate intensities, of the original constituents; and its return, or re-presentation, is not dependent, like recurrence of impression, on repetition of stimulus.[1]

[1] The primary memory-image, like the tied or sense-bound image that figures in preperception, continues its life-history, so to speak, when not attended to. It may recur in the field of consciousness, assimilated with a fresh impression, or as a 're-presentation'—when "it is accompanied by the reinstatement of those antecedent circumstances which were integrated with it by attention on a given occasion" (B. Edgell, *Proc. of the Aristot. Soc.*, 1919–20, p. 195). The writer just quoted observes that re-presentations and dispositions are processes possessing the activity of mental life, in that they rise above and fall below the threshold of consciousness; and also remarks that where the activity thus ascribed to the plastic continuum, and the activity [literal] of the subject, precisely begin and end, is a question as to which clearer teaching than has been forthcoming, is desirable. This is an important topic in relation to activity; and it has received some discussion in Stout's *Anal. Psychology*, I. 123 ff., 168 ff. It should be observed that the activity that is analogically attributed to mental processes, is not to be assumed to be inherent in them and to be other than the activity which must literally be predicated of the subject; though there is *some* truth in the assertion that the flow of ideas is determined partly by a "motion of its own". Attention is not transeunt causation, and association is not voluntary or selective, but quasi-mechanical; yet when, as in reverie, the subject is least conscious of mental effort, mental images do not "glide over the surface of the mind as a procession of moving bodies is reflected in a mirror". He is not merely a spectator or an endurer; and, to quote Prof. Stout again, "facile action is not inaction". Every step in the reverie-process is conditioned by interest as well as by association: attention bestowed, as well as the object on which it is bestowed, determines the power of each image to call up others. The flow of ideas is thus manipulated by subjective activity; apart from the active subject, it is an abstraction and a nonentity. Mr Johnson, in his *Logic*, also comments on the exposition of psychology as if in association, etc., quasi-mechanical processes went on, constituting a kind of non-ego over which the ego, as agent, is supposed to exert control now and again or not at all. This fission of experience, he says, often leading to suppression of subjective control altogether, is otiose and a misrepresentation. And it is through vicious abstraction of the stream of consciousness from its subject, without whom it could not be a stream, that the subject itself has come to be regarded sometimes as a logical abstraction, and its activity to be replaced by transeunt action of Objects.

Thus, between the sea-divided mainlands of the impressional and the imaginal, which differ so markedly, there are outstanding islands that seem to bespeak submerged connexion, now only observable here and there. Prof. Ward suggested that in the hallucination we have a case of-transition in the reverse direction, *i.e.* from image to percept. Dropping the theoretical insinuation involved in 'transition', we must retain the established fact that objects, intermediate in characteristics between the impressional and the imaginal, are presented. Whether this fact has import for theory of knowledge and ontology or not, it is well to recognise any facts that may prove relevant when we proceed to theorise.

The word 'imaginal' has been used, so far, in preference to 'imaginary', because the latter term suggests illusion or falsity: a notion which can only arise when individual experience is transcended, and psychology is replaced by epistemology. Illusoriness is properly a quality of certain beliefs about objects; *quâ* happenings, or objects of individual experience, images are as real (*i.e.* psychologically objective) as impressions. Even the impressional can be synthesised in such a way as to yield an unReal Object: as when the distant scare-crow is taken for a man. The error is simply in our judgement 'that is a man', not in asserting the presentation of the 'that'. And, generally speaking, an image is commonly called an illusion, because what belongs to the realm of objectivity is mistakenly referred to that of Objectivity also. Such illusions as the bentness of the staff in the pool or the juggler's swallowing of a sword, however, can be common to many percipients; and they bespeak no abnormality of sense-organs or of stimulation. Distinct from these is the hallucination; which is not merely a vivid image mistaken for a percept, because it contains somewhat of the impressional—the so-called 'subjective sensation', sensa due to 'inadequate' stimulus, or the organic sensa. There is abnormality, from the point of view of psychophysics, about the hallucination. The stimulation to which it is due, is often different from that involved in normal perception: the nervous system, secretions and blood-circulation being affected by poisons, drugs, etc. Hypnotic suggestion may produce hallucination; either positive, when the patient 'sees', etc., what is not Really there; or negative, in which case he does not 'see' what is Really before him.

The chief conclusion thrust upon us by the facts now set forth, is that imaging is in part a psychologically conditioned function: it is dependent on attention as well as on previous impressional presentation. It can no more be identified with sensing than can feeling, though it is apprehension of objects. Its objects have not admitted of Objectification into a cosmos, and there is no science of this secondary realm of objectivity. We can afford to ignore the imaginal, for the most part, in the conduct of life. That conduces to practical convenience and expedites the business of science; but it is irrelevant to a philosophy of experience. Metaphysics has scarcely deigned to discuss the ontological status of the imaginal. Perhaps the only use made of it by philosophy is to test the adequacy of theories of knowledge to account for the curiosities among facts: and certainly the forthcomingness of images, etc., puts some of such theories to confusion. Nevertheless, this slighted order is of immense importance for psychology of knowledge. All ideas—in the modern sense of the word—are derived from it; as is also the memory-thread, which is an offshoot from primitive free ideas, and a prerequisite of thought and scientific knowledge.

3. MEMORY.

Like most psychological terms in common use, 'memory' has been abused. We sometimes hear of "the memory of plants"; and processes in inanimate matter, such as hysteresis or recurrence of cycles of change, have even been rhetorically called instances of memory. Such "analogies" have indeed been commended to the psychologist, as calculated to lead him to treat of mental phenomena in a sound, scientific manner. Repetition of events, however, is not at all what the psychologist has in mind when he talks of remembering, but recalling of experiences; so the proffered analogies happen to leave out precisely what he is concerned with. A scarcely better approach to a description of memory is afforded by the phrase 'stored impressions'. Remembrances are not stored presentations deposited in the cellar of the subconscious, like the trunks in our box-rooms, lost to sight and to mind but persisting in their identity through the interval between our travels. What persists in memory is not impressional presentation, but effects thereof; otherwise memory would have none of its familiar capriciousness. Storage of impressions is an inadequate description even of retentiveness: for though that is persistence of the old, it is only the old in so far as it has been selected through the interest, and assimilated and changed through the activity, of the subject. The primary memory-image, again, is not the original percept either prolonged or reinstated. But retention falls far short of memory. What is remembered, is the central fact *plus* its setting. Memory involves recognition, while recognition does not involve memory. When, at the stage of experience at which memory and time-conception have become developed and explicit, one says 'I remember this place', one means more than 'I recognise it': viz., that the recognition awakens reminiscences or recalls circumstances which are dated in one's own experience. That is to say, the temporal signs, connected with the thing remembered, are intact enough to secure localisation in the past. Memory, then, involves some contrast of past and present. The memory-image is in the present, yet has the mark of pastness about it. Psychologically, it is as immediate knowledge, of the past, as was the original percept, of the present, though conditioned by the previous perception; and the original or temporally remote Object (as distinct from object) is not an original, of which the memory-image is a copy or an effect, but a conceptual construction involving or presupposing the memory-image. Incipient memory, in other words, is not founded on the assumption of a Real past: it is the first intimation we have, as to there being such a thing as a Real past. But, it has been asked, how do we know that the memory-image, which is a presentation now, is verily a *re*-presentation of a past presentation? We answer that, wonderful as immediate knowledge of the past may be, were there none, there could be no knowledge such as science; and further, that retention, the precursor of memory, and already possessing its wonderful element, is practically brief memory within the 'specious present', or temporally minimal actual experience. Here the bridge between past and present is visible to introspection. The trustworthiness of memory is thus doubly justified, as other than paradoxical: it is an actual precondition of forthcoming knowledge; in retention we actually experience or catch the lapse from past to present going on. Memory, then, is presupposed in all talk about records and repetitions; it is our only evidence that the first syllable in those words has significance. Records or memoranda are not memory, but its outcome. They may consist of physical traces, as the mnemic theory of heredity, invoking a physical *modus operandi* and 'engrams', suggests. But it is idle to speak of memory, unless we mean the functioning of a subject that remembers. The automatic in the organic world, after all, may be the outcome of experience.

Further, memory is a personal matter. My memories are revivals only for myself. In memory there is not recall of public events, save in so far as they were experienced by the remembering subject as in *his* past; not of events as such, but of events formerly presented to the individual remembering. Memory reproduces, not history, but private life-history or biography. It may be noted in passing, that memory thus plainly involves the numerical identity of the subject remembering with the subject who originally perceived what is remembered, and so is the main basis of our adult belief in a perduring self.

*R*emembering implies obliviscence between original perception and subsequent image. But this obliviscence is not, of course, other than temporary and supersedible. It is otherwise with the circumstances and setting in which we learned the items of our accumulated knowledge, which we commonly, but inaccurately, say we remember. The contents of stored learning are not dated, as a rule; there is, generally, irremediable obliviscence as to the occasion, etc., of acquiring each item.

We can now see how memory differs from imagination. In memory, we believe in the actuality of the remembered thing; in imagination, we do not. A reminiscence is concrete and circumstantial, and its constituent elements are fixedly grouped; while in the ordinary image they change uncontrollably. This fixity we can no more alter at will, than the impressional ingredients of a percept. Memory indeed, as well as what claims to be perception, is open to illusion; and it can then only be corrected by appeal to other memories, just as illusory perception can only be corrected by other percepts. It is in virtue of this characteristic of fixity, that memory yields *knowledge* of actuality, whereas imagination does not. Memory is involved, moreover, in all knowledge transcending awareness of present and passing impression; and unless some at least of the positings of memory were true, no universal knowledge would be possible: there would be no 'matter' of which concepts could hold. There is, however, no *a priori* principle to decide which memory-judgements are true and which are false: at bottom, 'knowledge' involves alogical trust, as well as interested interpretation of data. When experience has attained to the conceptual level, memory also differs from imagination in that it involves localisation in past time. Its implicit reference to the time-order can only be accounted for by interest and movements of attention, the sources of those temporal signs which impressions, as such, do not manifest, but out of which explicit knowledge of time-order is developed. Such is the significance of the fact, that when a child is reciting what he has non-intelligently learned by rote, and needs to be prompted, the word given to him will suggest what comes after, but not the words which went before. Memory here follows the original order of attention, and attention-traces are indispensable for explanation of the fact that memory-imagery differs from other kinds of the imaginal. The attention-trace bespeaks what has been called a 'functional inertia' in subjective activity; and a speculative explanation of imaging has been based on it.

4. IDEATION.

It has already been observed that reminiscence differs from stored knowledge, in that obliviscence of original setting generally characterises each item of our accumulated learning. Obliviscence is also involved in the transition from a string of memories to a chain of thought. It is only with the idiot, or the uncultured, that memory is a continuous thread; and that is why such persons cannot tell the gist of their news without reproducing every item of circumstantial setting. From the knowledge of the educated, such cumbersome settings have mercifully faded away. Also, in a train of thought, the single thread of memory is replaced by tissue; and the linear temporal order, by ramifying relations of another kind. For this transition, more than obliviscence is plainly necessary. Reduplications of the memory-train follow upon recurrences of partially like situations. The common portions of the train are thus strengthened against obliviscence, while the divergent portions will tend to blur and cancel, rather than reinforce, one another. At the same time the central representation will be rendered somewhat fluctuating, through now one, and now another, of these divergents more or less distinctly accompanying it. A memory-image, thus far fixed, will be ill-defined: particular, yet in its variability potentially general. Not general in the logical sense; for the general idea follows only on explicit distinction of the diversities comprised in the indefinite. But such a generic image will possess a salient core, corresponding to the common characteristics of a class, together with a vague and inconstant margin, corresponding to the specific features of individuals. It is therefore already a crude idea. It is no faded copy of a particular percept, but a re-complication of partial images. It still contains a nucleus of the concrete and particular; and it differs little from the percept in form. There can be no general image, because it is of the essence of the image to contain individual traits. But in the generic image, whose natural developement out of memory-image has been accounted for, as above, by Prof. Ward, we may see the first transition-stage from image to general idea. It remains to describe how the sensoriness, or percept-likeness, of the compounded partial images is distilled out, till nothing remains but empty form, capable of containing an indefinite variety of concrete sensory fillings: an inquiry important in connexion with the problem of knowledge of an external world.

This distillation-process is gradual. It is impossible, because of continuity of developement, to say where imagination or perception or even sensatio ends, and where ideation, culminating in pure conception, begins. There is embryonic conception implicit in the simplest perception; were this not so, there would be no psychological accounting for the existence of our developed knowledge. It seems a far cry from sense-perception and the sensory kind of imagination to abstract thought. In the course of the transition, the spatio-temporal order is transcended, the possible replaces the actual as central interest, and the 'what' or the essence of things comes to be dealt with in abstraction from the 'that', or the existence of them as posited in the impressional. But it has been seen that sense and understanding have a common root; and we have already come upon ideas in the making. Moreover, ideation does not always arise by way of memory-image, as previously described. In the fusion or complication of different sensa, which must precede association of such complicata; in the difference which repetition and familiarity make to impressions and motor-presentations; in recognition, with its implicit universalising of the particular; in the preperception of qualities not at the moment *in sensu*: we have found cases of 'thinking in the germ'. And in the primary memory-image, which is sense-bound and possesses the form, but not the identical matter, of the percept whence it is derived, we meet with something on the way to the sense-free idea. This primary memory-image is no replica of the percept, but it can stand for or mean it: in thus representing the percept, it fulfils to some extent the function of the idea. The prepercept functions similarly; and, like the idea, it gives the 'what' without the 'that'. Sometimes the 'that' which it avouches attaches to another 'what'. In other words, preperception may lead to illusion or error, as when "what was seized as booty proves to be bait". It would seem that it is largely through making such mistakes, or through preperceptions being displaced by brute fact, that the separation of 'what' and 'that' was thrust upon us or evoked from us, originally. Such indeed appears to be the humble origin of abstract thinking: trial and failure. When the distinction is explicitly recognised, as well as implicitly contained, and abstraction of essence from existence can be made, the free idea has been reached. "Instead of unquestioned preperception that 'makes the mouth water', we have alternative possibilities present as 'free ideas'; action also is in suspense, the alternative courses, that is to say, are present only in idea".[1] There is advance, on the cognitive side, from immediate assimilation towards mediate cognition; and, on the active side, from impulsive behaviour to deliberative conduct.

Thus may free ideas emerge one by one, and in greater profusion as perception grows in range and complexity. At first they are vague or indefinite rather than general; and, as such, their developement out of the imaginal and the memory-thread has been analytically and genetically traced. It remains to say a word as to the transition from the vague, to the clear and pure, idea.

Already in the image, despite its perceptual form, impressional constituents, essential to the original percept, are often dropped out: the visually imaged dagger cannot be clutched. Detail can also be voluntarily eliminated when it is irrelevant to a purpose:

[1] Ward, *op. cit.* p. 187.

e.g. when the triangularity of an Object is its only characteristic that calls for attention, the particular inclination of the sides may be ignored as much as size or colour. No more of the imaginal then remains than three-sidedness. A general idea has been obtained. This is no longer an actuality, or even an image, though it is an object; it has lost not only all the impressional, *i.e.* the sole vouch for actuality, but also the sensory or quasi-impressional visuality of the visual image. It is still objective: its derivation prohibits taking it for a subjective modification.[1] But, whereas the impression is thrust upon us, the pure idea is not. It cannot be presented, in the first instance, independently of prior stages in transition from percept to idea, or with *(ps)* immediacy. Though not a state or an act of the subject, the idea is subjectively derived or fashioned; and though not created out of nothing, but ultimately out of the impressional, it does not consist of the impressional.

Concrete filling distilled away, empty form[2] remains. The idea, so gotten, still has reference to actuality. Indeed, the loss of concreteness gives it a determinateness, in virtue of which it has utility lacking even to the generic image. Though no actual thing consists of three sides and nothing else, some actual surfaces are characterised by three-sidedness. The universal, triangularity, while *in re*, is thus a factor in actuality and, as such, needs to be reckoned with as much as the whole concrete percept. But, abstracted from the perceptual and regarded as *ante rem* or *in se*, it 'exists', so far as psychology knows, only in the mind of a subject or when thought of: *i.e.* when, on occasion, it is abstracted, and becomes an object of attention that is withdrawn from other factors, essential to the constitution of a determinate percept. In other words, the ideal (ideational) is not actual or real. But an idea will be *valid of* the perceptual *in which* it was implicit, and *from which* it has been abstracted; just as a frame will belong to, fit and suit, the picture it once enclosed. In this analogue, the

---

[1] The polemic of Reid against the idea as a *tertium quid* between subject and Object, was concerned with the idea as defined by Locke, etc., when its denotation includes the individual's percepts. It has no relevance to ideas, in the sense in which the term is here used, nor therefore to representational knowledge, as nowadays conceived.

If the idea, like the image, be an object, it is impossible to equate 'I have an idea of a circle' with 'I am thinking of a circular surface', as if an idea were a subjective act. We can work geometrical problems without thinking of actual bodies.

[2] 'Form', here, is some one ingredient of 'matter' to which attention is restricted.

frame is as actual as the picture; and here the analogy fails. For the empty idea is not actual as is the percept: validity is not to be identified with reality, but is rigorously to be distinguished from it.

With a caveat against the dangerousness of linguistic devices, such as the bestowing of a substantival name on an abstracted adjectival characteristic, we may bow to customary hypostatisation and say, *e.g.* that redness is an element in red things. For that reason, and for that reason alone, the idea of redness is valid, or holds, of things that have been perceived as red. But there is no guarantee that any idea, not obtainable from percepts of red things, will be valid of them; or that the idea of redness will be valid of any things not perceived as red. Concepts derived otherwise than directly from the percepts to which they are to be applied, *e.g.* from objects of constructive imagination uncontrolled by the perceptual, may or may not apply to things, and may or may not have actual or Real counterparts. There is no ground for supposing that they will or must. Hence the importance of limiting the scope or range of ideas to the particular contexts whence they have been elicited. Transcend that context, and ideas may become as irrelevant or invalid as they are empty or unreal.

Let it be repeated, as the matter is of first philosophical importance, that abstract ideas, or concepts, are devoid of the impressional content that is the sole direct criterion of actuality; and that, on this account, there is no psychological or scientific basis for the opinion that universals exist save *in rebus*, or for identifying the valid with the Real. For psychology, it suffices to say there are like things; if 'universals exist' be other than a poetical or figurative way of saying the same thing, the statement is without warrant in fact-knowledge and analysis thereof. Universals are obtained by subjects from the particulars in which they are implicit; we know of none that, in the last resort, are not so obtained. In the order of knowing, they presuppose thought: not thought, them. Consequently, universals are not known by acquaintance, or with (ps) immediacy; the (ψ) immediacy, with which they eventually come to be explicitly apprehended, is an outcome of process and practice. Thought or conception is impossible for us, without percepts; perception, without conceptual distinctions, is not impossible.

Conception is sometimes defined as explicit apprehension of universals. It is safer to describe it as formation and usage of abstract ideas. Unless mere recognition of a sensum as presented again, be called conception, the implicit presence of a universal element in a cognition does not render it conceptual. 'Conception' is rather to be reserved for explicit apprehension or usage of the universal, as such, and in antithesis to the particular. The ill-defined must be sharply defined or differentiated, and its particulars discriminated, before logical generality, with its clearness and distinctness, can replace indefiniteness. Thus reached, the general concept, specifying characters common to a class of particulars, is a kind of universal. It then denotes something Objective, entering into the structure of Actuality, or *in rebus*; but not necessarily anything that exists in isolation from either percepts or thinkers. There is no mystery about the applicability of the concept of length to long things, or as to its validity of long things: the correspondence of the thought with the things, hardly calls for the Divine intervention that Descartes deemed necessary. But there is no reason whatever to suppose that length, as an eternal existent, lay waiting till things not having length should come into being and partake of it, or till it could make ingression into 'possibles' and bestow actuality on them. The supposition seems as superfluous and as fanciful as the aeons of gnostic theosophy. Psychology can account for the origination of universal concepts, without resort to such speculation; and knowledge of mankind suffices to explain the perennial and endemic tendency of the human mind to hypostatise, by giving a substantival name, these mental abstractions into ontal beings. Knowledge as to how we have actually come by our abstract ideas, is the preventitive, better than cure, of what may be called 'the metaphysician's fallacy'. Whether any ideas hold of anything perceptual besides the percepts whence they have issued, can be ascertained only by experiment. Whether they hold of the imperceptible; whether any Real counterpart to the ideal form exists; whether there *is* an electron, *e.g.*, corresponding to the electron-concept popularly miscalled the concept *of* an electron: there is no immediate means of knowing. Thus there are *no thought-given realities*. There may be any number of thought-given fictions, and any number of systems of them; but so far as their *a priori* knowable relevance to being is concerned, these are all of equal value because possessing none.

Not to wander further from psychology into epistemology, let it suffice for the present to observe that ideas are mind-made tools, derived from the imaginal and therefore, at a further remove, from the impressional or perceptual: derived *from* 'what is in the senses' *by* 'the mind itself'. They are neither impressional, nor subjective modes, but non-impressional objects. Nor is the abstract idea an image. Berkeley's polemic against general images is powerless against general ideas. Moreover, some concepts emerge when specific relations are observed between the constituents of a complex presentation. Different connexions between the same constituents yield different concepts: consequently re-synthesis is involved in such conception, as well as analysis and elimination of the irrelevant. If the first characteristic of conception is abstraction of some or all of the 'what' from the 'that', involving transition from reality to validity, the second is the explication of relations which at first were but implicitly and indefinitely apprehended. As to the former of these characteristics, it is plain that its essence consists in its being an 'intentional', not a presentational and willy-nilly, process. Selection is always *ad hoc*, guided by interest and directed to an end. And the selective re-synthesis, performed in conception, is quite different from that involved in involuntary association of ideas and images. For the latter kind unites things as they occurred: the smell of box calls up, it may be, reminiscences of a garden and the friend we met in it; whereas, by conceptual thought, a connexion is established with bowls, with evergreens, or with the order Euphorbiaceae. The selection of what shall be included in a given concept, though convention, is not necessarily exercise of caprice; in science it is determined by Objective relations. But relevance and irrelevance are necessarily relative to some specific end.

Reproductive imagination, we have found, is revival—quite a different thing from repetition—of the impressional. From it to constructive imagination which anticipates possible percepts, is a long step. But in the fact that partial images can be fused into a new image, as in the case of the centaur, we find the beginning of a process of subjective manipulation, which has only to undergo developement, to yield the higher products of the human art which we call creative thought. In imagination, the matter retains its sensible form; in pure ideation or conception, the same matter is used, but its sensible form is exchanged for another, which is distinguished as 'intelligible'. Concepts have become imageless.

It is little wonder that before there was a science of genetic and analytical psychology, sense and thought should have been regarded as discontinuous and disparate. We now know that they do not differ in that way: nor in that thought is innate; nor in that thought is active while sense is passive; nor, yet again, in that thought is wholly determined by the subject. The thinking-process, as we have found and shall find more abundantly, is prompted and guided by the subject; form has to be invented or fashioned. But it also needs to be found to fit, if invention is to end in discovery. There is a limit to the extent to which form can be imposed by us on sense-matter. We may make and try our key, but the lock, not we, decides whether it shall fit; and possibly some other keys than those which our common sense and science have fashioned, would fit the lock equally well, or, in other words, would make a cosmos out of willy-nilly data presented to individual subjects.

In tracing the genesis of the concept, we have followed the developement of cognitive experience to a stage which it could not have reached, without the mediation of intersubjective intercourse and language. Words signifying complexes of other words, and possessing a meaning given by verbal definition, are indispensable to the attainment of our more abstract ideas. Language and developed conception presuppose communication: communication presupposes knowledge of other selves and, *a fortiori*, some knowledge of one's own self. In the next chapter these presuppositions will be discussed. Meanwhile it will be fitting to summarise the characteristics of individual experience, with which this exposition has hitherto been as exclusively as possible concerned, as they emerge when looked for by common knowledge. What is meant in these chapters by 'individual experience', is not merely the experience of an individual. All experiencing is necessarily performed by individual subjects: there are no others, in the strict sense of the word. What is signified, is the experience of the individual, while it is as yet unenriched by the effects of intercourse with other subjects, and before he has acquired the common point of view. Now that our adult knowledge is mediated and coloured by socialisation, involving transference to the over-individual standpoint, and by the self-consciousness and developed introspection which are only attained through intercourse, this individual experience is necessarily somewhat of an ideal, or of a tentatively recovered actuality. Unfortunately for the psychologist, no human being has been a Robinson Crusoe from birth; such a man, when socialised, would have much to tell that it would repay us to hear. Nevertheless, we can claim to have some indirect knowledge concerning approximately 'individual' experience.

In the first place, it is indisputable that perceptual reality, at its maximum of concreteness and minimum of "sicklying o'er with the pale cast of thought", belongs to individual experience alone. The individual's primary, immediate and impressional objects are necessarily private; and what is thus thrust on each man singly, is the ultimate datum, or brute fact, in which the real is first and immediately posited for us. *The* world, as phenomenal, may depend only infinitesimally on any individual subject; but *his* world depends upon, and presupposes, the existence of him. It is by manipulation of privately owned psychological objects, that the phenomenal world, and what passes for knowledge of a world *per se*, come to be. The word 'actuality' has here been used to denote what is presented to this and that individual subject. But, experience having once begun—and as to how it began there can be no scientific search—the individual object is not pure impression: it is incipient percept. And if individual subjects always remained non-communicating, the objective side of their experiences would be confined to percepts and images, reminiscences, etc., all characterised by the concreteness of particular positings. Such experience is presupposed by what is called universal experience. And universal or common experience, being but the experience of individuals enlarged and enhanced, cannot do more than establish or discover relations between objects within individual experience; for there are no other original data. Individual experience, again, would lack opportunity to arrive at explicit knowledge of many relations. Its syntheses would hardly be more than associative. It could know no difference between its percepts and the world, between appearance and reality, thing and memory-image. Its world would be one of sensible qualities; and the question whether the world, as it exists for an individual, exists independently of him, could scarcely arise, at this level. Such experience would not necessarily be solipsistic. Certainly not, if solipsism be understood to be the highly sophisticated supposition, that a subject's percepts are his own states or modes. There must be some intellective synthesis, even developed perception of one's own body and other human bodies, prior to recognition of other selves with which to communicate. There must be some measure of self-consciousness. It is no question of which came first, perception of bodies or self-consciousness, in finished form like hen and egg; but of *pari passu* developement. The distinguishable factors of sense and understanding were there from the first. Thus was provided the basis from which individual experience may rise to the ejective stage, and so to social intercourse. Knowledge of the self, of other selves, and of the world, advance together from a vague and humble first stage, by reacting each on the other.

Individual experience, then, while as yet unenlarged and untransfigured by intercourse, can advance far beyond the processes described as differentiation, retention and complication. It can attain to perception of things, involving reification and localisation; it finds for itself the cruder notions of substantiality and persistence, the germs of the categories of universal experience. It can reach the lower levels of self-consciousness.

CHAPTER V

The Self and the Soul

Sufficient account of the initial stages of the cognitive process has now been given, to prepare the way for study of the origin and developement of our presumptive knowledge of the self. This is therefore the occasion to hark back to self-consciousness, the discussion of which, though it is the primary fact-datum of adult experience, it was found necessary to defer.

1. Before there can be ejective knowledge of other selves, and intercourse with them can evoke the more advanced conceptions of self-hood and personality, there must obviously be in individual experience some rudimentary notion of one's own self. How this is gained, and how the subject, originally only conscious, becomes self-conscious, is our first inquiry.

Genetic psychology shews that the transition is mediated by differentiation of the body from other percepts. As perception developes, the body is perceived as one among other extended things. It comes to be distinguished from all other things, and to be regarded as uniquely one's own, chiefly through the organic sensa (somatic consciousness, coenaesthesis). Psychophysically regarded, the organic sensationes are not due to stimulation of the special sense-organs from without, but to stimuli within the body. They arise from processes affecting nutritive and other vital functions by invigoration or depression. Sensa such as are involved in hunger, fatigue, etc., generally lack the distinctness of those mediated by special sense-organs, and are more vaguely or confusedly apprehended; but some of them are ever with us, and are closely connected with appetites and pains. To them is due "our vague total awareness of bodily well-being or discomfort, our 'feeling well' or the reverse".[1] They largely condition feeling and conation; and their influence would be relatively more pronounced when experience was non-ideational and nearest to that of the animal status. Coenaesthesis might fittingly be called 'inner sense', had not that phrase been unhappily applied to

---

[1] See p. 234 of Stout's *Manual of Psychology*, 1913, of which use is here made.

introspection of mental states; for coenaesthesis is *sensatio*, not feeling. Largely determinative of the feeling-tone wrongly attributed sometimes to external sensa, it enters, without our awareness at the time, into what we call our higher feelings of contentment, etc. In so far as perception of the body is dependent on the organic sensa, we have another instance of the truth contained in the half-truth "there is nothing in the understanding that was not previously in the senses". That this dependence is fact, not surmise, is seen in that when, through disease, coenaesthesis is in abeyance, a patient will regard his body as a strange and inimical thing, not belonging to him.

The localisation of organic sensa, with all their affective influence, in the body, is then one cause—and a good reason—for distinguishing it from other perceptual objects. Another, is the discovery that the body is the one thing, action on which is accompanied by feeling, and the one that can directly be made to undergo movements satisfying conation. Thus the body becomes 'me', as distinguished from 'it': it is found to be a constant and unique possession. The first crude notion of self is that of the bodily self, implicit in awareness of embodiment. Self-consciousness, like the notions which become our primary categories of thought, is, as a matter of fact, mediated by the body. Whether we should have attained self-consciousness but for the accident of embodiment, is a question as to which speculation is possible, but knowledge will not be forthcoming, till we receive the testimony of a subject that has not known the bitter-sweet experience of being "clothed upon with our habitation which is from" earth.

When the ideational level of individual experience is reached, further developement of self-consciousness becomes possible. As Prof. Ward has observed, discernment of change within the bodily self leads to discrimination of an inner zone which, relatively, changes not. Trains of ideas compete for attention with percepts; and, in reminiscence and reverie, a generic image of the self is generated, again intimately associated with organic excitations and regarded as their seat. Hence the germ of the idea of a soul inside us. This synthesis of idea with organic sensa, like the earlier synthesis leading to awareness of embodiment, can be undone. The inner self then becomes alien, as if the body were indwelt by another self; while in such experiences as ecstasy, the outer bodily self may seem to be altogether wanting. Ideas may be influenced by coenaesthesis. In hysteria, such changes of mood occur, that a new self may seem to have arisen, with new tastes, etc., due to abnormal dominance of some set of organic sensa; and the old self may now reveal itself to the subject only through its acquired knowledge or skill.

2. So much of self-consciousness having been attained, the experient can advance to belief in other selves. This belief is generally held to be mediated originally through their bodily behaviour. One's own self being so far known through one's own body, and other persons' bodies being perceived to be and to behave like one's own, analogy suggests a like interpretation of them—in terms of selves as ejects. If knowledge of other selves be originally reached thus, it was attained not by a method comparable to that of establishing uniform sequences, but teleologically: its later self-evidence has been acquired pragmatically. This view needs but to be carefully stated, to meet by anticipation most of the objections that have been urged against it. For instance, the self, first known and then ejected into other bodies, must be but a very rudimentary self; and the analogical inference must at first be implicit rather than explicit: explication is a matter of later developement, and the initial reading-in is not to be confounded with rational inference, that is only possible at the level of socialised experience. Ejection, we have seen, has already been involved in developed perception of things; and a mother's behaviour is, to the young child, perceptibly different from that of other things. Knowledge of one's self, and knowledge of other selves, proceed *pari passu* from the humblest beginnings; wherefore, objections on the score that the infant cannot learn of its mother's displeasure from her facial expression, when it has as yet not beheld its own angry visage in a glass, are gratuitous. The theory that knowledge of other selves is mediated by sensible signs, interpreted by ejection, *i.e.* by incipient introspection and retrospection, is based on observable facts and is not challenged by any facts. But it has been opposed by another theory, as to which a word is called for.

It is sometimes maintained that other peoples' mental states or processes are directly apprehended, like sense-data; that we have acquaintance with them as with our own, and not merely knowledge or mediate belief about them: and that this is so in normal experience, apart from abnormal cases suggesting telepathy, etc. Generally, upholders of this view are content to assert its conceivability in the abstract: to argue that, though it is intrinsically impossible that one subject can have, or *erleben*, another's states, there is no absurdity in alleging that he can immediately apprehend them as parts of his acquaintance-environment. But the question is not as to possibility or conceivability in abstraction from circumstance, but as to matter of fact: which is not to be ascertained by balancing possibilities. And so far as the more highly developed forms of normal knowledge of other minds are concerned, where observation is feasible, there may be said to be no evidence forthcoming in favour of this supposition: while there is abundance to the contrary. We cannot tell what is going on in other persons' minds or know, when in the dark with them, what emotions, etc., they are experiencing, with the unfailing correctness that immediate apprehension should bespeak. And if we cannot discern thoughts and intents, how can we discern thinkers? Such facts are decisive. Further, when knowledge of other minds is called 'immediate', that word is used without discrimination of its 'psychic' and 'psychological' senses.[1] Direct acquaintance is asserted where familiar theory is sufficient: interpretative perception, or sympathetic imagination, has but the semblance of (ps) immediacy. Possibly there are beings in the universe that can directly read each others' thoughts; and apparently some human minds can be in *rapport* unmediated by sense or by body: but as to normal knowledge of the existence and operations of other minds, the facts leave no room for any view but that it is almost wholly, if not wholly, the outcome of analogical ejection, pragmatically justified so amply as to have become an inevitable and (ψ) self-evident belief.[2] On the other theory, our fact-data would

---

[1] See p. 46.

[2] It is another question whether direct acquaintance with other minds, such as is involved in alleged telepathy, is a faculty once possessed by mankind but now atrophied, as it were, in the majority of human beings, through disuse since the acquisition of language. As the special instincts are sublimated by intelligence, so, it may be conjectured, telepathy has been killed by speech, and become comparable to the rudimentary organ that in rare cases of atavism reappears in developed form. But infants do not appear to be telepathists before they have learned to talk, and instincts are not destroyed when sublimated.

not be what actually they are; while there should be forthcoming
a volume of data that, as a matter of fact, is lacking.

We may pause to measure the philosophical significance of the
truth which has here emerged. All presumptive knowledge, common sense and science, rest on an assumption which each of us
has to make, but for which no strictly and coercively logical proof
is forthcoming. It is the assumption that ejection of that subjectivity *erlebt* by one's self, into bodies behaving like our own,
yields knowledge, and knowledge such as we do not attain, in the
first instance, by any other way. The assumption is, of course,
abundantly justified, in the pragmatic sense; it is now inevitable,
conduces to a vast system of thought that tallies with impressional
fact, and so forth. The point is, that teleological interpretation, of
data derived through sense, which is neither direct apprehension nor formally logical, is part of the foundation on which all
common 'knowledge' rests, and is presupposed by all the thought
of which logic ascertains the framework. As we are seeking empirically to find out what knowing is, it will not be irrelevant
digression to note, by the way, that apriorism already dwindles to
a secondary affair; and that the rationalism or intellectualism that
would oust the teleological from knowledge, and contrast its own
'knowledge' with such 'mere belief', subsists only by gnawing its
own vitals.

3. The psychology of common ('universal') knowledge dependent on intersubjective intercourse, shall receive consideration
later; but the developement of self-knowledge, rendered possible
by communication with other selves, can now be sketched. At the
perceptual level, we have seen, the perception of the self had much
to do with construing, or shaping knowledge of, the not-self.
Things, that is to say, were comprehended and understood by
projecting into their elements characteristics of the self, such as
would later be denoted by 'unity', 'substance' and 'causality'.
At the intellectual level reached through intercourse, this ego-
centric procedure is exchanged for its reverse. The higher and
later knowledge of self is acquired by observing, imitating and
understanding (*i.e.* establishing sympathetic relations with) other
selves. The individual thus comes to regard himself as, and so
becomes, the social individual. He examines his conduct in the
light of the behaviour of others, and so acquires conscience: he

becomes, as it were, an external spectator of himself. Converse with others leads to taking counsel with himself, and the common weal suggests ends other than his fleeting self-gratification. Without further encroaching on the subject of moral developement, we may now observe that morality, and consequently what is commonly meant by 'personality', as distinguished from bare subjecthood, are conditioned by relations with other selves. Having attained the status of the willing, thinking, moralised person, the individual can regard the appetitive self as an outer self possessed, like property, by an 'inner man': no longer in the sense of inside the body, but as metaphorically interior to unextended objects presented to, and so distinct from, itself. The thinker is distinguished from its thoughts. The idea of the empirical self, as object known, and to which sense-perception is referred, will, according to genetic psychology, be a construction made by an inner agent. Thus the idea of the self culminates in the psychologist's notion of the perduring subject as pure ego: which is but a further refinement of the thinking and willing self.

This notion, as Berkeley shrewdly called it because of its derivation being different from that of empirical ideas in general, has been variously regarded: e.g., as an immediate presentation or intuition, an idea of reason, a philosophical fiction, a logical construction, an *a priori* condition of the possibility of experience. If the account that has been given, of how the idea has been attained, be in essence true, it will follow that the pure ego is the idea of the self that, in the order of knowing, is last to be reached, an outcome of developement of reflective thought; and to this may be due its clearness and distinctness, giving it the semblance of a (*ps*) immediate presentation. On the other hand, if the idea be more than a fiction, if it have a counterpart in Actuality, it is in logical order the first, because presupposed in all knowing.

4. This brings us to a new issue. So far, it has been left an open question whether, to the idea of the pure ego, there corresponds an Actuality: the centre of experience or of the concentric empirical 'selves' that have been studied, may be but an imaginary point, a limiting-concept. If it refer to an Actuality, how do we know of the Actuality? And what, in this case, does 'knowledge' mean?

It has been held by some, that the subject knowing is not distinguishable from the pure ego as known; and the pure ego, as known, is sometimes included in the denotation of the 'empirical ego'. If we reserve the latter phrase for the empirical self, or the personality, as already described, *i.e.* for the pure ego *plus* its states, relations and objects, or for the mental βίος and its owner, we shall divest our problem of one superfluous confusion; and we may avoid another, by disentangling the psychological issue from an ontological question. Psychologically, the I knowing, and the pure ego as known, are distinguishable: and logically, they are two terms, not one, viz. recipient and datum. Ontologically, they may be numerically one entity with two aspects, one substance with two rôles. Whether the ego, *quâ* a substance, can know itself, is not the same question as whether the ego, *quâ* knower, is distinguishable from ego, *quâ* known. The former, metaphysical, question is not just now before us.

How the pure ego is known is, so far as consequences are concerned, a less important matter than whether it is known. But, in faithfulness to our method, we cannot assume it to be known at all, till we have shewn how the knowledge is derived from experience.

As to this question, diversity of opinion prevails. One view is, that the subject apprehends itself (a different matter, by the way, from apprehending its states and acts) with the immediacy (*ps*) of acquaintance. Knowledge about it, or 'by description',[1] it is said, cannot be had without such acquaintance. The I describable as 'now aware of red', and the I describable as 'aware of that awareness of red', cannot logically be identified; yet their identification is necessary, if the I is to know itself by description. But the bridge which abstract logic cannot throw, actuality does throw. For the second I could not be described as it has been, were it not identical with the first. Unless the 'awareness of red' were *erlebt* by it, the second I could have no inkling of red having been sensed, or of sensatio having occurred. On the other hand, though awareness of objects cannot be had without acquaintance—for these are one and the same thing—knowledge about Objects, to which class the I belongs, can so be had: else geology would need

---

[1] 'Acquaintance' and 'knowledge about' denote the two kinds of cognition indicated respectively by *connaître* and *savoir*; *kennen* and *wissen*. A man blind from birth might know much about redness (optical science), but could have no acquaintance with its *quale*.

to be struck off the list of sciences. This negation of the possibility of indirect knowledge of the ego, involves two errors. It applies, to conceptual Objects, what is only true of impressional objects; and it applies to acquaintance with objects, what is only true of knowledge about Objects. Recognition of these errors, it may be observed, will stand the reader in good stead during the whole course of his study of the ego-problem.

On its positive side, the theory of direct acquaintance with the I is equally unconvincing. Acquaintance, in the indubitable instances of it that we have in impression and introspection, presents the *quale* of the object. Hence the qualitylessness, or transparency, of the ego suggests that it is known only by, or as, idea: as to its 'that', not its 'what'; its 'form', not its 'matter'. This is not a conclusive refutation: but we may go further. If the I be apprehensible to itself with (*ps*) immediacy, it is strange that all sentient beings are not fully self-conscious, and that the human. being only becomes self-conscious at a certain stage of his mental developement. We are thus empirically confined to the alternative view, that the pure ego, if known at all and not merely thought or supposed, is but known about, mediately and reflectively or intellectively.

This is perhaps the more generally received doctrine. Taking it now as a substantive motion, so to speak, instead of as an amendment, the argument for it may concisely be put thus: consciousness involves a subject; there is awareness of consciousness; therefore, as cognition does not create its primary objects, there is knowledge of the involved subject's existence. In other words: at the level of self-consciousness (the common-sense fact) consciousness, or perceptio, is presented, as directly as any sensum, to the subject thereof; this presentation *involves* the subject—for there are no perceivings, or other instances of consciousness, that are not acts or states of a subject—though it is not a presentation *of* the subject. The I is known *in* the me, agent in acts, cause from effects. Unless the me were a construction of the I, and a presentation to *it*, the me of self-consciousness could not be known at all. Yet again to repeat: the subject is present in all consciousness, but only at the level of awareness of consciousness (*i.e.* self-consciousness) is the subject revealed. It is not revealed, however, by 'inner sense', unless that phrase mean something different from what it would naturally be taken to mean. The apprehension of the I is neither *sensatio* nor acquaintance having sense-like immediacy and 'receptivity'. The I may have no qualities accessible to acquaintance; it may be noumenon without phenomenon: certainly it is not phenomenally known, or known as phenomenon. Nor is the I revealed, as apart from its acts, states, and even objects. The apprehension of it is mediated discursively, by construction rather than by pure inference, just as is knowledge of the external world. If this apprehension is still to be called inner sense, it is not coordinate with outer sense, as if a sixth sense. It is not a simple presentation of the present moment, but a construction out of the past, or out of residua, also. Indeed, it is not akin to sense at all, because it consists, in the first instance, in apprehension of *relation* between external objects and empirical self. Just as one finger cannot rub itself without rubbing another, so the ego does not know itself, save in knowing that objects are presented to it, and feelings, etc., are thereby evoked in it.

If this be the true account of the nature and derivation of ego-knowledge, Kant was right in teaching that internal experience is only possible through external experience. Yet Descartes and Locke were also right in affirming that we have clearer and more certain knowledge of our own existence than we have of the existence of things. For knowledge of ourselves is based on the *erleben* that is more ultimate than the knowing that knows either it or anything else. We can "feel that we are", so to speak, though this consciousness cannot adequately be described in terms of cognition, which is narrower than consciousness, and is but one particular kind of experience.

Another consequence of this doctrine is that cognition of the subject, precisely because it is knowledge as to the 'that' with nothing or but little as to the 'what', is noumenal and not phenomenal. The I that is unknowable to sense, is knowable to intellect operating on sense, though not to intellect operating independently of sense; and this intelligible knowledge of the I is not, like perception of the non-ego, dependent on immediate presentation of the object (in this case the I) itself.[1]

---

[1] If the pure ego is not directly presented in introspection, it does not follow that subjective states and acts are not objects of acquaintance, though they are not apprehended by inner sense or by any activity so akin to sense as to warrant but phenomenal

5. So far as the theory of the pure ego has as yet been presented, it will be seen to be derived, whether cogently or not, from facts: not through baseless speculation or from supposed *a priori* necessities, independent of empirical data. That it yields an unforced explanation and an adequate systematisation of the facts, its foes often handsomely admit. These demur to it on two main grounds: that the idea of the pure ego transcends the facts, and that it is a superfluity with which psychology can dispense. It shall now be submitted that the several theories that have been propounded as definite substitutes for it, are inadequate to the facts; whereas the pure ego, so far from being dispensable, is presupposed in the attempts to prove it superfluous. And by the pure ego, one does not mean a name for the unity (*i.e.* unifiedness) of a person's life-experience, the continuity of a mental βίος. Quite a different thing from such observed matter of fact is meant; viz. the bond which gives the unity and continuity, and explains what otherwise remains a mystery. It must be maintained that unless the enduring subject were an Actuality, the empiric fact-knowledge of common sense (our primary datum) could not be.

But before weighing the facts of this sort, and indicating the metaphysical interpretation for which they call, we may remind ourselves of the consideration, that a psychological problem must

knowledge of them. Dr Ward denied that there is acquaintance with attention, feeling or desiring, and asserted these to be known, like the I, only inferentially or reflectively. But if pleasure and pain, desire and aversion, differ respectively in *quale*, they must have *quale*; and *quale* is known by acquaintance, and not intelligibly.

This doctrine that feelings, and subjective modes in general, are not known with sense-like immediacy or acquaintance, has been found unassimilable by psychologists who may be said to belong to Ward's school. It certainly seems paradoxical and unproved; and it seriously jeopardises that master's vindication of the pure ego. We may agree that the pure ego itself, in abstraction from its states and acts, is not object of acquaintance, while maintaining that the states which involve it are immediately apprehended. Our discursive knowledge of the ego then becomes less roundabout and precarious.

There is another point at which Dr Ward may be suspected of error which weakened his case. The me and the I need not be represented as so distinct as he conceived them. It is, after all, only the bodily self, not the inmost thinking and willing self, that is empirically presented, and can be strictly called empirical ego, on Ward's presuppositions. The pure ego must be in the me: it is the sole subject. It is 'pure', only in the sense of having fewer empirical qualities. We need not cling to the name 'pure ego'; all that is here meant by it is the abiding subject, to which the name 'soul' can be given.

be dealt with from the psychological standpoint. It must not be answered or foreclosed by adopting presuppositions derived from another standpoint, and relevant only elsewhere. We must not assume, as instruments for the demolition of the ego, what may turn out to be products of the ego itself. Hypothetical or imaginary causal laws connecting the contents of a personal βίος, are sometimes invoked instead of an abiding *continens*; as if it could be straightway assumed that any such laws are knowable, without the previous activity of permanent subjects. If the *ordo cognoscendi* is to be followed, this is to put the cart before the horse. If the *ordo essendi* be intended, it should be remembered that psychology is prevented, by its unique nature and standpoint, from accepting that *ordo* as indubitably known. All other sciences, from physiology to applied mathematics, simply assume, for their own departmental purposes, a theory of knowledge which psychology is precluded from assuming to be sole or final. Again, it is an unbecoming fearfulness that refrains from employing, in psychology, concepts, should the facts indicate them, such as are neither physical nor mathematical. Reverence for methods and conceptions, relevant to sciences of those kinds, has led writers on psychology to describe the mental life in terms of 'series', etc. Continuance in one stay is as unwelcome a notion, to minds steeped in logic of the discrete, as activity is to those wont to think in terms of inertia; consequently the human subject has been of late more suspect than was God in the generation succeeding Laplace. To pass from generalities to particulars: psychologists should not allow themselves to speak of presentations as 'given', and yet suppress reference to that to which they must be given, in order to be given at all; to call the mind a stream of phenomena, while declining to specify to whom or what the phenomena, and the stream as a whole, appear; or to describe it as a series of 'events', in forgetfulness that every such event involves a subject. Abstractiveness, when taken more seriously than as parsimony in speech, is apt to issue in slavery to words; when we look rather for the meanings of words, it will perhaps be found that the notion of the pure ego is not easy to avoid, and that the pure ego is the one thing, involved in this controversy, that is not an abstraction.

One line of attack on the pure ego consists in the assertion that the formula for simple cognition, $M.p.O$, is sufficient to represent all knowledge, and that there is no need to resort to the I, as distinct from the empirical me (M). But it has been shewn earlier that, if $M.p.O$ covers cognition, it does not cover all experience, which is wider than cognition. Feeling and conation have immediacy other than that of sensatio; they are *erlebt*, whether or not they are directly presented. They are being that is prior to thought. And it is these subjective states, especially, that compel recognition of a subject, over and above a unity and continuity of cognitive consciousness; for they can only be known or known about, as distinguished from being *erlebt*, at the level of self-consciousness attained when experience is elaborated beyond a certain degree. At this level, however, $M.p.O$ expresses but fact *known*. It is inadequate to express the kno*wing* of it, because no term in it indicates the knower. It seems obvious that $I.p'(M.p.O)$ is required, and that the I is a concrete individual if $(M.p.O)$ is concrete fact. The only other ground, it would seem, on which the ampler formula can be discredited, is that, in any instance of self-consciousness, the I and the M are not different phases or rôles, not one subject regarded now without, and now with, its mental 'property' or empirical manifestations, but are numerically distinct existents; so that the ego of any moment does not know itself, though it does know another. If this be heresy, it is that of dividing the substance; while that previously refuted consists in confounding the persons, I and M.

Reminding ourselves that every single 'content' of the empirical self's experience, every single drop in the 'stream of consciousness', must have its subject,[1] our problem now takes the form: is the unity of a person's mental life (which no one disputes) possible, unless the subjects of the distinguishable contents are one and the same? The crude but undeniable facts from which investigation must set out, may be summed up under the heads: the temporal continuity, the unity and orderedness, the individuality, of what common sense calls minds or mental lives. The first of these facts, or systems of fact, is perhaps the most

---

[1] Perhaps it is only when this fact is temporarily overlooked, and lapse into presentationist terminology for expositional purposes is incurred by the non-presentationist, that the latter type of psychologist can succeed in making plausible to himself his scepticism as to the abiding ego. If so, the issue is then begged by a verbal device belying the facts.

important in relation to the problem before us; it shall therefore receive fullest consideration and earliest place. Anyone but the avowed presentationist is committed, and must be pinned, to his admission that each "mental event" involves a subject. Any theory as to the origination and the connexion of these mental events, must account for each of the groups of fact forthcoming. The unity of a mind is admittedly not comparable to that of a society of minds; it needs to be argued that it is inexplicable in terms of a series of successive subjects.

6. As to temporal continuity, we may first dismiss the attempt to describe psychological facts in terms of the 'instant'. This fiction of creative imagination may have its uses, like that of $\sqrt{-1}$, in pure mathematics: it has none in any science of the Actual. Observation would be an impossibility if events were instantaneous; or if continuity, in the sense of duration, were replaced by continuity conceived in terms of the discrete, as by the mathematician. An experience confined to a present instant, is a contradiction in terms. For experience *is* change, and, experience *of* change; so, even if change be conceived as substitution, at least two instantaneous events must be presented to one subject persisting through both, in order that such 'change' be observed.

As psychology is not a pure science, we may abandon the instantaneous for the momentary—'a moment' denoting a finite stretch of time. Contact with Actuality then becomes possible. This footing adopted, the sceptic as to the abiding ego sometimes appeals to the cinematograph; though he is apt to overlook some of the conditions of film-production. Given the perduring subject, we can analyse its experience into distinguishable portions of finite duration; just as, given a walking man, we can procure snap-photographs for a film. But if we begin with separate experiences, each owned by a different subject, to account for their unification into a personal life is as serious a difficulty as it would be to provide a cinema-hero, if the span of human life were but a fraction of a second. In lieu of the facts to be explained, a less recalcitrant set of fictions is usually dealt with, having little resemblance to the analytica of actual experience.

To admit that an empirical self is a series of momentary subjects —which is done when acts as well as contents or objects are recognised in 'mental events'—is to admit the thin end of a wedge which, it shall now be argued, proves shattering.

There is no gainsaying *cogito ergo sum*, when its ego is the ego of a single momentary experience. In spite of its *ergo*, the Cartesian proposition is then analytical. But this momentary ego-life, this minimal concrete present of actual experience, within which a subject does not distinguish prior and later parts, is itself no discrete happening, such as the instantaneous event would be if it could go through the form of occurring. The unit of actual experience, known as the specious or the psychic present, is "a saddleback, not a knife-edge", and is of variable duration depending on the subject and his degree of attention. Parts in it, that from the (ps) standpoint of science may be distinguished as non-contemporaneous, are presented as, and (ψ) are, simultaneous. It contains, *e.g.*, the primary memory-image, or after-percept, and the pre-percept: residuum of past, and anticipation of future, experience. To ignore this continuity with other specious presents, would be to refuse to face fact, and facilely to simplify our problem by substituting another for it. The momentary present is no discrete event, because each one overlaps another. The *terminus a quo* of any one specious present, is as arbitrarily fixed in time as is that of a wicket in space within the field, or that of a roach-swim in a river. Partitioning of a mental life into momentary lives, or replacing the abiding ego by a series of subjects, is rendered impossible by the *fact* that actual experience is not divisible into discrete portions, though it is resolvable into distinguishable phases. To take this methodological convenience as embodying mathematically expressible metaphysical truth, is like making theological dogma by literalisation of metaphor.

The temporal continuity of a person's mind, then, has no analogy with the spatial 'continuity' of a piece of matter, as described by physical science. There are no parts wholly external, each to the next. The continuity is that of actual duration; and to treat mental acts or states as discretely isolable, is arbitrary. The cinematographic method of resolution into static elements, in so far as it is but attending to one bit at a time, is a useful and necessary device. It is sheer falsification if taken for more than approximative method; if the unceasing flux of mental life is lost sight of; or if phases are treated merely as happenings, and without reference to their functions and psychological interdependence. We then but exchange facts for fictions. The specious present is the only experiential or actual unit, so far as temporal aspect is concerned, that psychology can find; and it, we see, affords no basis for the theory that the personal βίος is discontinuous. Like other kinds of cross-section, it can be taken anywhere. The mental life is no more actually built up out of separate presents, than is a living stem out of the sections into which a microtome can cut it. The abiding ego is the precondition, not the result, of the distinguishable experiences. Those who repudiate this ego can point to no actual discrete elements, a series of which would yield a mental life. They resort to conceptual or supposed elements in an imaginary βίος: they discuss mathematics, not psychology.

The indispensableness of the continuing subject is revealed first by the fact of retention. If in what is called 'my' experience of two successive impressions of blue, what really happens is that the first impression O_1 has a subject S_1, while O_2 is presented to another subject S_2, how is it that S_2, who ex hypothesi has not received O_1 as his impression and cannot know its quale (blue) save by impression, nevertheless recognises O_2 as like O_1, as 'blue again', and as familiar? How is comparison of O_2 with O_1, that was never seen, a possibility? And if the identity of S_2 with S_1 is not fact but appearance, to what does the appearance appear? Unless the ego have so much of duration as is required for retention or for implicit recognition and comparison, it would seem impossible for such experiences to be forthcoming, as they are. Many of one's mental states are what they are, only because of derivation from others; and at least in some cases the bond of connexion cannot but be their common subject. A piece of chalk may appear to be one thing, in spite of being a multitude of shells, each secreted by a different organism; but many of the analytica of a man's mind could neither be, nor be connected, nor appear to him, unless they were states or acts of himself, as one and the same subject. Thus an ordinary memory-judgement (proper), which is neither a historical judgement nor an event caused by an unperceived happening in the past, consists partly in implicit awareness of subject-continuity; neither assuming nor proving, but asserting it. The 'trace' is due to attention; and unless the same subject that formerly perceived, afterwards recalls, there can be no momentary reminiscence, let alone a life-long memory-store. There can be no psychological explanation of such an experience as disappointment in C, if the wish were A's and the non-fulfilment B's. If each organic sensum were presented to a different subject, it is hard to see why our 'sense of personal identity' should be mediated by embodiment. Perhaps it is un-necessary to bring up the heavy artillery of the facts that have evoked the theory of mental dispositions, or those concerning the connexion of ends into a system such that satisfaction of a par-ticular end is also partial satisfaction of a more general aim: though this interweaving of interests is one of the chief character-istics of human mentality. These complex psychoses, and their teleological connectedness, have not received from supporters of the theory of a linear series so much notice as the impressions and images, which *prima facie* are more amenable to serial treatment. Only one further difficulty for this theory shall be mentioned, for the present: there is continuity of attention even when it is suddenly diverted from one object to another; not a new discrete event. The subject may be aware of both the old and the new, and of transition from the one to the other. The end of the one process, and the beginning of the other, are con-temporaneous.

Thus the ego of Descartes is not merely momentary. If it were, there could not be that which we call a continuous self, with memory, etc., to analyse or to explain away. Ockham's razor (*entia non multiplicanda praeter necessitatem*), when applied to the pure-ego theory, chops only logic, and makes rough places smooth for the mathematician, not for the psychologist. But there is a more deadly weapon, the Actuality-razor, by which the empirical psychologist may make an end of the neat over-simplifications that have been imported, from the newer logic or algorithmic, into literature on the human mind. Ockham's tool, used in that sphere, procures economy of 'description' by razing what is significant in the facts to be described. *Res non minuendae*, is at least as important a methodological principle as *entia non multiplicanda*. This empirical knife cuts out many of the possibilities open to a pure science, and many logical suppositions that are entertainable only so long as Actual conditions are ignored. And when facts are not allowed to utter their determinative inwardness, or to speak for themselves, this razor seems to leave no course open but resort to mystery, coincidence, impossibility.

This will be found to be the case, when we examine forthcoming attempts to account for mental continuity otherwise than in terms of the abiding subject. One suggestion is that the series of separate psychoses is aware of itself as a series. Now the self-consciousness we presumptively know, is mediated by apprehension of relations between objects; it proffers no analogy, therefore, to the hypothesis before us. At any moment part of this series is future, knowledge as to which is impossible. If the series is involved in knowledge of each item, the whole becomes constituent of the part. But it is perhaps superfluous to expose the various contradictions inherent in this suggestion. Another view is that a man's mental unity consists in relation between successive items, as phenomena to one another in turn. The thoughts are the only thinkers. 'I think' means 'there is thinking in me': the me being the series of thoughts. In order to explain how the earliest thoughts or thinkers, a, b, are presentations to z, the me of the present moment, it would seem necessary to suppose that the whole past series a–y be accompanied by z: but then we are back at orthodoxy. James sought to save the series-theory from so sad an end by suggesting that each term "absorbs" its predecessor; each is born an owner (subject) and dies owned (object), so that the latest up to date "contains" all its forbears. Pruning somewhat the exuberant rhetoric that here does duty for science, we might reduce this snowball-hypothesis to the form in which it asserts the successive subjects to take over their immediate predecessors' accumulated mental inheritance, so that the latest owns its wisdom as unearned increment.

Some such hypothesis as this, it would seem, must be entertained by the adversary of the permanent ego, once he repudiates the notion of subjectless experiences or events, and acknowledges that subjective acts involve agents. And it must now be submitted that the theory on which he must rely, is as fanciful as it is audacious. It overlooks the fact that the relation of subject to object is non-commutative, like that of father to son. Instead of one subject that lives and learns, that satisfies all the facts and introduces no difficulties, we are offered an indefinite tale of subjects, conceived not at all after analogy with the empirical person, but needing to be magically endowed with far ampler powers. There is no resemblance between the apprehension, by S_2, of S_1 or of his states and objects, and the self-knowledge and knowledge of other selves, of which psychology traces the developement in persons: for these kinds of knowledge consist not in immediate discernment of subject *quâ* subject, by subject, but of object and object, each necessarily correlated with a subject. And if by 'absorption' or 'appropriation' be further meant the *erleben* of S_1's states and acts by S_2, that, as Ward remarks, is "the most impossible thing in the world". James himself taught that the breaches between "thoughts belonging to different persons' minds" are "the most absolute breaches in Nature". Yet these breaches must not exist for the mythical subjects of the series-theory. Each of those must not only know, but in some cases at least must have had, or 'enjoyed', the experiencings of its predecessor; *e.g.* acquisition of familiarity is inconceivable unless the subject made perfect performed the practice. It is another monstrous offence against fact, to suppose that, in any one psychosis of a person's life, all the previous psychoses of that life are 'contained'—whatever that dark term here means—or even known; and talk of appropriation, by a momentary self, of countless dead selves, is but invocation of the miraculous. Without appeal either to the marvellous or else to the abiding ego, it is, however, no easier to unify two momentary experiences than a life-time of them. Further, the momentary discrete experience is after all as much an intellectual construction, and a transcending of data, as the enduring subject. So far, the alternatives are on a par. But whereas the linear series of subject-objects explains nothing, actual experience does not seem to admit of explanation otherwise than in terms of the permanent ego.

Even Kant lapsed from his customary sobriety in discussing the continuous ego, sincerely as he believed in it. It is true the lapse occurs in but a footnote[1] and in course of polemic against a *bête noire*. But he allowed himself to imagine the successive selves, conceivably constituting the abiding self, as substances analogous to elastic balls capable of communicating their motion to one another through impact. Psychical *erlebnisse* being the last things to be conceived transferable, and elastic balls about the last things with which subjects can be compared, this suggestion

[1] *Kritik der reinen Vernunft*, 1st ed., p. 363.

is valueless to the psychologist. But it is possible that it prompted the obscurer and more rhetorical theory which James propounded: a theory which has importance thrust upon it, in that some or other variant of it would seem to be the only forthcoming concretely psychological alternative to that of the permanent subject. The theory implies that a subject can derive its images, reminiscences, etc., from another subject's percepts, if not its percepts from another's impressions; that it comes by its store of knowledge simply by arriving after other subjects have spent, each its little lifetime, in mastering a momentary lesson for itself. Perhaps these things may be; but those who can believe in them on the strength of the notion of 'appropriation', whether as suggested by Kant or by James, may fairly be called upon to account, by a supplementary hypothesis, for the mishaps which appear, on the commonsense surface, as temporary obliviscence of a familiar name. Obliviscence in S_2, of an item of knowledge possessed by S_1, somehow escapes transmission to S_3, who *ex hypothesi* derives the mental property of S_1 solely *quâ* that of S_2—in which the given item was missing. The ball-like subjects of Kant prove leaky of momentum, and acquire it otherwise than through impact: and on one paltry fact the theory is wrecked.

Far shrewder than some of his modern followers was Hume, who initiated scepticism as to the abiding subject, but sagely abstained from offering a better substitute. Hume merely recorded that he could not find the I among his impressions. This does not cause us surprise. But had he coupled his view, that impressions are subjective modes, with the platitude that acts involve agents, he might have found at least the momentary ego. He concluded that the I is but the me, and the me but a bundle of impressions. Yet all the time he needs—and the need is ominous—to distinguish the I from the me: *e.g.* in the words "when I enter into myself". It certainly would have been awkward to talk of a bundle of impressions entering into a bundle of impressions. Again, he might have found the I, had he looked for the string which bound the sensations into a bundle: had he examined memory, comparison, etc., more carefully. He assumed, like his recent followers, that the flux of a person's presentations must be a flux for an external observer; which is what a series, constituting the contents of a person's mind, is not. He tells us that he never caught himself without a perception; but he might as truly have said that he never caught a perception without himself: a subject never catches *an* impression that is not *his* impression, or without being there to catch it. Hume, in fact, failed to see the significance of his data; his cleverness exceeded his sagacity. Like all series-theories of the self, his obviously must presuppose that of the continuous ego, in order to get itself propounded; and like many, it sets out from the assumption that the series of psychoses is a linear series of cognitions only. This assumption bestows some plausibility on such theories; but at the expense of fact. For one fact included in the 'unity of the mental life', is that any momentary experience has three aspects, distinguishable but inseparable; cognitive, affective and conative. These are causally connected. Any one of them may, on occasion, be more in evidence than another, but from no actual psychosis does it seem that any is wholly absent.

7. The unity of the mental life is as inexplicable, in terms of the serial theory, as is its temporal continuity. Appeal is commonly made to causal laws subsisting between the successive discrete psychoses. But no one has had enthusiasm enough for his theory to undertake the investigation of such laws, and their particular forms have never been suggested. They subsist as yet but in the inaccessible realm of possibility. The only definite suggestions equivalent to them, those of Kant and James, have been argued to be, not causal laws, but conceits without warrant in, or relevance to, fact. And even these offer no more explanation than does epiphenomenalism, of the teleological, the genetic and— in processes of reasoning—the logical, concatenation or sequence of psychoses: of why, *e.g.*, when S_1 has played the first bar of a solo, S_2 who arrives as a bolt from the blue—perhaps as the result of a cerebral explosion—should devote his span of life to playing the next, rather than to any other conceivable life-work. That a person lives a more or less ordered life, shews character and increasing purpose, though there is no reason on the serial theory why he should not be a legion of incompatibles; that there is conspiration of innumerable irresponsible egos to issue in an orderly citizen: such facts call for a sufficient reason which the theory fails to suggest. Happy chance and unfounded coincidence, multiplied thousandfold, would seem to be the fount whence flow

the rationality and the moral stability of the man of parts. Credulity at its maximum is perhaps to be most easily found in the incredulous; or, as Wundt has said, the greatest sceptics are often the greatest mystics.

By the 'individuality' of a mental life is meant the fact that psychoses which, as we have seen, are not discrete, cohere into unities that *are* discrete. None of *A*'s 'conscious' psychoses enter into *B*'s life-experience, *A* and *B* being normal empirical persons. We speak, indeed, of two persons sharing a common sorrow. But all we can mean, is that they are similarly affected by the same Object. Their like 'affections' are two, not one; and neither's emotion, as a mental occurrence, is *erlebt* by the other. James, as has been already mentioned, recognised the absoluteness of this breach; yet the thoughts that are thinkers, by which he sought to replace the permanent self of common sense, have to surmount this breach, to achieve in some cases the appropriation of experience which yields continuity of βίος. If the serial theory be in earnest as to the subjective factor in each of its elements, it thus has to invoke the impossible; if it be not in earnest, and the thoughts be not the thinkers they have been called, it lapses into presentationism. Presentationism, however, also collapses when confronted with the fact of individuality: it can offer no reason why presentations should arrange themselves in particular streams, such as yours and mine, or why so much of individual experience should be, as it is, incommunicable. On the theory of an abiding ego, on the other hand, the individuality, like the unity and continuity, of a mind, follows as a matter of course.

Presentationism sometimes explicitly maintains that the ego is but a name for the body. Enough, however, has been previously said as to the psychology and epistemology of presentationism and behaviourism, to indicate the nature of the grounds on which this supposition is based. Consciousness *is* not material change; if heat be mode of motion, it is necessary to invoke mind, in order to get from heat to warmth. Emergence of consciousness out of matter in motion, is not traceable; unimaginable, it is also inconceivable in relation to what we know about matter and mind: which is to say it is unthinkable. And if such a derivation of the mental were abstractly conceivable, we should be no nearer to accounting for logical and teleological order in the mental, the physical antecedents being *ex hypothesi* alogical and mechanical. A theory of the mental should surely make it its first duty to explain the order-characters of mental process; any hypothesis that ignores them can safely be ignored.

8. The last of typical attempts to dispense with the ego-concept as superfluous, is the suggestion that the purposes for which the idea was fashioned, can equally well be served if the ego be taken to be not an Actuality but a logical construction, a non-existent subsistent, a class; and if for actual *rapport* we substitute logical relation. The principle of abstraction, suggested by Dedekind's theory of number, has of late been invoked for various philosophical purposes: to retain a realistic interpretation of the conceptual scaffolding (ethers, electrons, etc.) of theoretical physics, while renouncing the category of substance; to describe the mental βίος without hypostatising the ego-concept. It is not necessary here to discuss the resolution, involved in this principle, of adjectival identity into membership of a class definable, or even indicable, without presupposing the adjectival in question. It suffices to note that the principle, as applied in science, is confessedly "a heuristic maxim", a form of Ockham's razor. It affords, in fact, what is technically called description, preferable to interpretative explanation in virtue of its economy, especially its dispensing with the notions of substance and of possession of a common quality by a group of things. Economy, or paucity of descriptive apparatus, however, is not the prime concern with the student of Actuality; but rather, sufficiency. One *ens* more will not be eschewed by him, if its adoption prove essential to adequate representation of his facts. The whole truth, as well as nothing but the truth, is his paramount interest, though possibly it be none for the logico-mathematician. Now the class-concept, which the thinker of the latter type favours, when abstracted from its concrete instances, is not an existent or an Actuality. It is precisely an Actuality and an agent, however, that psychology requires, on which to bestow the name 'ego'. Kant shewed that the 'I think' must accompany each psychosis; and it has here been submitted that the I, thinking, cannot accompany certain psychoses unless it accompany certain others. It is something without which forthcoming *facts* could not be. We are not rash, then, in concluding that it, as well as they, is an existent. And we shall

be good Ockhamists if we use this one *ens*, indispensable for some and sufficient for all the facts, to cover all as well as some. If the pure ego were but a class or a class-name, it would not suffice to describe Actuality as it is; it would leave out the psychologically most significant features. Economy, void of significance, is as charmless to the man of science as it is misleading to the philosopher. In the case of the individual mind, to dispense with the permanent subject is to abandon the one sufficient bond by which the essential characteristics of a mind, and the connexions between its phases, are made comprehensible. Apart from its abiding subject, the individual mental life, or stream of consciousness, is no stream, no unity; and when the stream is abstracted from him, it is no wonder that he cannot be found in it, and that he 'transcends the facts'. The so-called facts that he is said to transcend, it must be insisted, are not facts without him, but artifacts and fictions. The hypostatising of an abstraction is not perpetrated by those who regard a mind as a synthesis effected by an actual agent, but by those who reify the abstraction consciousness into an agent; by those who speak of the mind's unifiedness, or bondedness, and repudiate a unifier or bond.

The view that the 'I think' is merely a logical form, and the I an idea that obtains hypostasis through the ontological fallacy, is sometimes alleged to be an outcome of Kant's first *Critique*. It is true that, in one section of that work, Kant asserts the thinking subject to be the "mere form of the consciousness", which "accompanies" all concepts, and all objects of consciousness. So he speaks on occasion. But the occasion is when he engages in polemic against the dogmatic rationalists, whom he supposed to have derived their doctrine of the soul from the *cogito ergo sum*, as an *a priori* truth independent of empirical fact. He rightly maintained that to think an idea, is not to posit an existent: to extract from 'I think', as a merely logical proposition aloof from empirical datum, the existence of the I, is like deriving the Actuality of a mermaid from the proposition 'mermaids swim'. But in putting this interpretation on *cogito ergo sum*, and in criticising such supposed use of it, Kant was attacking the ego, only as known in an *a priori* way, with which we have no concern: if indeed the pre-Kantian rationalist had. It may be observed incidentally that in the section on The Paralogisms of Pure

Reason, Kant deserts his own teaching in several respects. He confounds the subject with an object known, before he can argue that it is a form; he asserts that the I is known, like any other object, phenomenally. But, underlying the constructive part of the *Critique of Pure Reason*, and essential to its whole fabric, is the belief, common to him and the dogmatists whom he attacks, in the Actuality of the ego as unifier, rather than the unity, of experience. The synthesis involved in experience, he teaches, is the activity of an ego that needs must be permanent. He insists on the duality of experience, with which the notion of the subject as mere 'form' is incompatible. The unity of consciousness is not, for him, the ordered whole into which its contents are somehow brought, but the unifying process of one unifier: it is no category, but "the ground of all the categories". The idea of the ego is grounded in the fact of the empirical unity of all thinkings, and is the *sine qua non* for the possibility of the fact.

Perhaps the most important of Kant's pronouncements as to the self, is that set forth in the following passage:[1] "One may therefore say of the thinking I (the soul), which represents itself as substance, simple, numerically identical in all time, and as the correlative of all existence, from which in fact all other existence must be concluded, that it *does not know itself through the categories*, but knows the *categories* only, and through them all objects, in the absolute unity of apperception, *that is, through itself*". This sentence, the more emphatic in that the italics are Kant's own, may be taken to embody, not only the conviction uppermost in his mind at the moment of writing, but an inevitable outcome of the Kantian epistemology, despite his own desertion of it on occasions. We have found that its truth is confirmed by analytical psychology, and that no alternative theory is allowed by the all-decisive facts. And the conclusion reached is fraught with philosophical import. It means that the world is intelligible only when it is *interpreted*, and interpreted in terms of what the human ego, at its level of self-consciousness, knows *itself* to be—not phenomenally but noumenally: that all other knowledge is mediated by categories that are not thrust upon us *ab extra* but emanate from us, their source and their paradigm: that these categories

[1] *Critique of Pure Reason*, ed. 1, p. 402; M. Müller's tr., p. 347. In this exposition of Kant some use has been made of Ward's work, *A Study of Kant*.

are not endowed with necessity absolute and *a priori*, but with expediency dictated by empirical or Actual conditionings. Inasmuch as there can be no foundation for spiritualism, or even dualism, unless we know ourselves to be abiding subjects; inasmuch as, unless there be a spirit in man, it is idle for him to talk of a God in the world; inasmuch as there can be no knowledge that is not derived from the interpretative faith of *homo mensura* in commerce with his world-environment: the establishment of the Actuality of the perduring subject of personal experience, which has been undertaken in this chapter, is the laying of the foundation of the philosophy concerning the self, the world and God, in which our pursuit of the *ordo cognoscendi*, and its empirical method, will issue.

9. The pure subject, as distinguished from its objects, from the body which it controls, and from its manifestation in the personality—in short, from the empirical self—has been argued to be Actual, because it acts: existent, because experience, our prime fact-datum, is impossible without it. The concept is not superfluous, but indispensable. The ego is not a mere idea, but the Actual counterpart to an idea: Actuality involves its existence, as thought implies its essence.[1] It remains to shew that the idea

---

[1] The critical reader will perhaps lay the accusation that here I am confounding what Kant taught us to distinguish, and am taking a pre*supposition*, indispensable for our *thinking*, for a real *position* or existent: a regulative idea for a Real agent that is Actual ground of Actual functionings. Just as Kant forbade us to infer from '*we* cannot *think* the organic without a teleological category', to a mind internal or external to organisms or to the world, lest we mistake what perhaps is a limitation of our faculties, for a manifestation of a thing *per se*: so are we forbidden to infer from the indispensableness of the soul-concept to a Real soul. One can reply that enforcement of this prohibition, however logically salutary, carries the consequence of Humean scepticism. If a soul is not known to exist, on the evidence and reasoning that have been submitted, *a fortiori* neither is a tree known to exist and have a life-history. If we are to renounce the validity of substance and cause because they are suppositions, or postulates that are merely pragmatically 'verified', we must renounce all knowledge so-called: not merely alleged knowledge of the soul, but the knowledge on the strength of which, suspicion as to the soul is entertained. On the other hand, if we have any knowledge of Actuality as connected and determined, so that the world is not one of unlimited possibilities in which anything may follow upon anything, then we can not only say, *e.g.*, that the concept of memory analytically involves that of perduring ego, but also that the fact of memory involves an abiding soul. Those who base their scepticism as to the existence of the soul on the precariousness of the categories involved in the assertion of it—and scepticism generally reduces to precisely that—

is not empty, nor the ego so poor and bare as to be wholly un-knowable as to its 'what'. The ego is not to be dismissed, as by Mr Bradley, on the ground that it is a "poor substitute" for the empirical self. A substitute, it does not profess to be. "If the monad stands aloof", said this philosopher, "either with no character at all or a private character apart, then it may be a fine thing in itself, but it is mere mockery to call it the self of a man". The mockery is Mr Bradley's and is gratuitous. The pure ego is not the self or person, but the Actuality without which there could be no such thing as a person. And it certainly cannot be said to have no character at all, as we shall presently see. Nor is it to be con-founded, as by James, with the soul as conceived in pre-Kantian rational psychology: *i.e.* as self-subsistent, necessarily immortal, existent apart from objects and activities. Inasmuch as our em-pirically obtained knowledge as to the pure ego, or soul, is learned from what it does, its substantiality (when we pass to metaphysic) is not to be conceived in terms of spatiality, inertia and quasi-materiality, of the *in se* or the *per se*, or even of *res cogitans*, but rather in terms of the *conatus* of Spinoza and Leibniz. It is of no significance for us that Kant, in his first *Critique*, denied the sub-stantiality of his own thin abstraction.

In the light of facts now expounded, several assertions can be made as to the essence of the pure ego, or soul, as modern psycho-logy allows and requires us to conceive of it.

(1) It is simple, not a complex of subjects; numerically singular, and in that sense individual, atomic or monadic. It has no parts, as its states and even its objects have been miscalled. One subject cannot be divided into two, nor two fused into one. This, by the way, is the psychological finding on which traducianism founders.

(2) It is also an individual, in that it alone can have or 'enjoy' *its* states, or be presented with *its* objects—which are its *idia*. If such terms as 'fluidity', 'confluence', 'overlapping', 'interpene-tration', have any scientific, as distinct from poetical, significance when applied to personalities, they are certainly not predicable of pure subjects or souls. What is sometimes called "sympathetic thinking of oneself into another's experience", cannot mean having

should be more impartial in the application of it. They are welcome to flaunt Hume's conclusion if they will proclaim loyalty to his theory of knowledge. But they should not be Humeans in psychology, and Kantians, etc., in physics and physiology.

that experience, but only imaginatively reconstructing it. Transition from any psychosis to another is transition from, and to, the experiencing of the same subject. With every subject is correlated a not-self, numerically different from that correlated with any other: each has its world. In this sense, the ego is an impenetrable or impervious monad with its own 'point of view': which is not to say the soul is "windowless" or devoid of active *rapport* with objects, or that its experience is explicable as a series of immanent states.

(3) The ego is individual in a third sense: that of possessing idiosyncrasy. It thus differs from the mass-point or the electron, as conceived by physicists. Doubtless the differences between persons, of which we are wont to say there are no two alike, are conditioned in many ways; but the original feelings of pleasure and displeasure evoked by the sensa, whether external or somatic, of an individual, must be what they are, because the pure ego is what it is. Though in general we may thus attribute a *haeccitas*, a divergence from the conceptual type, that is not describable by any finite number of universals, there is, nevertheless, no need to commit ourselves to the doctrine of the numerical identity of indiscernibles, or to transcend empirically manifested diversity by affirming absolute or analytic necessity thereof.

(4) The soul is not a blankly receptive *tabula rasa*, nor is it exclusively cognitive. In virtue of the capacity of feeling, it is interested; and to be determined by its own feeling-response, is to be self-determined. This capacity of feeling, along with the faculties of attending to, and complicating, impressions, etc., deriving ideas, selectively fashioning concepts and performing all the synthetic activities involved in the complexity of mental life, constitute the knowable essence, or the 'what', of the pure ego, and account for the richness of personality which accrues from increasing commerce with ever-widening environment. Ultimately presupposed by such growth in individuality, through intercommunion, is the truth thus expressed by Spinoza: "any emotion of a given individual differs from the emotion of another individual only in so far as the essence of one individual differs from the essence of the other".[1]

(5) The pure ego is not an existent without an essence, then,

[1] *Ethics*, III. 57.

any more than it is an essence without existence. Nor need we suppose that the capacity and faculty, that constitute its essence, can be evoked or exercised in isolation from objects with which it has *rapport*. It is no such abstraction as that which critics have set up, and have demolished instead of the Real thing. Its *known* essence is to function: and though to suppose that its being is exhausted in functioning, that it must incessantly function in order to be, is perhaps to confound a psychological with an onto-logical issue, and rôle with player; still, a substance to which experience is only incidental, is an abstraction from fact, a mere possibility of which psychology can make no use. However, it savours of dogmatism to assert that in sleep, etc., the soul cannot be functioning, and therefore, after all, there can be no abiding ego; for there are operations beneath the threshold that may go on in states of what is commonly called unconsciousness. Again, when a mystic speaks of his ceasing to be, or of losing his self, he is not to be taken seriously. His attention has for a time been so concentrated on other Objects that his pure ego has been aware of no presentation of its me; but he must have been continuously existent, in order to concentrate, to become and to remain rapt, and to remember his mystic experiences when again non-rapt.

(6) The soul cannot be phenomenal. It is that to which pheno-mena appear, and is known otherwise than is the phenomenal. It is rather the one known being that must be called ontal or noumenal, if we are to avoid indefinite regress; or the one ontal thing that is assuredly known.

10. From such inferred knowledge as to the essence of the soul, we can pass to the metaphysical question of its substantiality. It is chiefly through association with some of the less relevant of the many meanings of 'substance', that the soul has been brought into disrepute. We may dismiss the concept of substance as that which *per se stat* or *per se concipitur*; as the self-subsistent and underived; as the indestructible as well as the indiscerptible; as static or changeless (the essence of substantiality before Leibniz); for con-tinuity of becoming may be the law of the soul's being. The soul may not be substantial in any of these senses, and yet may be called a substantial Actuality: not substance but *a* substance. It may be so called, if thereby we mean that it is (1) substantival—a

logical substance, (2) relatively permanent, (3) active or efficient: if, *i.e.*, substance be a 'real' category, and not an abstraction from concrete individual things and from causality.

(1) The distinction between substantive and adjective, the characterised and the characterising, is no mere dispensable convention of grammar incidental to the habit of mind of Aryan peoples, as has sometimes been represented. Language has derived it from Actuality. It is the outcome of thought on things. As an implicit distinction, it is a presupposition of effective thought; and we need not concern ourselves with thought of other kinds. This irreducible and inevitable distinction does not imply that the substantival and the adjectival are separable existents, but it embodies the truth that substantival beings are determinate. The relation of the substantival to its adjectives is unique. It cannot be replaced by any other known to logic. It is different from the relation of a substance to its states, which are not adjectival. The substantival and the adjectival are apprehended and defined by different thought-processes. In calling the soul substantival, then, we mean that it is a particular, characterised, not characterising; it cannot be an adjective of another soul, or even of God or the Absolute. When this latter view has been maintained, as *e.g.* by Bosanquet, adjectivalness has been confounded with relatedness, as of part to whole or member to group; while substantivalness has been mistaken for substantiality in Spinoza's sense. When the soul has been said to be but the aggregate of experiences (objects, acts, or both), or of vital functions—as by Aristotle— substantiality, as well as substantivalness, has been attributed to the experiencings: thoughts being hypostatised into thinkers, states into subjects. The case is similar, when soul has been taken to denote but the unifiedness of the experiences: the observable bondedness is then confused with the bond, fact with explanation. The soul is not the mental life, but is manifested therein. Both are substantival; the difference between them, and the substantiality of the soul alone, bring us to the second factor in the meaning of soul-substance.

(2) The soul is a 'continuant'.[1] It is not a collection of states

---

[1] This term is due to Mr Johnson, *Logic*, Part III, a work from which some statements in the foregoing paragraph are derived. The meaning given above to 'continuant', is identical with that which it seems to bear in some passages of Mr John-

or of occurrences, nor a class of members, even connected by causation transeunt between them, and 'immanent' to the collection as one whole. The unification of states, etc., into one thing, can only be explained in terms of immanent causation within a numerically singular entity. Hence (3) "substance is through and through causality", and the two categories of substance and cause are at bottom one, each implicating the other. Stability of nexus, and determination, which make conceptual 'description' a possibility and are (ps) presupposed by it, are explicitly ignored in scientific descriptions which (ψ) profess to have nothing to do with substance or cause. Dispensing with explicit usage of these categories, is a practical convenience in science; but, however conducive to departmental success, it renders scientific procedure, as compared with that of metaphysics, relatively facile. This is, of course, no defect of science, so long as it does not pose as philosophy, or so long as it does not pretend that what it agrees to leave out, is not there. It is not science, but exploiters of it in the interest of their philosophical predilections, who make that mistake, and who speak as if science had eliminated these categories from the structure of thought or knowledge. This is by no means

son's book, not with meanings apparently contained in others. It agrees with the following statements: a continuant is a unity into which 'occurrents' [*i.e.* states, acts] are constructed by thought, by means of the nexus of causality (Introduction, § 4, paraphrased); it "continues to exist through some limited or unlimited time, during which its various states and its outer connexions with other continuants may alter or keep unaltered" (Introd. § 5). It agrees with the assertion that this persistence is "something behind even the possibly changing properties" (ch. vi, § 2), if by this be meant that the properties are 'of', or inhere in, the continuant, and that certain first-order properties are not necessarily supposed to be changeable; also with the statement that the relation of the states, etc., to the continuant is unique (ch. vi. § 1)—if the relation in question be 'inherence', in the sense of immanent determination by the continuant. This selection of passages seems to imply that the continuant is numerically one substantival entity, the ground or immanent cause of its states: and this supposition alone seems adequate for the purpose for which the continuant is invoked. But there are other passages in which Mr Johnson would seem to approach the view, that the continuant is but a complex of states related to one another otherwise than as states 'of' one entity: and if this be his meaning, he cannot be cited as a supporter of the pure-ego theory which has here been maintained, but of a form of the series-theory which has been rejected. Dr Broad (*Mind*, N.S. No. 131) interprets Mr Johnson in the latter sense; but it seems to me, especially in the light of the explicit statement in Introduction, § 4, p. xix, that his doctrine of the continuant, applied to the mental, is indistinguishable from that of the pure ego as I have expounded it.

the case; though it is largely due to belief that it is so, that cause and substance have been for some time under a cloud. As Mr Johnson observes, a continuant, viz. the ego, is assumed in order to eliminate continuant and cause from the physical, because presupposed in alleging observation of continuity of changes in an Object; while, in order to resolve the psychic continuant into the nervous system, the physical continuant needs to be reinstated. In other words, immanent causation in continuing substances seems to be the indispensable explanation of that stable nexus in change, in the absence of which, regular determination in things, and consequently any science of things, would be impossible. Without it, our world should be one in which "anything may succeed upon anything", and unfounded coincidence should be the source of the world's intelligibility. The former situation does not obtain. The only forthcoming alternative to the latter incredible supposition, once substance-cause is repudiated, is the conception of the deterministic system, invoked by some writers as if it were relevant to empirical fact. In a deterministic system, as conceived by the mathematician, all proceeds according to law, the future states of a continuous process being as determinative of it as the past: but human experience is non-reversible. Again, in the deterministic system all the terms must be correlatable with numbers: but the distinguishable elements of a mental life are not. The mind is therefore no such system. It is the old story, that necessary truth is acquired at the expense of relevance to Actuality. Ockham's razor is of no avail against brute fact. Substance and cause may be superfluous in a pure science, and even in applied science, once it has discovered that to which it would give descriptive exposition: they are presupposed in all thought that would eliminate them from natural philosophy or psychology, and in all thinking that issues in a product such as can be expounded without explicitly invoking them. We are authorised then to see, in the abiding ego, a substance or continuant to whose immanent causation or activity, evoked in *rapport* with objects, is to be referred the connexion between passing states, constituting them one βίος. Only so, it would appear, can the selective, synthetic, activities involved in forthcoming knowledge, be explained without violence to fact and to logic. Transeunt action, as in volition determining sensatio, is equally predicable as immanent causation. Psychology doubtless purges away some of the attributes that once were bestowed *a priori* on soul-substance; but there is a residuum of the legitimate *a priori*, derived from the *a posteriori* as its necessary presupposition, which is indispensable. It is that of the continuant, of which feelings are states, and knowledge and volition are activities. We might retain the old notion of substance as *substratum* or support; for though thoughts, volitions, etc., are not accidents or adjectives, they may be said to 'inhere' in their subject. The continuing identity of the soul, moreover, is not adjectival changelessness, but numerical identity of ground. That would seem a *sine qua non* for explaining determination of psychosis by psychosis, without reliance on chance or miracle. States inhere, qualities characterise; and both require an Actual determinant. Substance is not to be decried as a useless notion, in that it does not explain how or why particular states inhere in particular continuants: something must be ultimate and unsearchable in data not posited by us. But determinateness being simply accepted as irresolvably ultimate, the substance-concept is the only sufficient ground of the unity, coherence and determination which psychoses observably manifest; one mental state cannot be supposed to create its successor out of nothing. Lastly, the concept denotes no logical or abstract 'form', because it is only an existent that can feel and be efficient, with power on its own act and on the world.

11. The individuality that has been ascribed, as an essential characteristic, to the soul or subject, may seem to be threatened, if there be scientific accuracy in such expressions as 'the soul of a people', 'the mind of a nation'; some notice of these phrases is therefore called for.

Doubtless there is such a thing as common, if not strictly universal, experience, the *Bewusstsein ueberhaupt* of Kant. A society is not an aggregate of non-communicating individuals. It may be doubtful whether there is such a thing *sui generis* as mob-psychology; but the mentality of a society, and of its several members, is different from what would be that of an unsocialised individual, were there any such adult human being. The phrases cited above express some truth, but they must be said to be figurative, rather than literally true. For collective experience, there need not be, and there is not, one experient like or parallel to individual selves; though thinking goes on in individual minds alone. The nation, for instance, has no soul but the many souls of its members. It is a common fallacy, when more than a poet's licence, to suppose that a whole of many parts or members can be taken for a macrocosm of the same order as its units. A system of subjects need no more be a subject, than a constellation of five stars is a sixth star. Resemblance is not numerical identity; analogy between a society and an organism does not mean that a society is an organism, but that it behaves more or less like one. A society is personal, but not a person. The social mind, then, is a hypostatised abstraction consequent on previous abstraction of the individual, who is actually a social individual, from his social environment.

But individual thought and action are affected by fellowship. The scope and nature of an individual's mentality become vastly enhanced and enriched through intersubjective intercourse. Nevertheless, all the thinking is performed by the individuals who give and take. What is common or is one, is neither the thinking nor the thinkers, but what is thought. 'Collective mind' is thus but a name for a characteristic evinced by individual minds, in consequence of their interaction and co-operation. Used otherwise, it is a superfluous and misleading phrase. An over-individual aspect is not a super-individual; souls do not coalesce into an over-soul. There is a position tenable between nominalism and realism; social consciousness is an Actuality, but it is not aloof from individual minds, nor to be hypostatised into a Subject.

12. The knowledge concerning the soul that we can claim to possess, important as it is, is scant. Psychology can tell us nothing as to the origin or the destiny of the soul, its pre-existence or its immortality, or as to how it became embodied. Opinion on such matters, to command respect, should be consistent with psychological science, but must be based on conclusions derived from a survey of a more comprehensive field of fact.

As to the origin of the soul, various theories are forthcoming. Materialism and epiphenomenalism assert what is beyond knowledge, and indeed beyond reason at its present stage, when they allege the soul—or rather mental events—to be derived from matter. If 'matter' means what it does in physics, such mystery has no relation to science.

Traducianism, according to which the soul is produced from the souls, as the body is from the bodies, of parents, may be said to involve a quasi-materialistic notion of spirit. The view that souls can be split into parts, can lose some of these parts without being essentially altered, and that such parts of souls can fuse together into a new one, not only implies that spirit is extended, but is inconsistent with the knowledge that may reasonably be inferred from psychological fact concerning the subject of experience. Traducianism also transcends observable fact, in asserting continuity of soul-plasm, analogous to that of germ-plasm. In thus satisfying the evolution-craving, and in accounting for the larger portion of the facts concerning mental heredity in terms of continuity, it has proved attractive. But it fails to account for individual peculiarities, which are as much in evidence as likeness in mentality between parents and offspring; and heredity of mental traits, we shall find, can be explained without the apparently impossible assumption that new souls are chips from old blocks.

Creationism, in turn, transcends fact. In accounting for the subject's idiosyncrasies, and in being free from psychological solecisms, it has advantages over traducianism. But it is not easy to bring it into line with the phenomena of mental heredity. With that end in view, Lotze propounded it with supplementation by the occasionalistic hypothesis, that God adapts souls to the bodies of organisms according to law, weaving successive generations into gradations of an inherent affinity. This supposition, in cases in which souls are implanted in ready-made bodies such as necessitate insanity from birth, raises the problem of evil in acute form. Also the view that the heir is created for, and appointed to, an inheritance lying unclaimed, is repellent to theists who are not dualists, as involving a ὕστερον πρότερον and as contradicting their idea of a Creator. On such grounds, and in order to satisfy the intellect's desire for continuity, others would place the creation of souls further back, and embrace the view of Leibniz, that souls have always had bodies of some sort. Pre-existence is postulated; and then theism is confronted with the alternative that souls are not created, but self-subsistent. On any theory, the questions how the soul becomes associated with the body of this life between conception and death, and what occasions μετενσωμάτωσις, are beyond the tether of fact-controlled speculation.

They will always remain so, unless the sciences of psychology and psychophysics shall make advances, the very possibility of which cannot now be foreseen. All that can be said by psychology amounts to rather less than Sir Thomas Browne said long ago: "There is a something in us that can be without us and will be after us; though indeed it hath no history what it was before us and cannot tell how it entered into us". It certainly is suggested by the facts that the soul was before us as besouled organisms; and that being so, we have no scientific reason to disbelieve in its continued existence after dissolution of the body which, in this life, conditions its inherent activities.

CHAPTER VI

The Empirical Self and Personality

Of the three factors which determine personality, one only has hitherto been indicated, viz. the pure ego or soul. That is the source of all that may be called idiosyncracy. What is evoked from it, in the way of interested response, depends ultimately on the ego's intrinsic nature; and there is the root of self-determination or freedom.

The second mental factor is the sum of inherited endowments, commonly known as the nature with which we are born; while the third is what is afterwards thrust upon us by social nurture and physical environment, with or without volitional appropriation.

1. *Heredity.* The term 'heredity' is derived from the sphere of law, where heir and inheritance, as person and property, are separate and independent. This separateness must be retained when the notions of heir and hereditament are taken over by psychology. But in the biological usage, which, rather than the legal, is wont to influence psychological thought, the difference is obliterated: metaphor replaces exact statement of fact. The inherited property is identified with its heir himself; it includes his idiosyncracies as well as his common nature: and what is said to be inherited, has but a superficial analogy with legal property, in that parents cannot divest themselves of their personal traits, as of their goods. What is chiefly meant in biological science by heredity, is the observed continuity of germ-plasm, the fact that like begets like. But, in the psychological realm, continuity of soul-substance is not observable: it appears that one's parents are but foster-parents of one's soul. Nevertheless, resemblance between parent and child obtains on the mental, as well as on the bodily, side. And so long as 'mind' does not mean or include the subject, which cannot be said to be transmitted, or to be a chip of soul-block, there is no inconceivability about connexion of the objective content of the unborn ego's experience with the transmitted germ-plasm. But it is important to observe that the

psychological subject is *called* an heir at all, solely because his mentality, as it developes, shews partial likeness to that of his ancestors.[1] Such likeness can only be transmitted in the form of bodily characters, conditioning the functionings of the underived soul. The so-called heir either-seizes, or else is appointed (and that not by the testator) to, the inheritance: and the mental characteristics that he inherits, are not subjective capacity and faculty, as such, but the objective side of his earliest experience which, as evocative of subjective reaction, conditions him and thereby contributes to make him a determinate individual. The inheritance does not include his idiosyncracies: these his parents did not possess, and could not bequeath. Nor is it talents and disposition, unless by those words are meant merely aptitudes such as preclude developement along certain lines and predispose to developements along certain others: tendencies, *i.e.*, to reproduce ancestral characteristics. The inherited mental 'property' is not of the subject's own synthesis. Synthesised by his ancestors, it is given to him and is for him (*i.e.*, is ψ), simple. Hence it is popularly called instinct. "It is anything but a *tabula rasa* in itself: it is such, however, for the concrete individual; for his experience—so far as we know—begins with it".[2]

'Instinct', however, is not an inclusive enough term aptly to designate this inheritance as a whole, and *Anlage* may replace it. The mental inheritance thus denoted, is not the body as Objective, any more than mentality as subjective action, etc. It is indeed not even the body *quâ* objective for its owner when his experience as an embodied soul begins, but rather as the largely unperceived medium for his intercourse with the Objective world. It constitutes, so to say, the 'point of view' for its subject, for whom it remains in large measure diaphanous or non-presented, while instrumental in mediating presentations: it is the body "in its intentional aspect".

It is not possible completely to distinguish, in developed mentality, effects of commerce with environment from self-unfoldings of the innate. For instance, temperament, often included in the mental inheritance, is a vaguely definable system or generalisation of moods, etc., dependent largely on coenaesthesis and affected

by secretions, by cultivated appetites, by disease. What is popularly
called temperament, is not so fixed, so purely and completely
innate, so constitutive of personality, as used to be supposed; and
it is only part of the *Anlage*, in so far as organic sensatio, evoking
affective and conative response from the pure ego, remains un-
modified by both ego and environment. Much that is sometimes
called instinctive belongs to this temperamental or dispositional
factor of the *Anlage*: emotions accompanied by motor expression
(such as the fear which issues in flight), appetites, aversions,
parental love, curiosity; and, some would add, gregariousness, or
the herd-instinct, the existence of which is disputable. If there
be any advantage in using 'instinctive' in this broad and indefinite
sense, there is gain in precision when the word is restricted to one
sole kind of inherited endowment, viz. the specialised instincts
which are not dependent on coenaesthesis, but on definite situations determined for the subject by external perception, and
which consist in actions that are not necessarily accompanied by
specific emotions. In this narrower sense, the instincts in man are
very few; and they play practically no part in differentiating one
person from another. Along with other elements in the *Anlage*,
they are largely sublimated, *i.e.* diverted to form habits remotely
connected with the instinctive itself. There are, again, no organised
talents in the human hereditament; only plastic capacities which
can be variously combined and adapted to circumstances. The
insect, in virtue of its elaborate and stereotyped inheritance, is a
consummate specialist of the narrowest type; but man, because
of the poverty of his legacy in respect of ready-made mentality
and dexterity, is the better equipped for coping with the changes
and chances of life. His long youth, presided over by parental
care, leads to suppression of some of the 'instinctive' as superfluous, and to the freer acquisition of diversified skill. Instinct
and intelligence, however, are not so nonconcomitant nor so
essentially disparate as Bergson would have us believe; for what
is now instinct once was not: and the recent tendency to find in
the 'instinctive'—in the vaguest sense of that abused word—the
paramount factor in human mentality, whatever other value it
may possess, yields no important or new contribution to theoretical
knowledge of the normal mind.

Instinct, even in the lower animals, is not to be identified hastily with reflex actions or with tropisms. It is arguable that these presuppose interest and subjectively acquired facility. Instincts have been defined as "original tendencies of consciousness [*i.e.* the conscious subject] to express itself in motor terms in response to definite but generally complex stimulations of sense" (Baldwin). They are inherited reactions to environment, markedly adaptive, fixed in the species; and their continued exercise requires provision for their fulfilment. They involve no memory, in the proper sense of that word, but only what is called race-memory; and they differ from other adaptive responses, however similar as external behaviour, such as are acquired by imitation or rapid learning on the part of the individual. As used in common parlance (and in theological literature when religion, prayer, etc., are miscalled instinctive), the word 'instinct' often means impulse: *i.e.* conation operating through its own intrinsic strength, and in independence of the system of mental life as a whole. It differs from instinct, as above described, in that it is not wholly, if at all, excited by external stimulus, but is initiated by a craving unaccompanied by an idea of the result, accompanied by which it would be a desire.

We commonly speak of inherited talents. What is then really meant, is capacities for talents or some of the constituents of talents, such as sensory discriminatingness, motor agility, quick tempo, peculiarities in respect of retentiveness or assimilation, and so, of association. It is by combination of some or other of these, that the talent, as an organised complex, results. The items may be there, yet never get combined. Talents differ from instincts in that they are individual variations, not fixtures of the species; and in that progress is their invariable mark, whereas instincts are perfected at birth and undergo no developement. The correlation involved in talent, is provided by the individual's intelligence: hence his precocity or pre-eminence. When talent is not wholly acquired—as it sometimes is—its ingredients are part of the *Anlage*; and, in that sense only, may it be said to be inherited. Ability or capacity, however, is wont to be distinguished from genius, *i.e.* marked inventiveness or originality. Statistics shew that talent-ingredients are inherited, but suggest that genius is not. Its marks are not those of heredity. It is innate but not inherited; in its pre-eminent cases it is "but a prerogative instance compelling attention to the fundamental distinction between the experient and his *Anlage*"—between inneity and heredity. Even in the sense in which everyone may be said to have *some* genius or originality, genius is the subjective activity which, as seen already, is the *sine qua non* of individuality or idiosyncracy, and of talent as a systematised complex.

For his *Anlage*, a person has no responsibility; nor has he any for the nature of his pure ego. "It is God that made us", as souls, if we adopt the creationist account of the origination of the soul; and "not we ourselves", on any theory. Here the theist comes upon one of the irresolvable elements in the problem of evil: one which is not wholly explained in terms of finiteness or 'metaphysical evil', because every ego is not only finite in general, but also determinate in intrinsic and individual nature. If free as a creator, it has, as a particular creature, a fore-ordained scope and direction for that devolved freedom which issues ultimately out of interest and affectiveness. Self-determination, in short, is the work of a pure ego whose intrinsic nature is not self-determined. The *Anlage*, again, is given ready-made to its owner; it is none of his making, but the ancestrally prescribed handicap with which he starts his earthly race. He is responsible only for what use he makes of the material assigned to him; not for his 'disposition' but for his 'character', to speak in terms of a familiar contrast. However, with volition and character we are not as yet concerned, save to observe that there is a period of the embodied soul's life to be lived, before will and conscience emerge.

Save in the merely zoological sense, man is at birth but potentially human. As to the "clouds of glory" which the infant has been said to trail, psychology discovers nothing that can be so described; no reminiscences of pure-soul life, no innate ideas of God-given reason: nothing but innocent tendencies of the stock, imparted to man by his brute ancestry. Appetites and various affective-conational dispositions are entrenched in human nature, before the personal and moral status is acquired. This *fomes peccati* is what has often been called original sin. Sin proper, it cannot be, of course: because what is non-volitional is not capable of moral evaluation. Nor, to the evolutionist, do these conative tendencies bespeak abnormity or derangement; they are biologically natural and necessary, belonging to man as it pleased

God to make him. If admitting of ethical valuation in respect of their instrumentality, they are in themselves neutral, in the sense that they are springs of virtue equally as of vice, when volitional attitude toward them becomes possible. But philosophers, *e.g.* Kant, as well as dogmatic theologians, have assumed that these propensities *are* morally evil, for no better reason than that they have commonly been called so. Accordingly, it has been taught that moral evil is already in us at birth, if only discoverable when our moral consciousness awakes; and resort has then been made to the notion of a fall, whether of the race in its first parents, or in each soul separately in a previous life or by a timeless act. Genetic psychology shews that there is no more need to postulate an innate propensity to evil, than an innate propensity to good: propensity to the non-moral, out of which the will eventually makes good and ill alike, is all that can be found, and all that is necessary to explain what every form of the doctrine of original sin confesses to be, for it, an ultimately irresolvable mystery.[1]

2. The third influence that shapes personality, is that of environment, more especially the social environment.[2] Enough, if but little, has already been said about this factor, to prepare for discussion of personality; more will be supplied in chapters dealing with valuation and reason. But before personality can be further described, another inquiry must be undertaken: that into fact and theory indicated by such phrases as 'mental disposition' and 'subconscious mentality'.

'Mental' is variously used. The primary and the narrowest denotation of the term, is the acts and affective states of subjects. Whatever else a mind or mental βίος may be said to include, it will contain subjective action and passion. These will literally be *in* the mind; and no such states, etc., of consciousness are known to occur, save in a βίος or mind in which they are phases. A commoner and broader meaning of 'mental', is that which includes also the objective side of experience: what is directly, and literally, *before* the 'mind' or its subject and is presented *to* it, but is not *in* the mind or *of* the subject, in the same sense that are subjective

---

[1] For a fuller discussion of the psychology of moral evil, as distinct from imperfection, and for explanation of the so-called 'universality of sin' in mankind, I may refer to my book *The Concept of Sin*.

[2] What is called social heredity, is in some respects heredity proper; but it is not heredity at all in the biological sense.

functionings. Again, it is only when 'mental' embraces this objective side alone and excludes the subjective, that we can speak of mental heredity: in that phrase, therefore, we distinguish a third current denotation. The former two senses of 'mental' do not necessitate inclusion of the subject itself, along with its functionings in 'the mind'. There is sense in calling the ego a substance, a soul, or a spirit; hardly, in calling it 'mental'. Hence it is usual, and indeed necessary, if we renounce rhetorical subterfuges dealt with in the preceding chapter, to speak of the mind, or the mental, as 'owned' by an ego, or as the mind *of* an ego. Nevertheless, 'mind' is sometimes used as a synonym for ego or subject, and sometimes to denote—what assuredly is the only concrete fact, and no abstraction from Actuality—the complex, consisting of subject, states, etc., *in*, and objects *before*, him or his 'mind', in the narrower sense. Similarly 'experience', which has been substituted for 'mind', is sometimes inclusive of experiencer, experiencing, and what is experienced. It is enough to call attention to these various usages of the words 'mind' and 'mental', and to observe that it has become difficult to adhere exclusively to any one of them. But, to say nothing as to the familiar antithesis between the mental (in any of the foregoing senses) and the physical, the whole question is complicated by a further issue. For 'consciousness' is naturally restricted to mental process, of which the self-conscious subject can be aware in normal introspection; while 'mental' is used to denote also processes which (often believed to be essentially similar in other respects) are not instances of the unique *erleben* called consciousness, or do not "shine by their own light" to introspective attention.

In this case, 'mental' or 'psychic' will include the unpresented, or what is not attended to, if 'presentation' and 'attention' are confined to immediate awareness, or direct cognition. 'Mental' will embrace more than 'the conscious', viz. what is called 'the unconscious': *i.e. rapport* between subjects and objects, of which the subjects themselves are not directly aware, and subjective functionings beyond the reach of introspection. It is consciousness, with its uniqueness of *erleben*, on which the assertion of mentality is based; but mentality, as subjective interaction with non-ego, is affirmed to occur where there is no such *erlebnis* at all, not to say where there is no reflective apprehension of it. It is in the 'conscious' that the peculiar essence of the mental *appears*; it is nevertheless present in the subconscious and the unconscious. The soul lives not by consciousness alone, and the mental βίος cannot be coherently described, without invoking mentality other than consciousness, such as traces or dispositions. This is hypothesis; but it has justification similar to that claimed for the doctrine of potential energy, which bespeaks the physicist's unwillingness to forgo pursuit of continuity or to cease walking when he cannot walk by sight. Nevertheless, there are psychologists who will not entertain the theory of subconscious mentality, and who would assign all disposition to the body, as distinct from the mind. Some of these (*e.g.* Münsterberg) base their denial on the assertion that a search for mental causes is futile, because there are none: but that is only metaphysical prepossession. As the issue is important in connexion with the discussion of personality, the facts, on which the extended conception of mentality is founded, must be briefly set forth.

We may start from the undisputed facts, that the field of consciousness, or of the supraliminal, contains the marginal as well as what is in the focus of attention, and that this relatively undiscriminated portion affects the whole field. What is ordinarily meant by 'attention', can admit of degrees; and the fact that there is continuity of variation of intensity of sensum with intensity of stimulus above the threshold, or the limit to the conscious, *suggests* variation below the threshold. Again, there is no antecedent difficulty about *conceiving* subjective *rapport* or mentality that does not evidence itself to its subject. However, fact is another matter, which cannot be decided by *a priori* possibilities or by extrapolation of continuity, as if the so-called law of continuity expressed more than a pious hope, a probability or sanguine expectation, such as experience has made inevitable.

Passing then to facts, and dropping the term 'subconscious' just now, because it has been spoiled by having been applied to the 'faintly conscious', or the marginal above the threshold, as well as to what is below the threshold: the first class to be dealt with, is that of subliminal impressions. The weightiest fact, in this connexion, is that the threshold itself has breadth, and is not analogous to a mathematical line. A sound emerges above the threshold, on stimulation of lower intensity than that of the stimulus at which audibility disappears below the threshold; and in case of both its appearance and its disappearance, on rising and falling intensity of stimulus respectively, there is 'flickering', and a margin of doubt as to whether sound is heard or not. Jastrow asserts that one colour is unduly often guessed rightly to be brighter than another, when discrimination between the two fails. He also states that the illusion of inequality between two equal parallel lines, when they are terminated by convergent and divergent arrows respectively, obtains when the arrows are too faint to be perceptible. The most natural interpretation of such facts, is that imperceptible impression produces an effect; but the experiments are hardly conclusive. Nor, perhaps, is the more commonly adduced observation, that, though we cannot discriminate what, on physical grounds, should be two distinct shades of colour, a and b, nor b and c, we can distinguish a from c; which is said to imply that there is difference between sensa, when there is no discernibility of the difference in sensatio. It has been alleged reasonably that the inference here rests on question-begging assumptions, and that Stumpf's experiment is irrelevant. More conclusive is the fact that the field of consciousness may vary, greatly and suddenly, with the amount and distribution of attention. We cannot be sure that presentations do not pass abruptly into, and out of, existence; but if they do, the intensity of a presentation would be a function of attention alone, and not of the objective side also: and as Ward observes, it should then follow that there is no such thing as non-voluntary attention; and that a man asleep could never be awaked, but must awake 'of himself'. This authority concludes, from the facts, that there are ultraliminal impressions which tell on supraliminal experience; and that the contradiction, said to lie in the notion of 'unpresented presentations', is but due to faulty terminology. If there were no facts in support of the theory, it might still claim antecedent probability: to assume that there are no presentations but those in the field of consciousness, is as arbitrary as to assume that there is no vision or hearing, save that mediated by human eyes and ears. We may conclude, then, that there may be mental modifications ('mental' will here include the objective) in which consciousness has no part. Existents can surely be known otherwise than by acquaintance, or our knowledge would be scant indeed.

Turning now to secondary presentations, images and ideas, it is again fact that, in the case of memory-images, the threshold has appreciable breadth. Other relevant facts, each of us can supply for himself: sometimes we could recognise a forgotten name, though we cannot reproduce it; the sad memory and dream-imagery can haunt, when not in the field of consciousness. Not all the traces of past experience are at the disposal of the self, as conscious, but they somehow persist: though dead, past mental events yet speak; or at least their works follow them. On certain conditions, they are revivable or become accessible to introspection.

It is only in terms of subliminal ideas that we can account for stored knowledge. These are sometimes spoken of as *residua* or traces, when actual persistence from the past is emphasised; sometimes as dispositions, when their potentiality as regards the future is suggested. But 'potentiality' connotes nothing Actual, unless it denotes *something* Actual. This denoted Actuality must be *disposita*, a combination or arrangement. 'Potentiality' indicates that something new may ensue on certain conditions being fulfilled, whether inhibition being removed or some causal factor being added; and this may be distinguished as *dispositio* or tendency. If 'disposition' be regarded on its merely structural side, as *disposita* abstracted from, or unaccompanied by, *dispositio* (latent tendency or functioning), it becomes doubtful whether such terms as 'subconscious' and 'psychical disposition' have any meaning. Storage is conceivable physiologically, as persistence of neural tone: there we can imagine *disposita*. But, on the psychical side, we cannot reasonably suppose that all acquired knowledge persists, item for item, just as first received; that separate ideas are retained, as such, in the form and order of their occurrence. Nor is it easy to allow the notion of the persistence, beneath the threshold, of wishes and other complexes, described as having all the attributes of their 'conscious' equivalents, save that the subject is not only unaware of them, but also inactive in them: as if, to speak in terms of an analogy borrowed from another writer, there could be subconscious red having all the properties of red, save that it was not a colour. Such notions have led to those of the censor and the subconscious dungeon into which even 'events' are said to have been repressed. These notions, as Mr Russell has remarked, are popular because mythological, and because phrase-repeating is easier than observation. However, such extravagances are not essential to the theory of psychical *disposita*. It is enough to assert that ideas, etc., do not persist as items, parallel one to one with cerebral *residua*, but as assimilated and elaborated; as implicit rather than explicit; as 'involved' and able to evolve in a variety of shapes and orders. The *disposita* may have several *dispositiones*; and dispositions need but be processes inhibited through relation with other processes or functions. As to their intrinsic nature, it seems that as yet we can further neither know nor conceive. But as to subliminal persistence in this assimilated form, though not as specific articles of stored lumber, there seems *prima facie* to be abundant evidence accessible to anyone, and theory scarcely goes beyond fact.

It is necessary to speak of the mind—the word being used now to include objective dispositions—as possessing structure; though 'structure' is but an analogical term, suggested by the physical. What it should mean, when applied to the psychical, we cannot say as precisely as when it is used of the physical. But there is a vast collection of facts that cannot be unified into a coherent system, or be made comprehensible, without invoking it: it is therefore probably some function of the truth. Structure, it has been hinted, is not the only thing involved in subliminal mentality, even if it be an adequate figure, in terms of which the implicitness, or involution, of subliminal secondary presentation may be described. If it were, there would be more to be said in favour of theories dispensing with the notion of the subconscious. As to these, appeal to habit or to association of ideas may be dismissed, because presupposing subliminal disposition. Indeed habit, involving retention and *disposita*, is practically synonymous with disposition. More formidable is the view that disposition is wholly explicable in terms of physiology, and that the resort to the notion of mental disposition is gratuitous, because modification of nerve is enough. Against this view, Ward adduces the following considerations. Physiological structure implies plasticity, and plasticity implies life. When function lapses, the molecular structure can no longer facilitate its recurrence. Functional activity determines structure; to reverse that order, is to resort to the materialist's *generatio aequivoca*. Moreover, plasticity is not merely biological; it is psychological fact, also; and to ignore this, is to become committed to the theory that mind is a collateral product of matter.

If physiology alone can account for *disposita*, it cannot account for *dispositio* or potentiality. The view accords to volition no more initiative in the grouping of ideas than belonged to non-volitional *sensatio*, and consequently issues in presentationism.[1] It might be added that the facts concerning memory cannot be explained, without invoking traces of attention, *i.e.* of subjective activity as distinct from the objective side of experience. Lastly, we may set against the purely physiological theory, the indirect evidence in favour of subliminal presentations, and a breach with the continuity that we are predisposed, by study of 'the conscious', to postulate.

Besides presentations, primary and secondary, we have to recognise processes or activities beneath the threshold, which can be inferred by the analyst, but cannot be 'caught' by their subject. For instance, there are the acts of complication, etc., whereby perception that is (ψ) immediate, is (ps) mediated; the unconscious correction of binocular vision and of presentations entering into perception of distance: results within the conscious are due to unconscious elaboration. Similarly, in association there must be unconscious linkings; an idea, *a*, will reproduce another, *c*, owing to both *a* and *c* having originally been connected with *b*, which is not reproduced. Thus, apart from dreams, hallucinations, etc., normal mental life involves interaction of supraliminal and subliminal. The latter kind of activity, as Stout and other psychologists emphasise, is an omnipresent factor in the stream of thought. As for non-normal experience, it seems to be an established fact that hypnotised subjects can perform arithmetical calculations while unconscious.

We conclude that the mind has dispositions, structural and functional, and may now observe that they do not exist in separation, but form an elaborated or organised structure. Our stored knowledge is a cognitive dispositional system; sentiments are emotional dispositions. The 'meaning' evoked by a particular percept, is the expression in consciousness of the coming into activity of a system of dispositions. The mind, in fact, appears to be a system of systems. Hence the inadequacy of the old 'method of ideas', which took, as typical, only the objects in the focus of attention, to the neglect of the marginal, and to the over-

[1] *Op. cit.* p. 101 and preceding pp.

looking of the subconscious and the unconscious. Its 'ideas' were not concrete psychoses, but conceptual artifacts. Their connective tissue having been destroyed, they could be but artificially compounded; and the method by which this was effected was altogether too mechanical. It assumed certain elements, discernible in mature experience, to be genetically prior and Actually separable. Although the old sensationist psychology is dead—it was buried by Dr Ward's great Article in the *Encyclopaedia Britannica*—some of its worst features have been imitated in the presentationism and behaviourism of today. The dispositional and subliminal factors in mind, without the postulation (if it be but postulation) of which the mental βίος is unanalysable and inexplicable, afford the basis of one of the strongest of the many lines of argument for the doctrine of an abiding soul; they cannot be accounted for by composition of focal presentations, nor even by storage of presentations, as such. The reluctance evinced, in some quarters, to entertain the supposition of the dispositional, save in the physiological sense, is largely due to the sceptical attitude adopted towards subjective activity, the causal laws of which cannot be traced. But we must distinguish between causal laws or the principle of causation, and the bare notion of causality. That we find little or no causal law in individual experience—for which reason we are said to fly to the supposed subliminal and unobservable in order vainly to seize imaginary laws—does not preclude immanent activity; that is compatible with the mind appearing but as a stream of unique events. It is just this uniqueness that defies explanation of the mechanical type, and which conative activity accounts for; while, as to the charge of vainly pursuing the imaginary, the persistence in mind of previous modifications, is not only fact, but an indispensable condition of all advanced experience.

The theory that the only dispositions are neural, leads to the view that mental events are collateral products of brain-changes; and this is the chief ground for its rejection. Epiphenomenalism implies presentationism, or the 'psychology without a subject', which has already been argued to arise out of epistemological errors and linguistic solecisms. Its merits are commended, with perhaps the maximum of persuasiveness, by Dr Broad,[1] who observes that it "has no need to deny that certain mental events

---

[1] *The Mind and its place in Nature*, pp. 470 ff.

stand in the cognitive relation to other things" or that "two mental events may be so related that one is cognised by the other". But is it not a damning fact, that what epiphenomenalism is thus said to have no need to deny, it needs to assert? Mental events *do not* cognise one another, or anything else; and cognitive relations are nothing, if not cognitive acts, etc., of subjects. The physical Object supposed to cast mental shadows, in so far as it is a conceptual interpretation and filling-out of sense-data, is itself a shadow of the mind's throwing. The theory overlooks the non-commutativeness of the subject-object relation; while the mind's unity, its teleological and other orderedness evinced in processes of reasoning, are left to chance. The only bond allowed, between mental events, is that of "unique and very intimate relations". But if 'relations' be used in its logical sense, relations do not bind into an *Actual* unity; we require *rapport*, causality as a 'real' category, rather than its formal substitutes such as temporal concomitance or sequence. The ambiguous word 'relation', equivalent to *Verhältniss* as well as to *Beziehung*, and including, *e.g.* resembling and murdering, has confused many plain issues. It seems here to beg the question. For the actual commerce which constitutes the mind a thing, as distinguished from a logical class such as the grains of sand in the world, is conceivable only in terms of substance and cause. It may be submitted, then, that epiphenomenalism gains its alleged advantage in respect of economy, by ignoring the significance of facts, committing epistemological blunders, invoking fortuitousness and mystery, and using an ambiguous term paralogistically.

There is another suggestion, calling for notice, that has been advanced with a view to dispensing with mental dispositions: the mnemic theory. This has been clearly expounded, and siftingly criticised, in Dr Broad's work just cited. Some of the points there made may be here reproduced. The hypothesis has the laudable object of keeping only to observable fact, and would avoid resort to the mental structure, beyond reach of introspection, involved in traces and dispositions. It would account for reminiscence, in terms of past event and present stimulus, without appealing to any mental Actuality persisting in the interval between the two. One condition of reminiscence is overlooked by it, viz. what we call normal health; for in certain states of the body, appropriate stimulus does not revive memory of the past. But the mnemic theory requires to make its own particular postulate—that of a special kind of causal relation. Like the theory of action at a (spatial) distance in the physical realm, it assumes causal determination at a temporal distance, or non-contiguousness in time between one of the causes that are involved and the effect which ensues. Traces have been postulated especially with a view to providing continuity; they are hypothetical existents invoked to fill gaps between observable occurrences. They may therefore be compared with the potential energy of the physicist, or with the 'substance' category by which we make transition from our sporadic sensa to a persistent thing. As they are hypothetical, the mnemic theory would dispense with them. It only does so, however, by representing that causal determination is reducible to regularity of temporal antecedence. This is obviously too general or abstract a construction of causal connexion; for there are cases of uniform antecedence and concomitance where there is no Actual influence or determination of occurrence, so far as knowledge goes. This will become manifest when causation is discussed.[1] The theory is therefore inadequate, as overlooking part of the conditions *sine quibus non*.

The Actuality of the subliminal or the dispositional having been vindicated, it is now necessary to repudiate estimates of its importance that (save in respect of therapeutic practice) savour of exaggeration, and unwarrantable speculative interpretations of the relevant facts. Typical of these, is the notion of the subliminal self, as elaborated by F. W. H. Myers and others. The unconscious, thus hypostatised, has not only been regarded as the source of the reasoning of the genius, but as a larger and richer self, of which the normal self is but a part. We have seen that genius does not require, for its explanation, the uprushing of ready-made insights. There is nothing to suggest that consciousness is a fall from an earlier kind of mentality; though it may be a rise, or have been evolved, from unconscious mentality, through the subconscious. On behalf of the latter view, speculative as it must be deemed, there is something to be said. For the nearer we approach the recovery of the first stage of experience, the more of the marginal, and the less of the focal or even of a field, would there seem to be

---

[1] See chap. VIII and Appendix, Note J.

in it. It would be difficult to account for our first sensation, if there were no consciousness without difference within the presented field; difficult also to suppose that consciousness arose discontinuously out of unconsciousness. But however this may be—and it is a metaphysical rather than a psychological issue—much, at least, of our subconscious and unconscious mentality is fragments of the lapsed 'conscious', or supraliminally organised, experience. There may be other springs than 'conscious' motivations; but there is no reason to believe that the subliminal is the manifestation of a finer self, buried, save for occasional emergences, beneath the rubbish accumulated by the normal self's mediocre activities. The erratic behaviour of the mentally abnormal, again, is not due to uprush of a heroic 'other', but to impairments which exist in all degrees down to the momentary obliviscences of the sanest; nor does hypnotic suggestion evoke the thoughts, etc., of a submerged 'other', but those derived from supraliminal and ordinary experience. The subliminal self, the dungeon, the censor, with which we have been made familiar, belong but to the world of psychological romance, save when acknowledged to be figures of speech. There is, again, somewhat of hyperbolism in the suggestion of James, that the subconscious is common to all experients, an ocean in which their supraliminal minds are waves, somewhat like the world-ground (M) of Lotze; also in the theological supposition that the subliminal is the medium for the transmission of divine grace to the human person. The truth on which James' suggestion may be based, is that there is not the same incommunicability about unconscious mentality as about the conscious. The 'unconscious' of a person A, may have its origination in his or in B's conscious experience, and may operate on the mentality of A or of B.

3. Eschewing all travesties of the theory of subliminal mentality, we may take it that the conception of an individual mind implies, as necessarily as it does an abiding subject, that process of consciousness is conditioned by prior process; that this is only intelligible if past experience leaves mental traces, and disposition involves 'unconscious' (not directly cognised) regions of psychic activity. The mind must be provisionally and analogically conceived as having structure, as a system of systems elaborated by one and the same subject. It is now the occasion finally to vindicate

this interpretation of personal identity and of the unity of the mental βίος, by dealing with an order of facts which *prima facie* militate against it; and, at the same time, to prepare for an adequate description of personality, by considering certain phenomena which illustrate the relative instability of its organisation, and otherwise throw light on its essential nature.

It has already been mentioned that, in pathological conditions, the sense of self-embodiment and of self-identity may be lost. When personality is more highly developed, more profound fission is possible. Whole intellective and emotional systems, of complex order, may become sundered from others; and the subject's awareness may, for longer or shorter time, be confined to but one or more of such systems. The resulting phenomena led to such views as that a body may be tenanted by several selves, that 'multiple personality' reveals the functioning of distinct subjects, that even the normal man may be polypsychic, or the whole race monopsychic. These facts, by the way, afford a psychological explanation of what used to be called demoniacal possession, of certain kinds of mystical experience, and (as some investigators think) of the 'medium' and 'controls'. Groups of subliminal states capable of functioning independently of others, when dominating behaviour and manifesting themselves energetically, would naturally suggest possession; and a self, invaded by automatic impulses and obsessions, would seem to be under the control of another subject. But it is important to observe that continuity is traceable from the extremest developement of mental disintegration in insanity, through the phenomena of dissociation, to cases of psychologically simple, and practically trifling, kind.

Thus, in the common abnormality of temporarily forgetting a familiar name, we may see the first stage of dissociated personality. Usually we can pass from item to item of dispositional storage, as when, while conversing on one topic, we are suddenly questioned about another. But on certain occasions this becomes impossible. Emotion will sometimes inhibit particular memories, when persons will be dazed and unable to recall events which, when calm, they can narrate in order. In ordinary absent-mindedness, again, concomitant with concentration of attention, we do not perceive, any more than does the hypnotic, things Actually presented to us. In normal mentality incipient dissociation occurs.

Impulses to action may spring from the subliminal, as in somnambulism; from detached elements within that 'part' of the mind, as in hysteria; from external suggestion, as in hypnotism; or from auto-suggestion, as, apparently, in the loss of self-awareness during mystical raptness. Similarly, in the dreams of sleep, when orientation, etc., are precluded to normal consciousness cut off from the impressional continuum, images and phantasms pass for the actual, and a mere fragment of possible experience dominates attention.

Further, certain variations in the state of the organism so affect the nervous system, that experiences acquired during its changed condition are not reproducible when it resumes the normal. "Philip sober" cannot remember all that was said by "Philip drunk"; but it is remembered when Philip again becomes tipsy. The somnambulist awake, and asleep, presents a similar case. Here are simple prototypes, more advanced than that of momentary lapse of memory, of alternating streams of consciousness. Each series is continuous with itself in respect of revivability, but discontinuous with the other, as to which there is amnesia. In yet other cases of functional detachment of dispositions, the subject, when in the one state, will look upon himself, when in the other, as a different person; and when with each state there is associated a developed and integrated memory-system as well as desires and sentiments, so that there are definite and recurrent cleavage-lines between the total states or series, 'divided personality' results.[1] The gaps between detached systems may become impassable, save through hypnotism and the devices of psychotherapy. But so long as sanity is maintained, the dissociation is functional, not structural; and restoration or re-synthesis into one undivided personality, is possible. Multiple personality, of the kind so far considered, is, then, a continuity of separate processes of attention to organised alternating disposition-systems, each accompanied by its own memory-system. Thus a mind, however much of a unity it be, can be spoken of as having parts. It is a system whose several sub-systems admit always of slight, and in pathological conditions of grave, dissociations. The phenomena may be speculatively explained in terms of rise or fall of threshold, of repression, of feebleness of synthetic capacity, or otherwise; but the facts

[1] For particulars as to one or two outstanding cases, see Appendix, Note D.

shew that personality has been integrated, stage after stage, by subjective synthesis, and is capable of being in all degrees disintegrated. Personality is made, not born; it is not always gained, and when gained can be lost.

There remains to be mentioned, another alleged kind of multiple personality, asserted not without evidence, but difficult to prove to be fact: the type that has been called the co-conscious, to distinguish it from that of alternating personalities. Here, one system (to personify it, instead of speaking of its subject) is subliminally aware of another when that is in 'occupation of the body': not cut off from all cognition of it. Of course, neither series can be subjectless: the facts concerning disposition-systems, so pronouncedly revealed in these pathological cases, are the last to admit of explanation in terms of presentationism, or of the theory that a mind has a series of subjects. But the phenomena of co-conscious sub-personalities, have suggested the notion of a plurality of subjects functioning in one such dissociable personality and in one body. This is a hypothesis which might be brought into line with Leibnizian and other monadist metaphysic; but psychologically, the important fact to be observed is the continuity that can be traced through the numerous grades of co-consciousness, as well as through those of alternating systems. If the so-called persons be all synthesised by one subject, there is no more marvel about co-consciousness than about alternation accompanied by amnesia. If the facts point to synthesis of the several 'consciousnesses' by one subject, it is superfluous to invoke several. There seems to be sufficient evidence for belief that dissociation is concerned only with the empirical self or personality; none, for the coexistence, in one embodied mind, of several individual subjects. If there were, the indivisibility of the pure ego would not be invalidated; we should but be driven to the view that a plurality of souls can inhabit and use one body. But the extremer, as well as the simpler and commoner, cases of abnormality, shew that it is from the material of the original and normal consciousness, that the subsequent abnormal experience is derived. The old material is drawn upon by all the developed sub-persons, yet it can be drawn upon only by the same subject that formed it. The sub-persons, moreover, are at least in some cases capable of reunification into one normal personality; and this precludes that they have been synthesised by separate subjects. There is one Actual subject, which is not dependent on the unification of all its habits, ideals, apperceptive systems and 'universes', but which is presupposed by, and functions in, all the systems or broken parts conditioning its manifestations, even those of itself to itself. Personality is a relative thing, an attribute of the empirical self, objective to its pure ego; while dissociated personality would seem to consist in a single subject's acting, for different periods, and even during the same period, according to different conceptions of its self (*i.e.* body and mind), due, in the first instance, to different 'body-feelings'. There is (*ps*) continuity of subjective synthesis, where there is loss of consciousness thereof, or where there is (*ψ*) discontinuity. The distinction between a sub-personality and a hypnotic state, is at bottom but arbitrary. Accentuating it to the utmost, we may speak, if we choose, of several minds, though it would be more correct to assert dissociated dispositional systems, in one body; there would seem to be no reason to indulge the hypothesis of a plurality of souls in one body.

4. *Personality.* The meaning of the word 'person' has changed during the history of thought, and that of 'personality' is today largely a matter of individual predilection. Originally used in connexion with the drama, the term 'person' was appropriated by jurisprudence, to connote possession of rights by a being capable of suffering wrongs. At this stage, individuality, as an attribute of the person, was perhaps nearer to explicit recognition than was rationality. Meanwhile, Christianity was attaching importance to the ethical aspect of personality, and value to the individual soul as an end in itself. The notions of individuality and rationality became more explicit through the developement of theology concerning the Trinity; though the 'Persons' of the Godhead have, save figuratively, nothing in common with the human 'persons' of ordinary parlance. At length Boethius defined *persona* as *naturae rationabilis individua substantia.* Thenceforward, as Prof. Webb has pointed out, the emphasis on individuality, substantiality and rationality, respectively, shifted according to the trend of philosophy. Thus, the Cartesian insistence on self-consciousness as the primary known Reality, and the growing distrust of ideas not clear and distinct (evinced in Locke's

suspicion as to the intelligibility of substance) tended to make *rationabilis* the central word in Boethius' definition. With Kant, on the other hand, the substantial soul became subordinate to volition, and moral responsibility was counted the essence of personality.

As a result of historical process, the term 'personality', however indefinite, passed into the common vocabulary, as denoting something more than individuality. Personality is not generally ascribed to the sentient animal or, save as potential, to the human infant. A person is more than a subject or soul, and the term 'personality' becomes superfluous if used to connote mere subjecthood; though that is the fundamental precondition of personality. Of this gratuitous obliteration of a useful distinction recognised by common sense, no account need be taken. There is practically universal consent to predicate personality, only where there is self-consciousness: and that is the essential ingredient out of which all the others spring.

It has already been argued that personality, as thus far defined, is conditioned by sense-knowledge of the not-self, by the body, and by social life that mediates reason and morality: we do not come into the world having minds furnished with innate ideas, developed rationality, or a divinely implanted *lumen naturale*. To be a person, is to know that one is a person; and an experient attains to the rank of personal being when he can regard himself, not only as possessing more or less a permanent identity, such as belongs to the physicist's mass-particles that have no 'insides', but also as having tastes, aims, character and so forth, in virtue of which he is unique. He is one who thinks, wills, loves, plays many parts, owns his body and mental qualities. Once full self-consciousness, mediated by intercourse, has been attained, higher refinements of the personal status become possible. Indefinite expansion towards an ever-increasing ideal is provided for, given the conditions: "it doth not yet appear what we shall be". An individual experient who has acquired self-consciousness, is as truly a person as he ever will be, though his personality may yet become enriched in content. In another sense of the word 'true', he may say to himself "I am not yet my true personality"; but his personal self, as such, exists. Personality is a matter of degree; and there may be all stages of it between man and God. It is a developing and, as we have seen, a fluctuating, status. It is commonly understood to include the capacities which Actually or potentially belong to self-conscious man: social and ethical relations, thought and conscience, which superimposed on continuity of memory, will, and the interweaving of interests into a system, distinguish the person from the animal and the infant, with their uncorrelated passing impulses. The frontiers of personality, just because it is a flux, cannot be drawn with precision; and its contents cannot be enumerated completely, just because it is capable of indefinite expansion. But, allowing for thus much of indeterminateness of detail, a specific, natural, unambiguous, if vague and comprehensive, meaning can be given to 'personality', if it be defined as self-consciousness plus anything that may be superadded through the mediation of social life. Narrower definitions are common; but in asserting that the essence of personality consists in some one or other of these conceivable and attainable adjuncts, they become merely arbitrary. For instance, personality is not "capacity for fellowship" (Richmond), though it presupposes such capacity; for that does not distinguish human persons from ants and wasps. Nor is it merely the power to subordinate the self of the moment to the wider self (Ormond), unless 'wider self' be a synonym for 'personality', and the definition becomes tautological. Nor is it merely a straining after an ideal, apart from which the self is many selves (Royce); for this is rhetorical, as well as inexhaustive, description. Nor, once more, is it membership of a system of real beings (Howison), without further specification. Besides being unduly selective and capricious, such partial definitions minimise the existential aspect of the self, and its intrinsic or non-instrumental values; they tend to reduce personality to a meeting-point of abstract relations, and to lose contact with matter of experience. It is exclusive attention to the relational aspects of personality, that has led some writers to ignore the element of impervious individuality, and the alogical core, in personality; and to speak of personalities, as if they not only had expansible or fluctuating confines, but also had no fixed centres and no individuality: as if they were entirely fluid and even non-substantival. Personality however, as we have seen, is the construction of an individual and unique subject, whose individuality is presupposed by all communication, sharing, imparting and overlapping. When 'non-imperviousness' or 'penetrability' not only denotes such processes, but also is absorbent of the agents that conduct them, the word becomes misleadingly rhetorical, because psychologically incorrect.

Of the application of personality, a notion obtained from our self-knowledge and relations with our fellow men, to God, this is not the occasion to speak. It is from our knowledge of self that our fundamental categories of identity, continuance, substance, causal activity, end, in terms of which we 'know'—*i.e.* interpret—the world, are derived. That of personality is in the same case; and it is our highest interpretative concept. For the theist, it is the key to the universe. It is in virtue of our possessing personality that "all things are ours". And inasmuch as personality is a product of the world-process, man being (save in respect of his soul or pure ego) organic to Nature, the world itself has made imperative the interpretation of itself in terms of this concept. If such interpretation promises anthropomorphism, it need be but in the sense in which anthropomorphism has already been represented to be the inevitable mould in which all human thought is cast, and by which it is shaped from first to last; because man, after all, is man, and must think as man, if he is to understand—*i.e* to assimilate to himself. At present, however, we are concerned only with the connotation of 'personality' and with the genesis of the concept.

There is one ingredient in personality, over and above self-consciousness, viz. volition, which may suitably be dealt with at this stage, because it is involved in exposition of the nature of both reason and valuation, subjects to which the next succeeding chapters are to be devoted.

5. *Volition.* Volition is not an innate function; it is the outcome of a developement which psychology is able, in keeping with observable facts, to reconstruct. Conation, the *erlebt* want of continuance or of change in presentation, which tends to bring about its fulfilment and is consequently causative, is determined by feeling. But as there conceivably may be feeling without conation, so there can be, and indeed is, conation and also conative action without volition. Instinctive conations, *i.e.* conations determined by 'uneasy sensation' that is mediated by the inherited *Anlage* and is innate for the embodied ego, are observable; and there are acquired involuntary conative activities. Change

of sensum or percept, is often followed by change of movement, or motor presentation; and the link between them, which psychology assigns, is feeling. The movement which happens to lessen pain, to promote pleasure, or to be in itself pleasing, can be discovered by blind or random, *i.e.* involuntary, 'trial'. When attention, thus prompted by feeling, is concentrated on such movement, a step is taken in the direction of volition, though volition is not yet. It is when ideation has been attained, and movement ensues upon idea, instead of upon percept, of motor change, that volition emerges. Volition is, in fact, on its objective side, a transition from the imaginal or the ideal (the non-actual) to the actual, which is a new perceptual presentation. In ordinary volitional movement, such as reaching for a pen, we have first an image or idea of the movement, which is followed by, or issues in, actual movement. The idea operates, not simply *quâ* mental occurrence, and so by a *vis a tergo*, but in virtue of its preperceptual element or intent, involved in purposive action. Such is the psychological account of the genesis of volition, though it leaves out detail presently to be filled in. Over against it is the non-psychological, or physiological, attempt to explain the volitional in terms of reflex action. Several nascent motor-changes, it is represented, may be prompted, which conflict with one another; one ultimately prevails, and though really involuntary (not dependent on attention and feeling) is called a volition: it bespeaks no activity of subject, selective or initiatory of presentation. Such an explanation assumes that definite motor-presentations are co-ordinated and associated previously to any conation, and that reflex-action is not racially degraded voluntary action. But it is the connexion of particular sensory and motor presentations, that needs to be accounted for; and the only psychological evidence we have of intimate connexion between sensory and motor re-presentations, is that furnished by acquired dexterities, which have always been preceded by conscious movement, the precondition of habit.[1] The assumptions just indicated, are an outcome of "the inveterate habit of confounding the psychical and the physical".

Adhering, then, to the psychological method of handling psychological questions, and to the guidance of facts, we may assert, as beyond gainsaying, that definitely purposive movements presup-

[1] Ward, *op. cit.* p. 52.

pose ideal 're-presentation' before actualisation; *i.e.* that conative acts dependent on ideation of their end, and produced in consequence of attention thereto, must be elaborated out of movements immediately expressive of feeling. They issue out of self-determination, therefore, as well as out of external presentation. Suggestion, imitation, etc., as Ward observes, shew how close is the connexion between attention and such movements; and it is change in distribution of attention—again subjectively initiated —which causes change in effective intensity of the motor presentation, or tendency to change of movement.

According to this analysis, volition presupposes sensory perception, feeling, conation, ideation, concentration of attention, and is the outcome of them all. And if the analysis be substantially sound, the venerable problem of the 'freedom of the will' appears to be one that was raised naturally enough in the time of psychological ignorance, but, from the point of view of modern knowledge, needlessly. It is due, like so many others, to the proneness of the sophisticated human mind to hypostatise non-Actual abstractions. Of these abstractions, more shall be said presently. As yet it has but been insisted that willing issues out of subjective feeling and subjectively originated distribution of attention, and is therefore obviously *so far* free, or subject-determined. If, on the other hand, it is occasioned or determined by external perception and, psychophysically speaking, is dependent on sense-stimulation, this is only so because ideation intervenes.

When trains of ideas, not wholly shaped by the circumstances of the present moment, have been developed, new actions become possible. We can then desire. We desire, when the new idea does not open out fresh channels for actual motor changes, but keeps attention directed to itself and evokes interested expectation. In other words, desire obtains so long as attention cannot, or does not, convert idea into percept, or replace idea by percept, as it sometimes may. But precisely what desiring and wishing cannot effect, volition does effect. Desire is impulse thwarted; though it is something more than mere impulse, because directed to an envisaged ideal end. It is not determined exclusively by the objective, yet on the other hand it is not necessarily a reason-directed functioning. Further, we can desire, wish, and even intend, without willing. And will does not only involve, in some cases, predominance of some universe of desire rather than a single desire, but also includes purpose, resolution and action. Volition differs from intention, in that it is energising, *i.e.* transeunt action. It not only anticipates an end, in idea, but consciously strives to effect the transition from the ideal to the actual. It is here that ideation, which distinguishes the voluntary from the involuntary, or volition from the elemental 'striving to do something', gives place to a further factor in the fulfilled act of will—the factor that distinguishes will from desire, and may be called 'efficiency'.

Before proceeding to consider this last factor, we may observe that in the adult man, possessed of both volition and conscience, the primary springs of action are interfused with the volitional attitude adopted towards them, so that they can be isolated only ideally in abstractive thought. But that is not the case in the earliest period of life. For then volition and conscience are non-existent; separation of appetite and impulse from volitional attitude, is then actual, because there is as yet no conjoining. Man, once he has become a self-conscious, volitional and moral agent, a person, is no longer ever a creature of mere impulse, though he always remains an impulsive creature; but, in the earliest stage of his earthly life, he is, like the animal, a purely impulsive being.[1]

If the activity already claimed for volition be not illusion, and be not reducible to what used to be called 'occasional cause'—*i.e.* merely, as Malebranche expressed it, "a prayer that is always heard"—then volition involves spontaneity: sometimes subjective choice, always efficient action. This doctrine needs now to be vindicated. If it can be made good, as against negations and criticisms, it will follow that the motivations—in one sense of that word[2]—or the 'springs of action' which prompt volition,

---

[1] This paragraph is reproduced from the author's *The Concept of Sin* (p. 138), in which the bearing of these considerations on the notion of original sin and the genesis of morality, is discussed at length.

[2] 'Motivation' sometimes refers to the grounds or objects of the choice, which precedes decision in cases where volition follows after deliberation; sometimes to the mental states, dispositions, etc., rational or non-rational, conative rather than affective, which prompt volitional action. As deliberation is an intellectual function, or an evaluation of alternative causes of feeling, 'motivation' is more appropriately applicable to the conditioning of the activity in which volition issues; and certainly confusion could be avoided if the meaning of the term were thus restricted. Motives, as will presently be seen, then become tendencies of the subject to act, whether with or without deliberation.

can only be called 'springs', in the sense that they supply indispensable conditions or occasions of volitional activity. They
are appropriately called 'springs', in so far as without them the
will cannot bestir itself. In thus talking of 'the will', one is, of
course, but adopting a convenience of speech, an economy in
words: such is the one use of personifying abstractions. Translation of short-hand is then imposed on the reader, if he is to think,
and to think about Actualities. Once and for all to illustrate:
'the will cannot bestir itself' means 'the subject cannot will'—
else nothing is meant. For there is no such thing as 'the will'—it
is but a word; there is only a subject that wills. To revert to
figurativeness, the will does not work *in vacuo*, or without motives.
But if the will be found to choose which of various promptings
or motives it shall adopt, the will becomes the sole 'spring', in
a more ultimate sense, of voluntary conduct. What have previously been called by that name, sink to the level of incentives
or of 'material', determining but the sphere within which spontaneity is exercised. Freedom of will is thus not complete indeterminism or capriciousness, willing without motivation; it does
not bespeak causeless eruption of activity in a pure ego devoid
of qualities. When this abstraction has been relegated to nonentity,
the freedom that is claimed for the will remains unscathed. It has
been denied, however, on various grounds.

The problem is as wrongly stated in terms of the dilemma
'determinism or indeterminism', as it is in the phrase 'freedom
of the will'.[1] Volition is of course determined; the question is,
whether it is determined by external necessitation such as is
assumed, though its nature is not defined, in the mechanical theory
of the physical, which renounces explicit use of efficient causation;
or by subjective feeling and activity; or in both ways. And there
are two distinct aspects of the problem, which have often been

[1] It is needless to say that quite another issue, sometimes identified with the one
before us, is indicated when by 'freedom' is meant moral unfetteredness to do good,
or superiority to motives to do evil. The man of stabilised virtuousness is indeed free
from temptations to which backsliders are liable; and so is the hardened sinner free
from checks which his higher self might impose on his self-seeking. Some theologians
have followed Augustine in confusing freedom, in the psychological sense called
for in the present connexion, with this ethical disposition issuing out of free volition,
and have, on the strength of this lack of discrimination, refused freedom of will to
'fallen' man. Kant, again, uses 'freedom' for the capacity to choose evil or good, as
well as for exclusively rational choice in accordance with moral law.

confounded, but which should be separated, so far as is possible; viz. that of choice, which is a case of immanent causation, and that of efficiency, which is a case of transeunt causation. Taking the latter of these issues first, we may inquire into the nature of the determination that is rightly predicable of volitional acts.

In the first place, 'determined' does not mean 'determinate'. Our future acts will certainly be determinate, but it does not follow that they are now determined, in any sense. To predicate determination of volition, leaves the mode of determination still to be settled; and that can only be decided, if at all, by psychological analysis. Rigid determinism, so called, decides the question by assuming that the determination of volitions must be a particular case of that which is involved, whether as fact or as postulate, in theoretical physics. It is expedient, therefore, to examine what may then be meant.

Determination of the occurrence and nature of an event, may conceivably be due to efficient causation; though *how* any cause produces an effect, is unanswerable, because activity is an unanalysable ultimate. Science, in its higher reaches, does not explicitly resort to that concept, whether or not the concept is a metaphysical presupposition of its procedure. Actual compulsion of this sort being repudiated, what is the character of the necessitation or determination of so-called effect by so-called cause? It is (admittedly, one may perhaps say) not the necessary connexion which subsists between ideas or forms of propositions; *i.e.* it is not logical necessity. It is, on any theory as to its nature, connexion according to law; but the validity of a law of Nature is not logically necessary. For law is prescribed by Actuality, the behaviour of which is calculable by us only after experience of it, and then but provisionally; it is not intuitively certain, nor deducible from intuitively certain premises. Again, the necessitation is not Actual, in the sense in which 'this is red' is an actually necessitated judgement of individual perception. Sequence of noise on blow—an Actual relation—is observed; constraining influence between blow and noise, is not. From *post hoc* to *propter hoc*, then, is a step justified neither by logic nor by immediate experience. Actual connexion or determination is asserted by interpretative faith, the only proof of which is its non-falsification hitherto. Moreover, if the Real connexion were observable in a given case, say *B* following *A*, there would be no logical ground for supposing that, next time an *A* occurred, a *B* would ensue. Additional metaphysical premises are required, before any connexion can be established between causal determination and causal uniformity.

Yet it is uniformity that science explicitly presupposes, while explicitly dispensing with Actual connexion of the 'efficient' kind. Whether there can be constancy of sequence, without a sufficient ground in constancy of Real connexion of some kind, is a matter which science can leave alone. But just as efficiency is a postulate, if it be not a fact, of individual experience, whence the notion of cause originates, so uniformity, or its modern equivalent, is but a postulate—a postulate that is 'necessary' *if* science be unconditionally valid. "There is one theory of the world, and one only, which would justify this assumption completely, and that is the mechanical theory. Accordingly the postulate of the uniformity of nature is frequently converted into the theorem that nature is a mechanical system; and thus a methodological principle becomes an ontological dogma."[1]

But in implicitly postulating universal determination, science leaves the nature of the determination undefined; save that it renounces, on its own surface, efficient and final causation. It assumes necessity: it is silent as to mode of necessitation. Some of its philosophical exponents, indeed, anathematise necessity as an intruder, though *hypothetical* necessity is a presupposition of science's logic; and 'descriptionists' profess to study but the *post hoc*, though their method incessantly involves reliance on the *propter hoc*. Renunciation of efficient and final cause, is, even methodologically, less complete in the spheres of biology and psychology. This fact, taken in connexion with what has been said, and also with the fact that the concept of inertia Actually (as distinguished from logically) presupposes activity, as *erlebt* and known, engenders suspicion whether, after all, the aloofness of science from 'real' categories is but practically convenient semblance or pretence. Perhaps the only definite attempt to justify the procedure of science, without resort to specific characterisation of determination in terms of efficient cause, etc., is that which makes

---

[1] Ward, *The Realm of Ends*, 1911, p. 277. Lect. XIII in that volume should be read, as perhaps the most illuminating discussion of freedom that is accessible.

use of the conception of the 'deterministic system', at which we
have already had occasion to glance. In connexion with the
problem before us, the only relevant question is, whether that conception suffices to explain determination in the mental sphere,
such as of volition. The conception has been expounded thus:
if, from observations of a system whose states can be described
in terms of quantities which are theoretically measurable, it is
theoretically possible to construct a functional relation[1] giving the
state of the system at any time, the system is deterministic or
determined. Since states of mind or, more precisely, feelings and
acts of attention, are not isolable or divisible, and are not analogous
to the intensive magnitudes of physics (*e.g.* temperature), constructed from Objective data: obviously the quantitative notions,
involved in the conception of the deterministic system, have no
relevance to volition. Detached states which interact with one
another, and are not states of some subject that acts in them, are
fictions devoid of significance for our empirical problem.

It is by this last fact that, perhaps, all the specific arguments
for necessitarianism are convicted of being based on a false premiss. They all imply presentationism and, in the last resort,
sensationism. When they rely also on the necessary connexion
between physical events, which science presupposes but refrains
from characterising, they assume—which science does not, save
as a guiding postulate—that the world (including the psychical)
is a closed system; that all change is change of motion, and that
such change can only be produced by the mechanical, or *vis-a-tergo*,
kind of causation which, however, is denied efficiency. To finish
with the latter type of premiss before leaving it, it should be
remarked that, just as efficiency has no logical relation to uniformity of action, so also the idea of uniformity is no exclusive
monopoly of the doctrine of mechanical causation. Conceivably,
the regularities of planetary revolution might be the outcome of
each planet's own volition, or that of an external controlling mind.
The relative uniformity of personal conduct, is therefore no necessary sign of causation such as common sense attributes to the
movements of material bodies; and the former uniformity is never

---

[1] Quantity may here be taken as what is measurable, *i.e.*, consisting of parts like
each other, correlatable one-to-one with numbers. A function is a relation such that
'*x* is a function of *y*' means that to every value of *y* there is a corresponding value of *x*.

a case of recurrence of the 'same' set of antecedents. Nor does like volitional determination of conduct by any means always recur in like circumstances. When a man possesses a formed character, prediction of his behaviour in given circumstances is possible within limits, as if it were the outcome of regular conditionings, like those which make prediction of the physical possible. But the limits are to be reckoned with. The unique, or once-occurring, is not scientifically predictable, simply because there was no previous case; and such uniqueness, as well as the common and the repeated, is characteristic of subjective activity guided by interest and end. Prediction of voluntary behaviour is, in fact, but statistical; each single occasion is unique, and the knowledge essential for prediction of it would, perhaps, often require the *erleben* of the subject. Character is plastic, not static.

It is to be concluded, then, that whatever be the nature, ultimately, of the necessitation to which Nature's regularity is due—and it may be akin to the causation claimed for volition—the scientific 'explanation' of its observable manifestation in terms, in the last resort, of inertia and conservation of momentum, is inapplicable to the facts concerning volition, at any rate before they have been clipped by abstractiveness to fit the theory. In volition, consequent on deliberation, are involved end and worth: factors which render physical analogies irrelevant.

When determinism, passing from theoretical physics and its supposed bearings, analyses the volition, it is wont to identify it with the motive or the strongest motive. Using this word, for the present, to denote conations such as impulse or appetite, it is to motive that is ascribed the efficiency (denied to the will, or subject willing) which produces or occasions the 'voluntary act'. The motive is then conceived as an Actuality distinct and separate from the subject. Motives act and interact, while the subject is but a spectator, if he be allowed to be anything. We have seen that the facts cannot be so described, until we encounter an impulse or an appetite that is not a state of some subject. In other words, the motives, invoked by the determinist, do not exist. An actual motive is the tending of a subject to act; a striving which involves a striver. He, not it, is the efficient agent.

In respect of their supposed independence of the subject, and of their efficiency, these abstractions (called motives) have been compared with the external forces of the mechanist. The analogy, however, breaks down at the essential points. For instance, there is no psychological theorem of the parallelogram of motives. While two forces have a resultant compounded of both, and their effect is as if each had acted separately from the other; in the case of motivation of the will, one only of conflicting motives determines action, and the rest do not count. The psychical 'forces', moreover, spring from the subject, and are not impressed upon him from without. Instead of his being compelled by them collectively, it is he that selects which shall be operative. Attention to primary desires modifies their attractive or repulsive qualities, and so the subject determines their final strength. No more fortunate is the comparison of deliberation with the behaviour of the balance, and motives with weights. The aim of this analogy is to eliminate choice from volition, and to resolve it into the quasi-mechanical preponderance of the strongest force. But there is no external standard, in comparison with which strength of motive can be measured. The weight of a motive depends on subjective interest: the subject determines its strength for him. And if strength were an objective matter, which is the stronger motive could only be known after the event of its prevailing; so that 'the stronger prevails' would mean no more than 'that which is acted upon is acted upon'. Choice is not thus disposed of by question-begging metaphor and by talking of subjective states, etc., as if they were pieces of matter.

Similar abstractiveness has engendered the apparently deeper argument, that we cannot really choose, because volition is determined by one's nature or character. So it is. But character is acquired by volitional acts; and if they in turn are determined by the original nature, the peculiarity of that nature, as we have seen, is largely due to the intrinsic qualities, capacities, etc., of its subject. The subject is already in the nature, as he is in his motives: his nature can be treated as if separate from him, no more than can they. Thus, if character were exclusively determined by what is distinguished from it as disposition, and by circumstances—which of course is not the case—volition would still be self-determination, activity determined by individual interest—*i.e.* choice. The only way, it would seem, of establishing the deterministic theory of volition, is to deny the existence of the subject, its states and acts.

If pleasure is subjective affection, if conation is subjective striving, and if attention, etc., are subjective activity, then assuredly the freedom, *i.e.* the subjective determination, of volition is beyond question. For it is into these elements that volition is analysable; it is of these antecedents that it is the consequent. Physical events are but its occasions or circumstances, and are often shaped by it. And herein is contained the reply to the last type of deterministic argumentation that need be mentioned—the appeal to ignorance. Just as the antecedents of a particular volition are not wholly beyond our control and indeed, when most relevant, are shaped by the subject; so neither are they beyond our ascertaining—at least theoretically. Spinoza asserted that men believe themselves to be free, because they are conscious of their actions and unconscious of the causes by which those actions are determined.[1] But we are not so ignorant. There may be more, within us and without us, involved in volition, than we know; but we may claim general knowledge of the various antecedent stages by which the volitional act is determined. Those are perception, feeling, conation, concentration of attention, ideation; and in all of them we find subjective choice or activity. If by 'freedom of will' be meant 'subjective determination of volition', and if 'psychology without a subject' be but a science of the non-Actual, there is no question as to freedom. And there is no deterministic or necessitarian theory that does not presuppose sensationist psychology, with its fictitious abstractions. It must therefore be ascribed to inconsistency, that some philosophers, while professing to repudiate such psychology, and to recognise that, in knowing, there is activity, nevertheless refuse to the subject the power to choose; especially as deliberation is an intellectual process. It also seems arbitrary to admit activity in knowing, and to deny it in alleged efficiency, where *prima facie* the call for it is at least as apparent. The grounds of the claim of psychology to know of efficiency in volition, are similar to those of the claim to know of subjective activity in intellectual functionings.

We may now add to our stock of knowledge concerning human personality and its pure ego, the item that conduct is determined by ends, and ends by the ego. It is because of its teleological determination that we can 'understand' conduct; and it is because

[1] *Ethics*, i. ii. *Note.*

of its 'intelligibility' that conduct has suggested deterministic theory. But that teleological intelligibility has nothing to do with this logical intelligibility (coherence through the relation of implication) or with scientific intelligibility (traceableness to uniform antecedents, or having an assignable place in a mechanical system). In the latter two senses, conduct is simply unintelligible, as we have seen.

But the determinableness of conduct by ends, has other significance, of the ethical kind. In that the idea of an end precedes moral action; in that the end adopted can be credited to the acquired character of the whole personality; and in that the end can be approved or disapproved by the subject, the person possesses responsibility. Thus it is that we can blame character that is the outcome of volition, in quite a different way from that in which we blame innate disposition; or, again, that we can experience remorse. The judgements involved in strictly moral blame and in remorse, imply belief that one could, in the same circumstances, have done better. So impartial a writer as Sidgwick pointed out that, if determinism be substituted for indeterministic theory, under the guidance of which our leading ethical conceptions were fashioned, the meaning of such terms as 'responsibility', 'remorse', etc., must undergo some modification: how profound the necessary modification, was better appreciated by Martineau. This does not prove that our conviction as to the possession of free choice, on which the historical usage of such terms depends, is not illusory: it but shews that ethics, as commonly understood, presupposes that volition is self-determination. But as to the former point, Sidgwick observed that he could not suppose the conviction as to free choice, to be illusory, without also conceiving his whole conception of what he called 'his' action, fundamentally altered.[1] It has been argued above that the alteration, here in question, is a *reductio ad impossibile*. The insinuation of illusion is therefore groundless; responsibility, in the sense imported into the word by the theory of self-determination, and ethics as founded on that conception, retain their relevance to personality.

---

[1] *The Methods of Ethics*, 5th ed., pp. 65–66.

CHAPTER VII

Valuation and Theory of Ethical Value

Corresponding to the developement from perception, through ideation to abstract thought, there is continuity traceable by psychology from individual feeling and desire, together with their cognitive concomitants, to aesthetic and moral sentiments, and acquisition of ethical principles. This developement is not self-unfolding of the preformed, but epigenesis, or growth out of what was into what was not. Hence there is no impossibility about the derivation of morality out of the non-moral, though moral judgements are not deducible from purely existential judgements; and no fallacious identification, of the moral with non-moral antecedents, is involved in the alleged derivation. The common belief that there is, implies an obsolete conception of evolution, according to which it should be impossible for a bracken-stalk to contain woody tissue, if there was none of it in the spore from which the fern grew. Moral consciousness, indeed, is not resolvable into feeling and desire, or into intellection: it may none the less be emergent from them, when they are compounded.

At the outset of our empirical study of valuation, it should be emphasised that psychological investigation of the origin and developement of morality, is to be distinguished from inquiry into the logical presuppositions of ethical judgements. Whether the former study has relevance to the latter, is a further question, which should not be prejudged, but decided after we have examined the process by which the finished product of abstract ethics is gained. Psychology of valuation, in a word, is not axiology. Axiology bears to it the same relation that non-genetic epistemology bears to psychology of cognition. Axiology assumes the standpoint of, not merely the over-individual, but the over-social, the impersonal or absolute: seeking the logical presuppositions of abstract thought, without looking its gift-horse in the mouth. Psychology (ps) describes processes, as they are (ψ) for individual or community. It cannot deliver itself in terms of axiological findings, because they involve what for it, while on the way out to abstract principles, are but dogmatic assumptions.

For genetic psychology, 'good' must be what this individual, or that society, at its own level of ethical developement, thinks good: there can be no self-committal on its part to the assertion, that any moral judgement is either right or wrong as to what is Really good.

For this Real realm is beyond the ken of psychology, until its work is finished; and then, so far as psychology knows in the meanwhile, it may (or may not) have to be pronounced a realm aloof from the Actual. The necessity of these distinctions between psychology and axiology, between (ψ) and (ps) standpoints, between the level of individual, and that of common, experience or that of abstract thought concerned with what is supposed to transcend, or be independent of, all experients, will soon become apparent. Throughout the history of theory of valuation, continual crossing from one or more to another or more of points of view that need to be discriminated, has occasioned question-begging refutation of both sound and unsound judgements.

The psychologist sets out from individual experience, distinguished as rigorously as may be from common or 'universal' experience, because it is from the former level that the fundamenta are supplied, for conceptual elaboration at the latter level. The primary fact relevant to valuation, that he encounters, is that a percept can evoke feeling, which in turn may excite conation. A patch of blue may please and, in virtue of the feeling caused, become an object appreciated, or of aesthetic value to the experient. No one disputes that feeling is a requisite for such appreciation, or even that over-individual valuation is causally dependent on feeling. Appreciation is not exclusively cognitive, though it is called apprehension of value. But it is disputed whether, in individual appreciation, feeling is constitutive of value, or only instrumental to apprehension of it. This is not to be confounded with the quite different question, whether over-individual valuation, such as moral, is constituted by individual feeling. The latter question may easily be answered in the negative, without the former being so much as raised. As to the former issue, which at present is alone before us, decision is an important matter, pregnant with consequence. For if individual appreciation of the simplest kind be constituted by feeling, and if social experience be a conceptual elaboration of individual experience, it will not be easy to maintain that complex affective-volitional dispositions are merely instrumental to cognition of Objective (over-individual) values. If the aesthetic value of a patch of blue, for the individual percipient, is constituted by his pleasure in it, then his judgement 'this blue is good', or 'has value, [forme]', goes beyond what his (ψ) experience, regarded (ps), warrants: viz. the fact that he is pleased with that blue. If, on the other hand, his feeling does but enable him to apprehend or cognise value, as something purely objective as is the colour-sensum, then, from a psychologist's point of view, he speaks literal truth and not in a figure: he apprehends value, and value is wholly intrinsic to the external percept, not even a *tertium quid* such as appearance of some intrinsic quality that is not value, but is evocative of valuation. Now feeling certainly *is* not apprehension of any kind of object; it is not cognition of the 'feelable', but an affective state. The instrumental theory, then, must suppose that feeling evokes in its subject the ability to apprehend what is neither impressional, nor a relation between impressions, nor a relation (of impression to subject) that is subjectively constituted: that feeling either excites a new species of cognitive activity or else, like a search-light, illumines a hitherto non-presented aspect, bringing it within the range of attention.

For the sake of argument, we may concede that there is no antecedent or inherent impossibility about this supposition; but it hardly commends itself as probable. Introduced into the psychology of common experience and knowledge of Objects, it fails to explain the fact that there is no accounting for tastes, while there is accounting for the agreement that salt has savour; that there is comparatively little unanimity in art-criticism, nothing but unanimity as to the gross properties of matter. It posits what is not assimilable with our established knowledge about cognition and feeling: it is psychologically groundless, unverifiable, mysterious. The view would not suggest itself to the psychologist studying, with open mind, the bare facts. It has the look of being dictated by the exigencies of an epistemological theory; because, psychologically, it is superfluous. To render the blue sky pleasing or aesthetically valuable to a percipient, it suffices that a sensory quality affect him pleasurably. No further objective quality, tertiary or other, requires to be postulated, nor any new feeling-induced cognitive activity to be invented *ad hoc*. We need but to refrain from rushing to the gratuitous belief that if the naïve experient deliver himself in a judgement verbally equivalent to 'that *has* value', he must be terminologically exact and philosophically profound. Whatever his words may 'mean' to the grammarian and logician, they may 'mean'—in quite another sense among the multitude that that term bears—no more than his experience barely warrants. He may take licence, verbally to transmute his subjective estimation into a character which he introjects into his percept, and, assigning value as well as colour to it, come explicitly to regard value as an intrinsic quality that the blue sky has, and that he immediately apprehends or reads off—not reads into it. Psychologists generally agree that this is the case with us; and their view cannot be psychologically impugned. Few will doubt that, when we speak of a readable book, a tedious discourse, a dull week, we are projecting qualities into things, while all that we can safely affirm is an affection of ourselves, and that our interest creates value such as 'exists' but for this person and not that. Psychology bids us regard all primary value as thus constituted. We can then understand why the same (common) thing has different values for different sentient beings; for appreciators with different interests, in different circumstances, at different stages of education of taste, and so on: facts which seem to receive no explanation, if some one or more value-qualities are credited, on a par as to objectivity and intrinsicality with physical qualities, to things. We can also understand why the valuable is always desirable; on the alternative theory, we can but assert that desirableness[1] *happens* to be a criterion of valuableness, without any apparent reason why it should be.

Value, then, in the fundamental form which we have so far examined, is not to be taken for another predicate of a thing, possessed by the thing previously to bestowal of it by the appreciator, over and above its primary and secondary qualities, any more than is existence: that would be an unwarranted intrusion of axiology into psychology. It has now to be shewn that the theory that such value is constituted by feeling, a theory which suffices for psychoogy of individual experience, is sufficient also for explanation of the developement of valuation of the over-individual kind; and

---

[1] 'Desirable' here means 'can be', not 'ought to be', desired: the latter is its axiological sense.

that value is a 'teleological' category to which there is no purely objective counterpart, though of course it is applied to Objects, is evoked by Objects, and, when thrust upon Objects, characterises them as they *are for* subjects.

Henceforth, it will be necessary to speak in terms of conation instead of feeling. There is no conation that is not determined by feeling, so the constitution of value by feeling will still be implied. But as valuation is here to be discussed in connexion especially with conduct and morality, and those are only developed in virtue of feeling issuing in desire or aversion, value may for our purpose be said to be constituted by desire.[1] The only kind of good, in primitive experience, is what is desired because it gives pleasure or serves some private end. But the judgement 'that is good', signifying (*ps*) 'I like', or 'I desire that', is not the same as the judgement which the experient would express in those words—a social product—when he shared the common standpoint: 'good' would then mean to him good for others also, for all, or perhaps good-in-itself. For this reason it is sometimes said that valuation, deeming good or bad, does not exist at the subsocial and subpersonal level, and that the simple appreciation, that has here been called valuation, is not valuation. Certainly it differs from the Objective valuation issuing from 'universal' experience. But difference, in this case, is not disparateness. To call things that differ by the same name, is generally to court confusion, but in the present instance it serves to indicate the continuity between them; and that happens to be the more important consideration. Private appreciations are the Actual source of public valuations and are the presuppositions, though not the logical grounds, of aesthetic and ethical principles. If, again, some writers would restrict valuation to the sphere of universal experience and axiology, because there it involves *e*valuation, or comparative estimation of better and worse desires, etc., it should be observed that evaluation itself begins in individual preference. The advance from valuation[2] (if the term may now be allowed to

---

[1] Aesthetic valuation, on the other hand, is based on feeling which does not issue in conative action, but in affective dispositions such as contentment, satisfaction, admiration.

[2] As a synonym for 'individual appreciation' from the individual standpoint, 'valuation' means explicit recognition that something is liked or disliked, produces feeling of pleasure or of displeasure.

As perceiving issues in the existential judgement 'it is', so the attitude of appre-

be harmless as well as significant at the level of individual appreciation) to evaluation, resembles that from tied to free idea, in that both are conditioned by the inevitableness, on occasions, of choice. Developement in conative, comparable to that in cognitive, experience, is rendered possible by the fact that, in a determinate individual, some continuity of specific interests is involved; but such interests will all be on one level till the subject recognises them as his: *i.e.* till a notion of the bodily self is acquired. Then the self becomes of paramount value relatively to momentary experiences, and to things already associated so constantly with pleasurable feeling, despite variation of moods, etc., as to be capable of being regarded as desir*able*. The self is, in fact, the condition and the standard of all primitive individual evaluation, and self-interest emerges with the rudimentary knowledge of self. Thenceforward, blind preference between pleasures—*i.e.* pleasureable objects—determined simply by intensity of feeling, can give place to choice that is intellectually grounded. Self-interest prompts deliberation; and some scale of values, according to psychological rank, can be established by individual experience, though of course but for it alone. When one has learned that what is good to eat is not always wholesome, intelligence alone makes possible a preference of the abiding pleasure of health to the fleeting, if intenser, enjoyment of a flavour. Life is found to have other pleasures than thrills; and temperance can impose on conscienceless prudence its expediency-imperative. That temperance is, at the level of universal experience, deemed a virtue, and gluttony a vice, is conditioned by existential fact—viz. that the human body happens to be a cause of unhappiness and inefficiency after over-indulgence: were physiological fact different, our ethical principle would be other than it is. And, speaking

ciating issues in a value-judgement such as 'it is good'. Our word 'valuation', we may observe, is used to denote the attitude, the judging, and what is judged; and 'value' stands for both the quality assigned to a thing, and the thing 'bearing' the value-quality. A further source of confusion in terminology was introduced into philosophy and theology by giving the name 'value-judgement', or 'judgement of worth', to judgements of other kinds than that just specified. Any judgement, as such, is a purely cognitive or intellectual act. There is no difference between the value-judgement and the existential judgement, save as to what they are about. And there is no hybrid between intellection and conation, such as "emotional reason" or "logic of the sentiments": there are conational dispositions toward intellectual constructions, and intellectual constructions of Objects of desire, etc.

generally, 'principle is better than impulse' is relevant to human conduct, in virtue of the fact that human beings can get scientific knowledge. It is owing to such germinal knowledge, that the individual experient can prefer one pleasure, in virtue of its abidingness, to another that is fleeting: the two being commensurable, because related to satisfaction within the same zone of self. When, however, the inner and ideal 'self' has been discriminated from the bodily and appetitive 'self', interests can also be organised according to their difference in respect of inwardness. Psychologically, a pleasure of 'higher' value to an individual, is one to which value is assigned only at a psychologically higher level of self-hood or self-knowledge. We always and inevitably prefer a more pleasurable, to a less pleasurable, experience; but as the self grows, the pleasures to be weighed do not remain the same *for it*. The 'harder' choice still "gives the subject greater pleasure, *i.e.* greater satisfaction, than the rejected alternative would have given. But there was a time when it did not and could not do so, and it only does so now because the subject has developed".[1]

Thus even before the individual is a social being, in the sense presently to be defined, he can apply some kind of norm to his preference and his behaviour; and this presupposes no new premiss, save of existential knowledge. Of course the rank, so far spoken of, is purely psychological; it bespeaks intellectual, not moral advance. But the advance is a *sine qua non* for acquisition of the moral status. Developed intelligence, increased ideality of motives, and consistency of conduct, may issue in moral goodness or in moral badness.

The conditions of arriving at the social, or over-individual, standpoint may now be pointed out. Though, perhaps, no two individuals are constituted psychologically alike, none are altogether different. None are isolated; in virtue of certain extra-regarding interests and desires, none are originally pure egoists; none unfamiliar with social restraint. Hence the possibility of some community of desire, and of co-operation towards a common end, is ensured. These simple facts solve some mysteries irresolvable by deduction from abstract concepts. They bridge the logical *impasse* between Objective ethics and the psychology of sub-personal interest. They indicate possibility of advance from

[1] Ward, *op. cit.*, p. 402.

valuation subjectively constituted in individual feeling and conation, to the socially or Subjectively constituted valuation that
assigns permanent values to Objects, deeds, dispositions, etc.,
desired by the social unit for social ends, independently of any
individual's private preferences; from the good, in the sense of
what is desired by a self for itself, to the good as what is desired
by an organic whole, composed of a plurality of more or less
co-operant and consentient selves.

When, through intercourse, the individual has come to share
common knowledge of a common world including other selves,
he does not merely become acquainted with new values. What
is of far greater significance, he cannot but adopt a new *standpoint*
from which to value himself, his desires and behaviour, and all
else. Baptised into the over-individual, he becomes a new creature
to whom all things are new. To have learned how others see him,
is to see himself as others see him. He can now be one external
spectator, among others, of his own conduct; he reflects their
approval and disapproval in contemplating his own desires. This
is *con*science. It is conscience of the jural kind. The individual
doubtless already expected things from others, but now he finds
actions are expected of him, and is aware that they are owed by
him as a contribution to the common weal. This is the original
'oughtness', though it is but recognition of duty or debt. The
individual is confronted with *mores*: indeed, he has attained the
moral status, in that now volitional conformity with social conventions is demanded of him, and he knows law that he can
knowingly transgress.

Doubtless it is a far cry from such crude morality, with its
externality and insularity, to that in which 'I owe' is replaced
by the categorical imperative 'I ought'; in which obligation and
law are inward and apparently unconditional; in which goodness
is no longer desiredness, by some one or many, of what is good
for something, but is conceived as an intrinsic quality of desirableness or of oughtness-to-be, independent of the conation, and even
the cognition, of all persons. We may, if we choose, bestow the
name of morality solely on this type: that is convention as to use
of a term, or as to where we draw a line. Actually there is continuity, if logically there is disparateness, between the advanced
and the elementary kinds; the axiological level, from which the

disparateness is discerned, is itself reached by idealisation and abstraction from the empirical value-judgements of social experience.[1] With the psychology of those intellectual processes and with the over-social or absolute standpoint, we are not now concerned; but the psychological continuity of morality-developement at the over-individual, Objective or common level, shall be illustrated.

Even before the standpoint of common knowledge was gained, the individual's conative experience could evince what has been called value-movement. But this process is of indefinite scope in social morality. Old values have been absorbed by re-valuation, transcended by discovery of new values, and transmuted from one to another kind. Intrinsic bads become instrumental, and in turn intrinsic, goods: as when labour, that is drudgery, is found conducive to skill, and acquisition of dexterity becomes pleasant in itself. Such mutation modifies the jointly intellectual and conative dispositions, sentiments, ethical beliefs, of societies and their members. One chief determinant of possible progress, from lower to higher morality, is knowledge and intelligence; and what is called moral insight, is largely intellectual discernment of existential truth, determinative of conative disposition. The ability to criticise custom, in which the birth of morality proper is sometimes placed, need be no more than that of acuter intelligence, or wider knowledge, than is possessed by the many. The prophet who occasions a social uplift, discovers a better than the old good, something more effective in promoting social welfare or conducive to the abiding happiness of a greater number; his criticism of *mores* does not presuppose, actually or logically, any new and unique conception such as that of absolute good or oughtness.[2]

---

[1] Ignoring this fact, as also the important distinction between (ψ) and (ps) immediacy, rationalism is wont to assert that there is no escape from the *a priori* grounding of ethics on the ultimate deliverance, both rational and immediate, of the moral consciousness that asserts the categoricalness, unconditionality, or absoluteness of its findings, such, *e.g.* as that rightness or goodness is the highest good. The immediacy in question has been acquired, and is not (ps) immediacy. The 'feeling of unconditional obligation', alleged to be the ultimate and indispensable essence of morality, owes its unique nature to its unique intellectual presuppositions. And these are involved, however much they may be abstracted from and ignored, in exclusive contemplation of the finished product obtained only by use of them.

[2] Relative implies correlative, not absolute, so far as Actuality is concerned. The unrelated is the All, or else nothing.

Nor does distinction between good and bad desires: so long as 'good' and 'bad' express social approval and disapproval. Such relative and mutational evaluation still involves reference to conative disposition. What was accounted good, may come to be accounted bad, and a value-judgement be reversed, because its 'reality presumption', or its intellectual presupposition, is seen to be inadequate. When it is discerned that all men, not only one's own tribe, are brethren, 'live and let live' can replace cannibalism as an ethical principle.

That growth in intelligence and existential knowledge accounts largely for moral advances, does not imply that increase of intelligence necessarily issues in moral progress; nor that ethical valuation is always, in the popular sense, utilitarian; nor that increment of knowledge is the sole cause of moral advancement. The next illustration of the causation of developement will serve to indicate another factor.

It has been seen that conscience, of a kind, is thrust upon the individual when he is socialised into a person. Developement from such jural conscience into the kind involved in spontaneous subordination of private interest to common weal, is unimaginable. Nevertheless, conscience that approves real altruism can be accounted for by genetic psychology. It is not descended from jural conscience; but the two are concomitantly descended from a common progenitor. The human individual does not enter into social life a pure egoist, who has somehow to acquire self-denial and inward approval of it. When con*science* is thrust upon him, he already knows sym*pathy*. There are propensities ingrained in human nature which prompt to altruism. Spontaneous sympathy or good-will is involved in the very sociality that confers jural conscience. Propensities that egoism should suppress, come to suppress egoism, because, in the developement of personality through acquaintance with others, 'identification' or 'unification' with others is involved, as well as 'differentiation' from them. Primordial sympathy, natural virtue, the element of humaneness in humanity, is a spring of equity such as mere justice can never inspire, and becomes constitutive of values different from that of duty, because constitutive of virtues that, from the jural point of view, are supererogatory.[1] That "love is the fulfilling of the law",

[1] Ward, *op. cit.*, ch. xvi.

is thus but the explication and amplification of what is written from the first on the table of the heart. Friendship or love of others is part, or an aspect, of the self, and counts in self-appreciation. The individual is able to desire or value what involves some self-sacrifice, and, on occasion, to prefer such sacrifice to the self-seeking in which at the ideational level he sees, and sees with disapproval, a seeking of his lower self. How evaluation of one's psychologically different 'selves', *i.e.* of the self as construed at different stages of self-knowledge, is possible, has already been seen. There remains, then, no mystery about the emergence of conscience such as acknowledges indebtedness or feels inward obligation, as well as yields external compliance with social duty. The external spectator of his own desires, is also internal sharer of external approbation, and is so constituted as to esteem approval from his kind. He can identify himself with the outward law, so that to him it becomes also an inward law, because its demands meet the responsive pull of his heart-strings. The "limitless possibilities" of ethical advance thus opened out to a reasoning being, can easily be imagined. It will therefore suffice to indicate the lines along which advance in valuation of conduct may proceed.

From the standpoint of social experience, at which sub-personal appreciation is transcended, moral valuation of the self, its dispositions and conduct, can take two distinct forms, assigning respectively 'personal' and 'impersonal' or 'social' values, as they have been technically named.[1] In both cases the values are borne by what is Objective, or known in common; and the affective-volitional attitude of the valuer is acquired by identification with that of others. But in 'personal' valuation the self is regarded as an end for itself, and its dispositions as of intrinsic worth; while in 'social' valuation the self is regarded but as a member, and its dispositions, etc., as instrumental to the ends of society as such.

'Personal' valuation calls first for consideration. The self has a

---

[1] What follows on this topic is in substance derived from Urban's *Valuation: its Nature and Laws*. Whenever 'personal' and 'social' are used in the special senses here given to them, they shall retain the inverted commas. That these terms bear other meanings, will impose on the reader the necessity to isolate their technical significations, and to guard against besetting possibilities of confusion.

self-interest that is inalienable, though capable of transformation and indefinite refinement: "what is a man profited if he shall gain the whole world, and lose his own soul?" A self can ever rise on stepping-stones, and the ascent presupposes, at each stage, the conception of a relatively more ideal self to be attained. This ideal and idea, a shared intellectual construction due to sympathetic participation, is one presupposition of all 'personal' valuation. In evaluation of this type, sub-personal appreciations are subordinated to those of the higher, rational or personal, self; the flesh to the spirit: but there is no subordination of the person's intrinsic values, constituted with reference to self-realisation, to those constituted by reference to the social end. It is in respect of the isolation of the idea of the self, as an end for itself, from the idea of the self as member of a society to which it is of but instrumental value, that 'personal' valuation possesses its second unique presupposition. To revert to the first, the successive relative ideals are imaginal or ideational constructions, original or suggested, reached by thinking away faults and shortcomings of which the higher self has already convicted the lower. As pursuit of personal worthiness progresses, the dispositions valued will cease, in some cases, to correspond with those that are of social obligation. To satisfy one's ideal of oneself, much more advanced developement of a given disposition may be required, than satisfies the demands of 'social' morality that has an eye only to the social good, and cares much about overt honesty, little about "truth in the inward parts". Cultivation of self, as an end for self, may conflict with cultivation of self, as a member of society: *e.g.*, personal holiness conceived monastically, if pursued by all, would be subversive of the commonwealth. Some of the saint's excellences may thus be not only supererogatory, but even offensive, from the point of view of public propriety.

The idealisation of the self, as end for self, can conceptually be carried to 'perfection'. Personal values would then be deemed absolute: their logical presupposition would be Kant's principle, 'be a person, and respect others as persons'. We are not as yet concerned with personal worths as conceived by wholly abstract thought, but only with realised and realisable values. These are relative and supersedible; and, carried to perfection, they may not only clash with others 'socially' constituted, but also become theoretically, as well as practically, unrealisable. To be well grounded, their fundamental presupposition of the isolableness of the aspect of the person as end for self, from the aspect in which he is a social instrument, must be practically possible. This, however, is so but relatively and partially. It should follow that universal validity, let alone unconditionality, necessity and absoluteness, cannot be accorded to value-judgements of this class.

Another condition of 'personal' value-judgements being "valid" of conduct, or admitting of application, is that the ideal self of ideation be at least theoretically realisable and relevant in all respects: that self-realisation should admit of specific and minute concrete description in the particular case. It is evident that self-realisation is hard to define, when we begin to ask what the vague conception should precisely mean. Whether it be construed as realisation of the rational self alone, or whether as realisation of the whole and complete self, difficulties present themselves; and of course the two construings are irreconcilable with each other. The former of them implies suppression of part of the self, and may culminate in regarding virtuousness as apathy. The latter of them overlooks that a whole or complete self, a harmonious compounding, without mutilation, of the sentient and appetitive, the higher conational and the rational 'selves', is a unification of incompatibles, and that the same appetitive propensities are the source of lofty sentiments as well as of vicious tendency. We cannot enter into moral life "whole": the question is, what kind of *a* whole we should strive to be. And there is no means, empirical or *a priori*, of ascertaining, in the concrete, what precisely, and how much of it, is to be suppressed in each particular zone of the concrete self, to yield perfection: while universalising would involve extinction of individuality.

The ethic which would see in self-realisation *the* highest good, grows out of exclusive regard for 'personal' values. Similarly, hedonism is based on exclusive recognition of sub-personal appreciation, and would describe morality in terms of it; while purely altruistic systems, in turn, are attempts to reduce morality to terms of the 'social' end alone. Each of these monistic systems, with its one primary concept or principle, and its one highest good, is necessarily incompatible with large tracts of ethical experience, because actually there are valuations from standpoints of which each theory would take no account. Whether *any* ethical system can transcend these partialities, while yet remaining monistic as to supreme principle and as to highest good, seems to be decided in the negative by appeal to fact. For moral valuation proceeds along the lines which lead to establishment of 'personal' and 'social' values respectively, and these lines seem sometimes to diverge into disparateness or incompatibility.

'Impersonal' or 'social' evaluation differs from 'personal' evaluation in presuppositional ideas and in criterion. It values personal dispositions and conduct solely in respect of their instrumentality to social ends. It is of course performed by individual minds, for there are no others; and it does not differ from 'personal' valuation in requiring the standpoint of common knowledge and of the outside observer. It differs in that it is concerned with the individual, not as an end for himself, but only as a means to a common end. A personal disposition that is good, as valued 'personally', may be bad, as valued 'socially'. Sentiments that are all-determinative in 'personal' approbation may be irrelevant for 'social' approbation. In concrete cases, 'social' and 'personal' ethic may assign different duties, which are incompatibles for the will. For instance: the 'social' duty of a general, aware that in his brain alone lies the plan of an imminent battle on which his country's destiny hangs, would be to keep alive in the meantime; but if a situation emerges in which, by risking his own life, he might save that of a humble orderly, his sense of honour and ideal of self-realisation might require him to do so. There would seem to be no higher court, *a priori* or other, to which to appeal for judgement, as to whether the one, rather than the other, of the two kinds of right thing, is Really right; no monistic ethic transcending the dualism of 'personal' and 'social' valuation. If so, the expressions '*the* highest good', '*the* absolute ideal', are meaningless. 'Be a person, etc.' is a principle inconsistent with the ethic of 'social' origin, which knows, save in the utilitarian sense, no respect for persons.

In the light of what has been said concerning the kinds and the mutations of valuation, it will appear that when psychology is denied bearing on the significance of the moral consciousness, 'moral' must be used in its abstractly axiological sense—presently to be considered—or else it is overlooked that there is

psychology of common, as well as of individual, conative experience. That Objective or common aesthetic and moral judgements are independent of any one individual's tastes or preferences,
goes without saying. But it does not follow that they are independent of the sentiments and other affective-volitional dispositions common to a society, or of shared attitudes towards the
ideal and conceptual constructions of the over-individual thought,
that is source of the rational element in ethics. Because Objective
valuation, at its highest level, is inexplicable in terms of individual
interest, at its lowest level, it is not to be assumed independent of
over-individual interests intellectually grounded. So long as
'Objective' means 'common to many subjects', and not 'independent of all', or 'valid *per se*'—and the meanings are none the
less wholly distinct, for being often confounded—the psychologically justified view that valuation, from first to last, is constituted by affective-volitional attitude, is adequate to account for
the developement of valuation that has so far been traced. Provided
the distinction, as well as the continuity, between individual and
social experience is recognised, and that 'good' denotes what is
deemed desirable for some Actual purpose or in relation to some
Actual interest, we have a workable theory. Judgements of personal merit, *e.g.*, are expressions of approval or of desiredness
of qualities which are expected by society from its members, or
from the Actual self by the ideal self. When 'I owe' is no longer
acknowledged to the Actual self or to contemporary society, but
to an idealisation of the self, to an idealised society, or to God;
and when an ideal law is constructed out of current *mores*, in a
way similar to that in which the triangle of geometry is distilled—
by idealising and abstracting—out of the visible surface: the
sense of obligation necessarily becomes inward and unconditional.
'I owe' is transmuted, *in virtue of its new intellectual or existential
presupposition*, into 'I ought'. Further abstractive intellection can
eliminate both the lawgiver and the I, and so arrive at the bare
concept of 'oughtness-to-be': which is determinative of ethics
proper, according to one view. From the desired to the desirable,
from the concrete good, that is good for something, to the good-
in-itself, from the subpersonal to the over-individual, and from
the social to what may be called the over-social or the absolute,
there is a way. But there is no deductive way back from high

abstractions, so reached, to particular moral judgements relevant to specific Actual issues. Necessary truth, in ethics as anywhere else, is purchased at the price of possible irrelevance to Actuality, and therefore—in one sense—of meaninglessness. Its logical grounds or presuppositions are a genuine quest; but such axiological or epistemological inquiry will not necessarily have relation to the ἀξία of things and persons, or to the ἐπιστήμη of human conduct. It may prove to be concerned with abstract concepts to which names can be given, but which have no denotation.

The origination of certain practical ideals has already been incidentally noticed. They are ideals in which processes involving feeling, conative disposition and ideation, come to temporary fulfilment. They 'exist' in and for processes of evaluation; and to those processes they owe all their significance. As abstracted from those processes, they do not exist; and verbal hypostatisation can confer no existence upon them. They are not independent of valuers. An ideal, to be capable of actualisation, must be specific and determinate; when idealisation runs on to 'perfection', and when abstraction arrives at the absolute, we are left without basis for particular and concrete judgements of value. 'Be a person, and respect others as persons', *e.g.*, is only unconditional when it is meaningless through its abstractness. Both 'personal' and 'social' values, it has been submitted, are relative to subjective standpoints, and are mutational and supersedible. When any is said to be universal or eternal, it is therefore implied that, in its case, there is no possibility of its lapsing through absorption or transmutation. As to the more specific moral values hitherto actualised, history warns against postulation of such a static condition; and for the generic the case is, theoretically speaking, the same. "It doth not yet appear what we shall be", and limits to transvaluation, here or hereafter, cannot be assigned. Charity may abide when faith and hope have become superfluities, especially if the class-name cover more specific varieties than we can as yet imagine; and progress is perhaps the one value for which there cannot be substitution.[1] But to eternalise any specific human value, is precarious in proportion to its specificness; and the fixity of class-

[1] If rationalistic monism and the doctrine of absorption into the One be true, not only faith and hope, but love also, shall be done away.

names is a fertile source of philosophical superstition. The notion of *a* universal ideal (the numerical singularity of which is impossible so long as valuation proceeds 'personally' as well as 'socially') and of its universal obligatoriness, involves the assumption that a disposition, having value with reference to some specified end, can be generalised into disposition applicable in all circumstances to all and for ever. Such an abstraction would seem to have no more relevance to human conduct than has the mathematical 'new infinity' to the physical world.

The word 'absolute' is often associated with terms such as 'universal' and 'Objective', in connexion with value; and its meaning now needs to be investigated. 'Objective' has here been used to denote the Experience constructed through inter-subjective intercourse, and its Objects as distinguished from the objects of individual, private, experience at the unsocialised level. The Objective realm is then the common: not necessarily the universal. Whatever is thus called Objective is, in the sphere of cognition, independent of any individual's perceptio; while in the sphere of valuation it is independent, as to its constitution, of the interest of any one subpersonal or personal individual. It does not follow that an Object of, or for, the many at the standpoint of shared Experience, or a value that is assigned by the many from the same standpoint and is consequently independent of the private experience of any one individual, is independent of, or is not constituted by, the Experience of the many. The assumption that it is, is made by naïve common sense: but so far as we know, pending the solution of a large problem, this is mere assumption for practical convenience, and, by the way, one which science that sets out from it has, at higher stages, to discard. What is over-individual, in other words, is not necessarily also over-social, existing *per se* and not constituted, as to its phenomenal Objectivity for social Experience, by any Subjective element in that Experience. Yet this is precisely what is meant by 'absolute'. The physical world, Objective for scientific Experience, is taken for such an absolute by naturalistic metaphysics. The realm of Objective values is, or presupposes, such an absolute, according to one school of ethics. Both systems seem to commit the same fallacy, or to make the same unwarrantable assumption. They take the same flying leap from the individual straight to the over-social instead of to the over-individual, and so, by illegitimate abstraction followed with hypostatisation, to what is supposed independent of all persons and all experience, cognitive or conative as the case may be. Ethics is then expounded in terms of a theory of knowledge which only could be justified, if it can be justified at all, after elaborate investigation, but is generally assumed without proof; and a theory which, applied in the field of cosmology, should issue straightly in materialistic naturalism.

Thus it is that we are often presented with the false dilemma: ethics must be either an affair of individual tastes, or else a science of absolute values. It has been argued here that it is neither, but deals with judgements that have Objectivity, in the sense of commonness and independence of this or that individual, though not unconditionality and universality. It is empirical, not *a priori*; normative, but not pure and deductive. Its data are intuitive inductions, such that apprehension in one instance is apprehension in all others of like kind; just as the data of physics are perception-judgements from the common standpoint.[1] But the ethical predicate differs from the existential. In ethics, as in physics, all significant propositions must be either true or false;[2] and they must be valid or invalid of some Actual or possible situation. The Actuality, in the case of value-judgements, is not the Objective simply as existing and 'perceived', but as valued: the value being constituted by more or less complex and common affective-volitional dispositions. That a value-judgement, such as 'that act is noble', has grammatically the same form as the judgement 'the

---

[1] The intuitive induction, as contrasted with approval or disapproval in the case of a present instance, is a judgement valid of all similar cases: *e.g.* that a certain act *is* vile or belongs to the class called vile. Such a judgement, in so far as it merely refers an action to a class, is purely logical: it is ethical in so far as the connotation of 'vile' is involved. From the common standpoint, an action is vile, whether or not it evokes abhorrence in a given percipient; but no action would originally have been called vile, that did not excite the emotion of abhorrence in the many. Intuitive moral inductions thus cannot be assumed to be deliverances of a 'moral sense' that reads off intrinsic qualities of actions, or qualities that actions have in abstraction from the affective-volitional dispositions of valuers. The action that is said to be preferred for *its own* sake, is first preferred for mankind's sake—*i.e.* on account of its relation to ends, desires, feelings, etc.; these being ignored, because tacitly supposed with unanimity, the preferability is naturally mistaken to be independent of valuers and their interests. "There's nothing either good or bad, but thinking makes it so": only "thinking" must include appreciating.

[2] This is what some writers (*e.g.* Dr Rashdall) mean by 'objectivity'.

sky is blue', disguises its nature: linguistically convenient, and practically harmless, it is philosophically inaccurate or superficial. And the value-judgements passed by individuals and societies, are true or false in relation to circumstantial setting, and especially in respect of what the ethical terms in them mean, or should (ps) mean, to those who make the judgements. It is, in fact, only in virtue of these relations or conditions, that such judgements are significant. If, *e.g.*, for a barbarous tribe, 'good' denotes whatever is deemed conducive to the tribal welfare, that welfare being understood as barbarians can understand it, then such a judgement as 'cannibalism is good' may be valid of Actuality and conditionally true: it describes a relation to an end constituted by social desire, etc., that subsists. That the judgement is not true, if by 'good' we understand what the axiologist might call 'really good', or that the judgement is not a universal and eternal truth, is irrelevant to its truth within the universe of discourse and on the presuppositions concerned: *i.e.* when the proposition in question is different from that of the axiologist. Again, if in 'X is the right thing for A to do, in his circumstances', 'right' be taken to connote 'deemed right by the society within which the judgement emanates', the proposition is significant and may be true. This is what, according to the theory here adopted, the proposition does (ps) mean, though not perhaps what it meant (ψ) to its bygone propounder, nor what it must mean (ps) to the axiologist in order to have, for him, moral significance. If the proposition be universalised into 'X is right for all men at all times, regardless of consequences and of all fluctuations in human enlightenment', it loses truth if not significance; and in the case where X stands for preference of death to untruth, as a 'personal' valuation it may then clash with 'social' valuation, equally Objective.

These illustrations are intended to shew that so long as valuation be regarded as constituted by interest of some kind, ethical judgements logically presuppose no one absolute principle or moral criterion or concept, in order to be true in the sense indicated above. Such a presupposition is only required if they are to be deemed absolutely true, independent—that is to say— of all interest, and corresponding with 'Reality' of some kind quite other than the Actual dispositions and situations, of which instances have been given. For any such deeming, it would appear, there is no psychological justification. It now remains to point out the consequences of assuming, despite psychology, that value-judgements have such a ground in the concept of the good *per se*.

According to this theory, value or goodness, aesthetic or moral, is a simple or unanalysable and ultimate quality. It has been compared, in these respects, to the quality of colour. But a colour can be ostensively defined by pointing to instances of it; and it can be indirectly described, in virtue of its correlation with wave-length and position in the spectrum. The value-quality, however, cannot be ostensively defined; it has no intuitable *quale*, like a colour; its presence appears to be discernible only by means of criteria, *i.e.* qualities that do not constitute its essence, but accompany it. Thus it is allowed that the good is desirable, and the greatest goods are said to be cognitions of Objects that evoke certain emotions, etc., though 'good' does not mean what can be desired or can satisfy elaborated conative dispositions. If good-ness is constituted by desire, etc., and the criteria *are* its essence, these correlations go without saying; on the theory under con-sideration, they simply are, "and there's an end on't": no explana-tion can be given. We may conclude then that 'good', unlike 'blue', is a "symbolically blank" word.

The non-intuitable, and therefore presumably noumenal, quality called goodness, is identified with 'oughtness-to-be'. To some this will not seem a meaningful expression, for several reasons. Without reference to some determinate universe within which a given entity is to be, with whose other constituents it should have a compossibility or compatibility on which its oughtness and fitness are dependent, such oughtness would seem to be as indeter-minate a conception as that of pure being, or that of possibility. Oughtness, abstracted from both debtor and creditor, is a relation between no terms; a nonentity like the phenomenon that does not appear, or the awareness that has no subject and is of no object. Inasmuch as 'oughtness' properly connotes something relational, it is treated with somewhat of equivocation when exploited for use as a synonym for 'goodness'; *i.e.* as a non-relational predicate, an intrinsic attribute, such as a thing may possess as its own essence and as independent of its relations to anything else. This synonym dropped, we are back at goodness as an adjective or simple predicate, and a word for which there is no synonym. It seems as if the quality 'good' has been assumed necessarily to exist, because there is in use a word for which there is alleged to be no synonym: there is a unique predicate, whether possessed by anything or not. It would then be a "linguistically generated phantom",[1] and use of 'goodness' for a verbally hypostatised abstraction would but give to airy nothing a local habitation and a name.

Propositions involving 'oughtness-to-be', and perhaps others such as Kant's foundation-formulae, must be asserted to be 'indeterminate propositions': i.e. not propositions, but propositional functions. These have no meaning, or are non-significant, and are neither true nor false. Any predication of 'true in all circumstances' is of this nature: it is concerned with formal, not material, truth or implication. If this be the case, nemesis indeed overtakes the demand for an absolute foundation of ethics. The fundamental 'proposition' is no proposition: it is of the nature 'X is a man', as contrasted with 'Plato was a man'. The science of the absolute 'good' is then as pure a science as meta-geometry. Empirically derived ethics, conversely, knows no absolute grounds, no unconditional and universal propositions, but only sufficient sanctions and well-founded Objective estimations. These are the 'practical absolutes' of the plain man of moral aspiration, and their unconditionality will perhaps be the more vividly believed by him, if his moral consciousness be permeated by religion. What has here been maintained, does not rob such a man of his practical absolutes. It only denies that they are literally and theoretically absolute, and affirms that they issue from, and are relevant to, life in the environment of Nature. If the psychology that has here been presented be sound, and if ontologism be fallacious, it would seem that the primary intuitions on which ethics is based are, ultimately, felt preferences common to the many and entertained in relation to common interests or ends, not assertions about hypostatised indefinables; that its principial judgements cannot be supposed to be independent of volitional-intellectual systems, without making ethics a non-applied science; that there is no good that is not good for somebody and good for something: that, apart

1 This phrase is borrowed from *The Meaning of Meaning*, by Ogden and Richards

from reference to valuers and their ends, 'the good' is but a name for nothing.

This psychological exposition of the affective and conative, or practical, side of experience, and of its developement in conjunction with thought or intelligence, has necessarily involved itself in criticism of the *a priori* method and of the rationalistic theory, as applied to ethics. Similar criticism will exude perforce when the empirical method is employed, in the following chapters, to ascertain the nature of thought and knowledge of the theoretical kind, *i.e.* concerning the existential. It will then be found essential to distinguish between necessary, eternal, truths of reason, and truth necessarily valid of Actuality. To revert to the difference, pointed out at the beginning of the present chapter, between logical presuppositions of pure ethics and genetic presuppositions of applied ethics, it may be observed, in conclusion, that the 'truth' of pure ethics, like that of logic and mathematics, is necessary and eternal. As Prof. Ward remarks, in his posthumous book on *Psychology applied to Education*, this 'truth' remains necessary, whether it can be applied or not; it does not become contingent truth because its realisation depends on Actuality; we did not make the realm of truths of reason by entering into it; nor can we explain, by genetic studies, the laws of thought or the principles of axiology. But in this connexion we should note two points which here, perhaps, Prof. Ward overlooked; so that he appears, when treating of pure ethics, to adopt a position which elsewhere, when pure mathematics is in question, he repudiated. These points are: (1) there is no eternal *prius* of truth, in ethics any more than in mathematics, into the realm of which we simply "enter"; (2) genetic studies at any rate reveal that the entities of which pure sciences are valid, such as the circle whose circumference is $2\pi r$, and the abstract good, are definitions or postulates that would not be forthcoming as ideas, were it not for subjective operations and human interest.

CHAPTER VIII

Thought and Reason

I. SENSE-KNOWLEDGE: "OBJECTS OF HIGHER ORDER".

The germinal thought implicit in perception, described in an earlier chapter, was found to be assimilation, subjectively guided by interest, yet objectively controlled by impression. Before perception is relatively developed, the only judgements possible are the impersonal, which we now express in such words as 'it rains'. These assert changes in the presentational field as a whole. Such change is the primary, or first apprehended, actuality; later it comes to be discriminated as specific changes. Otherness of presentations is the objective source of all knowledge of relations of space, time, number, etc. If verbs, as rudiments of judgement, are the first words that would have been coined by an imaginary soliloquist anticipating the social invention of language, nouns would follow when, from action, that which acts was learned: *i.e.*, when distinct percepts were formed. Perception-judgements, such as 'that is blue', could then be made; and in place of the first 'it' (the whole continuum) many kinds of 'it' could be asserted. The simplest percepts, sensa, are matter of fact as brute as fact can be; and their positing is the beginning of the cognition, of which thought-knowledge is a developement. Such crude, initial cognition has appropriately been called sense-knowledge. For though 'knowledge' is wont to be denied to sensatio because sense, alone, yields no cognition of things as continuously existent and inter-related, still sensa are not mere formless 'matter', and sensatio is therefore rudimentary knowledge. At any rate, before thought or knowledge, as 'perception of agreement or difference between ideas', can be forthcoming, and before the ideal can be abstracted or postulated, actual positings or fundamenta must be apprehended and assimilated. Again, in this sense-knowledge there is already implicit or relatively anoetic (hyponoetic) apprehension of relations, which, when explicated, becomes the categories of quality, resemblance, temporal and spatial order—the foundations of logic and mathematics, the *a priori* factor in 'universal' knowledge. Indeed, conceptual knowledge, to which the name 'knowledge' is usually restricted, differs from sense-knowledge less in its relations than in its relata: these, in the one, are concrete positings; in the other, ideal forms and postulations. Sense-knowledge, it may be observed, is marked by certainty and necessitation; but it is private to the individual, and is only of the here and now.

Thus recognition and distinction of sensa, precede explicit comparison and are actually presupposed by it. The concepts of those acts, on the other hand, logically presuppose the concepts of identity and difference. Primitive recognition, involving no logical analysis, is genetically prior, and essential to, explicit assertion of likeness. Thought may be the logical presupposition of all knowledge, as knowledge is usually conceived; but so far from thought determining things, it is things, or rather sensa whence knowledge of things is born, that determine all thought. Actual preconditions are one thing, logical priorities another.

The first function to be ascribed to the 'understanding', as distinguishable from sensatio or from the common root, is explicit apprehension of relations, as such. The child, bowling his hoop, has no definite concepts of circularity, rigidity or velocity; but he has a vague 'sense' of their content, that goes to make up his recognisable percept in which they are implicit. Similarly, relations such as number and resemblance, in their tied or implicit form, are vaguely 'perceived' before they are explicated. Explicitly apprehended relations were not originally apprehensible apart from percepts, yet they are not cognised in the same way as sensory qualities. Hume was unable to regard them as given, like impressions, to *sense*. When this, that and another colour-sensum are received, there is no fourth impression of three-ness; nor of identity or difference: the succession of the sensa is not the idea of succession. Nor can ideas of relation be generated quasi-mechanically by the conjoint action of sensa, as sensationism supposed: their forthcomingness is too fortuitous and precarious for that. Relations are not all originally read off as if data; they often fail to be read at all. Some of those we are wont to affirm, may be read in; others are certainly read between the lines, elicited from the sensa, or grounded on percepts, by intellective activity, such as comparison. Empirically founded, some of these kinds of relations are objective as their fundamenta, which *are* prime *data*; but they are objects of another and a "higher" order. They are not, on that score, separable or separate existents; indeed, no more are the terms between which they subsist. Neither term nor relation is before or after other, or *pre*supposes the other, save in order of emergence to cognition. Subsisting between percepts, and valid of them, relations enter into the constitution of actuality. Intellection does not merely invent them, but also finds them: even when it first needs to postulate them. Some few are read off, with immediacy comparable to that of sensatio. To find others, intellection needs to look for them; and that is where intellection begins to differ from involuntary sensatio.[1]

It is by establishment of relations between the percepts of a plurality of individuals, that transition is made from individual experience to common Experience, and from perception of objects to knowledge of conceptual Objects supposed to exist and interact while individual, and eventually even social, experience supplies no immediate vouch thereof. Ten men looking at the sun, see each a different object, yet See one and the same Object.[2] If we were to set out from common sense as sacrosanct metaphysics, we should ask how The Sun becomes an object to ten different percipients. If we take common-sense epistemology for but a practically useful working-hypothesis until we have found it to be anything more, we shall rather ask how each of the ten comes to know that to his object there correspond objects of the other nine. This is to pursue the *ordo cognoscendi* and to assume no particular theory of knowledge. The object of each man is private; no man can apprehend another's. These objects are not merely numerically diverse but also, we must believe at the standpoint of our common knowledge, qualitatively different—as is suggested by the prevalence, in some degree, of colour-blindness.

Now only what is common can be communicated. *A* cannot know that *B* sees the same shade of colour that he sees, nor indicate the colour-sensum that he himself receives: *B* may see grey where *A* sees yellow. But *A* can indicate—by gestures before language supervenes—that his 'sun' is like, say, 'that

---

[1] See Appendix, Note E, on Relations.
[2] 'See' and 'see' mean acts psychologically diverse, viz. perception overlaid with conception, and perception proper.

sunflower', and gather that such resemblance exists between
B's objects—sun and flower—if B gesticulates "same here".
That relation will still subsist, if A's objects be of yellow colour
and B's of grey. Thus it is relations between sensa or simple
percepts in individual experience, not impressional *quale*, that can
be known in common. Incommunicable sensa are the only data,
or original fundamenta, of all knowledge; and 'universal' Experience consists in the elaboration of relations between them, and
of concepts valid of them. But the relations that enter into common-sense 'knowledge' are not all like that of simple resemblance,
which can be immediately read off; some, that immediate apprehension or direct intuition cannot supply, have to be read in.
In universal Experience and the thought-knowledge that can only
be developed through intercourse, language, etc.; in the analysis
and re-synthesis (of individual percepts) that are essential for construction of knowledge of Objects: elements emerge that might
be called new fundamenta, were it that they are posited for us
like the impressional. They are, however, rather postulated than
posited, fashioned rather than received, suggested rather than
thrust upon us. An Object, such as the sun, stands to the objects
of individuals 'looking at the sun' in no such relation as that of
nx to x; and much more than comparison is involved in its
synthesis.[1] It is supposed to persist independently of being perceived, not merely by any one, but by all subjects; whereas the
objects from which it is synthesised are neither independent nor
persistent. For the existence of an object, we severally have *direct*,

---

[1] Thus the physical Object or, more generally, the external world, is not a symposium, or a sum, of objects for different subjects at different points of view; the
synthesis does not consist in mere addition or superposition of appearances of that
kind. Nor does it consist of the common element in the data, arrived at by mere
subtraction of the private and peculiar elements; for the data, while still concrete,
have no common and communicable elements. What is common, is not *in* the data,
nor therefore abstracted out of the data; it is read into them, suggested by them,
supposed or thought to be 'behind' them. No doubt the assertions that have just
been denied have some truth, when by 'data' we mean Objects of socialised experience,
and by 'appearances' we mean phenomena for science; but that is quite another
question, assuming a position which genetic epistemology would undermine. The
conceptual, interpretative and anthropic element in the synthesis of our 'knowledge'
of the external world, enters lower down than scientific realism suspects; it already
saturates the data from which science sets out, and consequently infects its ultra-
microscopic findings.

as well as coercive, sense-evidence. For the Actuality of the Object, we have not: we have what might be compared to circumstantial evidence, overwhelming in its cumulativeness. The Object is conceived, not perceived; and that again is no vouch for its Actuality: for a Euclidean circle is a concept, though no one takes it for a thing. Thus, in seeking to know what Actuality and knowledge are, we have to ask how the concept of a physical Object was got, and what grounds or causes there may be for taking the conceived Object of thought or of thought-knowledge, *i.e.* a concept, to have what some concepts have not—a counterpart that is as Real or Actual as the individual's object is actual.

It is unfortunate that physical Objects, such as the sun, have come to be called perceptual. For if the private object immediately apprehended or synthetically perceived by an individual, prior to intercourse, be perceptual, the common Object, *the* sun, is certainly not. The sun which we are commonly said to perceive, is not the flat roundish disc, about as large as a crown-piece, that is sporadically presented to each of us singly in perception proper. It is what we do *not* perceive, but *think is there*. This scientific thought, taken by realism to be thought-*knowledge of* the sun, however derived in the first instance from percepts, presupposes theory. We have found it impossible to draw any sharp line between conception and perception; but if any line is to be drawn at all, the individual's object must fall on one side of it, and the common Object, on the other.

The problem of knowledge of an external world is not now before us, save in so far as it is involved in any discussion of thought or understanding. It suffices to have pointed out that what is called knowledge of Actuality, is largely thought about things that are thought or supposed to be, but are not in the strict sense perceived to be. Naïve realism is deeply rooted in common sense, and is often unconsciously imported into the terminology of philosophers conscious of its assumptional nature. Common sense takes the surmised elements in the sun to be as real, as perceptual or sensible, as the perceptual sun-object of each individual's experience: and so it sets up, by unconscious metaphysic, its *ratio essendi*.

What has thus far been discussed under the name of thought or work of the understanding, it will be observed, is quite different from thought, in the usual sense of thinking or thought-process. We are as yet concerned only with the preliminaries to such thinking: with the construction of the Objects, causally related in space and time, which form the chief 'terms' about which we think. This constitutive function of thought may now be studied in further detail, and on the lines laid down by Kant; but 'understanding', as here used, will include the activities which he distinguished as 'intuition'.

2. THE FORMS OF INTUITION.

Of the Objects of higher order involved in thought-knowledge, the first to be considered are the "forms of intuition", space and time. These were rightly distinguished by Kant from the forms, functionings or categories "of the understanding": as concepts, space and time are reached by a different kind of synthesis. The intuition,[1] of which they are forms, is *developed* sensory perceptio; the resulting perceptum is the sole source of the 'matter', without which conceptual thought is empty. On this ground Kant could reject the views that geometry is merely logic, philosophy merely mathematics, and maintain that neither geometry nor philosophy is independent of [sensory] experience. He was again right in emphasising that space and time are forms of *our* experience and presuppositions of *phenomenal* knowledge: which implies that they are universally necessary frames, only in the restricted sense that they are inevitable for us in our environment, and for the specific kind of experience-organisation that we happen to have developed. But Kant was in error in regarding these forms as 'pure' and (in his sense of the phrase) *a priori*: i.e., as independent of sense-data, and as bespeaking, in their finished build, activities original to the subject and brought by it to the manifold of sense. They are not presuppositions of *experience*, such as an infant may have, but rather of the complex results of experience when, through intercommunication, it has become 'universal'. In other words, they are not forms of intuition, in the sense of individual perception at its lower levels. Indeed, the abstract concepts of space and time on which Kant operates, are rather forms of thought-knowledge of Objects for common Experience, in so far

---

[1] See Appendix, Note F, on the meanings of 'intuition'.

as this thought is based on, and valid of, minimally conceptual perception. Nor are they merely abstractions from perceptual space and time, *i.e. their* form with the filling left out: they are ideational constructions and ideals. If logically *a priori* as pre-conditions of our science, they have a genesis and a history. Localisation in public space and time are no more original activities, than space and time are innate ideas.

Space.

Our concept of space is not derived from 'pure' intuition, nor is it innate in the sense of lying ready made in 'the mind itself'. Again, it is not a 'logical' relation, such as similarity, that is directly read off from sensa; for to relate spatially, involves movements. It is not furnished by the subject alone, but by interaction between subject and objects. The form has some matter; at least if we adopt the view that even perceptual extension is elaborated out of the extensity of simple sensa. And it is a long step, from the visually and tactually mediated space or spaces of perceptual experience, to Newton's infinite whole, homogeneous and three-dimensional. Filled space is known before empty space; and it should be observed that these expressions are faulty, in that they imply that space is a thing in itself, occupation of which is an accident: they reify an abstraction. Lastly, the projective geometry and meta-geometry, that have developed since Kant's time, have killed the belief that the Euclidean concept of space is a logical necessity *a priori*; it possesses but applicability to experience, and even in that capacity it is neither unique nor perfect. What is called physical space, we may conclude, is not a pure and immediate intuition, but a concept reached gradually and discursively from sensa, by means of synthesis, abstraction and idealisation.

Time.

Time and space are not the twins they are supposed to be by popular thought. Psychologically, time is more fundamental; and the processes by which the two concepts have been elaborated out of primitive perception are diverse. Like space, time is not a logical relation,[1] as early rationalism believed; temporal

[1] See p. 171.

relations are unique.[1] Like space, again, time is a form in which there is involved an element of matter. At the lowest level of perceptual experience, sensatio, this is what has been called protensity, a *quale* of sensa; and, in virtue of it, duration (of the notion of which it is the precursor) has somewhat of concrete quality, of the nature of 'withstanding'.[2] Duration, the first temporal 'mode', eliminated in transition to conceptual time, is an essential factor in perceptual time. It imposes a limit to divisibility and succession. When it is eliminated, time becomes so abstract that it can only be talked of in terms of spatial metaphors. Perceived change is not substitution, such as may be represented by *abcd*, *lmno*; but gradual passage, such as *abcd*, *bcde*, *cdef*: *cd* enduring while *e* replaces *a*. Change is presupposed by time-perception, though the concept of change presupposes that of time. And change of presentation is not presentation of change. Change may be experienced without being apprehended as such, or explicitly. Duration can be, but cannot be known, without change, *i.e.* without the succession that measures it.

Succession, then, is a second 'mode' of time. It is to sensa we owe our notion of actuality; but mere sensatio could yield no awareness of the present *as* present, of now as distinct from here. When change is apprehended as such, it is apprehended with immediacy within the specious present, which (ψ) involves no time-reference. Awareness of present *as* present, is only possible when the present consciousness consists partly of memory-image and preperception. Neither one constant presentation, nor a series of substituted discrete sensa, could yield apprehension of time: for that, contrast of the new with the relatively enduring is essential. Unless the (ψ) present contained re-presentation of the (ps) past, and the subject were not wholly absorbed in the (ps) present, the

---

[1] While the order, *e.g.* of left to right, of points in space, is assigned arbitrarily, that of before and after in perceptual time is irreversible, given without option in immediate intuition, expressible in terms of intransitive relation. The theory of space-time, according to which temporal and spatial relations are arbitrarily divided by us but not Really transmutable *inter se*, takes no account of individual experience, and, in so behaving, reveals the fact that it is only a further developement of the economical 'description' which theoretical science pursues in its treatment of a common and conceptual world. That it conducts to ontology, is an error entertained by some expounders of Einstein's theory of relativity.

[2] Such was Ward's oral teaching.

relations of duration and succession could not become explicit. Distinction between past, present and future, depends on continual sinking of primary memory-images, and the rising of ordinary images of the member of a percept-series which is actual at the moment; also on previous adjustments of attention involved in expectation. These conditions, in turn, depend on formation of the memory-train and on recurrence of like sensa: if we never had 'the same' series of impressions twice, there could be no beginning of knowledge of a world.[1]

Succession, in perceptual time, has no uniform rate: rate depends on the specific *tempo* of the individual and on his interest. Thus there is in such time-experience, though not in conceptual time, an ultimate, inexplicable or alogical element: 'matter' or concrete existence, not reducible to pure or logical form. The case is the same with the order of sequence of the immediately and individually apprehended: the order is irreversible.

The third 'mode' of time is simultaneity. The specious present is all (ψ) present, though (ps) it is resolvable into successive phases. Indeed (ψ) it is not time, but rather temporal signs connected with change by movements of attention. Elements, distinguished (ps) as non-contemporaneous, are in it (ψ) simultaneous. In order that succession of b on a be perceived, both a and b must be within one psychic present, *i.e.* simultaneous; although the presentness of b involves the pastness of a, when succession is *conceived*. The notion of succession is thus the outcome of explication of the (ψ) simultaneous. There is of course no paradox here: discrimination between the (ψ) and (ps) standpoints, would have spared much dialectical labour spent on arguing the illusoriness of time-experience and the intrinsic inconsistency of the time-concept.

It is not necessary here to discuss further how the conception

[1] Such is Ward's teaching as to the origination of time-perception. He was aware that he was exploring a trackless and difficult region, and it should be mentioned that Stout at present thinks the master's exposition, as it stands, presupposes the thought-activity that it would genetically account for. I cannot see that more than retention, primitive memory, preperception and imagery, all precursors of thought, are invoked in so far as *perceptual* time-experience is dealt with, nor any ground for believing that, confronted with this particular kind of experience, the doctrine of the common root breaks down. The former of these issues is, however, one as to which only the psychological expert is entitled to have opinion.

of common time is genetically derived from perceptual experience; but the differences between the perceptual and the conceptual may be tabulated thus:[1]

PERCEPTUAL	CONCEPTUAL
1. A physiologically conditioned time-span fixes an absolute duration-block; duration is 'living', and a *quale* of duration or protensity characterises sensa.	1. Thorough and pure relativity. No duration: only succession of instants.
2. There is distinction of past, present, future, involving reference to a subject and oneness of *direction*.	2. There is only distinction of earlier and later, involving no reference to subjects, and only oneness of *dimension*.
3. Simultaneity of (*ps*) earlier and later obtains within the (*ψ*) present.	3. Contemporaneity, involving separateness of earlier and later.
4. Continuity is broken by attention-acts conatively, not cognitively, determined: *e.g.* long=tedious=involving irksome acts of attention.	4. Continuity is broken by division-marks such as clock-ticks, proximately derived from science, and arbitrary only at a further remove.
5. No regular rate: such approximation to uniformity as subsists, is imposed by our *tempo*, pulse, stride, etc.	5. Absolute uniformity or evenness of flow.

It will be seen that conceptual time is reached partly by leaving out factors of time-perception, partly by idealisation. Perceptual time is real as is change; and if experience *be* change, experience that knows not the form of time is impossible. But there is no reason to assert that abstract and ideal time exists apart from, and otherwise than, the Actualities between which temporal relations subsist. Like other creatures of our thought, Newtonian time is taken by common sense to be perceptual; and, some philosophers have taken the space-time of Einstein to be the Real condition of perception. So far are we from any necessity to conceive space and time as does common sense or as did Newton and Kant, *i.e.* as frames for all happenings observable or imaginable by us, that science is now using other notions of them, valid for all possible observers posted on stars travelling with various velocities or falling with accelerated velocity. The general theory of relativity

---

[1] A similar series of contrasts between perceptual and conceptual spaces might be pointed. The time, the spaces and the space-time of geometry and science, are all idealisations and abstractions, economic conceptual devices for co-ordinating perceptual experiences.

reverses Kant's position and goes further than Newton in the search for the absolute; though to talk of the absolute involves the gratuitous assumption that a frame, *common to* all possible observers, is as independent of all as of any, and so belongs to the world *per se* rather than to universal Experience. No conceptual time, space, or space-time is more Real, or even more true, than another: all are descriptive apparatus, differing only in range of applicability and degree of economicalness.

3. CATEGORIES OF THE UNDERSTANDING.

The categories are not concepts more general than other concepts, as tree is more general than oak. In the first instance, indeed, they are not *concepta*, but conceivings or functionings of 'the understanding', of which, or of whose outcome, once they are forthcoming, we form *concepta*. They fall into two main classes, known as the formal and the 'real' or (Kant) the dynamical.

A. *Formal Categories.*

These include (i) the mathematical, (ii) the logical, the only kinds of which pure sciences make use; whereas the 'real' are called for by sciences of the Actual. The fundamental category of the formal sub-class distinguished as mathematical, is that of singularity, oneness, or (in one of its senses) unity. Oneness is not sensed or apprehended with 'passivity'; but sense is, at the first, the occasion of the movement of attention, the act of differentiating, whereby this object of higher order is cognised. Explicitly to apprehend as one, is impossible when spontaneous attention is at its minimum. When whole field and focus of attention are undistinguished, the whole cannot be apprehended as one. Explicitly to unify, involves concentration of attention. It is to relate, in some sense. Our span of consciousness is such that we can apprehend more than unity at once; and a unity is whatever the subject differentiates and combines into a percept. Increasingly voluntary attention constitutes unities such as the 'thing' (though in intuition of sensa into a 'thing' more than unifying is involved) and even singles out particular aspects of things, as subjects of thought.

Plurality is vaguely and qualitatively apprehended, as by lower animals that cannot count, in the literal sense of correlating with numbers, before the explicit concept of number is attainable. Thus the mathematical categories are derived (by the mind) originally from the sense-given, not out of 'the mind itself' or from latent subjective faculty alone. Formal categories derived by reflective comparison,[1] are distinguished as the logical; and it is categories of this kind that figure in formal logic, or rather in such processes in the old traditional logic as constituted an exact science: in reasoning, in the sense of ratiocination issuing in certainty.[2] Among the many 'categories' of this class—other concepts than Kant's dozen have since received this name—those of qualitative likeness and difference, and of numerical identity and diversity, especially call for notice; if for no other reason than that, owing to the ambiguity of words such as 'same' and 'one', these couples are often confounded with one another. We speak of two brothers as having the same features and as having the same mother; of nations as of one blood, and a political party as of one mind: and failure to distinguish two different kinds of identity and difference, besides being the source of some philosophical tenets, occasioned much controversy concerning the doctrine of the Trinity, both in the Athanasian age and in the seventeenth and eighteenth centuries, that is, or should be, now of no interest to the theologian.

Qualitative likeness, as established by noetic comparison, subsists when some presentation enters as a common constituent of a plurality of others, and can only be predicated when numerical diversity of complex presentations is forthcoming: either several individuals are compared, or several presentations of the same thing, as at different times. On the other hand, numerical diversity does not necessarily bespeak difference of quality; the only conditions of otherness (of things), as yet conceived, are place and time. Two penny-stamps are for ever two individuals, though no qualitative difference is discernible between them; and there is no reason for Leibniz's principle or dogma, that absolute likeness in quality carries with it numerical identity, singularity or oneness. Qualitative likeness is matter of degree, and we can never, on the strength of perception, assert exact likeness between perceptual things, but only indiscernibility of difference. Exact likeness, or

---

[1] See Appendix, Note G, on comparison.
[2] See Appendix, Note H, on different kinds of logic.

qualitative identity, is a postulate, an ideal perhaps never realised: needful for thought, it is inserted into the 'necessary laws' of thought. Numerical identity, on the other hand, has no degrees. The latter unity is—as Dr Ward has put it—presentation of an individual; the former, an individual presentation. An individual cannot be identified, or have its identification established, by qualitative comparison alone: twins are sometimes indistinguishable, and the one might be hanged for the other, unless he could establish an alibi by calling witnesses possessed of sufficiently continuous observation of his movements. On the other hand, perfect likeness between a photograph, taken of a criminal at thirty, and the face of a suspect of the age of sixty, would be strong evidence of non-identity. The emigrant who returns home after long absence, is the same person, possibly changed beyond recognition; and this indicates that the logical category of numerical identity differs, not only from that of indiscernibility of unlikeness, but also from the mathematical category of numerical singularity: oneness or singularity can subsist when identity does not, or where there is no persistence through a plurality of moments. Self-identity appears to be the same category as continuance (involved in that of substance), which is compatible with adjectival changeableness.

The category of individuality[1] is important because of its metaphysical associations: the *principium individuationis*, the relation of the particular to the universal, and various other controversial issues, here suggest themselves. Logistic science operates with 'terms', each immutable, identical with itself and numerically diverse from others, supposed to be unchanged when 'entering into' different relations; but these are mere counters of a pure mathematic, to which probably no counterparts exist in the Actual world, whose essence is becoming or change. Within the latter sphere, and in that of ontology as distinct from logic, the category of individuality passes largely into that of a substance or continuant, and so belongs rather to the class next to be considered.

The formal categories, the more important of which have now been mentioned, like sense-judgements, give intuitive certainty and, unlike sense-judgements, even universality. But neither

---

[1] Several senses of this word have been distinguished in the discussion of the individuality of the soul: see p. 97.

yield universal and necessary knowledge as to common matter of fact: nor do both together. This enables us to appreciate Locke's doctrine, that science is probable belief. Knowledge of a common external world involves more than objective data of individual experience and formal categories of universal Experience. A further factor is the 'real' categories. Whether there is such a thing as necessary and universal knowledge, sensory as to fundamenta and intuitively certain and *a priori* as to form, depends, therefore, on whether the categories about to be dealt with are epistemologically on a par with those of the class just reviewed.

B. *Real Categories.*

Kant would answer the question involved in the foregoing sentence affirmatively. At any rate he regarded the 'real' or, as he called them, the dynamical, categories, though belonging to transcendental logic involving 'matter' other than sensible, as, equally with the formal categories, *a priori* forms of the understanding. It is not necessary here to examine his teaching in detail, nor to discuss its self-consistency. But there are errors in it, it must be maintained, that time has enabled us to correct. The 'real' categories, in their explicit form, are no more original to the understanding, and no more independent of sense, than the forms of intuition. It is a fiction that, while we should have no *knowledge* of Nature unless there were uniformity or recurrence in our sensa, we should nevertheless have an intrinsic capacity to *think* a category-ordered world. It is another fiction to conceive of the understanding as a faculty by itself, functioning in isolation from conation; as if we might devote our minds to unmotivated thinking. Psychology can shew that the 'real' categories originate in action, not in logic. They are not purely subjective furniture, but analogical ejects objectively prompted and, consequently, derived from commerce of subjects with objective environment. They presuppose the forms of intuition, and therefore feeling and moving as well as receiving impressions and reading off relations such as are represented by the formal categories. They are not original to each individual mind severally, but originate, in their explicated form, in self-consciousness as developed by intercourse.

Kant's dynamical categories are substance, cause and reciprocal action. Final cause, or end, is not included; and in its case there is doubtless less of objective prompting and of direct connexion with temporal or spatial determinations, and somewhat more of subjective contribution. Kant regarded the idea of end as 'regulative', thinking 'experience'—*i.e.* thought-knowledge—to be possible without it; whereas he took cause, etc., to be 'constitutive', or conditions without which experience is impossible. It is a source of confusion that Kant applies the word 'regulative', in quite another sense, to the dynamical principles, and therefore implicitly to the dynamic categories, in order to distinguish them from the mathematical which alone are constitutive of intuitions; though the dynamic categories are equally constitutive of 'experience', in that they condition the modes of existence of Objects. Reverting from this minor usage of 'regulative' to that which marks off the ideas of reason from the categories of the understanding, we may call in question the Kantian distinction. The dynamical categories, like that of end, must be asserted to be due to what shall be called the anthropic, usually spoken of as the anthropomorphic,[1] tendencies and inevitabilities of human thought. This is virtually admitted in another context by Kant himself; for as we have previously seen, he teaches that the subject derives

[1] 'Anthropomorphic' should be reserved for conceiving after the likeness of man, such as once was inevitable, but which riper knowledge puts away: *e.g.* of God as with body and passions, of the sun as rejoicing to run his course. The very power thus to think, involves potency to advance beyond it. Anthropomorphism is evidently erroneous when its attributions turn out to be incongruous, and is mischievous only so long as man is not alive to its element of falsity. But when anthropomorphic vestiture has been removed from our conceptions of other beings, thought or knowledge of Actuality is still inevitably human or anthropic. 'Real' categories enter into science. And if the notion of efficient cause be methodologically banished, as a fetish, from refinedly theoretical description, the conception of 'things', however refined, as self-like interacting existents, is retained. Partitioning into things, of whatever order, is not necessarily and always a reading off of absolute partitions; it is determined by human *tempo* and human ends. Explanation, of any kind, is a satisfaction of need; to be a philosopher, is not to cease to be a man. Knowledge is a 'function' of knowing subjects as well as of their objective data; and these data and their relations, as they appear in systematised knowledge, are not bare Reality seen face to face. Science, like common sense, is a search in the world for a ground of conceptions which take their rise in us and are projections of the attributes of selves. Knowledge can never soar above human interpretation; its *a priori* conditions are but conditions of human knowing, and their only necessity is inevitableness to man with his determinate subjecthood. So much is meant by the assertion that the anthropic element in knowledge cannot be abjured; but the philosophical bearings of this assertion, as of others issuing from our empirical investigation, must await discussion.

the categories from itself. Here we encounter the element of truth in the ancient doctrines "like is known by like", and *homo mensura*. Man is not (*ps*) the measure of all things. But man constitutes himself the measure, and (*ψ*) is the measure, of all things, because he is measure of them as they are for him, or as they are known to him and by him. At this point it also has at length become possible to describe explicitly what has hitherto been called knowledge, and has repeatedly been designated 'knowledge so-called', out of consideration for the possibility, pending investigation, that there is cognition superior to it. It now begins to appear that the knowledge, claimed by common sense and science, is not, so to speak, mental photography of the ontal, such as is alone deemed, by some philosophers, worthy of the name of knowledge. On the other hand, it is not necessarily a phenomenal caricature or a garbled rendering of the ontal, or a pretending that Reality is what it is not. Knowledge is assimilation, involving a kind of sympathetic understanding distinguishable from logical and necessary concatenation, whether or not it commits the pathetic fallacy. The anthropic origination of the 'real' categories, is fact. That they involve analogy, bespeak precipitancy and venture at the first, express belief rather than knowledge coming up to the formal standard, reflect man as well as the non-ego over against him, is also fact, from which neither logic nor science nor intellectualistic philosophy can get away. But the origination of knowledge, or of the categories constitutive of all knowing, in our anthropism, is no proof of their invalidity or irrelevance. If, as our understanding-functionings first emerged, they were merely humanly inevitable and even mythical, they have yielded forms which experience has found practically successful. They must therefore have some relation to Truth; and it may be they catch the meaning or revelation-significance of the Real, or of the Actual, though they may not mirror ontal structure.[1] Moreover, to call them anthropic, is not to insinuate that they are not *suggested* by relations—spatial and temporal, as they come to be known—between the objective presentations themselves, in which actuality

---

[1] Even Hume did not impugn their validity when he assigned them subjective origin. The knowledge, as to which he was a sceptic, is knowledge in the rationalist's restricted sense; *i.e.* synthetic *a priori* propositions about Actuality, characterised by universality and necessity.

primarily consists. These relations are the occasions, though not the source, of our ejectiveness and analogising; the external control which, though not coercion, is prompting or eliciting. And therein is the original warrant for our attribution of thinghood, permanence, substantiality, efficiency and interaction—all partial analogues derived from the self as paradigm—to the not-self in which by neither sense nor pure understanding-intuition do we read them off. Apart either from suitable material, on the one hand, or from our subjecthood and *erleben*, on the other, these 'forms' of thought could not have emerged. They have a foot in both worlds. They are not derivable, as sensationism found, from impressions by quasi-mechanical association; nor from functionings of the understanding such as might go on in an impressionless vacuum: but only from subjects in commerce with objective environment. Any more refined concepts by which theoretical science, logic, or philosophy of the type of 'nothing if not the logically necessary', would fain replace them, are also interest-motived and anthropic; it is but a question of degree. And perhaps it will appear that rationalism and logical realism go further than does common sense, in reading in what is not read off, and that with more violence and less reasonableness they "pretend" Actuality to be "what it is not". If by 'categories' we mean concepts, rather than functionings of the synthesising subject, the 'real' categories are neither purely read off nor purely read in; they are established by postulation that is subjectively derived but objectively evoked, and are principles of *inter*pretation.

Substance.

The category of substance has already called for discussion in another context, so that but few remarks need here be added. The notion of substances preceded the more abstract concept of substance; and it seems indispensable, whereas the higher abstraction has become useless and obsolete. The notion of a substance, in the sense of an abiding unity, is doubtless derived from knowledge of the self. It is knowledge of self, and of other selves, that encouraged the venture involved in believing things to continue a life-history when not being 'perceived'. Thus to conceive of things, is to personify, to assimilate to the self, to interpret scattered data in terms of self, and so to 'understand'. 'A substance' does not then mean a *collection* of discretes; it refers rather to their *connexion*. Quite another purpose than that for which this concept was fashioned, is served, as we have seen, by such objects of higher order as collection or series, by which the Humean psychologist or the logistician may seek to replace substance or continuant, and so construct 'psychology without a soul'. They ignore the fact-element which evokes this particular category, and invoke another category that is inadequate and irrelevant. Substance, as the category has here been expounded, indicates a ground or sufficient reason, such as reasonableness cannot dispense with, but which logical rationality, aloof from full-orbed fact, can superciliously ignore.

But there is a secondary and quite different concept, also named substance, which became amalgamated with that of a perduring, acting, individual, whether person or thing. Primitive experience distinguished between a specific thing, such as a bow, and the relatively indeterminate stuff of which the bow and many other things could be made. This notion was derived from things and read into the self, so that spirit was understood as breath or matter. Assimilation is here inverse: an instance of the give and take between objective and subjective in the subjective-objective construction called knowledge. Science has been quick to mark the shortcomings of the animism involved in applying substantiality, as predicable of the soul, to material things; it has been slower to observe similar incongruity in the application of substantiality, in the secondary sense of stuff, to selves. Hence primitive dualism and later tendency to materialism proceeded unrebuked. It is from this relatively abstract conception of stuff as underlying the thing, that the notions of substance in antithesis to accident, of substratum or invisible cement beneath a mosaic of qualities, and of the permanent as incompatible with change, were in time derived. A notion suggested or called for by material things, and eventually developing in the direction of abstract identity, immutability, inertia, came to be applied to souls or subjects whose essence consists in activity and the real duration that is presupposed in change and gives content to time. Things so disparate seem to have come to be embraced under one concept, for no other reason, forsooth, than that both alike are logical subjects.

Of these two primary meanings of substance, it is the second, in its abstractly developed forms, that philosophy, on becoming critical and clamorous for the clear and distinct, convicted of being a confused, ignorance-cloaking and superfluous notion. In getting rid of it, many philosophers think they have dispensed also with the quite other concept of substance, which was first mentioned. Substance, as unknowable substratum, can well be spared; for by resort to it we do not attain, as used to be hoped, to greater certainty of knowledge concerning things or subjects: but the concept of *a* substance remains indispensable. It assigns the *ground* of the conjunction of particulars, which resort to logical concepts, such as class or series, simply ignores. It is the determinedness, as to order, of our sensa, not they themselves or their mere occurrence (which might conceivably be fortuitous but is not), that suggests and calls for an interpretative concept. Thus the concept is not fashioned by the mind itself without objective call.

Cause.

Substance, it has been maintained, is a category with which we cannot dispense unless, in endeavouring to be rational (*begreifen*), we become fools, or sink to the level of "no understanding" (*verstehen*); and this category involves that of cause. The soul, which is the source of the 'real' categories, is immanent, or intransitive, cause of its own states and of acts, such as attention, that do not produce effects in the not-self; it is mainly on that account called a substance. Logically, we may distinguish between a subject and its activity, and make of its activity a new *logical* subject. But this is only a verbal device or a conceptual distinction; psychologically or actually, any separation of them is impossible. Neither subject nor activity is separately presented: "we are, being active". It is, however, by means of this verbal device alone, to the like of which all psychologies fain to dispense with soul and subject are ultimately due, that Hume was able to deny power or action to the subject, and to repudiate the common belief that subjective activity in volition is the source of the causality that we read into things. We have not come "by habit" to conjoin will or subject with mind or states and effects; the subject and its acts, etc., as effects, were never cognised separately in sequence, or in need of conjoining. Indeed immanent action, properly so called, is not resolvable into efficient and transeunt action; the transeunt action between parts of one system were better called internal than immanent to the system, unless we spoil an indispensable and univocal term. Action, then, is not exclusively effectuation. But it is action of the latter, transeunt, type, that is involved in the primitive notion of cause; as when we say the lightning causes or produces the thunder-clap. Such a concrete statement is an instance of the use of the causal category and, as such, is to be distinguished from use of the postulate, 'every effect must have a cause'—the non-empirical principle of causality—and from the empirical generalisation, 'like causes produce like effects'—the causal law. This category of cause, as Ward has observed, is not furnished by such functions of thought as are involved in formal logic, independent of time; nor by the modes of time which are independent of logic; nor by any imaginary 'schematism' of the two: but by our own doing and suffering. There is no direct apprehension of the causal nexus between lightning and thunder, as there is of their temporal succession. This last truth, and the further fact that the notion of cause and effect has some kind of subjective origin, and is then projected by us into things, were discerned by Hume. But he erred in thinking that association, arising out of repeated observation, determines us to attribute causal determination to things. He erred, partly because he confounded inquiry as to the origin of the category with inquiry into the ground of causal inference; partly because he was unconscious of twice invoking the idea of objective determination, in order to get it resolved into the only kind of subjective determination that he could sanction.

Attribution of causal nexus does not always wait on accumulation of instances; nor is it always the case that constant sequence obliges us to leap from *post hoc* to *propter hoc*. Hume's derivation being on these grounds abandoned, and the old associationism having become obsolete, psychology can now suggest no possible origination of the category of efficient cause, save that of projection, into the not-self, of what we experience when acting and acted upon. Effectuation is an ultimate, the notion of which could no more be forthcoming, unless the process were *erlebt*, than that of blue, unless blue were sensed. It is not analysable, though the concept of it is complex. In this sense it is unintelligible or alogical. Hence Lotze sought to resolve transeunt interaction into immanent causation; but that is equally unintelligible, in the same sense. Again, inasmuch as efficiency is not observable in things, and as activity in ourselves is no logical warranty of transeunt action between other things, the notion is discarded by physical science in its higher stages, when science is (ψ), but not (ps), non-metaphysical. That, however, has no bearing on the actuality of effectuation in experience; and transference of causation from selves to things, is admittedly analogical and interpretative.

There is another notion involved in the anthropic category of cause, besides efficiency of subject. It is that of necessitation of the effect, derived from the experience of effort, when we make a thing take the shape we want, and of being ourselves sometimes coerced. This, again, we read into things; but we have no evidence that they feel effort or constraint. Refining, somewhat, our anthropomorphism, we affirm causal connexion or determination when we observe conjunction or sequence, without explicitly imaging it in terms of effort. Now the conception of such determinedness of one phenomenon by another, or of dependence of one event on another, is less easy to dispense with than is the imagery in terms of which it was primitively expressed, or than the notion of efficiency. Science may ignore it in her expositions; but her very existence presupposes the apparent fact, as does all her experimentation. The concept of constancy of sequence may not logically imply that of necessary connexion or determination; but the fact of constancy of sequence, and of the non-emergence of effect unless the cause be forthcoming, bespeaks or suggests a sufficient ground. As reasonable men, we cannot dispense with the causal category as thus expressing determination of one event by another, whatever we may do as rational logicians. Our 'real' categories, let it be again insisted, are means to "make us wise", not as skilful workers of logical sums, but in respect of *savoir faire*, and as understanding the world so as to live on terms with it. And the understanding, of which they are categories, is not Kant's fiction of that name; it is the faculty, conative as well as cognitive, that man Actually possesses and uses. When we adopt the anthropic category of cause, we may be contenting ourselves with analogy where we cannot have logical cogency: with the 'regulative' where no 'constitutive' function is forthcoming. But if one then speaks "as a man", one at least knows what one is doing and what one is talking of. This is not the case when popular science speaks of laws of Nature having necessity; nor perhaps when science—whether above board or beneath—invokes the *apparently* non-anthropomorphic notion of determination, such as is not causal in respect of efficiency and compulsion. Logistic philosophy avoids talking of it knows not what, by not talking at all; it shelves causation, as such, and changes the topic of conversation to that of temporal sequence, deterministic systems, or anything but the aspect of the facts with which the causal category is an honest attempt to cope. Lastly, rationalism committed itself to identifying *causa* with *ratio*, effectuation with implication. But interactions between Actualities are not identical with logical relations between forms of propositions; and there is no implication between happenings. It is only after experience has revealed Actual connexions, that logic has any propositions to manipulate, and that its deductions are applicable. Then *causa* and *ratio* become *interchangeable*, in so far as such applicability obtains.[1]

The functions of the 'understanding', or more correctly, of 'the mind itself', that have as yet been examined in the present chapter, are not directly exercised in the process that is generally referred to when we speak of thinking. These forms and categories are rather instrumental to thought, in that they effect the experience-organisation presupposed by common thought-knowledge, and constitute or construct the Objects which presumptive knowledge takes or accepts, as its data. Certain others from Kant's list of categories have also been discussed, in various contexts, and it is not necessary to examine his table exhaustively. We have seen that these functionings cannot be ascribed to the mind itself (*i.e.* to the subject), as prior to experience, or in abstraction from the objects with which, in all experience, subjects are in *rapport*: they are evoked and also tolerated by the objective, not simply brought to it and thrust upon it. Of these forms some, viz. the formal categories, are 'reading off' with immediacy and necessity; others, viz. the 'real', are 'read in', and are of the nature of 'supposition' rather than apprehension of 'position'. The former categories, etc., yield knowledge of relations, characterised by univer-

---

[1] For a discussion of the various meanings which 'cause' has come to bear, and of the causal law and causal principle, Appendix, Note J may be consulted.

sality and necessity, such as belongs also to analytical judgements and to the judgements of individual sense-perception of the here and now. But they are far from sufficient for the forthcomingness of necessary and *a priori* scientific knowledge. Hence there can be no such thing as strictly 'positive' science, if that means impressional data knit together by nothing but formal relations. The individual subject's sense-knowledge is blind; the formal that may be universal is empty. Science, as conceived by Kant, must consist of synthetic, not analytic, propositions, with concrete content as well as *a priori* form. And in the light of our examination of the 'real' categories, therein involved but superfluous to pure mathematics, it appears that there neither is, nor can be, such knowledge: that desideratum is humanly unattainable. Our knowledge of the external world is, from its very foundations, a matter of more or less precarious and alogical analogy rather than of self-evidence; of hope and venture that have been rewarded. Its certainty or necessity is practical not logical; its exact intellectual status is that of 'probable' belief. To Hume's question, by what *logical* right do we derive universal judgements of fact from the impressions of individual experience, the answer is: by none whatever. And if, as Kant's theory implies, our minds make the Nature which they do not create, we have seen that the making is not done by pure forms of pure understanding—which is a fictitious abstraction—but by cognitive functions inseparable from interest, conation and will. So much of truth in voluntarism, humanism and pragmatism, seems to be psychological fact beyond gainsaying. Postulation underlies what is wont to be called axiomatic in deductive and inductive logic; and anthropic assimilativeness is involved in the very conception of an ordered world of interacting and mutually determining things in space and time.

4. THOUGHT AS THINKING-PROCESS.

From this consideration of the preliminaries of thought and knowledge we may pass to investigation of the thinking-process. By 'thinking' is here meant thinking about Actuality such as is conceptually constructed out of the impressional by the forms and categories; and something quite other than manipulation of the product of thought by syllogistic or other logical methods or ratiocination. Thinking of that sort is but a small ingredient in the processes by which knowledge of fact, and of relations between facts, is established by a thinker. No amount of comparison of ideas, or of judging by concepts, can suffice for the grounding of true or valid premises on which logic may subsequently operate.

Thinking, in fact, is experiment. It is a seeking for something often vaguely preconceived; search for a clue that has to be found and is not immediately espied but, like the answer to a riddle, is known when found. It is the solving of a problem of some sort. It is a means to an end: a continuous developement out of trial and error, under the impetus of practical needs, and largely unguided by considerations as to logical ideals of what it ought to be. Locke's definition, the perception of agreement or difference between ideas, is far from the truth. Thinking is not observation; nor is it merely logically relating, whether deductively or inductively. If it were, every university should teem with Newtons and Darwins. Thinking is a continuation of the same process as that in which the free image emerges out of the sense-bound image or the preperception. It is not observation of finished products, but the experimental producing of the products. Instead of pursuing the logical one line, thinking pursues many. It is discursive; and, paradoxical as it may at first sight seem, it is mainly alogical. Darwin's sagacity and insight consisted in imagination and association of ideas, such as enabled him to see significance, analogies, etc., which the ordinary naturalist, with as much travel, observation and reading, would fail to detect. It is the psychologically conditioned excursus along lines of *association* of ideas, not the logically conditioned confinement to the line of implication of propositions, that a thinker follows, whether he be genius or mediocre man. Emotional excitement, by quickening the associational flow, may do more to procure a successful issue, other things being equal, than may correct knowledge as to syllogism and fallacy. It is not until the goal is reached, that the associative procedure is exchanged for logical connexion. The thinker works like the detective; starting from a central idea or a clue, he is led, it may be, by chance associations, into many experiments or ventures that, actually indispensable for success, are ultimately seen to have been logically superfluous. It is only as the relevance of one item is established, that other items can be discarded as irrelevant. Indeed thinking, and especially scientific thought, consists essentially in elimination of the irrelevant *ad hoc*. As one line of association is opened, others are closed; as one is closed, others are opened. It will be seen that inattention and obliviscence are involved in successful thinking or discovery of fruitful combinations of ideas, as well as concentration and retentiveness in other directions. Ceasing to attend to the irrelevant, or non-interesting, is one aspect of selective pursuit of the salient, the suggestive, the significant.

The process of thinking, then, is one of shrewd guessing, of making mistakes and following blind paths before hitting on the right road, of entertaining things hoped for before grasping their substance. In so far as by thought or reason we mean discovery of valid premises as to matter of fact, reason is an alogical, as well as a logical, process. The finished products of thinking, the clear-cut and non-ambiguous concepts concerned only with the point and purpose in hand, and stripped of all irrelevant associations and reference to side-issues, the terms with which alone logic can work, are the outcome of a process that involves much more than logic and observation. Just as sympathetic *rapport* between persons, and interpretative ejection of ego-qualities into things, *i.e.* understanding of quite a different kind from that which Kant sought to distinguish from what he called reason, enter into the constitution of all our knowledge, so are alogically determined, or associational, mental processes involved in fruitful thinking. There is a kind of understanding (*verstehen*) that science cannot understand (*begreifen*), nor logic control and schematise, but which none the less has place in 'reason' in its wider, more usual and useful sense. If only we could wholly interpret the world through and through by its instrumentality, as of course we cannot, we should accomplish far more than a complete scientific description, logically concatenated, would put within our grasp. Ideas that are unintelligible, in the narrower and strictly logical sense, cannot be accepted by science nor be scientifically used: but facts that are in this sense unintelligible, may be so, just because in the other sense they are best understood; and logical manipulation, without discursive, experimental and associational thinking process, would be but a barren and feeble kind of rationality. If thought be the seeking of identity in diversity—and scientific thought is essentially that—its character is ultimately to be explained by the fact that the human soul and its mind are functional unities with diversities, and in that capacity are the source of all our categories. Knowledge is a relating of impressional data to the embodied soul and to the mind's demands. The 'real' use of the intellect, which we have already begun to distinguish from the merely logical use, is determined by what the subject, or soul, is. Thus we cannot know things nor acquire truth about them, independently of the relation of them, or of ultimate Reality, to our minds. The only truth accessible to us is human, because humanised, truth; and the world is only intelligible when interpreted in terms of what we have learned ourselves to be. This fact has already been insisted upon in connexion with the anthropic origination of the categories, and the synthetic work of the understanding in constituting Objects and World out of impressional objects and immediately intuitable relations: it will be more abundantly illustrated when inductive thought, the characteristics of which have as yet been but vaguely and incidentally foreshadowed, shall receive our fuller consideration; and when the continuity of understanding and reason, which Kant separated without psychological warrant, shall have been exhibited.

Meanwhile, something may be said as to the logical element which, if genetically secondary, is epistemologically indispensable to thinking process such as shall issue in science. It is to be said, not in the way of exposition of the rôle of logic as such, deductive or inductive, but by way of indicating the dangerous side of the treatment which concepts, or finished products of thinking-process, receive at the hands of logic. The understanding, in the narrow and technical Kantian sense, is concerned with but the sensory data of individual experience. It combines them in various ways, by means of its forms and its several categories, into what are data for common Experience and for a higher order of recipient, viz. the individual raised to the common point of view. But in thinking, as distinguished from such intellective synthesis, and as it is described by the older formal logic, one category alone, that of whole and part, becomes dominating. Judgement becomes solely comparison—of concepts; and comparison in one sole respect, viz. logical inclusion or coincidence, extension apart from intension. The categories or 'forms' of the 'matter' of thought, other than this of class-inclusion, are left out of account; and they have been shewn to arise not by abstraction, as logicians once believed, or even logomorphically—to use a word of Ward's coinage—as Kant maintained. Useful as this self-limitation of logic is, it is a severe restriction as to scope and adequacy, when thinking-process is concerned. Not every judgement is a comparison of ideas: not every judgement, consisting in comparison, involves but the one ground of comparison, and the one kind of category, to which the old logic confined itself. Logic, moreover, tends to resolve all concepts into class-concepts or substantive-concepts; it needs must do so when, however adjectival be the entity for discussion, it is made the subject of a proposition, receives a name, and is taken—even if it be an attribute or a relation—as a unity characterised by attributes, an S which is P. Logic, in fact, often needs to reify abstractions. This is harmless enough, as verbal economy and methodological device: it is pernicious when taken seriously and realistically, as it often has been, for purposes of metaphysic. Language, which is a necessary condition of all developed conception and thought, is unfortunately also a collaborator with logic in engendering hypostatised nonentities or reified abstractions. A word, once invented as a symbol for an ideal complex, is apt to be taken, not only to have intrinsic meaning when abstracted from the context of thought in which it originated, and to possess no other function than that of intrinsic meaning, but also to necessitate, by its forthcomingness, the existence or Actuality of the conceptual abstraction which it connotes: the fixed names employed by logic and language then become sources of philosophical superstition.

This observation, however, is somewhat by the way. It is more relevant to the present purpose, if less practically important, to remark that in the older and traditional formal logic, which takes S is P as the formula of simple judgement in general, and defines judgement as recognition of agreement and difference between concepts, thought is made consistent and its logical concatenation evident—ends desirable enough in themselves—at the expense of our being told nothing whatever as to the matter of thought, or as to the various forms of such matter. Yet this is of moment for psychology and science. Nor are we assured as to the validity of either premiss or conclusion: which is of chief moment for science and epistemology. The clearness brought into thought and knowledge, by formal logic and its attitude towards concepts and judgements, is certainly not to be decried. But it is somewhat illusory, in view of the fact that thought is first narrowed down to one specific form, the other forms being kept out of sight.[1]

It has now been shewn that the contribution of 'the mind itself', in what we call knowing and thinking, is not resolvable into acts of a purely cognitive faculty, such as may function in independence of conation. In so far as understanding consists in synthetic construction of phenomenal Objects out of sense-impressions, it uses, over and above formal categories, the 'real' categories which bespeak analogical symbolism, reading-in rather than reading-off. Both the plain man and the physicist are unconsciously poets. In so far as understanding further consists in judging, the process which supplies finished products and premisses for logical method to operate upon, is again largely alogical. Thinking is more than perception of formal agreement, etc., between ideas; it is intentional and teleological as well as intuitively cognitive.

5. REASON.

Used in their broadest sense, inclusive of all kinds of thinking-process, 'thought', 'understanding' and 'reason' are synonyms. These words also bear more restricted meanings, as to which more shall be said presently; but when *homo sapiens* is said to be a rational being, it is a more general capacity for discursive thinking than that involved in logical ratiocination, that is ascribed to him. That reason or understanding is the only instrument for acquiring truth and judging beliefs to be true or false, in any sphere of knowledge or opinion, is a statement to which all people of common sense, and perhaps all philosophers, would subscribe: so long as the meaning of 'reason' is left conveniently vague. And ambiguously enough has the term been used throughout philosophical and theological literature. Its signification has varied from common shrewdness to a highly and sometimes arbitrarily differentiated faculty; from the framing of a working-hypothesis

---

[1] Chaps. XII and XIII of Ward's *Psychol. Principles* have been freely used in the foregoing paragraphs.

to infallible intuition of the axiomatic or self-evident; from logical computation of agreement or difference between ideas, or between the forms of propositions, to the experimental discovery of matter of fact; from the conceiving of identity, everywhere we perceive variety, to any activity having an end in view or a moral motive behind it: it has meant the fashioning of clear and distinct ideas, the apprehension of universals and of eternal verities, the search for the ideal unification of all knowledges, the transcending of antinomies or of contradictions, and various other things.

Obviously the word 'reason' is worse than useless for philosophical purposes, till some specific and definite meaning is conventionally given to it. Some philosophers, e.g. Locke,[1] have employed it in a comprehensive sense, to include several of the kinds of activity just enumerated; others have favoured restriction: e.g. the pre-Kantian rationalists, whose usage shall be considered presently, the deists, Kant, and Coleridge. Roughly speaking, the words 'reason' and 'rational', as used in ordinary discourse and sometimes in philosophical literature, combine two essentially different types of signification; and it shall be submitted that Kant drew the line between them at the wrong place. These significations can be indicated, with sufficient approximativeness, by pointing out the difference between the 'rational' (in the sense of formally logical) and the 'reasonable'. The one is associated largely with the teleological and alogical, with the principle of sufficient reason, with induction and 'probable' belief, with satisfaction of conation: the other solely with coercive and deductive logic, with the principle of contradiction, with the requirements of pure cognition.

These two distinct and largely antithetic significations are included in one word, when we glibly talk of human reason or of the rationality of the world, without knowing or caring precisely what we mean. An analogous disruptiveness potentially exists, as we have found, in the understanding, as conceived by Kant. It is this fact which vitiates his particular delimitation of reason, as regulative, from understanding, as constitutive; and robs of its sting his polemic against teleology. The understanding, in so far as it gives 'real' categories, for introducing unity of form into impressional data and thereby constituting the phenomenal Ob-

[1] See Appendix, Note K, on Locke's usage of 'reason'.

ject, is already interpretative or regulative; and this characteristic of all human knowledge enters into it earlier than in the establishment, by 'reason', of unity among the rules of the understanding, and before the transcending of knowledge of the 'objects of experience'. Conversely, Kant's 'reason' is *as* constitutive as is his 'understanding'. It does not, like understanding, operate directly on sense-data; but it presupposes the work of the understanding which does, and which in part does so but regulatively. The belief and reasonableness provided by reason, as concerned with the world as a whole and with knowledge as a totality, does not outstrip in venturesomeness, save in respect of degree, the knowledge and rationality which Kant supposed to be mediated by the understanding. His distinction between understanding and reason, knowledge and belief, is thus psychologically arbitrary and unwarrantable. There is continuity where he would see a breach. The actual breach occurs between his formal and dynamical categories of the understanding, the latter of which have much more affinity with his 'ideas of reason' and with the category of end, than with those which yield the pure and deductive sciences.

Kant diverged from the rationalists as to usage of the word 'reason', in maintaining that reason does not yield certain knowledge. Reason, as he conceived it, does but round off and unify our knowledge, by invoking the unknowable and by supplementing knowledge with belief. The rationality which it thus seeks in the world, is itself but an ideal. Dogmatic rationalism, the "muddy stream of bad metaphysic", involved, in his opinion, an abuse of reason, in that it falsely identified reason with understanding. Reason, however, according to Kant, deals but regulatively with questions which the understanding raises, but cannot answer because they lie beyond its scope or bounds. We may fairly interpret him as implying that reason satisfies a demand that is reasonable, and satisfies it reasonably, but not rationally. We are now able clearly to see that reasonable belief does not begin where Kant thought positive knowledge and understanding ended. The knowledge of Nature which Kant mistakenly regarded as characterised by universality and necessity, is shot through, from its foundations upward, with regulative belief. He failed to entrench in Newtonian physics the rationalism that he had expelled from psychology and theology. If reason be so defined as to include acquisition of knowledge of fact and discovery of truth, it contains an alogical element as well as the *ratio* that is alone involved in deductive logic and ratiocination; and reasonableness is something quite other than formal rationality. Its essence is teleological and conational, interpretative and analogical. And there is no science of Actuality, of any kind whatever, from which alogical reason can be strained out. The physics in which there is "so much of science as there is of mathematics", is at least as remote from human ken as the metaphysical psychology and theology, of which dogmatic rationalism had dreamed before the age of Hume and Kant.

We may pass from the specific and definite sense in which 'reason' was technically used by Kant, to the other outstanding conception of reason that is restricted, rather than promiscuously general, viz. that of the rationalistic school. Reason, as conceived by rationalism, is a different faculty from that described by Kant; its nearest equivalent in his system is the understanding, as source of the formal categories and as instrument in deductive ratiocination. Rationalists of different ages, and even of the same period, have differed in their teaching as to what the faculty of reason is, but have been fairly well agreed as to the output of the operations which they ascribe to it. It has been identified with reminiscence of antenatal experience, with direct vision of timeless truth in this life, with innate ideation or knowledge, and so forth. There are also variations in opinion as to whether the unique faculty, called reason, should be ontologically conceived as the functioning, of a rational soul, in which the essence of human nature is evinced, and the 'image of God' consists; as a God-inspired, as well as a God-given, human power; as a 'spark' of Deity, as the divine reason or Logos immanent in man, and therefore as a divine, rather than as a human, energising. With such opinions, however, we are not here concerned. More to the point, are the ancient Greek views that reason is contemplation of the Ideas, a faculty independent of sense and sole source of real (or the higher) knowledge; that the νοῦς ποιητικός is intellect independent of both body and animal soul, and a participation in the divine. Christian theologians naturally took over such teaching: Augustine applied it to explain the human reception of supernatural truth, and the divine illumination of the mind of man. Apparently it was from Augustinianism and neoplatonism that Descartes derived his conception of reason. Outdoing most theologians in zeal to magnify the divine and to belittle the human element, he stultified as a theologian the theory of knowledge that he had elaborated as a philosopher. For he taught that reason, though God-given, must bow to revelation authoritatively mediated, and accept it even when opposed to rationality; while his implication that the connexion of things in our world is due, not to their stable qualities, but only to the inscrutable will of God in recreating the world at each instant, involves refusal to human reason of capacity to fathom anything. From such implicit scepticism Spinoza recoiled to the opposite extreme. For him, God is practically Nature's rationality; and the adequacy of man's reason to read this rationality, is as necessary a presupposition of his system as his will-less God.

In spite of such diversity, between representatives of rationalism, with regard to the functions, scope and ontological status of reason, there is general agreement that what they respectively mean by reason, is a faculty *sui generis*. It is often called *lumen naturale*, however supernatural its origination. This natural light, invoked by ancient and modern philosophers and by schoolmen who came between them, has analogies with instinct, in so far as it is supposed to be innate and ready-made, either in perfection or in potentiality. But it differs from instinct, in that it is intellective, independent of sense, and non-continuous with understanding or with the common root. The existence of such a faculty, often supposed, as by Descartes, to belong in equal degree to all men at birth, is the primary assumption of rationalism. The assumption was natural enough, and indeed inevitable, before genetic or evolutionary sciences were born; before history came to its own; before the immense difference between individual experience and common Experience was discerned, and individualism could give place to a view rendered possible by knowledge as to the factor of 'social heredity'. Early rationalism was ignorant of the over-individual nature of its concepts, and so regarded ideas, etc., that we now know to be the outcome of intercommunication, as innate or as acquired by each person singly. Hence reason seemed to be a special creation, an original faculty, or a divine substance in man. Psychology finds that there is no such faculty. Reason is made, not born: an outgrowth of the understanding which has a common root with sense. There are no pure sensa, nor any sense-perception that is not implicitly conceptual; no pure forms of intuition devoid of matter, no matter of thought without form; no understanding in the formal sense, *i.e.* no intuitive induction (the only 'rational' apprehension that is immediate as sense) without impressional data, in the first instance; nor any understanding, in the sense of use of 'real' categories, apart from conation and ejection; no pure and ideal science that does not arise by abstraction from, and idealisation of, the originally *in sensu*, nor any knowledge of Actuality that is not interpretative or anthropic; no deductive physics that is not at bottom suppositional and grounded on induction, and no induction that does not transcend logical computation by assuming the indemonstrable, the hoped for and the unseen. These conclusions have already been approached, by argument from the fact-data from which we set out; they will receive further corroboration when forthcoming theories of knowledge shall be reviewed. If they be sound, it will have been proved that *at bottom* there is no gulf between knowledge and belief, no separableness of developed cognition from conation, no distinction, that is not merely conventional, between understanding and reason. The only breach within the whole of the process that issues in human knowledge, is that between formal and 'real' categories, between where we read off and where we read in, between the logical and the alogical in reason or thought. That gulf is bridged but *actually*, and by the soul itself.

CHAPTER IX

Theories of Knowledge: (i) Rationalism and Empiricism

RATIONALISM.

Rationalism, in all its specific forms, involves more than denial that thought-knowledge is derivable from sense-experience. It is opposed to empiricism of kinds other than sensationism, and differs from the critical theory of knowledge founded by Kant, in which the rationalistic trend is at least as evident as the empirical. Both in the ancient and the early modern periods it was thought that knowledge, characterised by self-evidence and demonstrable certainty, was forthcoming, valid of the Actual world. The name 'Knowledge' was indeed bestowed only on what was deemed thus certain; no room was found, within science proper, for the presumptive knowledge or probable belief which, as a matter of fact, is all-important for the conduct of life. With rationalism, as with its opposite extreme, sensationism, the attitude was of 'all or none'. Universal and necessary knowledge, being underivable from sense or empirical observation, was said to be *a priori*, supplied by the unique faculty of the reason or *lumen naturale*, which was regarded as both genetically and functionally independent of sense. Knowledge, it was held, is thus spun from the mind itself, originating as innate ideas and truths, or as the result of operation of innate, if not perfected, functionings of the rational soul. Commonly associated with these tenets, was the assumption that ideas, in the old comprehensive sense of the word, are subjective states. Brought to the Objective, to the external (phenomenal) world supposed to be in no degree constituted by the human mind, ideas were held to be valid of it. Indeed one of the fundamental presuppositions of rationalism is, that the logical order and connexion of ideas is of the same kind as the Actual order and connexion of things: that *ratio* is *causa*. So the world was assumed to be wholly rational in the formally logical sense. The mind and the world are each a closed system, and they run parallel. The duality in unity of experience not yet being discovered, a dualism of world and minds was set up, verbally resolved by Spinoza into a monism of two aspects. The ultimate ground of this parallelism, and consequently of the validity of thought, was God; though how it was mediated by God, was conceived differently by Descartes, Leibniz and Spinoza. It was agreed, however, that our concepts have but to be clear and distinct, and judgements as to relations between them but to be self-evident, in order to yield thought valid of Reality. Indeed, validity sometimes came to be identified with consistency of the ideas, etc., with one another. In science of the Actual, no less than in pure mathematics, the sole arbiter of certainty was the principle of contradiction, or of incompatibility of the opposite. Leibniz diverged from rationalism of this purely intellectualistic type, in resorting to the further principle of sufficient reason, as ground of contingent truth of fact underivable from necessary truth of reason; but this rift was mended by Wolff. Reinstating the law of contradiction as sole sovereign, and deriving the other Leibnizian principle from it, this philosopher perfected the method of seeming to extract the Actual from the possible. The rationalism that was about to perish, was thus brought again to its perfection by the systematiser of the whole body of rational science or philosophy under the heads of psychology, cosmology and theology.

In this brief sketch of the general principles of the rationalistic epistemology, several dogmatic presuppositions have been indicated which, it shall presently be argued, are refutable by forthcoming 'knowledge'. Such ungrounded assumptions are those as to reason being a unique and original faculty, genetically and functionally independent of sense; as to its having provided any knowledge concerning the Actual, that is characterised by *a priori* universality and unconditionality; as to the rationality or purely logical intelligibility of the world; as to the mind being a closed system, capable of spinning concepts out of itself, which, without further ado, are to be regarded as necessarily valid of another closed system, the external world. Several of these presumptions are comprehended in the one false identification of thought with knowledge. Epistemology that has other than historical interest and value, may be said to have emerged with the recognition of the gulf of difference between these two products. Bacon, Locke and Leibniz had each contributed to prepare the way for Hume, who for ever placed the distinction in clear light by his investigation of the concept of causality; and Kant soon shewed more completely that though knowledge is preeminently thought, it is also much more. What rationalism had taken to be knowledge, turned out to be but thought. Its own method shut it up to concern only with *conditionally* necessary truth concerning abstract ideas, which is quite another affair than knowledge about the Actual, *i.e.* the 'historical', whose essential core is an irrational surd, or about Reality that is richer than thought. If Leibniz was the first rationalist of the modern period to renounce, from within, the sufficiency of rationalism, Kant may be said—if the bull be allowed—to be the first rationalist who shattered it from without. He discredited pure rationalism until Hegel revived it, transformed so as seemingly to present experience as a construction of reason, and once more identified the Real with the rational.

Rationalism, we shall find, went astray through turning a blind eye to the impressional or perceptual, and in assuming the rationality—in its own sense—of the world, for no other reason than that the assumption was to be desired to make it wise— again in its own sense: which suggests cold wisdom waiting on superfluous folly. When sense was again recognised and received its due—and more; when the actual was properly distinguished from the possible: the main problem of epistemology became that of accounting for such correspondence as subsists between the order and connexion of ideas, and the order and connexion of things.

These sweeping charges against rationalism are now to be made good by piecemeal examination of its structure. Therewith will be submitted reasons for the assertion hazarded at the beginning of this volume: that epistemology, such as concerns itself solely with the logical preconditions of the finished product of thought or knowledge, taken at its own valuation, with disregard of the genetic and psychological processes by which the product came to be what it is, and which are determinative both of its nature and its scope, is an unprofitable pursuit.

Rationalism, like any other theory of knowledge, is concerned to answer the several questions as to the origin, the nature, and the validity, of knowledge. These problems overlap, and the lines of their investigation are inextricably intertwined; but it may conduce to clearness of exposition, if so much of distinction as is feasible be introduced into discussion of them, and they be considered one at a time. By indicating the general attitude of rationalism to each of them severally, we may make a further approximation to an estimate of the theory before us.

Its account of the origin of knowledge has already been disallowed. We have seen that psychology is in a position to deny that there is in us individually, at birth, any such original faculty as reason, and to assert that no function that can be called reason, such as developes during life, can be evolved independently of operation upon the data of sense. Sense is ultimately or originally the *occasion* of all knowledge whatsoever; for without it the successive stages of perception, imagination and conception cannot be initiated. Sensatio is, from the first, incipient understanding, the germ of reason, as well as reception of impressions. Over and against the impressional there is, indeed, 'the mind itself', *i.e.* the subject, with its intrinsic potentiality of faculty and capacity, but not with perfected knowingness or rationality. Reason comes not so much out of, as through or by means of, sense. There is no ground for believing that, apart from sense-data between which subsistent relations come to be apprehended, universals are originally and explicitly apprehended as such. When universals are explicitly apprehended and receive substantival names, they do not thereby become endowed with existence independent of the percepts from which they have been abstracted, and of the thinkers who have performed the abstraction. Such ontologism is a groundless, a gratuitous or superfluous, and an unverifiable, dogma. It is a dogma that has been assumed by many rationalists and realists, and one about which in ancient, medieval and modern philosophy, controversy has centred. The facts out of which it has arisen, are (1) that in our world there happen to be things that in some respects are like, (2) that the human mind can concentrate attention exclusively upon some one aspect or quality of a thing. This element then becomes a conceptual Object, but not necessarily an isolated existent *ante rem*. That likeness exists, need be no more than a figurative way of saying that there are like things. Taken literally, it states more than the concrete facts call for; it is read into them, rather than educed from them. The resulting dogma concerning universals generally, is thus linguistically generated; a literalisation of metaphor. Man never knows how anthropomorphic he is, especially perhaps when he is an intellectualistic misanthropomorphist. To reject, on the foregoing grounds, the doctrine of the isolableness of substance and attribute, the substantival and the adjectival, is not of course to deny the *universale in re*, or its Objectivity.

If the ambiguous phrase *a priori* be taken in the primary sense that Kant imported into it, denoting what belongs to, issues from, is brought by, 'the mind itself' to sensa, then there can be said to be no originally *a priori* knowledge: only *a priori* capacities for knowledge when impressional data shall be presented. Even the forms of intuition, it has been seen, are not supplied wholly by the subject, nor imposed by it on wholly formless data. A judgement 'independent of' *any* (sensory) experience, is an impossibility. Without sensa as fundamenta, no objects of higher order can be established, no *a priori* synthesis can be elicited. There can be no apprehension of likeness, for instance, without data that are like. Thus there can be no knowledge that is *a priori*, or 'independent of' sense, if 'independent of' mean not presupposing actual sense-presentation; the *a priori* can only be the *factor* contributed by the mind itself, which is essential to knowledge but is not knowledge. Of course when experience is developed, and it is no longer a question of its origination, the elicited concept of likeness can be in the mind, or be thought about, without contemporaneous apprehension of like perceptual data: we can work sums without using counters. That is quite another matter. That the concept of likeness is *logically* and timelessly prior to the explicit judgement that this and that are like, is also true; but if the concept be called, on that account, an *a priori* condition of the judgement, it should be observed that '*a priori*' is now being used in quite a different sense from that with which we have hitherto been concerned. The phrase '*a priori*' will now signify some relation within truth: truth which has been derived, in the first instance, empirically or *a posteriori*, and not established by the mind itself, apart from sense. Concepts and universals, just because the impressional has been strained out by the mind in arriving at them or conceiving them, are in *that* sense 'independent of' the eliminated core—they are devoid of it—but not in any other. Knowledge about their logical relations will then no longer require resort to perception. Such concepts, however, are not existents in the same sense as are percepts, once they are abstracted from percepts; and whether truth about their logical relations— truth that is sometimes called *a priori*—ever amounts to 'knowledge', *i.e.* to truth valid of Actuality, it is obviously for Actuality, not for abstract thought, to determine. The abstract truth about relations of concepts and propositional forms, the sphere in which rationalism is most at home, shall later be examined. For the present we may confine ourselves to examination of the claim that such truth is necessarily knowledge of the Actual; and more especially, the claim that such pretended knowledge is obtainable by an innate faculty, capable of working apart from sensory conditioning or *in vacuo*.[1]

Continuing our gradual approach to a full comprehension of rationalistic theory, we may now advance another step by ascertaining, in outline, its doctrine as to the nature of knowledge. We have seen that perceptual cognition and inductive generalisation are ruled out of knowledge, as it is conceived by the rationalist. What he would bestow the name of knowledge upon, is not mediated by sense or by discursive thought thereon (διάνοια), but by immediate apprehension of self-evident, and consequently indemonstrable, yet necessary, axioms. From these, by use of logical principles, which are quite distinct from premisses or original axioms, theorems are derived that are characterised by necessity and by demonstrable certainty. Instances of this doctrine may be cited. Descartes regarded all knowledge as of one and the same nature, and held the knowing-process to consist in combining self-evident truths with other propositions, by steps, each of which is self-evident. His model was coordinate geometry. Spinoza presented his system in the form of theorems successively deduced from definitions of concepts taken, by himself, to be the presuppositions of all thought, and at the same time to be Real or existent. His model was Euclid. Leibniz had discretion enough to lack, in part, the rationalistic valour evinced by his predecessors. He is not so typical a representative of the school as his audacious disciple Wolff: he was a rationalist with reservations. In so far

---

[1] At this stage Note L may be consulted, dealing with the notions of *a priori*, necessity, contingency, etc., which are frequently involved in the discussion pursued in this chapter.

as he was rationalistic, his model was algebra. One may pass from him to Kant, who remained predominantly the rationalist, for all his contact with empiricism, and observe that he taught, in a work of so late date as 1786, the *Metaph. Anfangsgründe der Naturwissenschaft*, that only a rational or *a priori* theory of Nature deserves to be called science, so that empirical knowledge is only to be called so "in a figure". Again, in his first *Critique* he insisted that, whereas particular instances of physical law are gotten empirically, yet law, in Nature as known by us, is necessitated by our minds, which put it into the data.

The purer rationalists believed that reason supplied direct knowledge of the 'intelligible' world. Knowledge was neither of phenomena, nor of the noumenal through the phenomenal. What is known, is the world of archetypal ideas or essences, timeless truths of reason characterised by necessity: Objects existing independently of being known by reason, even if (as Augustine had argued) they must be Objects for a Subject, and so proved the existence of God. The first axioms were taken to be intrinsically necessary and self-evident; their consequential or derived theorems, to be formally deducible.

As for validity, in the proper sense of 'holding of Actuality', as distinct from that of internal logical coherence, it was *assumed*, as by Spinoza, that the order and connexion of ideas is exactly like that of the order and connexion of things; or it was held, as by Descartes, that the orders were made to correspond, by the Deity. Truth was generally conceived, as by Augustine, to be *adaequatio rei et intellectus*. God geometrises (Plato), or algebraises (Leibniz), so that the world is connected and ruled by immutable law, which reason can read as it runs.

We may now proceed to more detailed examination, and begin with the fundamental or underived premisses of all knowledge, as rationalism conceived it.

These are what have been called the axioms of the pure sciences. Their general characteristics are discussed in Note L, and need but be briefly mentioned here. Their all-important feature, with relation to our present purpose of inspecting foundations, is their epistemological underivedness. They must be read off with infallibility; and in order to be so read off, must be self-evident. But 'evidence' is an essentially 'epistemic' notion: it is relation to some knower. The particular propositions regarded by rationalists as having 'evidence *per se*', were those (ψ) evident to reason as it was developed and informed in their day: Descartes could take the scholastic causal conceptions as clear and distinct. Hence evidence, the notion of which seems nonsensical when reference to subjects is abstracted, has often been said to be but a criterion, by which necessary and underived certainty happens to be recognisable. Of necessary truths we have found, in Note L, two kinds: (1) intuitive inductions, which are valid of Actuality, and whose necessity consists in the external or objective compulsion, akin to that of sense-reception, of subjective recognition; (2) analytical judgements, whose necessity rests on the requisite convention that words and concepts shall serve only one use while employed in discussion, and is thenceforward a matter of logical identity or inclusion. The axioms of the sciences are not identical with the former class; it remains to inquire whether they are identifiable with analytical judgements. This would seem to be impossible; if for no other reason, because any judgement of existence is derived ultimately from sensory-perception, which rationalism excludes. An existential judgement is synthetic: an analytic judgement may have no reference to the existent. If, *e.g.* 'gold is a yellow metal' is to have application to things, gold must be a concept embracing 'perceptual' Objects of yellow colour, and not a concept such as, *e.g.* the instant or the philosopher's stone, which denote nothing Actual. Apart from such relevance to the empirical, a nominal definition is not a truth, but a convention; it cannot figure as a valid axiom, nor even as a principle of demonstration. The so-called axioms which form the alleged first premisses of sciences, appear to be of this conventional nature; and in these chosen primary definitions the whole theory thence derived, is contained. A definition, as Aristotle saw, never implies the existence of the defined; a nominal definition is but apparently made a real definition by means of the ontological fallacy, when not genuinely made one by finding empirical fact corresponding to the defined concept. Such was the case in the ontological argument for the existence of God; and again, though more veiled, in the sorites of Spinoza: God is a substance; substance is *causa sui*; *causa sui* exists by essence; therefore God exists in virtue of essence. Conceptual definitions only appear to yield axioms by masking postulates. They originate in our minds or in the subject, and could not do so without previous perceptual knowledge. The propositions which in the middle ages were called essential, and by Kant analytical *a priori*, are not immediately read by reason, nor underived. They depend on a nominal convention which is conatively conditioned, and on a judgement of existence which is sensorily mediated. So far from being eternal *verities* or validities, they only have significance—or are propositions—so long as the convention is retained, and when the existential judgement is derived from experience. That the angles of a triangle are together equal to two right angles, is a proposition that was wont to be cited as an instance of universal and necessary truth. As a matter of fact, its 'truth' depends on whether we define a line after Euclid, or after Lobachewsky: that is matter of selection, and of convenience for empirical physics. Such postulates, apart from empirical applicability, are neither true nor false; they are comparable with the rule of chess, that a bishop shall move only diagonally.

Take, again, the '*a priori*' truth that $2+2=4$. Inasmuch as numbers and numerical relations are in the first instance derived from percepts, the knowability of this truth cannot be said to be wholly independent of sense. The question, however, is rather whether, the numbers having been derived from things, the truth of the assertion of their relation is *a priori*. If *a priori* then mean independent of sense, it is so: the truth can be apprehended without counting four things. But whether the definition of positive whole numbers does not involve some postulation, then calls for consideration. In any case, the applicability of such *a priori* truth to perceptual things, so as to yield *knowledge* about *them*, will depend on the behaviour of Actual bodies, their persistence or annihilation. If all bodies behaved like drops of water, that $1+1=2$ would not be valid of Actuality; though, once numerical concepts are distilled from percepts, the relations between them would remain subject-matter for a *pure* science of defined, or mind-created, entities. It would not follow that numbers 'exist' as eternal Objects, independent of cognition, and ready for Actual things to 'partake of' them. Numbers and functions, however, have been supposed, even by writers who repudiate the *universale ante rem*, to constitute an order of subsistent essences, independent of being known or of our convention; as if mathematics discovered, not created them, as isolable; or as if they were apprehended by pure reason, and not derived by abstraction from sense-knowledge, supplemented by ideal construction or idealisation. This eternal realm seems to have been discovered by Pythagoras; Plato took it for the ὄντως ὄν. And, much as Dr Johnson argued the Reality of matter from its resistance to his foot, Malebranche maintained the Reality—*i.e.* the existence when not thought of—of these eternal Objects, from their resistance to a mind that would think them away. On this ground he asserted their priority and independence of our minds. What is thus independent, is not the entities, but the relations discernible between them. Why we do not so readily 'realise' imaginary, as distinguished from the natural, numbers, calls for explanation; and it has been somewhat harder to remain realistic since such imaginary numbers were invented. However, we can perfectly well explain the apparent independence of mathematical entities, and their compulsion of our apprehension and thought, once they are finished products of its activity. We may turn once more to the classic example of immutable truth, supposed to be independent both of Actuality and of human mentality: the proposition that the angles of a triangle are equal to two right angles. Its truth depends, not only on recognition of logical rules, but on choice as to notions and definitions: on restriction of the meaning of 'triangle' to that of 'rectilinear triangle', with a view to applicability to earthly bodies. That our minds are not wont to think about curvilinear triangles, or in terms of other than Euclid's definitions, is contingent fact; yet, apart from logical connexions, that is the reason why the Euclidean proposition seemed an intrinsically necessary truth. The compulsion ascribed to the eternal Object is but the force of familiarity with the sensible. If we set out from the definition of Lobachewsky, it is immutable truth that the three angles are less than two right angles. We are compelled by Euclid's reasoning, apart from its logical consistency, only because we voluntarily committed ourselves beforehand to his postulates, when we were free to choose others. We are not constrained by any timeless 'reals' independent of our reason; but by our free self-committal, by conatively determined positing of ideal Objects. Euclid's geometry is not pure, as rationalism used to believe. It could not have been constructed, had there not happened to be observable solid bodies to suggest it; nor could it have lent itself for mensuration, had the land been of the nature of highly fusible wax. But the truly pure sciences likewise originate in human conventions and ideal constructions; and when these are misread as axioms, or as necessarily and universally valid of the Actual world and all possible worlds, the nature of the pure sciences is misunderstood.[1]

Logic is in similar case with mathematics. It needs to adopt notions that are intelligible, in one sense of that ambiguous word, and which, just because in that sense intelligible or not nonsensical, though they are irreducible, are indefinable. Implication, the precondition of inference, is such an indefinable, involved in the logic of propositions. Logic also requires a number of indemonstrable propositions or "axioms", such as the three "laws" of thought in the older systems, or some ten as yet indemonstrable principles in the new kind of algorithmic. But as to these, we may say that there is no meaning in their indefinability or indemonstrability, when it is regarded by rationalism as, so to say, *per se*: any more than there is in self-evidence when similarly spoken of. Certain indefinables or indemonstrables being *selected* as basal for a given logical system, others may be derived from them; while if the latter notions be selected as basal indefinables, the former become in turn derivable. Save for the intuitive inductions mediated by perceptual experience, which are involved in the foundations of all logical systems, there is not, for any one such system, one, and only one, set of basal notions or propositions dictated by supposed intrinsic necessity. There are several; and one is preferred to another because of aesthetic simplicity, convenience for practical application, or some such alogical consideration. The three laws of thought may be taken either as ultimate or as derivable; and indemonstrables in general

---

[1] It should be observed that the words 'axiom', 'postulate', 'hypothesis', etc., do not indicate intrinsically differing forms of proposition. The same proposition may now be the one, now the other. They point rather the attitude of the thinker to a proposition. A proposition has the same form and content, whether it be derived or underived by subjects; proved, unproved or unprovable; guessed, and provisionally entertained as a guide, or immediately read off. Relations constituted by thinkers, are apt to be mistaken for adjectives intrinsic to propositions as Objects.

are such, only relatively to a certain adopted order.[1] What shall be taken for axioms, is matter of choice: so that the axioms are after all conventions, in so far as their priority, as distinct from their content, is in question. Modern logic differs from the older logic of concepts, in being founded on the consideration of individuals; and 'individual' is an indefinable. For logical purposes, an individual is whatever we *propose* to regard as one entity, identifiable and unique throughout a particular discussion. Whether there *are* any individuals in Actuality, is an irrelevance to pure logic; while the *idea* of the individual is a *sine qua non* for all definition and science of classes, relations, order, etc. Perhaps the principles of identity and contradiction, which are primarily conditions of thought, and secondarily become laws of things *in so far as things admit of being thought about*, fundamental and even all-sufficient for many rationalists, may be regarded as but expressing "rules of the game" we call thinking. They prescribe the convention that we will use words in the same sense, ideas with invariable connotation; that we will fix as static, for the particular purpose of thinking, the properties of a conceived 'thing', though perhaps there is no single existent thing that is

---

[1] We can at length conclude that all the characters—immediacy, derivedness, derivability, inferability, self-evidence, and their opposites—commonly spoken of as intrinsic to propositions, just as, *e.g.* sterility is intrinsic to some living beings and no matter of how they are mated, are subjectively constituted. To take such relativities for absolutes, to substitute single-term predicates for relations between pluralities of terms, to use elliptical phrases or abbreviations as if they were grammatical *res completae*, are linguistically engendered errors, which reveal themselves when we take the trouble to get behind words to their meanings. The involved ignoring of human subjects cannot be sustained.

What truths are immediate for *us*, as distinguished from the imaginable intelligent gnat or from omniscient God, depends on our time-span and *tempo*, the range of our discriminative faculties, what we happen to begin with *in ordine cognoscendi*, what we already know, perhaps on the temporary position of our threshold, and so on. We cannot escape from such psychological conditionings and contingencies. It has already been argued that self-evidence is necessarily conditioned by subjective reference, abstracted from which, it becomes a fiction or at least something that can only equivocally be called self-evidence. And perhaps enough has been said to shew that whether a proposition is derived or underived, is a matter of what origin, to use a mathematical metaphor, we select. If we adopt that prescribed by psychology as a science of the Actual, there is a sense in which we 'know where we are', though our origin is contingent and relative, not absolute. If we adopt others open to pure or abstract sciences, we but know that where we are, is where we have been pleased to put ourselves for the time being.

not incessantly changing. If so, these laws of thought are not *necessarily* laws of Reality also. Certainly many individual 'things' are but abstractions, when isolated from their environment for convenience of thought, and when the law of their inner being is ignored. The logical law of identity does not negate change. Even if these laws, as intuitive inductions, are formally certified, they are not premisses for metaphysic, but principles of reason*ing*. Entities that conform to the laws of pure logic, may not be Actual. And existents are not *a priori* bound to obey all our logical 'axioms': they are only so bound, in so far as they lend themselves to the designs of thinkers. The application of pure logic to things requires postulates over and above those needful for pure logic itself. These rationalism overlooked: *e.g.* that there is invariability in the ultimate elements of things, that these elements are discrete, and so forth. Dr McTaggart, to cite a modern representative of this school, argued that, inasmuch as we can know [know about] nothing by sensation apart from thought, any law for thought must impose itself on all Reality which we can either know or imagine; while to allow that the self-contradictory exists, is to inhibit all inference. But he did not assign an *a priori* reason why a world *must* be knowable by inferential logic. That our world does submit to mathematical and logical treatment, in large degree, and consequently admits of exploration and prediction within limits, is observable fact, but not *a priori* necessity. The latter view has obtained so persistently, it would seem, because of the perennial tendency to confound an abstraction, which by itself is not an Actuality, with a being of some higher order of 'Reality': the 'valid of Actuality' with the existent *per se*. Rationalism is largely logical realism; and its realistic aspect shall presently receive further attention.

The so-called axioms, or underived premisses, of the pure sciences, when not intuitive inductions, have been argued to be definitions or conventions; and, consequently, not truths or propositions proper, such as premisses should be. It must now be maintained that the 'axioms' of physical science, as it is rationalistically conceived, are disguised empirical generalisations, when not conventional definitions.

The parallelogram-law, as Dr Whitehead has remarked, is the chief bridge over which the results of pure mathematics pass, in order to obtain applicability to the facts of Nature. The law, as applied to forces, and as set forth by Newton, was empirically suggested; but zeal to exhibit mechanics as a deductive science, led rationalists, such as Daniel Bernoulli, to claim for this law a truth independent of 'experience'. Mach[1] has pointed out how this zeal deceived itself. He has shewn similarly that Lagrange's deduction of the principle of virtual velocities falls short of being a pure proof. Archimedes' demonstration of the principle of the lever, is another historical instance of a proof, involving empirical observation, being taken for one of *a priori* kind. Newton's laws, on the other hand, are partly conventions. Matter, defined as having nothing but movability and mass, is a definition akin to that of a point as having no magnitude, although it is the warrant for Kant's assertions, that there is only science where there is mathematics, and that hylozoism would be the death-blow to science. These laws are neither *a priori* nor altogether empirically derived truths. They are definitions in a conceptual scheme, and partly suggested by empirical fact. The latter conditioning is instanced in the first law, which, in implying that our differential equations shall be of the second and no other order, did but make use of Kepler's empirical laws of planetary motion, and ignored the possibility that quite another law might hold elsewhere. The second law of motion, in positing the doctrine of central forces, makes possible the deduction of principles of conservation and of least action, secures the timelessness of dynamical equations, and promises the reduction of physics to mechanics: it is therefore pregnant with import for rationalistic science. But the law applies rigidly to isolated systems alone: whether there are any such systems, or whether (as Laplace assumed) the world is one, is not knowable *a priori*. Again, then, a conceptual system is indicated, but no necessarily valid applicability of it to Actuality. Newtonian dynamics is not the pure or *a priori* science of Nature that Kant, less shrewd than Newton himself, assumed it to be.

The empirically familiar has over and over again been mistaken for the *a priori*, and inductions have been misread as necessary truths. The first principles of mechanics, the laws of equilibrium and of motion, during the seventeenth and eighteenth centuries, were commonly supposed to be axiomatic or deducible

---

[1] *The Science of Mechanics*, 1902, pp. 46 ff.

from the axiomatic; but the proofs have been found to beg what was to be proved, just as the axioms, on examination, turned out to be more or less applicable conventions. We have learned that science is only deductive at all, when generalisations have first been inductively established: then, indeed, further particular facts can be deduced and foretold. But science can only be thus wise, after the event of empirical observation of physical constants, etc. Its theorems are not deducible from such principles as those of contradiction and identity, nor from that of sufficient reason: not even from Newton's laws. Descartes professes to deduce his physics from an empty formula; but his 'deduction' consists in shewing that the laws are compatible with the principle, not that they are logical consequences of it. From the immutability of God and the divine perfection, or from 'some invariant' in Nature, he passes on, as if to an identity, to conservation of momentum; whereas quite other things than momentum would suit equally well. So Leibniz corrected him by substituting *vis viva* for momentum. Maupertuis rejected both these versions of the invariant that is conserved, adopting what he called 'action'; while later, Mayer and Helmholtz read it as energy. Nowadays physicists are relaxing hold of all of the numerous conservation-principles; and Poincaré believed that any such principle is a tautology. The general metaphysical dogma from which Descartes set out, will not yield his, or any other, particular theorem by mere deduction. Moreover it is *prima facie* equally compatible with atheism as with his theism. D'Alembert pointed out the futility of appealing to the inscrutable God, as the ground of particular physical laws; and it was perhaps he who, in an age in which God was the ultimate metaphysical concept of rationalistic physicists,[1] gave to science that atheous trend which became so conspicuous in the mechanics of Laplace. D'Alembert thought that physical laws were deducible from the concept of matter "left to itself", and that they were necessary truths; but meanwhile 'matter' has become as inscrutable as the God of rationalistic theology. The most abstract principles from which these professed deductions were made, have of course each an indefinite number of particular consequences: the one chosen as *the* 'necessary',

---

[1] At this time 'necessary' and 'contingent' commonly connoted respectively issue from the intelligence and from the will of God.

being, in each case of selection, the one that seemed to be required by the exigencies of the empirical. Spinoza's favourite method of surreptitiously reimporting the empirical into the abstract concept that had been distilled from it, yet was taken to be all-embracing, is usage of the word *quatenus*: by its apparently innocent means, he often bridges a logically impassable gulf, and simulates deduction. All first principles, from that of sufficient reason to Newton's laws of motion, are incapable of being premisses for deductive physics, until empirical research has established what circumstances and qualities are Actually irrelevant, and until it has ascertained, from brute facts, what the particular physical properties of bodies are. And then numerous intermediary hypotheses need to be invoked, in order to connect the various kinds of phenomena with the general dynamical laws of which they are cases.

It would seem obvious, with the history of physical science before us, that knowledge of Nature is not *a priori*, that physics is not a series of theorems deducible from self-evident axioms. Rational dynamics is as pure a science as metageometry; but mechanics and physics are empirical and inductive. The 'underived premisses' either are not premisses, because not propositions but definitions and conventions; or are not underived, because disguised empirical truths concerning sensible fact. It will not be necessary here to prosecute a similar criticism of rational psychology, which set out from an arbitrary and obsolete conception of the substantial soul; or of rational theology, which was founded on the ontological fallacy. Nor need more be said of the principles, logical and mathematical, by means of which theorems were deduced from the underived premisses, than has been remarked elsewhere. But if the alleged premisses of systems of necessary knowledge have been impugned, the necessity of the deduced theorems is *ipso facto* refuted. The premisses of knowledge concerning Actuality, are not eternal verities independent of knowers and of Actuality alike, as the rationalistic theory asserts. Indeed in earlier chapters we have seen that they emanate in individual perceptual experience, from which there is no transition to 'universal' knowledge, or to science of any kind whatsoever, save by way of conception and of anthropic interpretation of immediate data. The finished products of tentative thought, which rationalism took for unanalysable presentations, descended ready-made from the blue to be confronted by a ready-made rational faculty that reads them off with immediacy and infallibility, have already been found to be results of process: and of process involving other kinds of mentality than rationalism recognised. We have now to examine the realistic aspect of this theory of knowledge, whereby we shall discover the causes of the plausibility, for successive centuries, of rationalistic presuppositions.

It has been remarked by H. Poincaré, that realism is a theory of knowledge that expounds what science would be, were there no *savants*, or without the supposition that there were any. It has also been described as the theory that knowing makes no difference to [*i.e.* is not in any degree constitutive of] what is known; but the ambiguity of both 'knowing' and 'what is known', renders this pithy description somewhat vague. For present purposes it is enough to say that the realism on which rationalism relies, chiefly consists in the view that certain ideas and propositions exist or subsist, in abstraction from facts and knowers: thus constituting a realm of being that is timeless or eternal, and has 'Reality' of superior order to that of the sensible world. These Objects, being over-against minds or subjects (which is fact), are said to be also independent of minds (which is theory), as if fellow-members with minds, on the same footing, in one universe.

It has already been observed that the conventions that give rise to numbers, geometrical definitions, etc., being once generated by us, their offspring seem to live a life independent of us. They compel recognition of themselves and of their relations, just as a kicked stone compels muscular sensation. They often reveal properties that we did not expect and could not predict, and so suggest that they are not children begotten of our minds. These new properties, however, are derived from the original postulates. The 'logical *existence*' of mathematical and similar concepts, need mean no more than their constructibility, compatibly with the conventions which generate them, and their Objectivity when abstracted and attended to. It is a superfluous venture beyond fact, to assert their 'existence', save in this technical sense, or to endow them with being when not attended to, or not presented to subjects. Their logical priority to other presentations, does not imply priority of existence, or priority in rank of 'Reality', if 'Reality' denote, as it would here seem to do, a hybrid conception between existence and value. If they are *a priori* in respect of not being apprehended by sensatio, they are not *a priori* in respect of being apprehensible by reason alone, without—in the first instance, or before abstraction and idealisation—sensory occasion. There is no more reason, indeed, to affirm their independence of thinkers and thought-processes, than to allege that language existed before, and independently of, speakers: and a language, once formed, compels recognition of its syntax and idioms. That every idea 'exists', or has a counterpart that is Real as well as ideal, is dogma unwarranted by our knowledge as to how ideas are formed: and dogma that, at least in some cases, leads to conflict with knowledge of fact. But this realistic assumption is involved in the doctrine of the *universale ante rem*, and in rationalistic theory of knowledge, when it asserts a Real realm of essences. To cite an instance from another field: the same assumption is made when religious experience is said to reveal, or involve of itself, a "spiritual environment". That is to ignore all difference between a merely ideational environment, such as is Objective but not necessarily Actual, and an Actual environment over and above the ideational. What realism can rightly claim, is that concepts, such as the mathematical, are Objective, if ideal; hence their coerciveness for thought, once they are generated. What it unwarrantably asserts as dogma, is that all the (ideal) Objective is necessarily existent in independence of thinkers to give it birth. Every idea, even of a relation between terms, receives from us a substantival name for convenience' sake; and the human mind has ever been prone to regard as a substance, any such relation that has received a substantival name. Thus mass, which originally denoted a relation between moving bodies, became hypostatised into a quantity of matter; energy, into the world-substance; velocity, into a state of motion; value, into an intrinsic quality of Objects. The further assumption that to every word there must correspond a Reality, an assumption which ignores the origination and the function of words, engenders supposed indefinable Realities, such as absolute oughtness-to-be. Many nothings have thus found a name, and have appeared to usurp a place in the realm of Reality or Actuality. Language is indeed responsible for many illusions. Concepts derived from 'perceptual' Objects by elimination, in thought, of part of their Actual content, so that they become inadequate substitutes, save for some specific and restricted purpose such as the scientific, are often hypostatised into entities credited with "Reality" superior to that of the Actual context from which they have been extracted. Then what is not included in the resulting artifact, is denied a place in the Actuality: it is called mere appearance, and so forth. The features selected— *e.g.* mass—because, in a specific sphere of discourse, alone significant or relevant, become the 'essential', the primary, and even (as in mechanical ontology) the sole, features. The Object which is only what it is, in virtue of *rapport* with its environment, is conceptually isolated as a petty closed system. Aspects separately attended to but actually conjoined and inseparable, are endowed by imagination with separable and separate existence. And then the pseudo-problem of how to put together into a living whole the dissected members, engrosses minds that have wilfully and superfluously given it being. Thus, Leibniz's unrelated monads, as soon as born, begin to cry for pre-established harmonisation. A predicate having been abstracted from a percept when the inadequate concept was substituted for it, it becomes a puzzle how synthetic judgements *a priori* are possible. Abstraction of supposed things from the commercium, in virtue of which Actual things are what they are, creates the intractable causal problem, evokes Hume's scepticism, Kant's 'mind-legislation' for Nature, Lotze's world-ground. Suppositional antinomies produced by logic-chopping, have compelled resort to the inscrutable Absolute One, to effect, behind a screen of nebulosity, their reconciliation: and so on. Abstractiveness in thought is methodologically inevitable: to conquer, we must conceptually divide. But in putting asunder what God has joined together, which thought thinks it does when, ignoring its own approximateness and mere instrumentality, it proceeds linguistically to hypostatise convenient abstractions into immutable Realities, we may see the origination of many pseudo-problems. The Absolute One that has often been the issue of rationalistic philosophy such as pursues its thought without heed to the external control of the sensible, is useless for mundane philosophy, when found. For from it there is no deduction possible of the finite, the particular, the various; no explanation of the declension of its perfection into the imperfect; no sufficient reason for the specific nature of our world and what is therein, rather than for any other; no possibility of accounting for the illusion set up by the Absolute for the Absolute, in which our experience, which none the less arrives at knowledge of the Absolute, *ex hypothesi* consists. On the other hand, logical pluralism, which is another outcome of the same presuppositions and method, is equally irrelevant to our world. For Actuality defies analysis into conceptual entities and closed systems, of any degree of simplicity or complexity, other than as provisional, approximative instruments of thinking.

The faculty of reason, as invoked by rationalism, has been found to be mythical. The realm of *a priori* and self-subsistent ideas or truths, with which this faculty was supposed to be confronted, has likewise been submitted to be a creation of human ingenuity. It is not precarious theory or baseless dogma, but established fact, that human reason, in the broader sense in which it consists of logical and alogical ingredients, is a developement of a potentiality innate to the soul, and that this faculty cannot function, in its less developed state, apart from sensatio. Knowledge is grounded in sense-acquaintance; it is elaborated by functions which can be distinguished by the name of intelligence—the making of ideas, symbols, conventions. Beyond intuitive induction, the first office of explicit reason or understanding, the human mind displays no further invariable or universal architectonic. When we come to 'real' and interpretative categories of the understanding, selection, of those we have adopted, is largely determined by environment, in the widest sense of the word. The forms of our thought have been derived largely out of sensory matter. Such notions, when once familiar, seem inevitable and come to be accounted necessary in a logical, rather than a psychological, sense; found practically successful, they are taken as solely, universally, necessarily, eternally, true. But man is in the first instance anthropic, and in the second place he is embodied and environed; and his developed 'reason' is the outcome of interaction between his intrinsic soul-nature and the objective. Had he been placed in quite another sort of world, his geometrical and other apparently immutable *a priori* truths would have been different. The structure of our mentality is largely determined by the structure of solid bodies, and by the specific qualities and relations of the physical world. The truths which have been invested with necessity, and perhaps with bindingness for any possible or conceivable world, issue from conventions of our own creation, or else are generalisations of empirical discovery. They reflect the dependence of man's mental furniture on his physical and social surroundings, not their own independence of either the one or the other.[1]

This conclusion, of course, does not involve denial of the fact that mathematics and logic are in some measure applicable to the world of empirical fact. It rather means that there is no foundation for the belief that any world, in order to be, must conform to a *prius* of subsistent law, separable from things and knowable without empirical observation of their behaviour. In order that there be a scientifically, if but partially, knowable cosmos, there must be a relatively stable nexus of relations, likenesses and recurrences and so forth, rendering logic and mathematics in some degree applicable to some aspects of things. Such a world ours happens to be: there is no *a priori* necessity that it must be a rational cosmos as well as a world. And, as a matter of fact, the world is not rational—*i.e.* knowable by purely logical and mathematical intuition and ratiocination—through and through or without remainder. How far it is thus rational, is ascertainable only by means of experiment. If rationalism were true, experiment should be a superfluity, instead of a condition *sine qua non* of science. If exact science be science that measures or correlates facts with numbers, there is but a relatively small part of human experience and of natural knowledge that can be reduced to it. Moreover, as descriptive of what there is of it, the word 'exact' cannot have the same meaning that it bears when predicated of pure mathematics. Science deals with indiscernible differences, not necessarily with absolute equalities; and its exactness is but approximateness of high degree relatively to the range of vision, etc., in *homo mensurans*. There is plenty of clear and distinct knowledge that is not 'exact'.

[1] For several observations presented in the foregoing discussion, I am indebted to *Les paralogismes du Rationalisme*, by L. Rougier.

EMPIRICISM.

'Empiricism' is a less definite term than 'rationalism'. It is generally used to denote theories which deny the claim of rationalism to knowledge independent of sensory experience, and which repudiate the alleged faculty of pure reason as innate in perfected, or potentially perfect, form. In asserting that there is no knowledge that can be had without sensory experience in the first instance, empiricism is at one with the Kantian or critical theory, which aims at transcending both empiricism and rationalism by combining their positive, and rejecting their negative, tenets. The essence of the critical theory being that sense cannot yield knowledge, without elaboration through the forms or categories supplied by intellect itself from within, it might seem that empiricism, in order to be contrasted with 'criticism' as well as with rationalism, should mean repudiation of all formal factors supplied by 'the mind itself', by Kant's 'understanding' as well as by the pre-Kantian 'reason'. In this case, Locke, generally said to be the founder of the empirical school (forerunners such as Bacon and Hobbes being ignored), was not an empiricist. In spite of his doctrine of the *tabula rasa*, his "simple ideas" were by no means the only source whence he derived knowledge; on occasion, he invoked 'the mind itself' as much as a Leibniz could desire. Even Hume did not identify relations with sensa, however much he fell short of finding a sensory substitute for 'the mind itself'. If Hume is to be called an empiricist, and even a sensationist, it should be remembered that his fundamental doctrine of pure sensa, and of sensatio as passive reception, was not empirical, in the sense of being derived from experience, but a rationalistic creation of abstractive conception. It was not till after the passing of the pioneers of empiricism, in the vague historical sense of the word, that rigorous sensationism, or the mental chemistry of associationism, was developed: perhaps not before the paradoxes of recent presentationism and extreme behaviourism received ephemeral formulation.

In that, as an accident of history, empiricism has been associated with sensationism, it would seem that a fine name has been degraded to a low usage. It was hinted in the first chapter of this volume, that there is another theory of knowledge, or rather a method of pursuing epistemological inquiry, which may more aptly be called empirical. It is to set out from the only kind of fact or analysandum that is forthcoming before philosophical reflection begins; from what alone is other than of purely conceptual and possibly fictitious nature, and what, with all its need of critical sifting and analysis, alone *contains* the element of external control, the primary 'reality', by means of touch with which, science and philosophy can be differentiated from groundless and futile speculation. It is to abide by these facts, to let them speak for themselves, to search for their significance and to respect it when found: discarding all metaphysical predilection while seeking their implications, testing every analysis by recomposition of analytica, and, above all, refusing to manipulate linguistically derived nonentities—such, *e.g.*, as mental events that cognise others—instead of studying Actualities and their subsisting connexions. The *forthcomingness* of common-sense knowledge is the foundation-stone of this kind of philosophy: a stone which many builders have rejected. The *ordo cognoscendi* prescribes its method. Psychology is its first science, the propaedeutic to its theory of knowledge. To set out from common-sense knowledge on the assumption that in it, as refined by science that works with the self-same presuppositions not critically sifted, there lies to hand a *ratio essendi* known, so far as it is known, with anything like finality, and 'known' in a sense that stands in no need of being precisely ascertained, is to begin with ungrounded, albeit developed, metaphysic already presupposed, instead of with the all-determinative reality in which is first touched, if only at the fringe of its garment, the Reality that is the quest of metaphysics.

This method, for which the name of empiricism may be appropriated, has not been pursued, in purity and entirety, by any historical school or by any great individual master.[1] It has features in common with Locke's empiricism,[2] Kant's 'criticism',

---

[1] Empiricism such as characterises scientific method, but not explicitly grounding philosophy in psychology is, however, frequently advocated and pursued by philosophers. It is commended, *e.g.*, in Prof. Carveth Read's *The Metaphysics of Nature*, 2nd ed., p. 33: "We must begin with experience, since otherwise there is no problem; and return to experience, since otherwise no solution is made good; and proceed on the analogy of experience, since otherwise there is a failure of that continuity and resemblance in which explanation consists."

[2] Locke's psychological epistemology was inadequate, because he worked with the

recent humanism, and other types of philosophical adventure. Perhaps no individual philosopher of first rank has used it in greater measure than (implicitly) did James Ward; but whether he would have endorsed, in whole, the programme set forth above, is very doubtful.[1] Perhaps because this kind of empirical philosophy, genetico-analytical and pledged to the order of knowing, is especially concerned not to transcend the knowable scope of ideas when they are knowably valid of, or presupposed by, known Actuality; and because it issues in a definition of knowledge that represents knowledge to be interpretation: it will be disparaged as pedestrian. Pedestrian it is. It keeps a foot on *terra firma*; and it escapes the fate of Icarus.

It is in recognition of the nature and of the limits of knowledge of Actuality, that the difference of empiricism from rationalism fundamentally consists. Empiricism, as just described, can recognise that this world is largely ordered according to logic and mathematics; it denies that there is any *a priori* necessity about this state of affairs, and that the logicality is complete and exhaustive. In insisting on the alogical residuum that the rationalist can never absorb into his nexus of relations, and that may, from the standpoint of value, be the most significant factor in the world's constitution, empiricism does not become irrationalistic, in the sense of disparaging the rationality that rules in logic and mathematics: but only in the reasonable sense of asserting that, in anything that can be called knowledge of Actuality, much more than such rational thought-processes is involved. Whereas the critical philosophy recognised the alogically posited sensible matter of knowledge, which rationalism despised and rejected, and then rationalistically took all the rest to be *a priori* and akin to the logical and mathematical, the investigation of knowledge that has here been pursued, has issued in the conclusion that the very Objects known, the data of science, are already constituted such by 'interpretative' categories, aptly so called because due to give and take *between* man and his world of primary reality;

psychology of individual experience alone. There is now a psychology of common Experience, unknown to the British empiricists, but available to empiricism. By means of it, the apparent need of an *a priori* supplement to Locke's imperfect empiricism is done away, and certain tenets of rationalism may be shewn to be erroneous as well as superfluous.

[1] See p. 160.

that in all knowledge there is a kind of understanding, that is neither logical comprehension nor yet nonsensical, though alogical. And, as for the alogical in the external world, empiricism enforces recognition of it, when it insists on the impossibility of one and all of the following reductions or derivations, which rationalism has prided itself on making: the actual from the possible, existence from essence, qualitative diversity from identity, the qualitative from the quantitative, the finite many from the infinite or absolute One, the perceptual from the conceptual, the historical from the timeless, causal *rapport* from logical or from factitious relation, change from immutability.

The third historic type of theory of knowledge specially concerned with the question of the origin and nature of the knowing-process, viz. the critical theory of Kant and his followers, need not here be discussed; already its essential features, and some of its shortcomings in respect of consistency with now known fact, have been considered in previous connexions. It will, however, demand further notice when, in the next chapter, the remaining epistemological problem of the nature of the Objective element in knowledge, or *what* it is that is known by knowledge, shall receive attention.

CHAPTER X

Theories of Knowledge (continued): (ii) *Realism, Idealism, Phenomenalism*

1. It has been contended that epistemology, in order to be a *science* of knowledge or knowing-process, must set out from Actual, observable fact-data, and seek, in the first instance, their actual preconditions. It is only so, that we can ascertain *what* knowledge *is*, in all its stages from sense-perception to theoretical science and metaphysics; and it is only thus, that we can define the known scope and the relevance of ideas, the conditions of validity of propositions. It may similarly be argued that, though epistemology is not identical or coextensive with ontology, it is the sole approach thereto; that no theory about the nature of ultimate Reality, or what exists independently of the knowledge-processes of knowers, can be other than unverifiable speculation, unless it be grounded on results of inquiry as to what the knowing-process is, and what status is held by the respective kinds of 'objects' that are over against knowers, at the various levels of experience-organisation. Our only approach to knowledge of being, is through being, as known; and if we are ever to have an inkling as to what Reality is when out of the knowledge relation, we must ascertain the nature of the knowing-process, the factor that we would eliminate. However, the attempt to determine the Real by deducting all the contributions of mind, is, as we shall see, impossible in practice.

The epistemological theories discussed in the preceding chapter, are concerned primarily with the origin of knowledge and its psychological nature. There is another group of alternative theories, whose predominant interest is as to what it is that knowledge knows, the object known; its dependence on, or independence of, the knowing of knowers; and as to whether or not, or to what extent, knowing constitutes, or makes difference to, that which is known. Of course other issues are involved in the theories about to be considered; but those just indicated may be said to be paramount and most immediately concerned, in the doctrines called realism, idealism and phenomenalism.

It may be observed at the outset that the problems about to be discussed, are some of the most intricate with which philosophy has been concerned; and that the literature dealing with them is often bewildering. One chief source of confusion is the lack of distinguishing between individual and common cognition: another is the ambiguity of the word 'object', which has so often been used, even by the greatest masters, as if it had only one denotation. The impressional or perceptual datum apprehended in the sense-knowledge of private or individual experience (o), the conceptual 'thing' of collective or common Experience (O), and the noumenal or ontal Reality behind either (ω), have indiscriminately been called 'object' of knowledge. Consequently, statements are wont to be made about some one of these entities, that are only relevant to another; and about cognition of one of them, that are only applicable to a different type of cognition, pertaining to some other of them.[1]

2. Following, so far as expositional method is concerned, yet without begging thereby (as does common-sense realism) any

[1] An illustration will perhaps make clearer what is here meant. Dr Ward taught that in the process of examining a flower, attention, involving retention and fusion of residua with new sensa, alters the object; not only are differences apprehended, but new differences are produced by interaction between subject and plastic objective continuum. He here speaks, of course, of the psychological object, o. But his teaching has been challenged on the ground that attention does not generate the differences between stamens, pistil, etc.: the object, viz. the flower, is not plastic, nor do differentiation, retention, etc., take place in it. What the critics here call 'object', is obviously not o, but O: they are discussing another topic, on which Ward would completely agree with them.

Anticipating the argument of a later paragraph, one may observe at once that the o is not a supposed *tertium quid* between the subject and a certainly, or immediately, apprehended Real O. It is the o's of individual experience that are the sole primary realities: O is the *tertium quid*, and its Reality has little in common with reality. It is O that is in the first instance *supposed*, however convincingly the supposition be afterwards justified by its pragmatic fruitfulness. O is constructed or conceived in terms of o. It is a practically convenient interpretation of facts about o's; so that *the* world, for an individual subject, is a conceptual 'comprehension' of *his* world of sporadic percepts. The O is a half-way house between o's and the ω of which even O is so-called phenomenon. This ω, according to theoretical science, is a group of electrons; according to metaphysics it is, perhaps, a group of monads.

Similarly, to puzzle oneself as to how a real existent directly appears in sensatio to the individual, and yet does not appear as it really is, while it comes to appear more really and truly as conceptual thought about it developes, is to take the word 'real' as if it bore but a single sense, as well as to assume a particular theory of knowledge as established, which for us is at present *sub judice*.

ultimate question, the empirical or analytico-genetic kind of investigation and the *ordo cognoscendi*, we may set out from the first reached analytica of presumptive knowledge as to the simplest kind of individual cognition. There only have we ground beneath our feet, some sort of external control to keep us in touch with some 'function'[1] of the truth, and from being beguiled into fruitless discussion of our own fiction. In other words, the first thing to be examined, with a view to comparing the merits of the theories of knowledge now before us, is the actual relation of the individual subject to his sensory object: sensatio, simple perceptio or acquaintance. This examination has already been made to some extent in chapter III, parts of which may be re-consulted with reference to the present discussion. It was there found that the kind of object with which we are now to deal, is private; it may, therefore, henceforth be clearly distinguished by the term *idion*. As an irreducible part, isolable by attention, of the individual's presentational continuum, this is the simplest datum—or, rather, analyticum—of his experience. And an actual datum is a datum received: indeed a datum *as* received, if the statement be other than a pleonasm. The question here before the schools, is whether in receiving this datum, whether in the act of becoming acquainted with, say, a colour-sensum, the reception 'makes a difference', not to the *idion* or sensum—that is impossible, for the *idion* is what now *is* over-against the subject, as his object—but to some supposed or conceived thing *per se* which may be denoted by ω, and not by *o* (*idion*), and is grievously miscalled 'object' if that term have the denotation already assigned to it (*o*). Conceivably, the subject may "make a difference" to such an ω. Or, more precisely, he may directly apprehend an appearance of ω, in receiving, through *rapport* with ω, an *o*: just as one makes a difference to white paper if one grasps it with inky fingers, or, in the case of visual reception, one wears blue spectacles. Assuming for the present that there is an ω existing when out of cognition-relation, it is as yet an open question whether, so to say, the subject wears blue spectacles of which he has no means of being conscious, and whether ω is not blue but the subject 'blues' it

---

1 I have repeatedly used this word to express something *like* what is meant by it in mathematics. In so far as unlikeness obtains, the word 'version' might sometimes be more apt.

in the act of cognising it.[1] All we can know, is that the datum received is blue; or that ω appears blue, if it be colourless when not sensed. That ω *is* blue, that *idion* is identical with ω, that mental vision is 'through plate-glass' and makes no difference, is an assumption for which there is no more basis, either in (ψ) immediate apprehension or in (*ps*) introspection, than for the opposite statement. Direct knowledge on the issue is precluded; and opinion can only be tested, if it can be tested at all, by remoter consequences and compatibilities. If a subject and an ω, the potencies of both of which, when not in the *rapport* constituting cognition, are *ex hypothesi* unknown and inscrutable, cooperate in producing an *idion*, we obviously have two or three unknown quantities on our hands, and but one equation between them. Realism and its alternatives here alike ignorantly guess; the only scientific question is, which guess is subsequently justified. The only items of fact relevant to the direct issue, it would seem, are that the effective intensity of a sensum is partly conditioned by degree of attention; and that in cases of negative hallucination produced by suggestion, there is no sensatio or sensum, when presumably there should be an ω in *rapport* with the subject. The datum, o, seems thus far to be constituted by subjective activity. If so, we can never catch or isolate a 'pure' datum. What comes into—*i.e.* before—'the mind', depends to some extent on the mind's tension; so that the mind is comparable to a slit in an elastic pouch, rather than to a slot in an iron automatic weighing-machine. Thus fact utters warning to the realism which presupposes sensibles, exactly like sensa save that they are unsensed; and which, by means of such 'terms' invented in order to give logic a foothold, would take the kingdom of actuality by violence, and compel its amenability to logical computation. So far as guessing has as yet been confronted with fact, there seems to be a verdict in favour of the phenomenalist, rather than of the realistic, interpretation of sensatio; but we must await possible appeal to a higher court.

Meanwhile, in deference to the maxim that it is the first step that costs, one may make the primary issue clearer by restating it, even at the risk of some repetition.

Our knowledge as to sensory acquaintance, in which we have

[1] A blue-sensatio is not to be mistaken for a blue sensatio, as by some objectors.

seen there is always some tincture of 'knowledge about', and which may be (ps) mediate though (ψ) immediate, is expressible by the formula $S.p.o$. We cannot ever observe sensatio, p, without its o, nor o without its $S.p$. We cannot therefore directly ascertain how much of the characterisation of o is due to p, save in respect of intensity, and how much, if any, is due to an ω. We cannot tell directly whether p in different instances, such as seeing green, seeing red, hearing noise, has a different quality or 'content', as some psychologists assert, or has always the same character of diaphanousness as bare apprehension. We can, by conceptual thought, distinguish sensum and sensatio, but we cannot resolve $p.o$ into separate genetic components. The *idion* is the *ne plus ultra* of (ψ) immediate simple perceptio; and analysis of it into p and o, assigning specific characterisation to each factor is, so far as psychological science goes, hypothesis not directly verifiable. Realism assumes o and ω to be identical, and, lodging all quality in o, makes p comparable to exact colour-photography. Phenomenalism, on the other hand, takes p to be comparable to vision through irremovable and undetectable coloured spectacles; so that o is an appearance of ω, and ω has a nature about which we can speculate but cannot know.

The third theory forthcoming, subjective idealism, cancels ω as superfluous; and maintains that o, like a feeling, is a mode or state of S. Of this view, Berkeley is usually regarded as the typical exponent. He certainly does sometimes appear to abolish the distinction between sensum and sensatio, and generally to imply that sensa are what we should call subjective modifications. But he is not consistent enough, or at any rate does not sufficiently commit himself with explicitness to the notion of subjective modifications, to enable us to pin him down to such subjective idealism. For instance, in *A Treatise concerning the Principles of Human Knowledge*, §49, he denies that the *idion* is in the mind, as mode of the subject, on the ground that there are no such things as modes; and other passages might be adduced in which he suggests that the relation of o to S is unique. Nevertheless, whether or not the sensum is a mode of, or is of one substance with, the subject, the subject is for him its *substratum*. He leaves it clear, at any rate, that he did not regard sensa as self-subsistent, and that he did not hold that sensa are created by their subject, or that they well up uncaused. If their *esse* is *percipi*, it is also *a Deo causari*. This latter element in his doctrine is no more directly refutable by psychology than is the view of realism or phenomenalism. But no philosopher has worked out a coherent system of subjective idealism; certainly not Berkeley. In order to avoid solipsism, he needed to postulate other selves or spirits, whose *esse* is not *percipi*, but *percipere*; and he had then no right to stop at his fellow man. On the same grounds that we assign a soul to a man, we must assign one to his dog; and continuity then carries us on indefinitely, till perhaps all "the furniture of earth" is back as Real, with existence for self as well as for God and man.

The question 'are sensa mental?' is not to be confounded with the question whether they are appearances of spirit, and is meaningless till we have fixed the connotation of 'mental'. As presented, as apprehended, sensa may well be appearances either of spirit or of non-spirit; certainly they are not subjective modes or states, and are distinguishable, though not separable, from the subjective acts of sensatio. They are objective; but their objectivity does not involve their existence when not sensed, their identity with 'Reals' or so-called 'objects *per se*', here denoted by ω. Their ontological status, in fact, cannot be decided by the psychology of individual experience.

3. It is only at the level of common Experience, where consequential issues of the various guesses just indicated crop up for discussion, that surmises, as to the relation of the objective to Reality, can possibly be weighed and compared. There we pass to quite a new sense for the word 'object', to a different meaning for 'cognition' or 'knowledge', and to a different set of problems with which realism, idealism, etc., are confronted.

Some of the differences and the connexions between individual and common cognition have already been discussed, and the reader may here be referred back to chap. VIII, p. 163 and chap. II, p. 20. There are, however, one or two other preliminary topics to which it is now necessary to invite attention.

It was shewn in previous contexts that *idia*, the fundamenta between which common knowledge establishes relations, are themselves incommunicable. Two subjects may agree in what is communicable, and yet there may be great qualitative difference between their respective objects. If we restrict the word percep to *idia*—and it can bear no unique meaning unless we do—it follows that the perceptual, at its lowest level, is of the here and now only, is blind and dumb; and that the common Object, such as The Sun, is not in this restricted sense a percept. We can extend the comprehension of 'percept' to include the 'thing' in which perception, developed without aid from intersubjective intercourse, issues for the individual; but no further, without blurring all lines of demarcation. Even then, the developed percept will already be a synthesis effected by use of implicit or vaguely defined 'real' categories, and will be the outcome or reading in, as well as of reading off.[1] Much more so will The Sun, as Object common to a plurality of percipients, be a conceptual elaboration. And if such an Object be called, as it generally is, 'perceptual', it is important to protest that it can only so be called, because perception suggests it, in the first instance, or because each individual reads his *idion* into the common concept. It is palpably miscalled so, if thereby it be implied that The Sun is compounded, or is a symposium, of percepts or *idia*. Some physicists of first rank have made this blunder, as it must be called, and have grounded the realism in their interpretation of science upon it. Whatever common sense may be, it certainly is not common *sensatio*. And now we come to the precise point at which the assertion that the sun is a concept, will be found by common sense to be a hard saying. When we affirm that the Objects and contents of common Experience are concepts, we may seem to be declaring that the sun and this earth are not even so substantial as the stuff that dreams are made of; that they are more rarified than images presented in sleep, and have but the same ontological status as Euclid's points. The realist will then reply that, though the concept of the sun may be a mental elaboration, it is still a concept *of* the sun, and is not the sun. The sun is a 'Real' thing, known by conception as surely as blue is known by an individual in perception. The concept may be a social creation; the sun is not: it was there before there were conceivers. We do not prove universal Experience to be 'a wider solipsism', nor find that the sun, or that space, is 'unReal', in the sense that their *esse* is *intelligi*, by shewing how the concepts of them have been

---

[1] If the realistic interpretation of the barest *sensatio* were possible, it could not be extended to developed *perceptio*. See chap. IV, pp. 44, 49.

acquired. The question, in short, is whether the sun, or the concept *of* it, is constructed by minds.

This question is pertinent though, as it stands, it begs itself. It is pertinent, in that it reveals the ambiguity of the word 'concept'. This term, in our niggardly language, has to do duty for the abstract idea, constituted by subjective attention and 'existing' only in and for minds, as well as for the supposed Object (whether O or ω) that is a Real counterpart of this idea, and is that which the idea is concept *of*. But experience teaches that we cannot assert such a Real counterpart to every idea or concept. No one believes in the Reality of the round square; some physicists do not believe in the Reality of the ether, though they employ the concept; the atheist believes there is no God, though his belief involves his possession of the theistic concept. Apparently there may, or there may not be, a Real counterpart to any given concept; our possession of the sun-concept, of itself, no more implies a 'Real' sun, than the God-concept implies (as the ontological argument sought to establish) an existent Deity. In either case the alleged existent is what, for certain indirect reasons, is supposed to be there. *The* sun, as distinct from *idia*, let it be repeated, is not perceived or sensed in individual experience, any more than is God: despite the implication of universally used, but treacherous, language to the contrary. *The* sun is what is *thought* to exist, in order to account for, and to coordinate, what *is perceived* or sensed by this person and that: and God, whom no man hath perceived, is thought to exist, in order to account for, and coordinate, facts of another order. If 'known' mean read off, as blue or likeness is, then the Real Sun is not known to exist. This is what some forms of realism would wish 'known' to mean: they assert that, in the sun-concept, we have certain cognition of a qualitatively characterisable, permanent existent. That the sun-concept is concept of a Real Sun, implies such a meaning of 'known'. But if previous argumentation have proved the indispensableness of 'real' categories, with their suppositional interpretativeness, in all 'knowledge' of, or about, permanent things such as the sun, this claim is untenable. We cannot advance a step from individual and fleeting sense-knowledge to what is generally called knowledge, whether common sense or science, without resort to supposition or belief; however compelling be the motivation, and however successful the venturesomeness, of the supposition. The grounds and causes of belief in the sun of astronomers, are coercive enough. But for all that, the sun is not that contradiction in terms, a common percept; nor an Object whose abiding existence is read off in conception with the maximum of (*ps*) immediate certainty: it is an Object which we have good pragmatic reasons, of a roundabout kind, to *think* existent and continuant, while the *idia* or percepts proper, of which it is a concept, are sporadic and transient. Further, if the *idia* of individual percipients may be appearances of things *per se*, which is not an absurd theory, the sun, as an existent temporally prior to sentient beings, is not to be assumed to have possessed in itself the characteristics of the *idia* which we receive when we 'look at it'. The *idion* is only 'independent of' its subject, in that it is not his subjective state, but is his object; objectivity does not imply that *idion*-marks characterise the ω which we conceive, or think existent, in order to account for the forthcomingness of the object. We can safely believe only that the ω corresponding to the sun as now 'seen' by us, was, before we came into being, such that, if human beings had existed on earth, they would have experienced such and such sensa. What the astronomer and geologist tell us about the pre-human world, is not repudiated as fiction by others than realists, nor needs to be denied; it is but translated into appropriate ontological terms. What is repudiated, is the identification of phenomenon with noumenon, *o* or *O* with ω; or the self-contradictory notion of the phenomenon *per se*.

The foregoing remarks were called for, in view of the common opinion, shared by some representatives of natural science, that divergence from realism, in the direction of phenomenalism or of idealism, involves stultification of physics. It rather appears that, if our theory of knowledge led on even to spiritualistic ontology, no fact or generalisation, as distinct from a postulate, of natural science would in the least be called in question. Science can ignore the Subjective factors that are everywhere present in common Experience, just as it can ignore the objective factors of individual experience; though its own existence presupposes both. It is not justified, however, in exalting the Objective factors of common Experience into absolute independence of all experients, or in professing knowledge as to the nature of a world *per se*;

still less in asserting the world *per se* to be identical with the world as conceived by theoretical physics. Such mistakes, indeed, are not made by science that knows its own business. But they are made sometimes by writers who would extract realistic philosophy out of science. As Taine remarked, Nature, apart from the human mind or other than as phenomenal, is "isolated by abstraction, separated by fiction, maintained as a distinct reality by a distinctive name; and the mind, having forgotten the origin of it, thinks of it as independent and becomes the dupe of an illusion which itself has made".

To return to the point whence we set out: the world in which our thought lives and moves, is a conceptual world. It is so because we are social beings and need to 'compare notes'. The conceptio by which it is fashioned, is not abstraction alone, but also interpretative supposition pragmatically 'verified'. The new fundamenta which replace, in common Experience, the *idia* of individual Experience, are concepts evoked by the *idia*, and coordinative of them. Some kinds of realism, apparently without any ground, assume that such conceptio is plate-glass vision of naked Reality. Phenomenalism takes it rather to be symbolic interpretation of the ω-world that assuredly exists independently of our knowledge, but as to whose nature we can, for the most part, only conjecture. Idealism cancels ω, and, asserting the *esse* of the world to be *intelligi*, bestows the name 'Reality' on the conceptual that is concept *of* nothing, and on the One or the many spirits that conceive.

"*Pas de discours, pas d'objectivité*" [*i.e.* Objectivity], said Poincaré; or, in the more pregnant utterance of Comte, "*entre l'homme et le monde il faut l'humanité*". Commonness, since Kant has become almost a synonym for Objectivity; and the conception of community in cognition now calls for sharper definition than as yet it has here received. Prof. Baldwin's investigation, in this connexion, has brought some inner detail into focus. Two individuals A and B can both possess the same piece of knowledge, or have it in common, and yet not know each that the other holds it: here (ps) commonness is not (ψ) different from privacy. A may discover that B shares his knowledge, and the knowledge is now common from the (ψ) standpoint of A; but till B discovers that A has this knowledge, there is no common knowledge that the

tem is common. Suppose C is aware of A's knowledge that a
act is known by A himself and B, and that C is also aware of a
ike situation in the case of B: what is (ψ) private to A and to B,
s then known to be (ps) common to them by C, who is now aware
)f an aggregate of private cognitions as to a (ps) common fact.
There is a possibility of C being mistaken, for his is (ψ) knowledge
)f the (ps) standpoint. And it is only when all members of such a
group have attained to this awareness of the (ps) point of view,
hat we have a case of thinking common thoughts, and thinking
hem as common: in other words, of public knowledge or perfect
ommunity. Thus, what should be meant by community in know-
edge, and by the common and (ps) point of view, is much more
han the mere fact that what is often called a perceptual Object—
nd should properly be called a conceptual Object—is cognised
)y a plurality of subjects individually. Yet this is perhaps all that
he more naïve kinds of realism understand by commonness.

The physical Object, which may be regarded as a hybrid
)etween an ω and an *idion*, or as the former entity into which
ach subject reads his own *idion*, has been said to be a supposed
xistent, counterpart to a known and constructed, but non-actual,
lea or concept. It serves a purpose. But it is not necessarily the
nly such concept that may serve the purpose of philosophy and
heoretical science, though the most suitable for the practical
hought of ordinary life. Indeed, substitutes for it have been
roposed. The physical Object of common sense, with definite
oundaries, and the source of many appearances (o), may be re-
laced by the notion of an Object which *is* wherever it acts, and
qually 'owns' all its varying appearances in varying circum-
tances. This view has been advocated, though it presents diffi-
ulties. It involves expanding the physical Object into an aspect
f the universe, and leads to a monistic interpretation of the world.
`o speak of 'things', should serve no purpose; whereas it does,
nd science is built on the practice. Another theory is that a
hysical Object is replaceable by a class of appearances (o),
guratively and conveniently called 'its' appearances. But this
gistic device realistically posits innumerable entities, as instances
f one kind, however economical it be as to kinds of entity; it
ives no sufficient reason why aggregates of *idia* are combined
nto such particular unities as evoke the postulation of a common

Object; it does not explain the occurrence of the act of perceiving nor the psychophysical fact that perceptio is conditioned by the body, itself—on this view—a 'function' of sensibles; and it dogmatically identifies what may be appearances with constituents or class-members. The laws of physics cannot be stated in terms either of *idia* or of classes of them. From individual experience alone, as we have seen, there is no way to the 'Real' world of common thought. Epistemology, from Descartes and Locke to Kant, was an exploration of blind roads seeming to lead from private psychology to public science. Explicated 'real' categories are as inevitably involved in science, as they are certainly suppositional; and if the logistical purist would pronounce them fetishes or figments, he can only avoid them by resorting, in his turn, to verbal figments, and to such as lack the virtue of explaining the significant aspects of fact. He returns to the pre-Kantian blind byways.

These attempts to replace the physical Object of common sense by other constructions, have served to make it evident that the *idion* is not identical with the Object, nor a quality of it, nor a part of it. The *idia* of different percipients looking from different positions at a coin, not only differ; they are not supplementary parts of a whole, but incompatible with the so-called Real shape; the tactual or visible spaces, in which each percipient locates his percept, moreover, are not synthetically compatible. Whatever be the status of the physical Object, *e.g.* the Real circular coin, it is certain that it is no perceptual symposium. It has no claim to actuality like the *idion*: the Actuality accorded to it, is metaphysical or noumenal. When common sense and science seek to explain *idia* in terms of a physical Object invoked as their cause, or as the Reality of which they are appearances, they no doubt propound some subsistent relations; but not, with any truth, those which they affirm. They would explain the more certain in terms of the less certain, the original in terms of the derived, the given in terms of the relatively precarious interpretation thereof. But if the physical Object be relegated, as by theoretical physics and by metaphysics, to the rank of appearance of more ultimate Reality (ω), such inconsistencies are avoidable. *Idia*, as immediately apprehended, utter nothing but their own occurrence; it is their relations of likeness, order, regularity, etc., which suggest a 'source' beyond them. The physical Object, or thing, was conceived in order to supply common sense with a Reality, the same for all precipients acquainted only with their private objects. It asserts what is supposed to be abiding while *idia* are fleeting, what provides a "permanent possibility of sensations". It accounts for continuity and developement, and supplies the terms between which causal laws obtain. It is a 'function', though not a logical but largely an alogical function, of the only primary actualities, the *idia*; and one which is practically a more service-able, and pragmatically a more highly justified, convention, than any other that is forthcoming from logistically sophisticated in-genuity. It may therefore be regarded as some version of ultimate truth; but it remains to inquire whether epistemology can eventu-ally supersede it. Henceforth, in investigating the 'source' of sensa, it will be necessary to refer to the problem of the relation of body to mind, as body seems to condition the very perceptio by which the body itself and all objects are known. The source which we would explore may be threefold, comprising the subject, external Reality, and the body which is a uniquely functioning part of external Reality, in that it is an instrument for cognition of other parts.

4. The extremest type of realism is that which has been called, by Dr Broad, the instrumental theory. We have already encountered it in discussing sensatio. It annuls the distinction between ap-pearance and reality, taking sensa as ultimate reals, or things *per se*, even when regarded from the (*ps*) standpoint. The theory further denies that the body or the sense-organ, however profoundly its normal functioning may be affected, and however various its spatial relation to an Object, is anything but an instrument for apprehension of Reality. The body makes perceptio possible, but in no way conditions the percept or the quality of the perceptio. The physical causes of dreams, drugs, etc., the complicated mechanism by which physiology and physics tell us that external perception is mediated, make no difference to the *idion* appre-hended; in all cases alike, the sensatio is diaphanous apprehension of the Real, and all that is determined by these psychophysical conditions is, whether or not we have a perceptio at all.

We have now attained that stage, in our discussion of theory, at which speculation may be confronted with its remoter consequences; and the first observation that suggests itself, is that the instrumental theory involves that the Real world is a vastly more complicated affair than common sense and science have taken it to be. That is not, philosophically, a fatal objection, however disconcerting. But we should have to believe in the existence, when unperceived, of all the indefinite number of elliptical shapes, *e.g.*, presented when a coin is looked at by a plurality of percipients from an indefinite number of positions; of all the different shades of colour when a flower is seen in different lights; of all the different pitches, loudnesses, etc., apprehended when a sounding body, moving relatively to hearers, is heard; of all the sensa of 'subjective sensation', those seen when the eye-ball is pressed, and so forth; of all that is apprehended in delirium, dreams, and after taking drugs, which become thereby means of extending our acquaintance with the Real world. A world may be of infinite complexity; it may be endowed with the six dimensions that have been assigned to it, in order to allow this indefinite tale of 'reals' to expatiate. But there is such a thing as external control to be reckoned with by the pure speculator; and when confronted with it, the instrumental theory does not fare well. It needs to abolish the distinction between actuality and illusion, for which psychology, no less than common sense, assigns grounds. It fails to account for the practical and scientific usefulness of the conception of 'things'; for the similarity in relations between the *idia* of different persons, when engaged in 'looking at the same Object'; for *idia* grouping themselves, as they do, with rhyme and reason; for the fact that some objects, *prima facie* purporting to be Real as others, are not such as to lead to the synthesis of Objects from them, while the others are. The world, according to this theory, should hardly be so amenable to physical science as it is: the practical and theoretical success of science would seem to be fortuitous, a little oasis of order in a vast desert of chaos.

It is, then, with good reason that common sense has shrunk from the severest type of realism, and the inexhaustible complexity which it involves. Common sense has resorted to what has been distinguished as the causal theory of perception. The physical Object is considered to be the cause of perceptio and *idion*, and the *o* to be appearance of O. In its crudest form, such naïve realism (as it is called) holds that in normal, though not in abnormal, perception, the appearance or *idion* resembles the Reality of which it is appearance: it embodies, in fact, the copy-theory of perceptual cognition. Science abandoned this primitive tenet of crude realism, in its distinction between primary and secondary qualities, and in maintaining that only a few more general and ubiquitous characters, such as extension, are intrinsic to physical Reality, whereas colour, etc., are 'subjective' or read into Reality by subjects. Naïve realism, which it would be equally correct to call a kind of phenomenalism[1] when thus far sophisti-cated by science, became more pronouncedly phenomenalistic. The physical Object, in fact, that naïve common sense had taken for an ω, for science became in turn a phenomenon; and the Real (ω) behind it, was frequently identified with the insensible or conceptual entities, in terms of which physics was expounded—atoms, ether, electrons, etc.

Whether the causal theory takes the form of naïve or of scientific realism, it has two main implications. One of these is that sensa, as well as sensationes, are caused, whether by O or by ω; the other is that sensa, as well as sensationes, are conditioned by the body and its organs. It thus differs from the instrumental theory, as also in asserting *idia* to be appearances, whether copies or not. But it is important to observe that the causal theory only limits the sphere of application of the instrumental theory, and does not repudiate it altogether. To distinguish between appearance and Reality, is to admit the thin edge of the idealistic or of the spiritual-istic wedge; and to prevent its own ultimate destruction, realism (so-called) of the causal type must retain the services of instru-mentalism, so far as to enable itself to remain realistic towards the primary qualities of matter. One of the points at which the general instrumental theory breaks down, we remember, is the forthcomingness of illusion, the imaginal and the hallucination. Having learned wisdom, causal realism admits that *idia* of these kinds do not exist when not presented: it teaches that they are caused by the body, or by body and mind, not by external Reality. It thus must cling to the belief that normal perception, at least of primary qualities, is caused by imperceptible events or changes

[1] 'Phenomenalism' is used throughout this chapter in its historical sense. It is unfortunate that the name has recently been applied to the doctrine of Mach, etc., which has more kinship with subjective idealism and solipsism.

within the Real. That secondary qualities are unreal, like the imaginal, is not necessarily implied by the theory in the abstract; but such becomes its issue, if it adopt from science the view that colour, etc., are not intrinsic properties of Real matter, *i.e.* of mass-particles, atoms, electrons, etc. From the point of view of psychology, there is no basis for assigning fundamental difference, as to ontological status, to primary and secondary qualities; it must be inquired, therefore, on what other grounds scientific realism presumes to entertain the important distinction. Idealism and phenomenalism naturally put this question; and causal realism does not find it easy to give a satisfactory answer. In whatever psychological respects they differ, the normal and the illusory *idion* are in *quale* much alike. Both, says psychophysics, are produced by the same mechanism. In what is commonly called 'perceiving' a Real Object, the total cause, according to the view under consideration, is O (or ω), body and mind (S): the O (or ω) being pre-existent. In illusion, there is a similar process in body and mind, and a similar *idion*, and yet no O or ω : the *idion*, in this case, must therefore be produced by body and mind alone. Then why not treat all cases alike? asks the idealist; why should not all kinds of *idion* be produced by body and mind, or by mind alone, if body be a particular physical Object, since some are admittedly so produced?

The issue has already been narrowed down to the question, whether scientific realism, or refined common sense, can retain the instrumental theory for primary qualities.

And now realism can be pressed further. Science does not apply its realism to all manifestations even of primary quality. Shapes and sizes in *idia* are generally as 'unreal' as colours: how, save by convention, are we to discriminate between the Reality of the circularity of a coin regarded from a point vertically above it, and the unReality of the ellipticity apprehended from any other situation. Perhaps it will be said, by appeal from sight to touch, the one sense that escapes illusion and apprehends Reality without phenomenalising it. But if extension be thus assured of Reality, what is it that is extended, or how can extension be conceived to exist without some other quality coexisting? Can temperature be excluded from the Real? More to the point is the fact that it would be all one for science, if this ultimately primary quality were, in turn, but appearance. That admitted, the case is given away: gross matter may as well be appearance of spirit, as appearance of occult quasi-matter, ether, or electric charge. The Real, or ultimate, constituents of physical Nature, as assigned by theoretical science, have been, from the first until now, in a state of flux; and there is as yet no promise of stable finality. In other words, science throws, and can throw, no light on'the nature of ultimate Reality, or the ω-world. Its 'knowledge' is equally compatible with a spiritualistic or a dualistic metaphysic; and if dualism be speculatively preferable, which is disputable, science can know even less as to the *per-se* nature of ontal matter, than psychology can claim to know as to the nature of spirit.

What is called realism, either naïve or scientific, has been argued to be inconclusive as to the essence of the ultimate Reality, of which the Nature of common sense or of science, is appearance or interpretation. Opportunity may now be taken to consider the presuppositions on which that type, called the causal theory, rests.

The one of these is that sensa are caused, either by the physical Object, or, if that be resolved into phenomenon of higher order than the *idion*, by the Real or ontal entity, of which the Object is appearance.

Some philosophers have objected to the category of causation being applied to sensa or *idia*; but the grounds of this objection stand in need of a little sifting. Certainly, for psychology proper, sensa are ultimate and inexplicable. There we are confronted with the subject-object relation; and that cannot be called causal, if by 'causation' is meant a relation within the objective continuum or, as is more usual, a relation between Objects. The subject-object relation is more fundamental than the causal, and may well be unique and inadequately describable in terms of any derived and more special relation. Still, subject and object are not merely logical correlatives; besides relation, some Actual *rapport* must exist between them, or be involved in connexion with them. And if we repudiate instrumental realism, the object or *idion* must be supposed to be constituted by *rapport* or interaction between the subject and some Real entity, whatever be its essence, denoted by ω. The critical philosophy prohibits, whether with good reason or not, the application of cause, or any other category, to the ontal; but if the essence of the causal notion be action, or even conditioning, it would seem to be but a verbal question, whether we speak of the ω as the *conditio sine qua non* of perception, as an agent cooperant with the subject, or as a Real cause (along with the subject itself) of the presentation and the essence of his *idion*. Unless 'cause' be assigned some other acceptation than this last, there would seem to be no reason to prohibit its application to subject and ω jointly. It is when the physical Object is assigned as the cause of percept and perceptio, that we may begin to demur. For, as we have seen, the physical Object itself presupposes, so far as Actuality and order of knowing are concerned, sensa such as it is supposed to cause. Psychophysical teaching as to causation of sensatio and sensum by stimulus, must indeed involve truth of some sort; but, as it stands, it assumes a particular theory of knowledge which, from the point of view of psychology and the *ordo cognoscendi*, is a mere prepossession. The physical Object, indeed, has suffered fluctuation, comparable with that of science's Real matter-constituents; and we have no certainty that the *ratio essendi* set up by common sense, and taken over by psychophysics, is known and final truth. If the physical Object be, as higher science takes it to be, phenomenal and provisional, it needs to be replaced by its ω, before the Real external source of percept and perceptio, cooperating with individual subject, can profitably be discussed.

The other presupposition of the causal theory is, that the body and sense-organs play some part in constituting the sensum or percept that is apprehended with (ψ) immediacy by the subject. They are part of the 'source' in normal perception, and sole source or cause in abnormal experience, in which the objective factor is not synthesised into a physical Object or referred, from the (*ps*) standpoint, to an O or an ω.

The psychophysical accounts of the mediation of sensory experience, normal and abnormal, may with sufficient accuracy for the purpose in hand be tabulated, as on the next page.

It should be added that, in the case of hypnotic suggestion, all the first five stages of I presumably occur, yet the sixth does not ensue. In III, the external source or stimulus is not cognised as it is in I; while in II and IV, the external is not involved at all, though there is apprehension of an impressional *o* as in I. In I, dependence of sensatio (and sensum?) on the body, is not to be identified with dependence on the mind or subjective act. This is forcibly exhibited by the physiological fact that, in I. 4, diversity of stimulation is apparently annulled; the only observable difference, however much the stimulus may vary in quality and intensity, is difference of frequency with which some change in state of nerve-substance is propagated along a nerve that is but a prolongation of a brain-cell. How the brain reintroduces diversity which, in transmission through the nervous system, has been thus reduced or apparently cancelled, and out of which the

I. Normal Perception	II. Dreams, Hallucinations	III. Sensation due to 'Inadequate' Stimulus	IV. 'Subjective' Sensation
1. Changes in the spatial 'real'—*e.g.* the sun—or the ω of which it is appearance, cognised in stage 6	—	1. Changes in an ω or O *other* than that of which stage 5 is cognition	—.
2. Changes in the transmitting environment (air, ether, etc.) external to the body	—	—	—
3. Changes in sense-organ	1. Drugs, etc.	2. Changes in sense-organ	1. Changes in the body
4. Changes in nerve	2. Changes in blood or body, *not* in sense-organ	3. Changes in nerve	
5. Changes in brain	3. Changes in brain	4. Changes in brain	2. Changes in brain
6. Sensum and sensatio: (*ps*) reference to conceptual O	4. (ψ) object, imaginatio, etc.	5. Sensum and sensatio	3. Sensum and sensatio

mind or subject can make impressional variety, is as yet as unknown, as the making of colour-vision out of ethereal vibration, is unknowable. It is also mysterious why 'seeing the Sun', the last stage (according to the scientific and causal theory) in a long series of processes initiated millions of miles away and eventually carried on in the rods and cones of the eye, should be the psychical resultant: why the remotest cause in the series should be the one, and the only one, to be immediately apprehended after such complicated mediation, and when all the causes in the long chain are scientifically on a par. The nervous system involved, is as much a physical Object as is the sun, and as much a cause of vision; yet it is diaphanously seen through, while the sun is seen. Such facts, together with the setting up of the *ex post facto* criterion of Reality by common sense, which is psychologically as arbitrary as practically it is serviceable, shew that common realism, on which natural science is originally based, has made a tangle for epistemology to unravel. Neither in the instrumental nor in the causal form of the theory of natural realism, have we an account of the mediation of perception that is consistent with all the facts. We have seen in chap. IV that the causal theory, and the criterion of Reality to which it is committed, arise through selectiveness from among the data which experience affords; and we now see reason to believe that, were the theory true, some of these data should not be forthcoming.

It may be easy for realism to explain what is properly called illusion, *i.e.* faulty interpretation or reference of sensa consequent on normal stimulation of normal sense-organs; but hallucinations, dream-objects, etc., consequent on stimulation from within the body and on abnormal states of the sense-organs and body, while wrecking the instrumental theory, also throw doubt on the necessity and the sufficiency of the causal theory. It appears that perception cannot be accounted for by endowing the Real alleged cause thereof with primary qualities alone; while science can equally well be accounted for, if primary qualities be as phenomenal as secondary qualities. Sensa do not yield knowledge of physical Objects, as these are conceived by common sense; rather are Objects conceived in order to interpret and to correlate sensa. These Objects are, in turn, resolved by science and philosophy alike into appearances of the ontal. The instrumental theory requires us to deny that the body, or its ontal equivalent, is part of the source of the sensum. Thus it implies that, when the taking of santonine makes one see all things yellow, either the trees, the clouds, etc., are thereby affected, or the wave-length of light is altered, or the mind's eye is opened to discern hitherto unsensed sensibles, and apparently precluded from apprehending others: and such consequences are, from the scientific point of view, absurdities. The causal theory, in turn, cannot account for dream-objects, etc., without weakening its case for belief that, to our supposition or concept of the sun, there is a Real counterpart, causing the sun-percepts of different beholders, and possessed of such and such definite qualities common to it and to *idia*.

So far, realism has been examined in its two forms, known as the naïve or natural and the scientific, corresponding roughly to the instrumental and the causal theories of perception. These theories are concerned only with knowledge of the external world. There are other types of realism, mostly of wider reference than to the physical, such as Plato's doctrine of universals, logical realism, the new realism and neo-realism. Their more essential tenets have been dealt with in contexts where discussion of consciousness, ideation, analysis, logic, rationalism, etc., has been undertaken. In one or another of them is contained doctrine or assumption that has previously occasioned criticism, because conflicting with the alleged facts which it has been necessary to present, or with the analyses and the implications that have been expounded, in the attempt to ascertain what knowledge is, and how it is mediated. It is therefore unnecessary, here, systematically to examine these several realistic theories, and enough to indicate the broader philosophical consequences in which some among them issue. They generally imply the negligibility of the difference between individual and common experience, and of that between the (ψ) and (ps) points of view; they assume conception to be as immediate knowledge of the insensible, as perception is of the sensory. Hence conceptual analysis is taken to be isolation of existent constituents, and by it are reached the 'terms' of a radically pluralistic universe on which logistic can operate. Relations are external; unities are aggregates; abstractions are Real. The 'real' categories are renounced; classes of 'entities' replace things and souls. Interpretation is eschewed, and sufficient reason is scouted as a demand of sentimentality. The cold dry light of the formally logical understanding is alone professed; and redemption of the pluralistic universe or multiverse from unknowable chaos is, with equanimity, implicitly attributed to ungrounded coincidence. It has been maintained in foregoing chapters that there is no knowledge possible on these presuppositions, and that the presuppositions are severally baseless. In the present chapter it has been submitted that the fundamental tenets of realism, viz. that object is independent of subject; that knowing sets up no difference between ultimate Reality as unknown, and as known;

that there is no distinction between appearance and Reality: are disputable. 'Independence' is an ambiguous term, and has but been arbitrarily defined by realists to include the relation of object to subject, which there is every reason to regard as unique. The theory has been argued to break down when confronted with facts concerning the apprehension of objects, of various kinds, that do not lend themselves to synthesis into Objects; and it has no explanation to offer of retention, familiarity, gradual differentiation of the objective, etc. There are thus forthcoming facts, with which the theory is incompatible; consequently, the empirical razor removes it from the list of alternatives to be reckoned with.

Naïve realism, or crude common sense, on submitting to refinement required by advance in knowledge, passes into scientific realism: which is already nine-tenths phenomenalism, and knows no means of saving itself from lapsing completely into theory of the latter kind. The inevitableness of this transition may be illustrated by reference to the history of modern philosophy, in which the problem of knowledge of the external world for the first time came to the fore, and could at last be propounded with such unartificial definiteness as to make advance possible.

In the century before Kant the important distinction, between the individual and the common standpoints, was not recognised. Hence it was, that rationalism often read the finished products of common knowledge into the individual, as innate or *a priori*. Descartes set the example, followed with scarce an exception to the present day, of confounding psychology with psychophysics. Locke, while inaugurating psychological procedure in epistemology, frequently pursued it from the common, when he intended to use the individual, standpoint. Berkeley, with equal ignorance of the vital distinction between these points of view, wrote spiritualistic metaphysics from that of individual experience. Progress in theory of knowledge, during this age, was also hampered by unsuspected assumptions, since shewn to be false: *e.g.* that 'ideas' (objects) are subjective modes externally caused or, according to Leibniz, produced by their subject from within; that the datum of experience is a manifold of discrete impressions, rather than a differentiable continuum. Again, the intellectualistic tendency to focus attention solely on the cognitive side of experience, prevailed. How these confusions and misleading presuppositions were gradually put aside, is a story instructive for our present inquiry.

Locke, as a representational realist, dealt with two kinds of 'object': the psychological object of individual experience, or the *idion*, and the physical Object. The object was within the circle of "ideas", and said to be 'in the mind' of the individual. The Object was taken to be public, external to the mind, or Real. Inasmuch as o was identified with a subjective state, it may equally well be denoted by σ. The individual, in so far as immediate or first-hand apprehension is concerned, being shut up to his circle of ideas, the problem was: how to get from o or σ to O, its alleged cause, and know that o is a copy of O. If in sensatio we have simply, in the first instance, $S-o$ or $S-\sigma$, either solipsism or subjective idealism should result. Why is o, an effect of O, a 'knowledge' of it? How can we know it copies an unapprehended original? How does the notion of an original arise? It was through thinking Locke's theory out, that Berkeley was led to idealism. Locke avoided this consequence by *assuming* an external O; in his distinction of primary from secondary qualities, he may be said to have adopted a kind of scientific realism. His position may be indicated by the figure

$$S-o)-O):$$

o is on the circle of ideas within consciousness, the *tabula rasa* contemplated by S, and is representative of O: which is on the circle of 'things' external to consciousness. Berkeley abolished O, as a superfluous *tertium quid*. He made o identical with 'thing', and referred its causation to God. *If* he regarded an o as a σ, he was a subjective idealist; if not, he should be a solipsist so long as he was self-consistent. In the former case, his formula, as also that of Leibniz, should be $S-\sigma$; in the latter, $S-o$. Reid, on the other hand, repudiated o, as the superfluous *tertium quid*. He took perceptio or sensatio to be (ps) immediate apprehension, not of an *idion*, but of a public or Real thing; and so upheld a natural or naïve realism, described by $S-O$. This view, ingrained in unsophisticated common sense, dies hard even with physicists, psychologists and philosophers. We observe that none of these pioneers was able to transcend solipsism, save by assumptional conjecture or by confounding the (ψ) and (ps) standpoints; and we have already seen that their respective ventures, especially those of Leibniz, Berkeley and Reid, bring them to insurmountable difficulties, or to conflict with facts. Solipsism is impossible for us, only because we have interwoven into our individual experience the results of intersubjective intercourse, on which all transcending of o or σ depends. It was Kant who first clearly recognised this truth, despite his clinging to faulty current prepossessions. What alone can be communicated, is thought: the conceptual, as distinguished from the sensible, or from the perceptual in which the conceptual element is but tied or implicit. Hence the great importance of Kant's conception of Experience, or *Bewusstsein überhaupt*. Equally important is his insistence that the *tabula rasa* is the subject itself, an active and synthetic agent rather than a passively recipient wax. But S_1 is practically a windowless monad till it communicates with S_2, etc. Then it becomes possible for several individuals, previously confined by their respective circles of *idia*, to *conceive* a common O. This situation is represented by

$$\begin{matrix} S_1 - o_1 \searrow \\ S_2 - o_2 - O. \\ S_3 - o_3 \nearrow \end{matrix}$$

Kant saw the great gulf between o and O: that o without O is blind; and that O without o is empty, because conceptual form without impressional matter. Hence he could escape the misidentifications made by his predecessors. In so far as he taught that O is 'phenomenon'—it may henceforth be denoted by ϕ—he goes farther than Locke's scientific realism, even to complete phenomenalism. Had he advanced no farther than ϕ, he would have given us but a 'wider solipsism' or a kind of idealism (*i.e.* mentalism). That, however, is not the last stage in his theory. Behind O or ϕ he puts the Real, the thing *per se* (ω), of which ϕ is phenomenon. Using Σ for society, or for the individual S_1 who can adopt the points of view of S_2, S_3, etc., and consequently the common and the (ps) standpoints; and taking ϕ to be the schematism, or forms of intuition and understanding, applied to the actual matter o: Kant's complete theory of common knowledge is denoted by $\Sigma - \phi - \omega$. Kant deemed ω to be unknowable, save as to its existence. Here, as shall be argued presently, he was

unduly modest and even inconsistent. That we only know phenomena, and only know them because we constitute them out of
sense-data, is hardly an adequate expression of the outcome of the
Kantian epistemology, as it may be viewed by others than its
author himself. For Kant's prohibition to apply any categories
to things *per se*, is a counsel of perfection which makes ω but
a useless limiting-concept when it is posited: and a counsel by
which he himself did not abide.

5. Meanwhile, the relation of the Kantian theory to others may
be stated; and it shall be submitted that, when its doctrine of the
categories is revised in the way indicated in a previous chapter,
and its inadequate conception of the thing *per se* is amplified,
this theory of knowledge is by far the most satisfactory of those
as yet considered. The difference, as well as the continuity, between
the functionings of S and Σ, substantiated by psychology, when
once recognised and taken into account as by Kant, renders all
previous theories obsolete. It seems that in the terms S, o, Σ, O
or ϕ, and ω, we have the minimal number required for adequate
statement of the forthcoming facts; that therefore any theory that
would dispense with one or more of them, is self-condemned.
Retention of o is the saving element of empiricism, maintenance
of touch with primary actuality, whence issues all that can be
called knowledge. It is o, as the 'matter' or posited nucleus, round
which ϕ is a conceptual concretion, that saves ϕ from being mere
empty form; and though o is not subjective modification (σ), it
involves its correlate S. Here subjective idealism and forms of
neo-realism are eliminated. The necessity of the transition from
S to Σ, for any explanation of common knowledge, implies the
futility of all attempts to construct O or ϕ out of *idia* alone, or
out of the unaided activities of S. Consequently Reid's naïve
realism ($S-O$) is to be dismissed; also logistical new realism,
solipsism, and the idealistic sensationism of Mach, K. Pearson, etc.,
often miscalled phenomenalism. As ϕ involves 'real', as well as
formal, categories, there is no need to reckon with positivism or
any de-anthropomorphising proclivity, such as seeks to account
for common knowledge in terms of *idia* and formal categories
alone. The science, so called, that some decades ago was commonly
taken to be tantamount to materialism, or to imply that kind of
metaphysic, is convicted of epistemological worthlessness, in that

it ignored Σ as well as S, and reduced ϕ to the purely quantitative. The ω in Kant's completed formulation of individual experience, expressible as S—o—ϕ—ω, was an addition needed to obviate the charge of idealism; and it has already been maintained that neither o nor O can be substituted for ω, without conflict with fact and knowledge. The thing *per se* was, however, left so shadowy and otiose in Kant's own version of phenomenalism, that it invited abolition, as a superfluity, from the thinkers to whom empirical fact and external control made feeble appeal: hence the rise of post-Kantian idealism and the revival of rationalism. But the *idion, o,* is metaphysically inexplicable, save by resort to miracle, unless it be constituted by *rapport* between S and an ω of some kind: a theory which leaves out ω, is therefore no theory of *knowledge*, whatever else it may be. Some of the newer Kantian school seem to take O as if equivalent to Kant's ω, and to be the cause or source of o; whereas O already presupposes o, and is no more, in so far as it is known, than conceptual form given to o by the socialised mind. The cause or source, therefore, is obviously not O, but the ω of which O is 'phenomenon' (ϕ). ϕ, again, is the meeting-point of relations implicit in S—o, explicit in Σ—ω. It is empty, an ideal nothing, without its content o. It therefore cannot be identified with ω, or be an existent, save in the sense in which the purely ideal is said to 'exist'. Hence rationalism, denotable by Σ—ω, and involving supression of o and ϕ, is precluded. Rationalism erred, as we have seen, in ignoring the difference between Σ and S: attributing what can only be the outcome of intercourse and explicated categories, to S, as innate or *a priori*. Dualism *assumes* O (refined by science) to be identical with ω; and, like abstractionism and absolutism, it *assumes* that, because ϕ is independent of S, it is also independent of Σ: assumptions which knowledge forbids, and logic should brand as superfluous.

Before proceeding to evaluate and to supplement Kant's conception of the thing *per se*, it will be well to bestow further attention on definite theories such as would dispense with it. One typical instance is Mill's suggestion of the "permanent possibility of sensation". This notion presupposes nothing but the actual and the possible sensa—in the latter case they will be unsensed *sensibilia*—of purely individual experience: no physical Objects, and no things *per se*, distinct from these sensa. It has been maintained by recent adherents to a doctrine akin to Mill's, that what our propositions concerning physical Objects truly assert, is that in certain conditions we shall apprehend certain sensa; and that our propositions are theoretically, though perhaps not practically, translatable into very complex statements involving sensa only. The question rather is, however, whether, without more than sensa and solipsistic experience, any such propositions could have been forthcoming for translation. We have already found reason to believe that such is not the case; and more shall presently be said on the subject. But as for Mill's formulation, we may ask whether a permanent possibility is anything at all. The word 'possible' may denote the potential, which involves *some* Actuality as already forthcoming; and if the individual subject be regarded as a Leibnizian monad whose sensa are its own modes, or its own creations by purely immanent activity, it is with some significance that we can call its future states possible, because their ground is existent. But this is subjective idealism ($S—\sigma$), not solipsism ($S—o$), and is open to the objections previously set forth. The only other meaning that 'possible' can have in this connexion, unless the potentiality be lodged in an existent ω which the theory expressly repudiates, would seem to be the abstractly conceivable; and that is not necessarily existent. The theory is then on a par with the Wolffian rationalism that would educe the actual from the possible, *i.e.* something out of nothing. The unsensed sensible, we have seen, is as suppositional as an ω that is not a sensible: indeed it is one kind of ω. Mach, K. Pearson and others, recognise no data for science other than sensa, and assert that physical laws are statements about sensa. But if a datum is what is received and used, the data of science are certainly not sensa, but physical or common Objects, events, etc.: scientific text-books do not allude to sensa. And if *idia* were the sole constituents of knowledge, each of us should be a solipsist, unable to use an alleged other subject's alleged sensa, or any testimony. Nor should we be able ever to predict our own sensa, much less to arrive at formulation of physical laws. Such theories presuppose much information about common Objects, if not as to things *per se*, in order to prove that no such knowledge is possible.

Physical laws cannot be reached, unless we assume processes to be going on when we are not individually attending to them;

without, in fact, usage of 'real' categories. These, however, are rejected by Mach and his school. Sensa are said to be our only data and our only knowledge-constituents. Concepts, whose origin is not accounted for, and for which place is found only by inconsistency, are taken to be but signs or symbols; and their function is said to be merely that of economic arrangement of data. Sensationism generally goes hand in hand with nominalism. Mach and some advocates of new realism hypostatise the abstraction, sensum; and he himself often fails to distinguish between it and the sensatio. The physical Object becomes then a symbolic construction of sensa, 'class' replacing discarded 'substance'. But the pure sensum is as much a conceptual abstraction or fiction as the atom, on which Mach bestows these terms. The sensationist has no right to believe in the Reality and permanence of functional relations, or of laws of any kind; nor to suppose that functional relations, which are systems of concepts, are Real, while the concepts, of which they are systems, are symbols to which nothing Real corresponds.

We may conclude, then, that the physical Object is an indispensable factor in the presumptive knowledge of common sense, which takes O to be an ω characterised more or less by o-qualities. As to this particular characterisation, common sense may need correction: but the ω, characterised in some way, is the essential core of what is required, over and above subjects and their mental functionings, in order to yield knowledge of a Real world.

Now to come to the thing *per se*. Kant, it has been suggested, was over-modest in his characterisation of it. He teaches that its *existence* alone is a necessary supposition: without that, our phenomenal knowledge could not be forthcoming. Sensa are due to its co-operation with our sensibility, *i.e.* with the subject in the act of sensatio; yet we are not to apply categories to it. Kant himself could not forbear at times to speak of it as causing our sensations; and unless we can do so, or at any rate unless we can speak of *rapport* between us and it, and so credit it with one or both of the category-like notions of activity and conditioning or determining, which we have found the causal concept to contain, it is plain that the thing *per se* is useless when reached. Even on Kant's shewing, then, we know more of the ω than that it exists.

Were it not further knowable, it would be unknowable as to its existence. It must then be of such nature as to 'cause' our sensatio. If we are to refrain from designating the subject-object relation as causal, in any sense that is applicable only to phenomenal Objects—and that is but wise in that the relation of S to o or ω is unique and more fundamental than that of such phenomenal causality—we cannot be prohibited from calling the S—ω relation causal, in the sense just now indicated. And further, unless the mind 'makes' Nature out of bare and structureless 'forms', or spins most of the world's diversity out of its own states (as subjective idealism teaches), there must be a one-to-one correspondence between phenomenon and noumenon, in respect of detail. Unless we create phenomenal variety *ex nihilo* and without external provocation, there must be as much of structural detail in the thing *per se* as in the phenomenon thereof.[1] True, we only 'know'—in one sense—this detail, in and through its appearance, or as seen through the mind's spectacles; but the detail must be there in order to have appearance. It is of the essence of the phenomenalist theory, to assert that the subject has spectacles and that they are not, so to speak, colourless or plane. That is only to say that sensum or percept is not identical with thing *per se*. But while we thus have *acquaintance* only with the sensible or phenomenal, we are having *rapport* with, and phenomenal knowledge of or about, the noumenal. We do not, in this latter sense of 'knowledge', know the phenomenal only: rather, we know the noumenal through the phenomenal. And we only know

---

[1] As Herbart said, *wie viel Schein, so viel Hindeutung aufs Sein.* Taking 'structure' to denote the sum of relations subsisting between each and every term in a system, abstracted from, and independent of, the terms that conceivably may be changed without affecting their structure, there must be correspondence between the structures of the noumenal and of its phenomenal manifestation. There must be at least as much of detail in the Real as in the phenomenal, to account for phenomenality: there well may be indefinitely more, of which sensatio makes nothing, because sensatio is not evoked by it. Reality may be richer not only than thought, but than experience in the widest sense. There cannot be mere, or wholly subjective, illusion in our phenomenalising. That our minds make Nature out of electrons, may be conceivable; that they make it out of structureless or undifferentiated space-time, as some would tell us, is psychologically unimaginable and scientifically unthinkable—*i.e.* non-correlatable with our forthcoming knowledge. The Real and the phenomenal must have more in common, or be more alike, than is commonly supposed by those who observe distinction between them.

phenomenally, or by phenomenalising, when the Object is primarily sensible. This has already been argued, in connexion with the knowability of the subject itself or the soul. We know the soul's existence only through its activities and states, which could not be what they are, as observable actualities, unless the soul be active or Actual. We do not know it phenomenally, however, as is the case with the physical Object, or rather its underlying 'Real'. It is from the soul as permanent and active, that is to say as, in certain senses, substantial and causative, that, as Kant emphasises, we derive our categories of the understanding. 'Like only knows like' may be but baseless dogma or antique prejudice; but 'like understands like', or understanding consists in assimilating, is truth that psychology may be said to have established, and that is presupposed in all attempts to deny it. One need not be green, in order to become acquainted with green; but we must be active and relatively permanent, in order to be cognisant of a course of Nature, or to have phenomenal science of an external world. Such knowledge, it has here been contended, could not be forthcoming, even as presumptive, unless there were human souls in commerce with other souls and with other Real beings, whether analogous to souls or not.

Kant's phenomenalism is again in need of correction when, as is implied by its title of 'transcendental idealism', it teaches that the thing *per se* provides but the formless matter of sensatio, while the mind does *all* the making of Nature out of the chaotic matter and, in imposing its categories, spontaneously and dictatorially 'legislates' for Nature. Kant recognised that our causal laws are the scientific explication or classification of vague, primitive rules, involving *propter hoc* as well as *post hoc*; he failed to see that these empiric rules are evoked from us, and already involve the thing *per se*. If ω must exist, in order to account for the existence of sensa or phenomena, it must equally be invoked, in order to account for their relations to one another. If we do not set out to discover scientific laws such as those of dynamics, until Nature has educated us by thrusting empiric rules upon us, it is presumptuous to say that we prescribe laws to her. The thing *per se*, we conclude, must be credited with far more of responsibility and character than Kant, influenced by rationalistic and idealistic propensities, meted out to it.

It has been submitted that phenomenalism of a richer kind than the half-hearted form taught by Kant, is the only one of the theories, dealt with in the present chapter, that satisfies the facts. It alone recognises that the two vital questions, in the problem of knowledge of the external world, are the transitions from (1) impression to idea and from (2) individual to common standpoint. It alone offers a translation of the original datum of presumptive knowledge: the others are free compositions, speculative guesses contemning external control of significant fact.

6. Just because it repudiates realism and rationalistic idealism, phenomenalism involves some form of the doctrine of the Relativity of knowledge. This doctrine must now be considered.

It is necessary, as usual in discussing philosophical questions, to distinguish between the several meanings of the terms with which we are to be concerned. 'Relativity of knowledge' is a phrase which, on account of its ambiguity, has been a source of confused, and sometimes of sophistical, usage. We have already found that 'knowledge' means several psychologically distinct processes and products. 'Relativity' is similarly dangerous.

(a) The first sense of 'relativity' to be mentioned, can be distinguished by resort to the name 'comparativity'. What is then meant by the phrase under consideration, is that we only know relations, differences, etc., not objects or terms as such. It is true that knowledge about a thing consists largely in knowing what a thing is not, its difference from, and its relations to, other things: all determination is negation. But this comparativity of knowledge cannot be applied, as Bain at one time sought to apply it, to acquaintance or apprehension of the simplest percepts. We must apprehend sensa before we can compare them; we must apprehend the *quale* of red and of blue before we can allege that the colours differ. The thorough-going 'relativity' of science, which can speak of the ever less and the ever more in magnitude, cannot be applied to sense-knowledge; for there we come upon absolute limits in *minima sensibilia*, specious presents, and so forth. That all knowledge, including acquaintance, is relative, in the sense of being a matter of comparativity, is thus not tenable.

(b) That knowledge is relative, sometimes means that it is

limited; that we "know in part", and know only what we have the faculty to know. This is but a truism. Knowledge certainly is limited both by our senses, faculties, etc., and by what is presented to them. There well may be more things in heaven and earth than are known in our science, or even than are dreamed of in our philosophy. The existent is not necessarily co-extensive with the known or the knowable, *esse* with *percipi* or *intelligi*. Idealists (mentalists) have sometimes leaped from the tautology 'what is known is known' to the dogma that what is, is known or knowable. They have relied much on pronouncements such as 'one cannot conceive things to exist apart from consciousness'; which, accordingly as we punctuate, becomes tautology or dogma. Realists, with more justification, equally transcend "the egocentric predicament", when they assert that there exists more than is, or can be, known. There is certainly no reason to the contrary; and assuming this to be so, we can assert the 'partiality' of knowledge.

It has sometimes been insisted that the known limitations of the range of the human senses, as compared with the sensibility of other organisms, must render our knowledge partial. This is true as to acquaintance: were our range of colour-sense, etc., wider, the world would certainly be different for us, as artists. But if scientific 'knowledge about' be in question, the assertion is disputable. We know much about magnetism though we have no magnetic sense, and about infra-red and ultra-violet light beyond the limits of visibility. Scientific knowledge, which has advanced from sense-data to relations between them, probably does not suffer from the limited range of our sensibility, and indeed is accessible to the blind and deaf.

(c) We pass to a more important meaning of relativity, and one especially connected with phenomenalism, viz. what Dr Ward in unpublished lectures, distinguished as 'impurity'. The doctrine of the relativity of knowledge now becomes a denial of realism such as would abolish distinction between reality and appearance, and refuse to assign 'coloured spectacles' to the mind. If the ontal (ω) be not known in its native purity, but only with additions or modifications due to our organs of sense and the capacities and peculiarities of our intelligence, then things are not what they seem, and all knowing is the converse of seeming *i.e.* is symbolising. Assuming phenomenalism to be true, know-ledge—or at any rate sense-knowledge—may be either an additive product, analogous to the air which chemists call a mixture, or a heteropathic and 'emergent' evolute, comparable to water that is formed by combination of its constituent gases. In the former case, it should be theoretically possible, provided a sufficient number of equations were obtainable, to eliminate the bodily and mental terms, and to arrive at the ontal; in the latter case, the subjective contribution or factor could not thus be eliminated. Phenomenal knowledge, however far extended, would then bring us no nearer to apprehension of the thing *per se*. Hence Hamilton was led to maintain that we have no absolute or pure knowledge of anything, and no knowledge at all of the absolute or of the ontal. He taught that we only know the phenomenal; and if knowledge be taken to be nothing if not pure—seeing face to face and not through a glass, darkly—it then follows that we can really or purely know nothing. Thus Kant's phenomenalism was de-veloped into the agnosticism of Mansel and Spencer, and into a scepticism similar to that of Hume.

It is of course implied, in this form of the doctrine of relativity, that our knowledge, because of its impurity, does not come up to some standard; that it falls short of the ideal of the purist. We should be better off, it is insinuated, if we could see the ontal, as it were, through plate-glass; even better off, if we could *be* the things we know, *erbeben* their *Erlebnisse*, as some mystics claim to be the case in their knowledge of God; or if we could have creative rather than discursive thought, and so see things as God sees them. Such 'intelligible intuition', positing the objects which it apprehends, is a conceivable ideal that surpasses so-called knowledge that we have; such also is face-to-face vision of the noumenal. The other kind just suggested, is obviously in-compatible with subjecthood in any form, even that which the theist, as distinct from the pantheistic absolutist, ascribes to the Deity. Hamilton seems to have been discontented, not because we are not gods, nor because we cannot transcend the law of contradiction; but because he thought that knowledge, in order to be knowledge, ought to copy the ontal. That knowledge so-called does not do so, is the deficiency in virtue of which he disparages it as obscure and impure, or—in his terminology—relative. It is only as not possessing purity, then, that phenomenal knowledge is deemed to be gravely at fault.

That there is any fault at all, of pernicious kind, in such relativity as phenomenalism bespeaks, is disputable. We have already substituted for the dictum that we only know phenomena, the more correct statement that we know the noumenal through the phenomenal. The phenomenon is, so to say, the utterance of the ontal *to us*; if the noumenal shines forth, or appears to us, as the phenomenal, it cannot be totally unknowable. And why should the appearing be assumed to be a veiling, rather than a revealing, a distortion or caricature, rather than representation? Philosophers have been wont to assume that phenomena only serve the purpose of deception. But their pessimism is groundless. What matters, is whether knowledge is *relevant* to Reality, not whether it is a pure copy thereof. If the very *raison d'être* of things *per se* be to mediate meaning or significance, it may be that the nature of the naked thing *per se*, which because of our coloured spectacles we can never view as it is, is the least significant and valuable thing about it. It does not matter that my map of Lakeland fails to reproduce the coloured scenery, if, by its correspondence with the country, it guides me correctly in my walks and climbs. Or again, if paint and tinsel, cardboard trees and houses, would confront us on the theatre-stage as the 'realities', this is beside the mark if, as visible from our seat in the stalls, their appearance-effects entertain us with a drama full of meaning. It is the play we go to see, not stage-mechanisms. And if phenomena are what we make of things *per se*, they may be to us the more expressive, significant and relevant utterances, because *ad homines*; just as English is the most expressive language to the insular Englishman. Possibly we should not understand the scenery and drama of life in this world any the better, if our knowledge were non-phenomenal. Our phenomenal knowledge, if relative, may be 'to the purpose'; and that is all that matters, and gives knowledge its value. The noumenal essence may be hidden from our eyes, and yet the world's 'meaning' be readable. Phenomenal knowledge is biologically sufficient for finding our way about the world: it may be philosophically sufficient for both worldly and spiritual wisdom. We have already found that knowledge, as a matter of fact, is essentially 'understanding', not in the sense of reading off formal relations, but in the sense of establishing *rapport* by anthropically assimilating or sympathising, and so making ourselves at home in our environment. We need not then, as phenomenalists, be dismayed by the fact that our knowledge is relative in the sense of impure, if we can still believe that our knowledge is relevant to Reality, while its impurity is an irrelevancy. If we have no absolute or pure knowledge of anything ontal, or none save in the case of our partial knowledge as to our own souls, it cannot be maintained that we have *no* knowledge *of* the ontal, even of the ontal other than our souls.

7. Of the three general kinds of epistemological theory that have been discussed in the present chapter, one calls for more than the fragmentary notice that as yet there has been occasion to bestow on it. This is idealism. The word 'idealism' is popularly used as having reference to ideals; it has also become a synonym for spiritualism in philosophical literature: here, of course, it bears neither of these meanings, but in its broadest sense denotes theories as to the identity of being with subjective states or with thought (mentalism). The simplest form of idealism is that called subjective, according to which the *idion* is a mode of the subject. It is as impotent as sensationism to account for common knowledge and for thought. Closely akin is the 'problematical idealism' which maintains that internal or subjective states are of higher 'degree of reality', are known most immediately, and are the data from which 'objects' of any order or kind are only precariously inferred. Kant's rejection of this teaching, on the ground that reflective knowledge of mental states presupposes objects and is only obtainable through their mediation, has in an earlier chapter been found to be psychologically justified. These simpler forms of idealism logically end in solipsism, from which there is no way out; and, coupled with the sensationism which in varying degrees accompanied them in the systems of Berkeley and Hume, they issued also in scepticism. Berkeley, in his later writings, passed from an idealism represented by *esse est percipi* to one expressible as *esse est intelligi*. As intelligence was not derivable from his sensationist presuppositions, he needed to resort inconsistently to a doctrine of archetypal ideas, such as Plato taught; and to an assumptional theory which is idealistic in asserting the objects of knowledge to be ideas, realistic in affirming them to be ontal.

Kant's impoverished phenomenalism is sometimes called transcendental idealism: which further illustrates the elasticity with which the term 'idealism' has been used. For Kant expressly avoided an idealistic theory of intelligence or of 'universal' knowledge, by his resort to the notion of the thing *per se*. However much he overestimated the function of mind in making Nature and legislating for it, he was far from identifying being with thought. The ontal, or ultimately Real, for him, was independent of our thought. But in overhastily accusing the thing *per se* of unknowability, he made the descent from phenomenalism to idealism easy for his successors. Again, in mistaking 'objects of higher order', *i.e.* relations grounded in the objective, for purely subjective and *a priori*, he prepared the way for T. H. Green's theory that the world is a nexus of relations alone; also for the rationalistic, as well as idealistic, tenet that the valid is identical with the Real, or that validity is *per se* and not *of* Reality. The idealism that passes over into rationalistic realism, has already been accused of employing the ontological fallacy; of dogmatically hypostatising abstractions; of supposing, without any psychological grounds and with violence to the suggestions of psychological facts, that universals 'exist' *ante res*, and independently of thinkers and thinking. Its simpler forms, derived from considerations as to the *idion* of individual experience, seem to be due to misreading of psychological fact, or to confounding psychology of individual experience with metaphysics. Its higher forms, where concern is with common knowledge and the ontal, are the outcome of speculation such as is heedless of facts and data, and of abstractionism which, in place of facts, sets up figments. When, at the extreme limit, reason is abstracted both from reasoners and matter reasoned about, and is discussed as if it were a Real being, with a life-history that is timeless and a developement that is but of logical stages or 'moments', it should perhaps be classed with allegorical poetry, rather than with philosophy such as sets forth from science.

8. If phenomenalism be accepted, as the only theory as to the relation of knowledge to ultimate Reality that is consistent with itself and with the *prima facie* facts, it follows that the individual's experience, or commerce with his private world of *idia*, passes into participation in knowledge of a common world, in virtue of

ejection—whereby belief in other selves is first hazarded, and then pragmatically justified—and intersubjective intercourse. The categories, etc., then made explicit, are largely our human version of our *rapport* with the not-self. That 'universal' experience is not a 'wider solipsism', *i.e.* an intellectual idealism as distinct from a sensationist idealism, is necessitated by the not-self, as indispensable source of our cognition. Common knowledge, then, is anthropic or racial interpretation of *rapport* with the ontal, which is seen in a mirror darkly, and not face to face. We can never transcend the human standpoint and mode of viewing. Perhaps we should be helped towards absolute or pure knowledge of the noumenal behind phenomenal Nature, if we could compare notes with non-human beings. Such parallax-methods are, however, as yet beyond the reach of mankind. We are shut up to framing hypotheses and testing their compatibility with the heteropathic product, phenomenal knowledge of the ontal. Thus is vindicated the dogmatic statement made at the beginning of this chapter, that we cannot determine the bare nature of the ultimately Real by deducting all the contributions of the human mind. To know Reality, it is not necessary to become it; indeed, to know, and to be what is known, cannot be the same. Nor is it necessary to create or make or constitute it, whether out of nothing, out of subjective states or ideas, or out of formless data. It is enough to be in *rapport* with it. Nor, yet again, is it necessary to identify knowing with pure finding. Knowing, according to phenomenalism, is neither making, alone, nor finding, alone; but finding by making, or giving and taking. We do not make the ω-realm at all. We receive from it *ad modum recipientis* (in what other mode could we receive?) its utterance *to us, singillatim*, as embodied souls, and have sense-knowledge, or *perceptio*, each of his peculiar *idion*-world. Out of these worlds, which we *cannot but* 'make out of' the ω, we collaborate in 'making'—in quite a different way—the so-called phenomenal World of common sense and conceptual science; and we 'make' it, in order to comprehend the many *o*-worlds. But the *O*-world (to speak as if there were but one of the class) is still made 'out of' the one ω-realm and the *o*-realms many. The *O*-order has a foot in both worlds, ω and *o*, but is to be confounded with neither. It is some 'function' of ω; it is some function also of human souls. It changes with the progress of science, with the refinement of common sense. And if science should aspire to attain by its own methods to pure intellectual vision of ultimate Reality, the phenomenalist can only say that, while "ever learning" science is "never able to come to knowledge of the truth". Neither science, nor mysticism, nor yet algorithmic logic, can divest the human version of its anthropic characteristics.

CHAPTER XI

Induction and Probability: Knowledge, Belief and Faith.

1. INDUCTION.

If the general propositions that were regarded by rationalism as universal and *a priori* premisses of science, are disguised definitions or conventions when not inductions from empirical facts, it follows that there is no pure or *a priori* knowledge of the Actual world. Generalised premisses must be inductively obtained from the results of observation and experiment, before science can begin to be deductive. It has been represented, however, by philosophers and logicians who reject both rationalism and Kantian doctrine, some of whom would claim the name of empiricists, that unconditional and universal knowledge of Nature can be established by empirical and inductive procedure. J. S. Mill, *e.g.*, maintained that inductively obtained judgements may be rigidly demonstrable and certain, rather than merely 'probable'. He, and other logicians of the last century, endeavoured to provide what rationalism had in vain tried to establish, by a method other than that which rationalism had pursued. Rationalists had claimed knowledge of the universal, not dependent on sense-particulars. These 'empiricists' sought to extract the necessary out of the contingent, the universal out of the particular: setting out to bless empiricism, they ended by deserting it. Sometimes it was taught that induction is a simple and direct process of arguing from particular to particular, without the mediation of a general or universal premiss: such general truth being conclusion, not premiss. There is no doubt that human beings, like the lower animals, 'reason' in this way; but it hardly needs pointing out that what thereby is yielded, is alogical expectation or surmise, not anything that can be covered by the term 'knowledge', elastic as it is. There can be no logical transition from particular to particular truth, save by a general truth connecting them; or without the mediation of a universal or an identity, as a bridge. The particulars were indeed said to be really differences within the universal, though this could hardly be affirmed to be self-evident. And it was *assumed* that the 'medium' of the general was in the particulars, waiting merely to be read off or analytically extracted, as if all induction were of a piece with the particular kind distinguishable as 'intuitive'. Whewell was sensible of a defect in this account of induction current in his day, and saw that the inductive logic, used by science, included a mysterious step from particulars to generals, such as he could not adequately describe in words. The magic process in question was given the appearance of rationality by opportune transition from a term such as 'unvarying', to which the empiricist had some right, to one such as 'invariable' or 'unconditional', to which he had none. Induction from past to future, in order to be demonstrative or rational, and not merely evocative of sanguine expectation, needs to assume that past observations yield complete knowledge, and that the same conditions will, or must, hold in the future, as obtained in the past. In other words, empiricism needs the same assumptions as rationalism, in order to arrive at similar conclusions. It is of some interest, in this connexion, to note that Hume, the critic or sceptic when writing the *Treatise of Human Nature*, became Hume the rationalistic dogmatist when writing the very un-Humean essay *Of Miracles*. In the former work, he based all reasoning, concerned with matter of fact, on the principle of causality, and that in turn on custom and psychological motivation; arguing that we have no logical right to regard the world as other than one in which anything may succeed upon anything. In the essay, he begs, for his purpose in hand, a fixed order of Nature: assuming that past experience yields such exhaustive knowledge thereof that any alleged event incompatible with it "ought" *ipso facto* not to be believed. And so, in his zeal to deny the credibility of the miraculous, he implies the bounden duty of rejecting every new scientific discovery as nonsense, because a breach of customary sequence. Unless customary sequence be in fact the fixed order that Hume, in his essay, confounds it with, it can have no veto as to alleged occurrences, or our right to believe in them. That we *expect* a sequence, observed many times, to obtain the next time, is a purely psychological matter, an affair of alogical conditionings such as association of ideas. Whether we have any reason or right to entertain a positive or a negative expectation, depends on whether Nature is known to be uniform:

a matter of physics and logic. Hume fell into the common error of confounding logical certainty with psychological certitude, reason for belief with cause of believing: a confusion which it is perhaps hopeless to try to extirpate from unreflective common sense, but avoidance of which is essential to clear thinking about induction. Allusion has been made to this past history because it is Hume, unconsciously posing as the rationalist, rather than Hume, the critic and empiricist, that inspired much of the inductive logic of would-be empiricists in the nineteenth century, with whom we have more immediate concern.

'Induction' is sometimes used as comprehending the whole of scientific procedure, practical as well as ratiocinative, between observation of isolated facts and arrival, by hypothesis, deduction, experimental verification and generalisation, at laws. It is also used for the purely logical process of passing from particular facts to generalisations; for inductive, as distinguished from deductive, logic, or—to include all kinds of opinion—as a particular kind of deduction. This double usage is natural; for the kind of induction that is especially employed in the sciences, involves, we shall find, use of particular hypotheses, guesses, *anticipationes Naturae*, as well as fundamental postulates. This escaped Mill, who was a logician rather than experimental investigator, and whose account of induction shared to some extent the inadequacy of Bacon's. Tabulation of accumulated items of fact, with elimination of the irrelevant and retention of the constant (the essence of Mill's rules), are not sufficient for discovery of a law such as that of gravitation. Without conceptual anticipation of a possible order, the Actual cannot be 'known'; induction requires a postulate, in order to render its own 'proof' possible. The induction chiefly used by natural science, of the kinds presently to be distinguished as 'demonstrative' and 'problematic', begins when the rough work of classification is done; it is more than logical generalisation such as is formally certified. It is conclusion from 'some A is B' to 'all A is B', that what is true at one time is true, in like circumstances, at other times; and so on. Hence Claude Bernard described induction as "conjecture by means of deduction"; and Jevons treated it as the invention of hypotheses, until one is found whose deducible implications coincide with the results of experiment. The particular fact is first conceived or supposed to be an instance of universal law; induction (in its wider sense) discovers this law, establishing the general premisses or preconditions from which the fact follows, and so is the inverse of deduction. According to Mill, induction does not extend knowledge, save in the sense of explicating what was implicitly apprehended already; it contains no element of hypothesis or of postulation; it is not confined to probability (whatever that word may turn out to mean), but yields demonstrable certainty: if an induction is subsequently falsified by fact, this is not because induction itself is problematic, but because in the particular instance some logical error has been committed. Whether or not the prevalence of logical doctrine such as this, in the middle of last century and later, was due to Mill's work, several logicians such as Bain, Hobhouse and Bosanquet endeavoured, like Mill, to extract from induction the same kind of certainty, about Nature's uniformity and the reign of law, as the rationalists of earlier generations had deemed deducible from *a priori* truth. Empiricism, or rather what called itself by that name, as if somewhat overawed by the progress and prestige of physical science employing inductive methods, tried to swell itself out into a logic mediating unconditional and universal knowledge. It was sore put to, however, in its endeavour to steer between the *a priori* necessity and the conjectural postulate, as fundamental presupposition of induction. Mill argued as if many particular inductions proved the universal one, commonly indicated in the principle of uniformity; whereas each of them, taken singly, could only be deemed true, on the assumption that the principle was proved.

Bain lapsed from logic to psychology in asserting deviations from a law such as gravitation, to be "incredible", rather than impossible. Hobhouse mistook consilience of 'probabilities' for necessity or logical certainty, and needed also to blur the line between such Objective certainty and Subjective certitude. Bosanquet taught, in his earlier period, that a connected system (Hume's logically demolished, but controversially invoked, fixed order), though not given by the facts, is demanded by them; while subsequently he inclined to the doctrine that this nexus is given in the particular facts, and not imported into them by generalisation or otherwise. These writers may be said to have implicitly assumed what they are concerned to prove: to have argued in a circle. They evince the growing sense among logicians, that induction is not bare reasoning from the particular to the particular, but implicitly, at least, involves a presupposition—though they profess it to be an outcome—such as was vaguely stated in the principle of uniformity. They also testify to the fact that the inductive method, or inductive logic, is indispensable for the acquisition of scientific 'knowledge'. But, as Poincaré remarked of that principle which is either presupposition or outcome of induction, it is as difficult to justify it as to do without it. In order to be able to speak of scientific inductions as logically demonstrated knowledge, coming up to the Kantian standard in universality, necessity and unconditionalness, it is plainly necessary to be able to assert invariability of Nature; yet no finite number of cases of the hitherto unvarying, is sufficient to yield invariability. Bosanquet, and the more empirical school of Mill, may have refrained from speaking of the principle of uniformity as a major premiss, and from identifying, by that means, induction with syllogistic deduction. But in asserting that induction directly reveals the necessary connexion, the invariability, the universal, of which particulars are instances, and in endowing inductive logic with the same coerciveness as characterises deductive logic, they must be said to transcend genuine empiricism, and to be victims of unconscious rationalistic proclivity. It shall now be argued that recent advances in knowledge have made their case far less tenable than it appeared to be some decades ago.

Whatever may have been the doctrine of logicians, as to whether induction is syllogistic use of the uniformity-principle as major premiss, scientific investigators during the latter half of the nineteenth century, or such of them as wrote about the method of science, may be said to have been unanimous as to that principle being fundamental in all scientific procedure. And the first fact relevant to our present discussion, is that, during the same period, logicians were realising that this principle is impossible to state, in a form that should admit of applicability and not be tautologous or else false. We have seen, when examining the notion of cause, that when the causal principle is made logically precise, it becomes practically useless. We shall presently find that inductions are not syllogisms at all. But if they were, they could not be syllogisms derived from a common major premiss: for, as Dr Broad has remarked, in that case if the minor premisses were statements of equally careful observations, all inductions ought to be equally probable—which they are not. And again, if there were one major premiss for inductions, and one principle underlying all scientific procedure, this could not be the old vague principle of uniformity. Before passing on to consider the several independent principles which have lately superseded the now obsolete and useless one, we may at this point take note of the results of examination of the genesis of the time-honoured principle, and of human belief in its validity. This will be to observe chronological order as to the influx of new knowledge, and will also be in keeping with our persistent determination to turn the searchlight of genetic study, decried as it is wont to be because deemed irrelevant, on the finished products of thought-processes.

Before the logicians had finished refining the principle of uniformity to tautological transparency, the psychologist had stepped in to testify to its humble origin, its mediacy, and to the gradualness of its coming to inspire pragmatically that (ψ) certitude, or to acquire that convincingness, which perhaps led the school of Mill to regard it as readable between Nature's lines with (ps) immediate intuitiveness, comparable to that which discerns a whole to be greater than its part. Genetic studies, wont to be ruled out as irrelevant to logical priorities, at least in some instances reveal that the finished products, manipulated by abstract and formal thought, are not entitled to the name of knowledge, in the sense in which the rationalist would use that term; and so it is here. Ward has observed that all science must have originated in belief and faith-venture. Mankind did not begin its intellectual career with knowledge or knowing, but with learning; and that, chiefly through doing.[1] Learning came sometimes by success, sometimes by failure; and in either case man ventured before he could have. Without this primitive faith or credulity, mankind would never have started on its acquisition of science and civilisation. The causal law, or principle of uniformity, is not written so large or so legibly upon natural phenomena that, in the time of man's primitiveness, he who ran could read it off. On the other hand, had it not been hoped for or expected and tentatively assumed, here a little and there a little, line upon line, the principle could

[1] Of course, ultimately, doing presupposes *some* knowing; but everyone will understand what Dr Ward meant.

not have become 'known'. The "father of the faithful", in leaving his Mesopotamian home, forsaking the Nature-worship of his ancestors, hearkening to the inward summons to go out not knowing whither he went, was not only a prophetic type of the religious history of Israel, but also an allegory of the intellectual progress of the race.[1] Had man not similarly believed and trusted the regularity of Nature, while as yet it was undiscerned and unverified, and while what afterwards was to become familiar was as yet mysterious: the thing unseen, yet hoped for, would never have obtained substance or relevance to life. *Credo ut intelligam* or, in the vulgar tongue, "nothing venture nothing have", has been, and necessarily must have been, the attitude of mind, in virtue of which the 'rationality' of the world was gradually discerned. Mankind attained his science, as his religion, and in particular his belief in uniformity, as pragmatic substantiation of the hoped for and unknown, of what was desired to make wise. And we shall find that this plucking from the tree of knowledge, even in the case of the knowledge we call science, has proved a courting of logical trouble.

The genetic study of individual experience, pursued in earlier chapters, leads to the same conclusion as this brief glance at racial developement, the details of which are provided by historians. Science's progress is due to its quasi-religious faith that this world is amenable to human reason, though there can be no *a priori* reason why it should be. Science has maintained that hope against the world itself, throughout its struggle with the obstinate brutality of fact. It has consequently succeeded in establishing, in certain tracts of Actuality, a reign of law. But when it knows its own limitations, and derives its logic from its own practice and not from text-books, it refrains from speaking of "laws that never shall be broken": or of law, in any sense but that of problematic generalisation of empirical knowledge up to date.

Whatever 'uniformity' in Nature may precisely mean, it is evidently postulatory, not a principle formally certifiable either deductively or inductively. The only 'verification' it can receive, is experimental; and that is confined to limited reaches in time and space, and but to parts within the whole content of experience. Moreover, we shall find that it is circular, if 'verification' be taken

[1] Had Abraham been a mere adventurer, without inward 'call', this analogy would be still more apt.

literally, or as identical with logical certification: from which it is distinct, in that it evidences applicability, not exclusive or sole applicability.

A stage has now been reached, at which it is necessary to clear away any possibility of confusion that might ensue on continuing to speak of induction, as if it were but one kind of logic or reasoning. So far, it has only been hinted that induction is of more kinds than one; we may now distinguish between the types that have been enumerated and described in the recent work of Mr Johnson.

I. *Intuitive Induction.* This has already received some notice, as the process that establishes the fundamental principles of inference, and the self-evident, *i.e.* the immediately read off, 'axioms' which form some of the first principles of logic and mathematics. The formal intuitions differ entirely from conventional definitions, assumed rules, or imperatives thrust upon us by social authority. They are imposed with as much of external control as sense-data, once we understand the propositions from which they emerge; and the immediacy of their apprehension is (ps), as well as (ψ). The conclusions of these inductions, *e.g.*, that 'some A's are B's' implies 'some B's are A's', are as certain as their premisses. Besides the formal kind, such as have been instanced, there are also experiential or sense-provided intuitive inductions: *e.g.* the judgement, from a single instance, that in all cases an equilateral triangle is also equiangular. We have already remarked on the important, the lonely or unique, position which these intuitive inductions, if the account given of them be accurate, occupy: they alone yield truth that possesses all the several characteristics of being (in the case of the experiential kind) derived from the perceptual, apprehended with (ps) immediacy, imposed with necessitation, valid universally as well as in the particular present instance. We can understand, while we must withstand, the tendency to regard, as belonging to this class of self-evident propositions, certain that belong to other classes, because not possessing some one or more of the characteristics just mentioned: *e.g.* problematic inductions, presently to be distinguished.

Inductions claiming to be universal, yet not merely problematical, should hold a pre-eminent place in the structure of human knowledge. It therefore behoves us to make sure that this claim is justified: in other words, that the description given of them is, in all relevant particulars, flawless. There would seem to be no possibility of error as to their universality, nor as to the absence of any underlying postulate such as could render them problematical. But as to the absoluteness of the immediacy generally attributed to them, comments may be made; and to make them, if they have any cogency, will serve to shew that the virtue of intuitive inductions is not contained in their immediacy, but that such immediacy is irrelevant to their universality and certainty. These inductions have been described above, in deference to authorities, as if they were cases of what may be called 'intuition in a flash'. And it may be submitted that here we are presented with one of those finished products of developed or adult experience, which the logician and the non-psychological epistemologist accept as data; but which the epistemologist, who approaches his subject from psychology, will insist on scrutinising in respect of their genesis. Intuition in a flash, may be outcome of practice; of rapid imaginal experimenting and inference; of subliminal synthetic process. Even (ps) immediacy, as distinguished from that of the (ψ) kind, is but affirmed by reflective psychology with due reservation as to the relativity of the distinction between the psychologically macroscopic (the observable or verifiable) and the psychologically microscopic, or non-introspectible. There are no literally instantaneous intuitions, of course; but possibly there are mental operations too rapid to be differentiated by introspection. It may be, as Rignano suggests, that intuitive induction, recognition that one case suits all—*ex uno omnes*—as in Euclid's proofs, is 'instantaneous', *i.e.* very rapid, recognition that if we imaginally repeated experiments, such as constitute demonstration as to the figure before the eye, on imaginal figures differing only in certain (irrelevant) respects, the result would be the same. If this be so, the distinction, drawn by Mr Johnson between intuitive induction and a type of geometrical 'induction by simple enumeration', which he regards as imaginal experimentation, and as to which something shall presently be said, seems to vanish. Nothing essential, however, is gained or lost if, as to this detail, Mr Johnson be found to be in error. But we may observe that (ps) mediateness passes into (ψ) immediateness, at all rates: from the slower, involved in reflective processes, to the higher rapidity such as would characterise, if Rignano be correct, 'intuition in a flash'. Rapidity being always relative, it serves no epistemological interest to regard what, for psychology, is extreme rapidity, as if it were an absolute limit such as recent physics ascribes to the velocity of light. Rapidity of mental synthesis, or of intake, is irrelevant to the truth of the proposition synthetically reached and taken in. In so far as immediacy is a matter of time or velocity, it is of no import for epistemology; and if the beatitudes wont to be lavished on immediate apprehension, as if it necessarily possessed superior truth-claims, be evoked, not by mere rapidity of process, but by supposed absence of *all* linkage or mediation (such as inferential procedure), whenever psychological science can empirically find none, they are doubtfully well-bestowed. The (ps) immediate is to the (ψ) immediate, we may grant, as science is to convictions of cranks. But just as phenomenal science is not pure vision of ultimate reality; neither is such (ps) immediacy as psychology may assert of inductive cognitions, necessarily absolute: indiscernibility of mediation is not necessarily absence thereof. Unless, however, these two things be identical, there would seem to be no more epistemological significance about the immediacy of intuitive induction, than there is physical significance about Fahrenheit's choice of 32° for the freezing-point: so long, that is, as epistemology is conceived as isolable from psychology, and truth as independent of knowers or interpreters. Immediacy is always relative; even the psychological absolutes, such as *minima sensibilia*, the specious present, etc., are but relative to *homo mensura* and his contingent discrimination-limits. Equally in faith-philosophies, 'enthusiasms,' mysticism, rationalistic intuitionism, Kant's practical reason, Bradley's intellectualism and Bergson's anti-intellectualism, the appeal to immediacy—evoked by failure to find comfort in the mediated, and assuming either (ψ) or (ps) immediacy to be the pre-eminent criterion of truth—has been futile: it is something gained, therefore, if we can exempt intuitive induction from any dependence on it.

II. *Induction by simple enumeration: perfect, summary induction.* This kind has sometimes been excluded from induction proper, on the ground that its conclusion is no wider than its premisses, or that it does not yield universality. That, however, is not always the case; at least it is not so, if we include in this class mathematical inductions such as the axiom that two straight lines, intersecting in one point, cannot intersect at any other point. Here the conclusion exceeds the perceptual observations. It is only made possible by our supplying what Mr Johnson calls the necessary "imagery"—'ideation' is rather called for in connexion with infinity of positions and indefiniteness of extension—of a line revolving through 360°: so it obtains universality of application. Such geometrical induction to non-enumerable cases has been classed under intuitive, and also under problematic, induction. It differs from the former kind, in connexion with which it was just now incidentally referred to, if that be always rightly described as being attained through one or two perceptual instances, without aid from the imaginal or ideal instances essential for the induction now under consideration. It differs from problematic induction, in that the conclusion does not go beyond the examined cases, which, in this type of geometrical induction, are "imaginally" apprehended, as Mr Johnson points out, in their infinite totality. This special type excepted, the method of simple enumeration does not reach beyond the observed examples. Consequently, it is used in science, only as a preparatory step to unlimited generalisation, such as is not characterised by the same certainty. There we come upon an element to which the Baconian canons did scant justice: the difficult matter of discovering the colligating concept, so different from passing from instance to instance and then inferentially extending to unexamined cases. For this, hypotheses are requisite: sometimes those which emanate only from the imaginative genius; who should be superfluous, if Bacon's, and even Mill's, account of induction were adequate.

III. *Demonstrative Induction.* This type is placed next to those which have preceded, because in it, as in them, the conclusion follows with necessity. In this respect it likewise resembles deduction. Unfortunately it differs from intuitive and summary induction, and further resembles deduction, in arriving at necessary implications of premisses, the truth of which it does not establish: it does not guarantee, therefore, the truth of its conclusions. Unlike simple enumeration of perceptual instances, it yields generalisation wider than its premisses. It might perhaps more correctly be called inductive demonstration than induction; for it is not generalisation of a particular minor, though for its minor premiss a single instance may suffice. Its major premiss varies from case to case according to the phenomena concerned, and so is not the principle of universal uniformity, though presupposing something like it. This major involves an assumption, 'established' by accumulation of instances and by problematic induction: it is, in fact, what logic technically calls a hypothetical judgement. In this respect, the more natural place, on a list of kinds of induction for this type (if it is to be called induction at all), is after that which remains to be considered.

To cite an example given by Mr Johnson: every specimen of argon has the same atomic weight; this specimen has the atomic weight 39·9; therefore every specimen of argon has the atomic weight 39·9. The authority whose teaching is here being reproduced, points out that the particular processes that yield the major premiss, involve the elimination of irrelevant facts of prescientific observation. This premiss, at the hands of science, becomes assertion that the character of the phenomena in question depends on a *limited* number of variable conditions, variation in each of which must be independent of variations in the others; and on the *simplicity* of the characteristics into which the total character of the phenomena have been resolved. Thus assumption is introduced, as to which Mill was unaware. The specific major premiss is assumed to have been established; and, as we have yet to shew more clearly, 'established' can only mean established as 'probable'. Demonstrative induction, it will have been observed, resembles deduction in requiring two types of premiss. Its major premiss is always universal, its minor is particular or instantial.

IV. *Problematic Induction.* This kind of induction, employed in providing one of the premisses of so-called demonstrative induction, differs from that kind, in that the instances compared are not determinately analysed, with respect to the variable characterisations on which the proposed generalisation may depend. When the differences between the instances are not exhaustively known, it is possible that unforeseen differences may exist. If there be no antecedent knowledge as to the conditioning of black colour by one or more of the other characteristics that constitute a crow, it is only by multiplication of instances of black crows, that we can gain any appreciable 'probability' for the conclusion that all crows are black. In this kind of induction, then, accumulation of instances is requisite to confirm the hypothesis that the characteristic p, possessed by the observed individuals $S_1 \ldots S_m$ really characterises the whole class $S_1 \ldots S_n$, so that all S is p. The precariousness of conclusions thus reached, is obvious. If m S's are p, that the $m + 1$th will be p, is 'probable' *relatively to the data*, and may not be true: a white crow may turn up after millions have been observed to be black. And to accumulate more instances, will but slightly increase the very small 'probability' of the conclusion. Hence science works chiefly with demonstrative induction: problematic induction is useful only at the first stage of investigation, when there is little scientifically organised relevant experience to draw upon. Increase of definite knowledge concerning the instances examined, is of far more importance than multiplication of instances without reference to circumstances, Actual conditionings, irrelevant accompaniments, and so on. To be included in the class S, the unobserved instances must, in spite of individuality, resemble in many details the observed S's that are p: and in details that are essential and not irrelevant. Hence the inductive method of science rather concentrates on the analogy between the instances, as disclosed by more and more refined analysis, than on the number of observations in the rough. It is demonstrative induction, which takes its rise out of the problematical, that is pre-eminently characteristic of the method of science. To this important logical method, and its epistemological nature, we must presently revert; but it is now expedient to indicate the chief differences between induction and deduction, in general.

In deduction, the conclusion is generally (there are said to be exceptions) no wider than the narrowest premiss and, in order to be universal, requires universal premisses. In induction, except the kind called simple enumeration, which, by the way, is reducible to deduction, the conclusion goes beyond the premisses, and is from the known to the experientially unknown. Induction, for instance, infers from 'some S is p' to 'all S is p'; it is generalisation of the particular. Deduction, again, is direct and definite, towards a conclusion that is one or, as it is sometimes described, unique: as from 12×12 to 144, two forces to a sole resultant, definite causes to one definite effect, two premisses to one conclusion. From 144, on the other hand, we can obtain several pairs or groups of factors; to a sole resultant we can assign an indefinite number of component forces; to an effect, perhaps a variety of possible causes; and so on: and it is in this direction that induction works, needing to eliminate indefiniteness how it can in each case. Deduction depends on the logical relation of implication, characterised by necessity and certainty; induction—of the kinds III and IV—yields conclusions that are 'probable': a term which, so far in this chapter, has been used to connote absence of certainty, and nothing more definite than that. The statement that these kinds of induction are probable, will be explained presently; when also the previously made assertion, that such induction uses hypotheses and rests on postulates, will be made good. Lastly, the particular kind of deduction known as the syllogism, and induction of the types III and IV (save for the particular syllogistic factor that appears in the third kind), differ in that they make use of different 'principles', as they have been technically called by Mr Johnson. The syllogistic principle asserts that, provided a certain relation holds between three propositions p, q, r, inference from the premisses p and q *alone*, will formally justify the conclusion r. This principle is not an additional premiss. If it were a premiss, the principle would be self-contradictory. It is therefore not coordinate with the premisses, but it is used or involved in the inference-process: syllogistic inference is *from* the two premisses alone, *through* the principle. The principle is established by intuitive induction; and some would perhaps on that account call it *a priori*. It practically means that, what can be predicated of every member of a class to which a given instance belongs, can be predicated of that instance. The inductive principle, through, but not from, which inductive conclusions are obtained, is different, and is stated thus: what can be predicated of all examined members of a class, can be predicated, *with higher or lower probability*, of all members of that class. Using this principle, induction argues: all examined instances characterised by a certain adjective, are characterised by a certain other adjective; therefore, with higher or lower probability, we can predicate of all, what is predicated of all examined, instances. Deduction and induction require each its own principle, and the inductive principle cannot be deduced from the other. It is the element of probability expressly mentioned in the inductive principle, that renders 'problematic', and also 'demonstrative', induction problematical. In order that an induction, of these kinds may be known to be certain or actually, as well as nominally, demonstrative, the problematic element would need to be replaced by self-evidence, or else by rigid proof. This is what some logicians of the 'empirical' school sought to effect; but as we shall find, it is impossible.

The uncertainty or probability of problematic induction, which henceforth may simply be called induction, used commonly to be indicated by the name 'hypothetical'. But inasmuch as, in formal logic, the hypothetical judgement is distinct from the problematical; and as 'hypothetical' is not univocal, when used in connexion with inductive demonstration: the term 'problematic' is preferable. The ambiguity of 'hypothetical', may be illustrated by reference to Jevons' treatment of induction; which also possesses intrinsic interest for us, at this stage, because of its intermediate position between the inductive logic of Mill and that which is the outcome of recent investigations, presently to be expounded.

Jevons asserted induction, such as is used in science, to consist of three processes, or to have three stages. The first is formation of a hypothesis: which here means formulation of a proposition that is provisionally entertained, a working-hypothesis or unproved guess, a generalisation to be established, a *demonstrandum*. The second stage is deductive: the implications or consequences of the hypothesis are deduced. Such deduction does not prove them true or demonstrate them; as yet they are established only as, in the technical language of traditional logic, 'hypothetical' judgements—of the nature: '*if p* is true, then *q* is true'. Here we encounter a second sense of 'hypothetic'. The third step is 'verification'. Deduced, and now anticipated, consequences of the original hypothesis, are experimentally found to tally with Actual occurrences; the hypothesis itself is, accordingly, verified. Verification, however, is not logical certification: if it were, induction would not be problematic, or uncertified, which Jevons held it to be, and is what he meant when he called its conclusion—in a third sense—hypothetical. Verification can only mean transition from a lower, to a higher, degree of probability. This is an important point. What in science is called experimental, or inductive, verification, is far removed from certification, for several reasons. The process is of the form: if h (original hypothesis) is true, q_1, q_2 ... (deduced consequences) must be true; experiment shews they are true; therefore h is verified. But h is not certified by its implication of q_1, q_2, etc., which are true; to be certified, it would need to be the *only* possible hypothesis implying q_1, q_2, etc. To prove that is generally impossible. Inductive science, in its wave-theory of light or its atomic theory of matter, certifies only that Nature has for a certain period of time behaved as if these theories were true. There is no logical certainty that they are true even within that range of time, let alone their immutable truth: but there may be overwhelming psychological certitude as to such theories. Practically equivalent, these entirely different things are commonly confounded; and the natural man is tantalised when told that logical uncertainty attaches to laws that he finds very reliable. Logical diffidence and sanguine practical confidence are not incompatible, however. Indeed we shall presently find that reasonableness consists in combining them, while no great acumen is needed to distinguish them.

Again, there is unavoidable circularity about scientific verification of the working-hypothesis. Experimental control itself involves assumption of generalisations, established only by problematic induction. To verify a hypothesis in one science, it is necessary to assume hypotheses adopted in other sciences; an isolable hypothesis can nowhere be found. For logical certification, as distinguished from scientific verification, it is not enough to say, as Prof. Dewar said in an address to the British Association in 1902, that "no theoretical forecast, however apparently justified by analogy, can be fully accepted as true until it is confirmed by actual experiment". The electron-theory may be applicable to physical facts, without there being such existents as electrons. As science well knows, the true is sometimes implied by the false, and verified theories sometimes become falsified. Verification, moreover, is a matter of our capacity to acquire 'knowledge'; and the unverifiable is not to be identified with the untrue. But, to return to what more directly concerns us, the important point is that, though verification may vouch that a theory is 'sufficient', it cannot shew that no other theory may 'satisfy' the facts. Experiment, and the inductive reasoning described by Jevons, can never prove the truth of a 'hypothesis', or attain to known certainty. If knowledge be defined in terms of certainty, logically derived from immediately read off fact, we must not look for knowledge in scientific treatises. A 'scientific' fact, such as that the heating effect of an electric current is proportional to the resistance and to the square of the strength of the current, is nine-tenths theory, hypothesis or idea. Mill was not unalive to the importance of the 'appropriate concept', nor to the instrumental value of hypothesis; but he set out with a tendency to separate unduly the fact, regarded as source whence the idea is extracted by comparison, and as if independent of idea or hypothesis, and the idea that becomes primary in respect of giving significance and order to facts. Jevons similarly regarded fact and hypothesis as if they arose more independently of one another than they do, so that the one could be verified by the other. And when he tried to justify induction (the 'hypothetical' or problematic nature of which he fully recognised), by means of the probability-calculus, and as probable in the mathematician's sense, he made unwarranted assumptions. He also failed to see— what perhaps Venn alone of the nineteenth-century empirical school discerned—that hypothesis, such as is essential to the inductive demonstrations of science, arises in human needs.

It has already been hinted that if induction is to yield certain knowledge, or is logically (as distinguished from psychologically) to justify belief in scientific predictions, we must be able to claim knowledge of some one or more general statements about Nature. Various fundamental 'truths' or assumptions have been offered for the discharge of this function. Some rationalistically inclined logicians have invoked the principle of identity, or a principle of necessary connexion according to which the given is necessary; but *a priori* foundations have previously been argued to be inadequate or irrelevant. 'Empiricists' have pointed to the law of causation, or the principle of uniformity; but empirical attempts to demonstrate any such universal law have been shewn to be obviously circular. A more rationalistic endeavour with the same end in view, is that of Hamelin and other French writers who have maintained that, were our inductive presupposition untrue, the agreement of scientific thought with Nature must be ascribed to chance; that unless the hypothesis were true, the consequences would not follow or be verifiable. But this, as we have just seen in another connexion, is a *non sequitur* from the point of view of logic—our present sole consideration. Once more, the American logician, Peirce, taught that, the world having a determinate constitution, we can avoid resort to any principle such as that of uniformity, and draw probable conclusions from 'fair samples' of given collections. Here, indeed, the probability or problematic nature of induction is not repudiated or transcended; but the justifying principle assigned, is to be rejected. It seems to depend on confusing two different senses of 'fair': viz. chosen at random without bias or selectiveness, and representative of the whole collection—as if samples, fair in the one sense, were necessarily fair in the other.

From the failure of these several attempts, we may gather that unless induction be formulated in terms of probability, it involves fallacy; while we have no logical right to believe in the universal truth of inductive conclusions unless *some* premiss or premisses, other than such as can be furnished empirically, are true. What these presuppositions are, it has not proved easy to ascertain. Nevertheless, it may be said that they have at last been discovered, by the recent investigations of Mr Johnson, Dr Broad and Mr Keynes.[1] The first of these logicians, as already observed, points out that the major premiss of what he calls demonstrative induction, *i.e.* of the analogical induction constitutive of the essence of scientific method, assumes that the characters of the phenomena depend on a limited number of variable conditions, variations in each of which must be independent of variations in others; and that the characteristics, into which the total character is analysed, must be simple, or further unanalysable. It may be taken as beyond question that these propositions are logical foundations of analogical induction; and that the conclusions of inductive arguments cannot be known to be true, unless these propositions can be known to be true. Until the last volume of Mr Johnson's *Logic* shall appear, we must turn for fuller explication of these foundations to the writings of Dr Broad and Mr Keynes, who in all essential points agree with one another and with Mr Johnson. The propositions in question are specific and independent of one another; and, together, they yield in

[1] See *Logic*, by W. E. Johnson, especially Part II; Dr Broad in *Mind*, N.S. Nos. 108 and 113; *A Treatise on Probability*, by J. M. Keynes.

definite and precise form the relevant contents of the old vague principle of uniformity, within which they were fused and concealed, and for which they are the modern substitute.[1] They are assertions about the ultimate constituents of physical Reality, about substances and causes.

The first of them asserts that the variety of Nature's ultimate constituents is limited. Mr Keynes is content to say that the first logical requisite for analogical induction is: that no Object is so complex that its qualities fall into an infinite number of independent groups, such as might exist apart from one another, as well as in conjunction; or, rather, that none of the things about which science generalises, are as complex as this. Dr Broad is somewhat more exacting in his statement of this principle of 'limitation of independent variety', and is therein perhaps more precise and thorough in the interests of both logic and science. He affirms that induction, to be logically justifiable, presupposes that there be but *few* 'natural kinds', or substances, out of which Nature is built; and that all instances of any of them be exactly alike and completely permanent. This rigorous statement is essential, if we are to abandon vagueness and approximativeness. Its non-empirical nature at once strikes us; exact likeness and complete permanence are ideals, for ever beyond the reach of the most exact science that human measurements can furnish. We see now that logical rigour in inductive science theoretically requires that invariability in Nature, into which Mill and others tried to expand observed unvaryingness, as plainly as we see that such invariability, complete permanence or exact likeness, can never be a matter of either empirical, or *a priori*, demonstrability.

The second presupposition on which induction logically rests, is that each of the elementary changes, into which a macroscopic change can be analysed, must be independently caused. The set of characters which condition the inductive generalisation, *must* not be a possible effect of more than one distinct set of fundamental properties. Otherwise, inference such as science seeks, is precluded; and scientific inductions become merely statistical, rather than universal. We may regard this second proposition as an application, to substances or physical (non-phenomenal)

---

[1] See Note M on the principle of uniformity and on uniformity.

ultimates, of the parallelogram-law: which is not 'purely' demonstrable, as we have seen, in its original sphere of application. Or, once more, the second presupposition may be taken as equivalent to a denial of plurality of causes, or of the theory that Nature is what is called an organic whole.

That these foundations of inductive logic have their equivalents, in the practical procedure of physical science, will have been observed. Science works on the supposition of 'atomic uniformity', or of the superposition of small effects; that bodies, or the physical elements that figure in natural laws, are such that each exerts its separate influence, and produces its invariable effect, independently of others, as if they were not present. Thus a change of state in the whole world, is treated as if it were compounded of a number of separate changes, each of these being due to a separate portion of a preceding state. As to limited variety in Nature's ultimate constituents, science has ever indulged the *hope* that *all* actual diversity will become subsumible under conceptual identity. Her ideal and goal is to describe material things in terms of one sole kind of ultimate matter, and all changes in terms of change of its configurations alone. She would geometrise matter and kinematicise physics. In investigating change, she uses a method which, at its ideal limit, implies there is no change save of place; and it is startling enough that the method has met with much success. That has been the case, however, because, while hoping for identity, science has worked with limited diversity. She has avoided a practical *reductio ad absurdum*, by leavening her rationalistic procedure with a saving grain of the alogical: by adopting the judicious compromise provided in the *limited* diversity of Mr Keynes and Dr Broad. The modesty that asks for identity, in any measure between all and none, does not seem to bespeak the thorough-going logicality, unity and simplicity, desired by rationalistic metaphysicians; it is rather suggestive of practical hygiene for preservation of sanity. And indeed, we shall shortly encounter reasons for believing that the 'rationality' to which man owes his proudest achievement—his science of the physical universe—only escapes absurdity and self-stultification by becoming partly alogical 'reasonableness'.

The two independent principles by which the old principle of uniformity, shrewdly if vaguely taken to underlie, as a major premiss, the separate inductions of science if these were to allow of unification or systematic coherence, are admitted by all three of the logicians to whom we owe their discovery and precise formulation, to be neither self-evident (*i.e.* immediately intuitable) nor capable of proof, whether *a priori* or empirical. They are postulates. Of course they are suggested by Nature; and the more thoroughly Nature has been investigated, the stronger has grown the conviction as to their truth. Nay, the more definitely they have admitted of being formulated, the more exact appears to be Nature's accord with them. They cannot be logically *certified*; but they are pragmatically, if with circularity, '*verified*'. Scepticism of the academic kind with regard to them, must be tempered by the reflection that epistemological science is as yet incomplete, necessarily tentative, and far from commanding unanimity or claiming finality; it does not follow, from their uncertifiableness, that these postulates are untrue, or even deserving of cold suspicion. No similar warning need be uttered against scepticism of the practical sort; such an attitude is not likely to invade the complacency of common sense, or the sanguineness of the scientific investigator. Nowhere, perhaps, will absence of logical or 'rational' certification have less effect than here, in engendering scepticism. The postulates, because presupposed in inductive science, will be believed to be true, so long as they cannot be proved to be false. If caution be called for, it is in the converse direction. Applicability to Nature, as known in part and up to date, is not the same as validity, universal and immutable; pragmatic 'verification' is not logical certification; certitude of practical conviction, however overwhelming, is not certainty of logical implication. That common sense harmlessly confounds, and will confound, these several alternatives or disparates, because of their *practical* equivalence, is no reason why the philosopher should not render them the discrimination that is their due. That academic scepticism —*i.e.* suspense of judgement where certainty is not forthcoming— will not deter science, is quite irrelevant to philosophical recognition that the certainty of our 'most certain' inductions, the basis of our largest convictions, is hypothetical: *if* Nature be constituted thus and thus, then scientific laws, etc., are of universal validity. As Locke taught long ago, our 'knowledge' of Nature is probable belief: recent research has but furnished more cogent justification of his doctrine than was forthcoming in his day. It has also enabled us to broaden Butler's pregnant saying, that "probability is the guide of life", into the assertion that probability is the guide of science. Scientific 'knowledge' rests on indemonstrable belief: it is not, in the stringent sense, 'knowledge' unless certain beliefs are valid: which, in turn, and again in the logically stringent sense, are not 'known' to be valid. In science, as well as in other fields of thought, we have to purchase rationality—*i.e.* reasonableness—with belief which, used in all proving, is itself incapable of being proved: *credo ut intelligam* is an attitude that science did not drop, when it put away the childish things of man's primitive credulity.

2. PROBABILITY.

Probability will have been increasingly felt to be a notion of first importance in connexion with induction; and in the later stages of the foregoing exposition of the various kinds of induction, the reader will doubtless have been desirous of clearer intimation as to what the term means. Explanation has hitherto deliberately been deferred, because it can be given more clearly in the light of the recently acquired knowledge about induction, that has just been set forth.

There are a few preliminary observations to be made before the bearings of this new knowledge receive discussion. As Mr Keynes remarks at the beginning of his *Treatise on Probability*, the word 'probability', when commonly applied to events, is used vaguely and incorrectly. No event is probable or improbable in itself, as if the likeliness of its occurrence were an intrinsic quality. When we talk as if this were so, we but speak elliptically. An event is probable, only in relation to other events: indeed, only in relation to known events, and therefore to knowledge. But the ascription of probability to events is a derived application; henceforth we shall be concerned with its predication of propositions and of belief, waiving for the present which of these uses is primary. According to Mr Keynes and other recent writers, probability is a relation between propositions, or rather between sets of them. The relation is said to be Objective and logical. In these respects it is analogous to the relation of implication, though different from it. What exactly is meant by this assertion, and whether it is tenable, are questions bound up with the already mentioned issue, whether probability is strictly and primarily predicable of propositions in themselves, or only of propositions as believed. For the moment, we are concerned with the relativeness of probability to some datum. It will eventually be found that there is one class of propositions involved in induction, professedly 'probable', to the 'probability' of which this relativity cannot similarly apply; but it must certainly be said to be an essential characteristic of the probability of all other propositions or beliefs. The probability of a given proposition, being relative to knowledge-data, will change as knowledge enlarges: what was probable, relatively to known grounds, may become untenable or be found to be untrue. Probability, again, has all degrees between the bounds of impossibility (o) and certainty or necessity (1). If knowledge be defined in terms of certainty or demonstrability, it follows that there is no probable knowledge, but only probable belief. It also follows that knowledge, as to probabilities, cannot help us to knowledge of the certainly true; while, to be probable in any degree, a belief must have *some* foundation in 'knowledge'. The probable belief, in other words, lacks rigid demonstration, yet is not groundless. It is, therefore, always a species of what logic calls the problematic judgement, instanced by '*A* may be *B*'. An *A* must either be, or not be, a *B*: the problematic judgement seems, therefore, to be but assertion of ignorance or incomplete knowledge concerning fact; while the probable judgement makes the same assertion, coupled with the reservation that impossibility, on the one hand, and necessity or certainty, on the other, are ruled out. Probability, in so far as it is relational, or relative to data, arises out of ignorance which is partial knowledge, not absolute nescience. But all that has so far been said of it suffers from indefiniteness or ambiguity, because the controversial issue has been avoided, as to whether probability is a wholly Objective and purely logical relation between propositions; a wholly subjective and purely psychological *rapport*, such as doubt or certitude entertained toward a proposition; or some compromise between these two extremes. No definition of probability can possibly be given till this issue has been discussed. Those who hold the view that probability is a logical relation, affirm that it is indefinable. There are of course indefinables; but some of them, we have in other connexions been led to suspect, owe their indefinability to abstraction from their 'epistemic'—*i.e.* ultimately, their psychological—factors. There is reason to believe that this is so in the present case. Certainly there appear to be difficulties involved in the supposition that probability is an Objective, logical relation between propositions as such. The probability-relation is of course distinguished from the contingency-relation, *i.e.*, Actual *rapport*, or interaction between the Real elements of the world.[1] It is also sharply distinguished from the logical relation of implication, fraught as that is with necessitation. The probable conclusion does not follow with logical necessity from its premisses: how then can the probability-relation be conceived to be logical? It is useless to resort to any of the definite substitutes for the puzzlingly indefinite statement, that there is a *logical* relation capable of degree. The conclusion cannot, for instance, be said partially to follow: 'partially' and 'follow' are incompatibles. To 'follow', in logic, means nothing, if not that the conclusion is necessarily true if the premisses are true; and necessitation is a matter of all or none. Partial following is therefore a self-contradictory notion, comparable with that of moderate chastity. It is not partially true that the Kantian and Hegelian philosophies are identical because Kant and Hegel held some philosophical tenets in common; it is not the trueness of the proposition that is partitionable, but the complex proposition that is partitionable into a multitude of sub-propositions, some of which are true and others, untrue. Certitude of conviction admits of degrees: certainty of logical relation does not. Nor can 'partially follow' mean follow sometimes, not always: that equally negates the meaning of 'follow'. Again, a mathematician may cherish the hope that a certain theorem will prove deducible from first principles, while as yet he cannot find the deduction: his belief may be probable; and according to the view under consideration, there is a logical relation of probability subsisting between this theorem and the axioms of the mathematical science. Should the deduction be afterwards forthcoming, we must then believe that, in the past, the theorem was logically related at once in two different ways—probability (known) and necessity (unknown)—to the same principles.

---

[1] *'Relation'*, *in virtue of its ambiguity, often conceals the distinction here indicated: hence my frequent resort to the word* rapport.

From these inherent difficulties we are saved, if we adopt the view that probability is originally and essentially a characteristic of beliefs, rather than of propositions abstracted from belief, and from degree of belief, in them. 'Partial following' will then be a misnomer for partial conviction as to logical nexus subsisting where it cannot be seen. We are also enabled to give some explanation of the fact that additional data, while not increasing the probability of a conclusion, increase the weight of the argument in favour of it. It is not rational—if rationality be solely matter of logic—to prefer an argument of greater weight or strength, to one of less weight but of the same logical probability. The preference, however, may be due to belief in the determination of particular occurrences by finite sets of conditions, and to the reasonable surmise that few data may not happen to include relevant but unfavourable facts, while a more exhaustive collection of data is less likely to be unrepresentative by omission.[1] Weight of argument, like strength of motive, seems plainly to be psychologically conditioned. Evidence cannot affect external Reality; it can only influence our confidence. Inasmuch as logical certainty is beyond the limits, is in fact a bound, of probability: probability would seem also to be a characteristic of opinion, and therefore necessarily to be a degree of psychological certitude.

It is generally agreed that probability is not subjective, in the sense of caprice. A proposition asserting 'probable fact', at the level of common (Objective) knowledge, is necessarily independent of any one individual's subjectivity. But just as there is unbroken connexion between individual appreciation, or taste, and Objective valuation; or between individual sensatio and knowledge about a common world: so is there connexion between individual certitude, on which probability may ultimately be based, and the probable 'knowledge' or belief that guides social life. The only subjective element that Mr Keynes will allow, in probability, is relation to a corpus of 'knowledge', as distinguished from 'unknown truth'. Knowledge, as distinguished from 'unknown truth', involves knowing subjects: so far is subjectivity allowed to be concerned,

---

[1] Dr Broad (*Mind*, N.S. No. 121, p. 78) inclines to this explanation; though apparently he shares the view that probability is a logical relation between propositions. Some of the foregoing criticisms of this latter view are suggested in an article by Mr Joseph in the same journal, No. 128.

but no further. For the rest, probability is Objective relation: the measure of belief, not which we individually happen to have, but which we "ought" to entertain, or which it is "rational" to entertain. It is the alleged Objectivity and logicality of the probability-relation, that lead the writer just named, so strongly and frequently to emphasise the 'rationality' of belief, where demonstrative proof is lacking, and of being guided in action by preference of the more probable to the less probable judgement. It must be submitted that 'rational' here should be replaced by 'reasonable'. In common speech these terms are synonyms: in the present discussion it is essential to use now the one, now the other; else important issues will be begged through ambiguity. What 'reasonable' ultimately means, is a question that has been raised by the new knowledge concerning induction, with more definiteness and insistence than ever before; but it is one which the logicians, who have supplied the increased knowledge, have as yet left almost entirely unanswered.

This question calls for discussion, to some extent, at the present stage of our inquiry. For one of the implications of the theory that probability is a logical relation between sets of propositions, is that probable belief is rational; and the theory may prove vulnerable through its implication. We may proceed, then, to examine the meaning of the common-sense statement, that there is, and must be, a 'reason' why a belief is probable. Doubtless this statement refers to the relation between probability and evidence; to the grounding of the belief in facts known. We can readily concur with Mr Keynes when he says that probable belief is "rational" [I would substitute 'reasonable'] because it has *some* grounds in "knowledge", and so may be contrasted with irrational belief such as is the outcome of mere association, inherited 'instincts', etc., or is produced by entirely alogical causes of any kind. But when we begin to look beneath the surface, we are led to doubt the rationality of this reasonableness. Assuredly it is not the rationality involved in formal logic, the seeing of necessary connexions between ideas or propositions. Perhaps, when we are confronted with alternative indemonstrable propositions, the only 'rational' procedure is to suspend judgement between the more, and the less, probable of them. But in actual life, choice is often thrust upon us: then we not only account action on the more probable judgement to be a mark of reason-ableness, but feel urged to it, as it were, by a categorical, if not a moral, imperative. For all that, however, the probable judgement is not, strictly speaking, rational. For the whole corpus of so-called knowledge, relatively to which our belief is probable, and on account of relatedness to which our probable belief is said to be rational, has itself but probable grounds. Thus if probability is rational, the rationality is in turn problematic. Probability becomes a logical relation to probabilities. Why the latter pro-babilities are believed, is not a matter of logical grounds or 'reasons', with which alone 'rationality' should be coupled, but of the alogical: of non-rational, yet reasonable, certitude deter-mined psychologically.

The theory that probability is a logical relation between pro-positions, has been found not to be above criticism. We may now leave it and go on to shew that what even logicians call probability, is not always a relation, of any kind, between propositions. The corpus of 'knowledge', of inductively established science, is now admitted, as we have seen, to be only hypothetically entitled to the name of 'knowledge', in the stricter sense in which many people would fain use the term, but in which the term unfortunately has no denotation. It rests on specific basal propositions concerning the constitution of Nature, which are not demonstrable. These are called probable; but the word must then have quite another meaning than that which has hitherto been assigned to it. So far, probability has been discussed as an alleged logical, if indefinable, relation between a proposition and a set of propositions within the corpus of 'knowledge'. The basal postulates cannot be pro-bable, in their turn, in the same sense; for there are no more ultimate propositions to which they have relation. Their 'proba-bility' is non-relational: at least, to any knowledge independent of them and more certain than are they. Either, then, logicians must cease to regard relativity as an essential, universal, charac-teristic of probability; or they must find another name than 'probable', by which to characterise the basal postulates of induction. The latter course would secure terminological exactness at the cost of meaning; for it would remain fact that every man of science would regard these postulates as so 'likely to be true', that he would stake his life-work on them. Indeed the truth seems to be, that the 'probability' of these basal propositions *is* relational after all: though not to prior principles, but *to their own problematic consequences.* The corpus of 'knowledge' is probable relatively to them, and they are probable relatively to it. Logically, this is of course mere circularity: and to such circularity common sense and science are committed.

We may dislike the name 'pragmatism' because of its evil associations; but there would seem to be no escape from the outcome of inquiry into the nature of induction, that pragmatic 'verification' of logically indemonstrable, and even logically non-probable, assumption, is the Actual basis and 'justification' of all our science and 'knowledge' of any kind. Probability is, in the last resort, a matter of the downright alogical, the psychologically inevitable, the vaguely-called instinctive, the expectation based on usualness, the hope that springs perennial: our corpus of so-called knowledge is at bottom non-cognitive. Reasonableness is thus largely non-rational. If probability be the measure of belief that is reasonable, or one's moral duty to entertain, reasonableness and morality in this connexion consist *ultimately* in being alogical in one way rather than another. The alogical element in reason is generally overlaid with truly logical superstructure: hence the plausibility of the rationalistic and intellectualistic accounts of knowledge. It has also been wont to be hushed up, as an indecency, when philosophy has detected signs of its operation; but that is no longer possible, now that impartial logic has testified to its all-pervading presence. Even this testimony, in explicit form, is as yet given as if grudgingly and of necessity, not cheerfully: the left hand, indeed, not only knows what the right hand gives, but takes it back. The logician has but observed, as to the probability of induction-postulates, that it is not numerically measurable. As we have seen, more needs be said than that. To say it, may be to court the opprobrious charge of revelling in irrationalism, and insulting proper human pride and aspiration. But human pride of intellect has already been convicted of being overweening; and we have found converging and cumulative reasons to regard human knowledge as essentially anthropic interpretation. Discovery of the alogical basis of induction, is but in keeping with those results of study of the knowledge-process; and it will not be so staggering to those who regard presumptive knowledge as some function of the truth, whatever be its logical deficiency. We shall but have established, in the case of science, what was long ago discerned within the sphere of religion and theology: that faith and hope are more fundamental than the knowledge which is to "vanish away" and which indeed, in a very real sense, has already vanished away. Whether as scientific 'knowers' or as religious believers, we must be content to "feel that we are greater than we know": to recognise that it is trust of some such feeling as this, that, in all our knowledge (such as it is) and in all our reason (whatever that be), has prompted and guided our intellectual search; that the superficial success of the reason that is everywhere thwarted and baffled in its quest for certain knowledge about the world, is the substantiation of things hoped for; while if it be also the evidencing of things unseen, that evidencing is, in the last resort, a matter of psychological certitude, not of logical certainty. So far as we can as yet discern, the reasonable is what stands in the relation of probability to presumptive knowledge: this knowledge rests on belief: the belief is grounded on expectation or hope.[1]

It was remarked just now that recent logicians have owned that the probability of the fundamentals of induction is not numerically measurable. No account of probability can cover the subject, that does not contain some notice of the quantitative usage of the notion, and indicate the limitations of its scope: a few words shall therefore be said on the matter. In Todhunter's *Algebra*, the following statement is offered as equivalent to a definition of the meaning of 'probability', in mathematical works such as treat of the calculus of chances: "if an event may happen in a ways and fail in b ways, and all these ways are equally likely to occur, the probability of its happening is $\dfrac{a}{a+b}$, and the probability of its failing is $\dfrac{b}{a+b}$". The algebraist is cited for the sake of his words "equally likely". They serve to indicate that for all calculations of probability, in the mathematical sense, a definition of the equally probable (suppressed as if superfluous in Todhunter's

---

[1] There is here some citation of an article which I contributed to *The Quarterly Review*, Jan. 1924.

statement) is presupposed. The definition furnished in the classic work of Bernoulli, equates equal probability with absence of known reason for one alternative rather than for another. A different conception of probability thus underlies the mathematical calculus, from that which passed over from common sense into philosophy. Locke, Butler and Hume based probability on 'knowledge' derived from past experience; the probable, roughly speaking, was the usual. Bernoulli's method, resting on his 'principle of non-sufficient reason', applies where there is no past experience. When brought into connexion with experience, the fractions representing probabilities were assigned significance by being supposed to express the Actual proportion of occurrences: which suggests that experience can be translated into algebra. Laplace supplemented Bernoulli's theory by a law providing for numerical measurement of the influence of experience, however scanty. Consequently, the course of Nature seemed, to some of his followers, to have been rationalised by being brought within the probability-calculus; and knowledge, to have been derivable out of ignorance. The extravagances and absurdities to which this kind of mathematical theory led, have been pointed out by various logicians: as have also the errors, in virtue of which, Jevons was beguiled into representing scientific induction to be reducible to the probability-calculus. Mr Keynes, from whose treatise some of the statements in this paragraph are derived, has recently indicated the conditions that were ignored, but which must be satisfied before the Laplacean method can be applied. It now appears that probabilities are measurable, only when the possibilities can be divided into alternatives that are mutually exclusive, exhaustive, and so forth: as in the problems concerning dice-throwing and the drawing of balls from bags, which figure in text-books on algebra. Such cases are rare in the field of natural phenomena. Indeed it is now generally recognised by inductive logicians that 'initial probability', or relation to some ground in 'knowledge', is indispensable for application of the calculus, and obtainable only from experience. Any conception of the probable that is of use to science, presupposes knowledge. This, in turn, presupposes law and necessary connexion, such as are specifically indicated in the induction-postulates. The Laplacean definition of probability, *prima facie* independent of causality, must implicitly have reference to certain causes as non-existent, if it is to admit of application to the Actual; the principle of non-sufficient reason, or of indifference, and Todhunter's "equally likely", involve judgements as to *irrelevance*, which are of fundamental importance for inductive method. The method of Laplace, etc., is indeed still adopted in some quarters, but apparently without concern as to philosophical implications. Prof. Karl Pearson, *e.g.*, makes no appeal to the postulates underlying induction, or to necessary connexion; prior ignorance and Humean scepticism are sufficient basis for the 'probable' knowledge such as his method provides. The world is then tacitly assumed to be one of pure chance and of unlimited possibilities; accordingly, science is conceived as but tabulation of observations and curve-plotting. For science's capacity hypothetically to predict and to 'verify', there is on this view no justification: the fact is ignored as if of no significance. It may be concluded that if 'probability' have a definite technical meaning in algebra, it is not one for which inductive knowledge of Nature has much use: there the calculus is futile without some 'initial probability', based on experience eked out with postulation.

This conclusion is confirmed by Mr Keynes' examination of the empirical theory of probability presented in Venn's *Logic of Chance*, where we find a meaning, an interpretation in terms of Actuality, given to the probability of the algebraist. Nature is found to contain classes of phenomena, and series of events, having characteristics in common; and occasional attributes are found by observation to occur in a certain definite proportion of the whole number of such cases. A kind of probability, to which experience is the sole guide, obtains in the world, which may be defined or indicated thus: that an event, having a certain character, has a probability measured by a/b, means that it is one of a number of events, of which a/b Actually have this character. Probability, in fact, is statistical frequency, the proportion of instances actually occurring in the long run. Some logicians hold that, only in this definite and limited sense, is probability a logical relation, numerically computable, an assertion of fact and a justification of reasonable belief. While admitting that probability, thus defined, is something definite, and allowing that it partakes of the characteristics claimed for it, other logicians decline to grant it monopoly in all of them. It is more important, however, to observe that this theory is of very restricted application. Dr Venn himself needed sometimes to use 'probability' in other senses than that which the term acquires in his definition. The probability that is the guide of life, and that is involved in analogical induction, contains elements not wholly derived from past experience, and is much more than statistical frequency. Statistics indeed yield but approximate generalisations of specific and limited range: laws and universal inductions must be otherwise based. Statistical returns do not enable us to predict an individual's length of life, or manner of death; science has predicted innumerable specific events and phenomena, which subsequent experience has observed. But, even in science, 'probability' seems but to refer to subjective confidence: by a trick of grammar, it is made to seem to be a quality of things or propositions.

The importance, for philosophy, of the results of inquiry into induction and probability, does not require further indication than has been here given by the way. They throw light on the nature of human 'reason', on the nature of 'knowledge' and its relation to belief, on the subjective element inalienable from probability, on the hypothetical character of natural law: on the postulatory venture, and the alogical but pragmatic 'verification', involved in all inductively 'established knowledge'. It has been found that the propositions, underlying all inductive demonstration, possess *no* antecedent probability; if by 'probability' is meant logical relation to certain knowledge. If, however, 'probability' means their capacity to evoke sanguine *trust* from human subjects, that certainly increases with the progress of science. The confidence we feel toward a particular induction, is now largely due to the increasing regularity that science has revealed, in Nature as a whole; and there is no circularity involved in the *reasonableness* of confidence in a clue that is leading somewhere. But if, for reasonableness, we would substitute logical rationality, our wish proves vain. It seems quite impossible to *know* that, in the postulates of induction, there is the requisite finite initial 'probability', in the sense of logical relation to certainties. It is admitted by the logicians who have ascertained these postulates, that it is difficult to see how such knowledge is possible; and the only suggestion put forward, is that in some way we do see directly

KNOWLEDGE, BELIEF AND FAITH

this probability, though the epistemology involved is wrapped in mystery. This appeal to mystery, passing understanding, seems to be a dubious refuge. Psychology and epistemology may be far from exhaustiveness and finality; but they have nevertheless investigated all known knowledge-processes, immediate and mediate. And they hold out little hope that some hitherto unsuspected 'faculty' will swim into our ken, such as enables us to discern, with immediacy of intuition, the necessary validity of abstruse assertions as to the non-physical, that have till lately escaped discovery by the curious. There is no mystery, on the other hand, if we recognise that, in making transition from the probability (relatively to the induction-postulates) of laws, etc., to the probability of the postulates themselves, we are exchanging one meaning of 'probability'—the logical—for another—the psychological.

This is the solution indicated, not only by particular items of knowledge, but by the whole history of science. Perhaps logicians as yet shrink from adopting it, because it would imply that the feet of science are part of logical iron, part of psychological clay. Shocking as such a deliverance might be to rationalism, and to the equivalent 'empiricism' that would see, in physical generalisations, an expression of universal and unconditional knowledge: it would not be taken as offensive by most scientific investigators who have given themselves to pondering the method of science, as they understand it. They are not apt to take generalisations for more than historically conditioned, and by no means presuppositionless, assertions, capable of revision; still less, to regard conjectures as to the microscopic structure of Nature's framework, as more than representations of her behaviour *as if* she were so constructed. It is rather philosophers that, century after century, have adopted a current physical theory as the last word of science, and made it a foundation of a metaphysical edifice. Hence, in the past, the mechanical theory, and then energetics; and in these days, the exploitations of relativity and space-time, which inspire new theologies in Gifford Lecturers and other writers. The plain lesson of history not having been read, the philosopher, and even the theologian, has sometimes received rebuke from scientific authorities, for mischievous propagandism of pseudo-science: *i.e.* of false notions as to what science is, and of extra-scientific interpretations of theories, etc., used in science. There are, indeed, rationalistically and realistically minded scientific investigators who cherish the beliefs that scientific laws are universally true and logically demonstrable, and that theoretical physics is metaphysic. But the majority of the representatives of science would not be perturbed at hearing it to be a discovery of logic, that science walks by faith and cannot give a 'rational', but only a 'reasonable', reason of the hope that is in it. The news would not seem to them new. However, no appeal to majority in numbers is here intended: the issue is dependent on the argument that has been presented.

3. KNOWLEDGE AND BELIEF.

Belief, and its relation to knowledge, can be discussed with profit, only when the distinction between psychological and logical (sometimes called 'epistemological') treatment is carefully observed. 'Epistemology', conceived as a higher logic aloof from psychology, is not concerned with believ*ing*, but with *credenda*: with propositions, their logical grounds, Objective certainty, etc.; with a logical structure, a finished product, abstracted from believers and treated as independent of whether it is believed or not; with what ought to be believed, and why. Psychology of individual experience, or reflective study of a person's experiencing as it originally is for him, is on the other hand concerned with belief as mental process, with its causes, with certitude,[1] the convincedness of the believer, and the criteria of its genuineness. Psychology is not concerned with the truth of beliefs, but with the believing of them; logic is not concerned with believing, and deals with beliefs only as propositions. Unfortunately, both sciences often use identical terms with quite different meanings. Grounds and causes, certainty and certitude, criteria of truth and criteria of good faith, are distinct; but they are apt to be confused, which of course leads to paralogisms.

The epistemology of beliefs has already been dealt with in

---

[1] 'Certitude' and 'certainty' are terms commonly treated as synonyms, which spoils their usefulness. Here 'certitude' shall be appropriated to a state of mind, the convincedness such as is affirmed in 'I am certain that...'; and 'certainty' shall be reserved for the Objective character ascribed to propositions independently of whether they are believed, as in 'it is certain that...'.

connexion with logic, probability, etc. The psychology of belief, or rather a few points connected with the psychological aspect of belief, may now receive attention.

Belief, in the sense of believing, is a unique or irreducible subjective attitude. Its essence is bare assent. It is thus distinguishable from apprehension of the meaning of a proposition; we can understand, and can suppose, without believing or disbelieving (which is believing the negative). Assent is not necessarily accompanied by, or inclusive of, any emotional element such as 'welcoming': we may believe and rejoice—or tremble—and we may believe and be left cold. In belief, as contrasted with mere supposal and contemplation, there is some degree of certitude, which is simply *erlebt*. And when this certitude is at its maximum, belief becomes psychologically identical with knowledge, certitude is correlated with certainty, seeing is believing. Logic and epistemology, speaking from the common standpoint, distinguish belief and knowledge as different in kind, in virtue of their being private and social or impersonal respectively; they decline the expression 'probable knowledge' and allow only 'probable belief'. But psychologically, or from the (ψ) standpoint of the individual himself, the difference is but one of degree. Unless there be cases in which certitude is correlated with certainty, there is no such thing as self-evidence; no truth that is directly apprehended; no knowable absolute certainty anywhere. Such cases, however, are forthcoming.

In these, the subjective certitude is objectively determined; and that is why certainty can, nay must, be predicated. Convincedness, here, is literally being overwhelmed or forced; assent is willy-nilly; no option is left; no room for doubt, or even reflection, is open. The fundamental case of certainty, whence all other certainties such as the certainties of thought, issue, is 'sense-knowledge', which is prior to and independent of all other cognition. In sensatio, the object is posited, presented, and simply is. Illusion cannot enter till sensatio passes on to perception-judgement, and more is alleged than is sense-given. Of course sense-knowledge can be denied the status of knowledge: that is a matter of verbal definition. And 'belief' can be, and generally is, used so as to exclude knowledge, certainty, and certitude at the maximum possible: that again is a matter of definition, from the epistemological level. We are now only concerned with psychology and its actual continuities, before reflective thought dismembers and defines.

The next case of concomitance between certitude and certainty, is that of apprehension of the simpler 'objects of higher order': which, in that it is not sensatio, though presupposing it and grounded on it, must be referred to the understanding or intellect. This type of cognition, and the intuitive induction that is closely connected with it, have already been studied. Here again "seeing is believing"—a phrase which, epistemologically taken, is a contradiction in terms; and again certitude is objectively compelled as in sensatio, and consequently yields certainty and self-evidence: this time, of truth, not merely of being.

Lastly, memory or reminiscence, or at least retention where possibility of obliviscence is *nil*, is as constraining as the sensatio which, in the specious present, it overlaps; and the constraint is again wholly objective. But in reminiscence, as distinguished from retention, we begin to encounter subjective certitude to which epistemology cannot always grant accompanying certainty. Memory, unlike sense and immediate apprehension of relations of ideas, is fallible even when its subject is "absolutely certain"; he may be still objectively constrained, but the objective is now of the imaginal or ideal kind, not the impressional or the impression-sustained. Once this order of the objective, whether as presented or as used in the way of an interpretative instrument, has entered into experience, epistemology can no longer allow any necessary connexion between certitude and certainty; and it has good grounds in psychological fact for refraining. It will be argued in a future chapter that so long as this ruling is not obeyed, all discussion of 'the validity of religious experience' is but a beating of the air. To revert for a moment to memory, where the rift between certitude and certainty first appears, it may be observed that from the fallibility of memory "it does not follow that such subjective certainty [certitude] is never right; and in fact, if it never were, experience such as ours would be quite inexplicable".[1]

Certitude, at the maximum degree which alone has yet been considered, is plainly involuntary. Its consent is not that of the will, and, in the case of such belief, there neither is nor can be

[1] Ward, *Psychol. Principles*, p. 352.

any 'will to believe'. Belief is thrust upon us. But there is such
a thing as wish to believe; and that brings us to the subjective
causes of belief. When to believe is to get rid of doubt or suspense,
it causes the emotion of satisfaction, in which is contained pleasurable feeling. And this effect of belief may in turn become a cause
or motivation of future believing. We can be persuaded as well
as convinced; otherwise the rhetorician would find no use for his
art. We can by no effort of will come to believe what we know
to be false; but we can be psychologically moved to believe what
we wish to believe, and we can come to take for fact what is not
fact, and so entertain erroneous belief, in consequence of several
kinds of subjective motivation. Just as in dreams the imaginal
imposes on us as if it were impressional, because we cannot confront it with perceptual reality that would give it the lie, so when
we attend passively to the working of imagination so as to ignore
Actuality and let it lapse into oblivion, the imaginal and plausible
may obsess, and option may be put in abeyance. There is then
objective constraint or fascination, which results from selective
attention. The pleasurable aspect of a situation so dominates
attention, sometimes, that a person at first will not, and at last
cannot, see the other side. It is selective attention, in fact, controlled by individual interest and uncontrolled by consideration
of the over-individual, or thought shaped by desire and emotion
and unchecked by doubt and proof, that is the source of personal
bias, as distinct from reasonable conviction. And, in this connexion,
the disconcerting fact should be noted, that a large proportion of
defects, that we are wont to account intellectual, are at bottom
moral. Shallowness is generally self-indulgence; unthoroughness,
impatience; slavery to words, idleness; special pleading, in-
sincerity; facileness, or the simplification of problems by ignoring
their difficulties, is an immoral abomination of complex nature:
and the inevitable limitations of the ability and agility of a person's
intellect have little to do with such mental habits, which often
accompany what is called brilliancy. Their absence is conditioned,
rather, by the expulsive power of the affection which may be called
loving truth with a love like the love of home. Thus there is much
justification for the general assertion that Objectively true belief
(believing) is morally conditioned; but it needs qualification. It
does not apply, of course, in cases in which certitude is compelled

wholly objectively; and there is exaggeration, as well as somewhat of correctness, in the statement that 'spiritual' (*i.e.* presumably, ethical-religious) truth is 'spiritually' discerned. That certain sympathies, refined appreciations, moral discipline, etc., are conditions of insight into certain kinds of values, goes without saying; that character conditions the attitude one will take towards the *cui bono* of the historical and axiological, is plain; that purity of heart is essential to right judgement in some matters, has been already observed; that the open mind, personified by "the little child", is requisite for reception of truth, is beyond question. But sincerity, in so far as we can judge of its presence, does not always, in this life, "see God", nor necessarily carry with it apprehension of truth in other matters. It is a condition, but not the only condition. And there is no Gospel-beatitude on either credulity or foolishness. There remains, when all has been said as to ethical conditions of the believing of true beliefs, a purely intellectual element, distinguishable though inseparable from subjective motivations of any kind, that is involved in all apprehension of the existential: an element whose function cannot be performed by any other faculty or capacity that goes to make up "the whole man".

If the open mind be a requisite for truth-seeking and truth-finding, the disposition to doubt is equally essential. 'The method of doubt', as much as the primitive credulity that was previously mentioned, has from the beginning of human history been indispensable for acquisition of knowledge, or systematised probable and verifiable belief. Primitive belief, credulity as yet unsophisticated, was venture or hope arising out of action and need to act. Its underlying supposition, to reproduce Ward's citation from Bain, is "that we are working to a lead, following out some end, by the means that experience suggests" but does not entirely warrant. And this teleological factor, we have come in this chapter to see, is the essence of human reasonableness, in so far as that includes more than logical rationality—an after-acquisition. But this pristine assurance was met by checks from brutal fact, which led to new insight. The seemingly open way proved not to be so open; Nature was found not to be entirely plastic to human ends. Thus doubt was born: and doubt, the antithesis to belief and disbelief, is the corrective of credulity. It evokes the proving of all things, before holding fast that which is true. It is the cure of both ignorance and folly; a good that is instrumental to knowledge, though not quite the sole instrument to advance in knowledge. It arises when *cons* are discovered in addition to *pros*; and also when in a given situation there are neither *pros* nor *cons* as to what may be expected or believed. Thus, the open mind that is not also a doubting, and consequently an inquiring, as well as a critical mind, is not equipped for the transition from credulity to reasonable and reasoned assent. Nevertheless, doubt has been decried frequently as an evil; and this comes about from more than one of the plurality of standpoints from which ethical judgements may be passed.[1] The uncertitude ensuing on discovery of uncertainty, and engendering doubt, is an evil for individual experience; at least at the subpersonal level, because occasioning discomfort and perplexity. From the social standpoint of *e.g.* a church, taking its dogmas as infallible and regarding acceptance of them as necessary to the soul's health, an individual's doubt will be apt to be construed, not as a 'personal' instrumental good and a mark of rational or reasonable manhood, suppression of which would dehumanise; but as a 'social' evil—infidelity—or as an absolute 'personal' evil (ensuring damnation): however instrumentally good as an organon of knowledge. Reflecting this 'social' valuation in his own, the individual may regard his doubt as an evil: not merely as recognition of uncertainty and the personal discomfort of uncertitude, but as a soul-destroying sin. He may thus be self-inclined, as well as externally admonished, to stifle his doubt by resort to what *for him* must be credulity, the poison for which doubt is the sole antidote. Such credulity is not to be confounded with the faith by which the just shall live, nor with belief. Belief, such as falls short of maximum certitude, is doubt-sifted credulity; and belief, worth calling belief, must often "be purchased with the sweat of the brow".

In its narrower, commoner and less technical, sense, 'belief' is confined to assent that is not exclusively caused by the impressional and the impression-sustained: when alone it is certain, and certitude may be asserted to be at its maximum. Believing, as commonly understood, is not such 'seeing', but is acceptance that is in part

[1] See pp. 149 ff.

conditioned objectively—and now objectivity includes the imaginal and ideal—and in part subjectively. External constraint is but partial, not overwhelming; the judgements accepted are 'probable'. When theoretical considerations compel neither belief nor disbelief, which psychologically are the same, with change of 'sign', but leave uncertainty, there may be said to be a right to believe, or at least, to hope. This is perhaps all that is meant by the doctrine of the 'will to believe', in which, otherwise, it is difficult to find sense. Some of the subjective motivations to believe, such as selective attention and wish, have already been touched upon; and it is perhaps unnecessary to do more than mention other causes, as distinct from logical grounds, of belief. Suggestion, which is of much wider application than to hypnotic treatment, and is practised by advertisers, shopmen, and lecturers, is one such cause; and with it may be coupled auto-suggestion. Tradition and authority are purely causes, only when blindly swallowed; when acceptance of tradition is reasoned, and the credentials of authority are submitted to private judgement, belief has grounds as well as causes. Such grounds, however, are but partially or relatively logical, as we have seen when discussing probability. In science there is much logical connectedness of propositions; but there are fundamental propositions involved from bottom to top, which are themselves not formally certified but only pragmatically 'verified', and whose 'verification' circularly involves the propositions in question. In other words, there is no antithesis, no hard line to be drawn, between knowledge—or what passes for 'knowledge' most worth having—and belief: the 'knowledge', with which belief was wont to be contrasted, does not exist. Nothing logical constitutes the 'probability' of science's presuppositions; it is constituted simply by faith, of which belief is actually an outcome. The way to religious faith is open to all; and the rational justification of faith, is the fact that without it we lack assurance that the world is reasonable, in the sense of not being meaningless. But without faith, that in essentials is akin to that of religion, there is no scientific 'knowledge' possible as to the Actual.

4. BELIEF AND FAITH.

There is need for the word 'faith' in addition to the word 'belief', though they are often used as synonyms. 'Belief' serves to emphasise the cognitive, and 'faith' to lay stress on the conative, side of experience involving venture. Belief is more or less constrained by fact or Actuality that already is or will be, independently of any striving of ours, and which convinces us. Faith, on the other hand, reaches beyond the Actual or the given to the ideally possible, which in the first instance it creates, as the mathematician posits his entities, and then by practical activity may realise or bring into Actuality. Every machine of human invention has thus come to be. Again, faith may similarly lead to knowledge of Actuality which it in no sense creates, but which would have continued, in absence of the faith-venture, to be unknown: as in the discovery of America by Columbus. There is, of course, no necessity as to the issue of faith in either actualisation or knowledge. Hopeful experimenting has not produced the machine capable of perpetual motion; and had Columbus steered with confidence for Utopia, he would not have found it. But when faith succeeds, it is defined with psychological accuracy as the substantiation, or 'realisation', of things hoped for and unseen. The religious writer who gave us this definition, goes on to enumerate instances of the heroic life which faith enabled men of old to achieve: of the gaining of material and moral victories, the surmounting of trials and afflictions, solely in virtue of their souls being possessed of faith. The fruitfulness of an idea or a hope, for the spiritual life, is indeed not the same thing as the Reality or existence of what is ideated. The former of these distinct kinds of fact, is dependent on certitude as to the latter, and certitude is sometimes at fault; while the latter is a question of certainty. But, as we have found, there is no absolute certainty about the bulk of what passes for positive science of the Actual or existent, because its very foundations are but matter of certitude, and their verification is ultimately pragmatic, in the same sense (if in different degree) as is that of religious beliefs. Indeed there has already been occasion to cite the most impressive of the instances of faith supplied by the author of the Epistle to the Hebrews, as a figure of the intellectual progress of the race, a concrete embodiment of the principle "nothing venture, nothing have"—which underlies acquisition of all presumptive knowledge. We might, accordingly, extend this writer's roll of the faithful, and say: by faith, or by hope, Newton founded physics on his few and simple laws of motion; by faith the atomists of ancient Greece conceived the reign of law throughout the material world; and so on indefinitely.[1]

'Faith' is thus not a word to be confined to the theological vocabulary. Epistemology that would go to the root of its matter, cannot dispense with it. So-called knowledge, our working substitute for 'certain' knowledge that is not forthcoming, presupposes belief that commands only certitude, though called practical or moral certainty; and the belief that underlies knowledge, is the outcome of faith which ventures beyond apprehension of data to creative ideation or supposal, and justifies its venture by practical actualisation. Analytical and genetic investigations both yield this conclusion. Theoretical propositions were preceded by practical maxims, and learning has issued out of doing: when scrutinised, these propositions are found to involve faith-presuppositions. This does not merely mean that "there is more in life than logic"; it means that there is more in 'knowledge' than logic, and more in reason and reasonableness than ratiocination and rationality. Conation is genetically a source of all knowledge higher than involuntary sense-knowledge. Analytically, induction is found to contain postulation or faith-venture, creative imagination, pursuit of end; and its verification is discovery of applicability, not logical certification of photographic correspondence with Reality.

[1] For all his exclusively religious concern, this writer would doubtless have sanctioned an application of his definition of faith to other departments of knowledge. Unlike other New Testament writers, he does not conceive of faith as if it were an attitude distinctive of the Christian, or of the peculiar people; he includes Rahab the heathen among the faithful. And the Object of faith is not God alone, but the indefinite realm of the unseen, by which some scholars have taken him to refer to the Platonic world of ideas. On this interpretation, there is the closer similarity between his teaching and that contained in the lines of Hartley Coleridge:

> "Think not faith by which the just shall live
> Is a dead creed, a map correct of heaven,
> Far less a feeling fond and fugitive,
> A thoughtless gift, withdrawn as soon as given;
> It is an affirmation and an act
> That binds eternal truth to present fact."

It was found, in a previous chapter, that some of the categories of the understanding are but interpretative. We now see that the category of end enters into the very foundations of the edifice of 'knowledge', as much as do the mathematical and the dynamic categories of Kant.

Faith is venture dictated by human interest: it is not mere prudence or probability, for these cannot be, till faith has substantiated somewhat of the hoped for; it is not confined to the realms of moral value and religious ideas, but infects all existential and theoretical knowledge. The Objective situation, alone, determines with compulsion neither the probabilities of science nor the creed of religion; at most it suggests. In either case, it is a particular subjective attitude toward Objective situations, that is determinative and originative. Without more venturesome response from human subjects than is involved in infallible reading off of the self-evident, there would have emerged neither religion nor science. The fundamental belief in which knowledge or science indulges, is a following of an end and a satisfaction of a human need, as much as is the fundamental belief which issues in theology. It involves the determination, once it has gathered content, to be guided by such experience as we have, rather than by none at all; it equally involves the determination, before its Actual content has been secured, to venture into the realm of the possible and the ideal, and to experiment there. Science postulates what is requisite to make the world amenable to the kind of thought that conceives of the structure of the universe, and its orderedness according to quantitative law; theology, and sciences of valuation, postulate what is requisite to make the world amenable to the kind of thought that conceives of the why and wherefore, the meaning or purpose of the universe, and its orderedness according to teleological principles. Both are necessarily interpretative, anthropic, interested, selective.

Inasmuch as all reason, involved in the acquisition of 'knowledge', is leavened with faith, it seems arbitrary to deem the one kind of postulation and tentative verification less reasonable than the other, neither being fundamentally 'rational'. It sometimes happens that two different keys fit the same lock; while it is the lock alone that decides whether either, or neither, or both, shall fit. As for the scientific and the theological interpretations or keys, the world may be amenable to both; for they are not mutually exclusive. It shall be argued in the sequel, that the theistic interpretation of the world is but a carrying to completion, and an explication, of the implicit belief of science in what is vaguely called the rationality of the world. So far, we have enabled ourselves to recognise that *if* science be true, *something* more must be true, though it may never be precisely ascertainable; for analogies never prove existence, and what is necessary for our thought about things, is not, without more ado, necessarily existent.

The essential meaning of 'faith', as epistemology needs to invoke it, having been expounded, we may now briefly notice various other acceptations of the term that have been prominent in the history of theological thought. Faith has already been distinguished from the soul-destroying credulity, the *dernier ressort* of baffled thought and uncomfortable uncertitude, that has sometimes been recommended to persons in perplexity. It is equally far from the certitude, of which reason, in the narrower and merely logical sense, is the only foundation. Yet faith has been so described by rationalistic deists: Toland taught that all faith is entirely built upon ratiocination. A similar notion is implied in the denunciations which faith received from agnostic writers of the nineteenth century, who insisted on the depravity of faith or belief where we do not see: "It is of no use to talk to me of analogies and probabilities", said Huxley; "I know what I mean when I say I believe in the law of inverse squares, and I will not rest my life and my hopes upon weaker convictions". From this, as a representation of the nature of science and the ethics of unbelief, it could easily be deduced that "there is none righteous, no not one". But it is only fair to Huxley to observe that, though he wrote before the epistemological regress in science had overtaken Britain, his own philosophical excursions diminished his confidence and increased his 'knowledge', causing him to recognise that the certainty he had ascribed to scientific law, pertained only to private sensation here and now: "our sole certainty is momentary".[1]

Between the extremes of blind credulity and objectively constrained certainty, other attitudes have received the name of

[1] *Life and Letters*, III. p. 163.

'faith'. By some writers, faith of the religious kind has been identified predominantly with trust, confidence, *fiducia*. This is certainly conational and emotional, and so far resembles faith and differs from belief. But it presupposes belief in an Object already established; whereas what has here been called faith, is the positing of that Object as idea or possibility, and subsequent actualisation of it by energising, or else arriving by 'verification' at knowledge of, or belief in, its Actuality. Trust, again, is a venture, like faith, though of a different kind.

Despite features in common, trust (in God) and faith are so essentially different, that it will not conduce to clearness to amalgamate them into one concept: *fiducia* toward God pre-supposes *fides*; *fides* involves but the *fiducia* or trustfulness that makes *any* knowledge possible.

The more general tendency has been to identify faith with belief. The distinctively conative attitude which is appropriately called faith, is then lost sight of, and the name becomes superfluous. As sometimes used by Tertullian, for instance, 'faith' means in-tellectual assent to doctrine promulgated by recognised authority; not individual insight, venture and certitude. Aquinas strikes a middle way, when he defines faith as an act of the intellect which is moved to assent through the will; but even so defined, faith is psychologically identified with belief. Of ancient writers, per-haps Clement of Alexandria, who recognised that all 'knowledge' presupposes the venture of faith, comes nearest to the accuracy that modern epistemology shews to be desirable. The 'reasonable' theologians of the eighteenth century, who, like Locke, wavered somewhat between the rationalism on which they had been nurtured and the empiricism that their souls desired, equated faith with probable belief: faith stood to knowledge in the same relation that probability stood to certainty. Intuitionism of any kind in the sphere of religion was then suspected of 'enthusiasm'; and so the venture into the realm of the ideal and possible, indispensable for 'knowing' the Actual, was overlooked or disparaged along with the vagaries of mystics and possessors of alleged 'inner light'.

Lastly, repeated attempts have been made to find the essence of faith, at least of religious faith, in the attitude of valuation alone, and in valuation such as is only possible at a relatively

advanced stage of experience. Whereas dogmatism had based
faith on knowledge, Kant based religious faith on the *moral*
postulate. An unconscious precursor of the recent epistemologists, who find that knowledge is founded partly on faith, Kant
was withheld by his ineradicable rationalism from advancing to
the discovery which he otherwise might easily have made. He
would then have felt no need to narrow down religious faith, or
faith in general, to an exercise within the field of moral experience,
exclusively. His deficiency in historical sense further accounts
for his insularity. The subjective attitude to the Objective, in
which religious faith is born, we shall see later, is not that of
moral valuation, and was historically antecedent to morality such
as Kant talks of. Moreover faith, of which religious faith is but
a variety, has other Objects than God and those corollary to the
theistic idea. Kant might be supposed to argue thus: having
ideated the possible or what can be, morality says it ought to be,
therefore faith says, it is. But faith did not, and need not, wait
for morality's 'ought'. That moral valuations are closely intertwined with the developements of religious faith and practice,
is historical fact; that the essence of faith is worth-appreciation
of any kind higher than what is involved in satisfaction of practical
need, is too limited a description of faith to be adequate. Moreover, unless theological dogmas, in which religious faith ultimately
issues, be existential propositions, underivable from value-judgements pure and proper, they cannot be more than pictorial rules
for conduct. Kant was at least logical in so construing them;
other teachers who have based theology on valuation or on
"feeling", have been less consistent. Spiritual efficacy, or capacity
to promote pious and moral life, is one thing; Reality of the ideal
Objects figuring in efficacious doctrines, is another. It is in
asserting the Reality of such Objects, that faith essentially consists: not in appreciating the value of statements concerning them,
while their ontological status is left a thing indifferent. Faith,
as distinct from credulity and superstition, affirms its Objects
only so long as 'knowledge' leaves it an open way; if reasonable
belief in their Reality becomes inhibited, faith must renounce
them as nonentities or mere ideas, whatever worth or edification-
value may attach to belief in doctrines about them. Hope may
be blind: faith is not. Though faith contrasts itself with sight, it

does not profess to be antithetic to knowledge. It is self-confessedly fallible clairvoyance, to be tested by self-instigated and self-directed verification or actualisation. And if faith be taken to be as it has here been represented, religious faith being essentially the same in *nature*—whatever difference there be as to verifiability, etc.—as the faith that has been found to be intrinsic to the foundations of all 'knowledge' whatsoever, several important consequences command acceptance. It follows, firstly, that *ultimately*, or apart from comparative verifiability and capacity to inspire alogical certitude, science and theology are of the same epistemological status: both are substantiations of the hoped for and the unseen: the electron and God are equally ideal positings of faith-venture, rationally indemonstrable, invisible; and the 'verifications' of the one idea, and of the other, follow lines essentially identical, accidentally diverse. Theology is no nebulous, emotion-distilled haze beyond the horizon of a sunlit champaign of self-contained and self-explanatory science. To change the metaphor, and to abate grandiloquence appropriate enough for bombastic dogma, theology's opportunity does not first emerge at science's extremity. Alike human interpretations, science interprets in one fashion a relatively narrow, and theology interprets after another fashion a relatively more extensive, range of observable fact: they are complementary, not mutually exclusive or needful of any 'reconciliation', and can lodge in unity, domiciled within one mind content with reasonableness when it cannot have rationality. It is only when faith is construed as the conative source of all knowledge, however, that this happy state of things can obtain. On any other construing, religion and theology become unreasonable or baseless, from the point of view of a scientific mind.

Secondly, it follows that theology, founded on faith, is essentially metaphysical dogma. A theology that would eschew connexion with metaphysic, *ipso facto* removes itself from possible contact with Reality, and even with the Objective control of Actuality. It becomes an affair of the purely subjective or, at most, of subjectivity claiming such objective control as is possessed by the imaginal and the unactualised ideal. There is then nothing left to differentiate reasonable religious belief from credulity and superstition, theology from pragmatic recipes for pious behaviour, or from symbolical expressions of pious feeling entertained towards Objects that, for all we know or care, are nonentities or fond imaginations. 'Fideism' and similar subjectivisms can have no attraction for 'the faithful'.

Again, to resume a previous topic, if theology is thus an existential science, it cannot be derived from considerations as to values alone. The existence of a Reality, cannot be inferred from the worth of an ideal Object, or from the value of doctrine concerning ideal Objects. That theology derives its *apologia* largely from considerations as to values, is of course true; but these valuations must be appreciations of the existential, and so presuppose existential and theoretic 'knowledge' of the world and man, in order to gain purchase and to yield any theistic argument; while there is no room but for blind hope in their conservation, till the universe is theoretically found to be of such nature as at least to admit of their conservation being possible. Reasonableness would even demand a shewing of the 'probability' of their conservation. That they *ought* to be conserved, is irrelevant to whether they *will* be conserved (which is theology's interest), until the world has been found 'reasonably believable' to be teleological, so as to guarantee reasonable hope that higher human aspirations are destined to be fulfilled. In short, theism must be established before we have any right to its moral corollaries. On the way out, so to say, or while pursuing 'proof' rather than expounding the 'proved', moral considerations are but the coping stone of teleological argument, not a substitute for it. The several attempts that have been made to construct theology out of the moral, the value-judgement, the 'immediate feeling', etc., reveal easily, to scrutiny, their instrumental invocation, as a foregone conclusion, of what they profess to prove. Had Butler's suggestion been followed, that probability is the guide of life; and had the deistic tenet, that revealed religion presupposes natural religion, not been evaded: the nineteenth century would have done better than expend much of its theological strenuousness in pursuing blind roads that had the look of short cuts, and eventually, in sheer weariness, beating the tracks of superficial pragmatism and airily nonchalant subjectivism.

If the modern demand is 'back to experience', to experience by all means let us go. Genuine empiricism would go nowhere else. But it would go to experience, as the unmutilated whole out of which the knowledge-process has been fashioned; not to this or that analytical element in it, abstracted from setting or context. Unscared by the breakdown of rationalism and its professedly logical proofs, empiricism would rely on that 'reasonableness' which the eighteenth century confounded with 'rationality', and which the nineteenth century, perpetuating the confusion, largely deserted for 'irrationalism' that is in antithesis to both. Empiricism can now claim to have discovered, in faith, the common root of scientific 'knowledge' and religious 'belief'; in reason, a teleological, as well as a rational or logical, factor. The theologians who, in the nineteenth century, propounded the doctrine of 'the whole man', built more wisely than they knew: they arrived, generally by fallacious arguments, at a true conclusion.

CHAPTER XII

Religious Experience.

I. NORMAL RELIGIOUS EXPERIENCE.

It has been taken for granted in the preceding chapters that the only original 'matter' of knowledge, is the sensorily impressional. The simplest percepts are the only ultimate actual analytica of which psychology knows. They are the fundamenta between which relations are first read as subsisting; from them the imaginal, ideas and universals, are derived; by them feelings and conations are in the first instance evoked, themselves the source of valuation that issues in aesthetic and moral sentiments and principles. It is sense that furnishes the essential core of the primary meaning of reality, involved in the distinction of knowledge from thought; and it is only by conceptual supplementation of sense-data (and the subjective states they evoke) by minds which, through intercommunication, have attained the common standpoint, that there emerge the notions of Reality, phenomenal and ontal or ultimate, the physical sciences and metaphysics. Religious beliefs and theological doctrines also, according to such science of knowledge, can only be derived indirectly from study of the sensible world, man's soul and human history.

One challenge to this teaching has already received consideration in the foregoing pages; viz. that of the rationalism which asserts thought-given data, independent of sense, and equally original as the impressional. But another challenge to official psychology, and its epistemological outcome, is delivered from the quarter of religious experience: and this it is necessary to consider; on account both of its possible retrospective bearing on the psychology and epistemology previously expounded, and of its significance for future discussion of theological problems.

It is alleged that in religious experience a genus of the objective, other than the sensory and the sense-derived, is apprehended with immediacy; and though the assertion of this immediacy is made without distinction of the (ps) and (ψ) senses, vital as that distinction is, it is generally the former of these senses that is intended. This objective realm is held to be evocative of emotional attitudes that are qualitatively unique, and to be the basis of knowledge as to ultimate Reality, such as is not otherwise mediated: the forthcomingness of which knowledge, renders that derived from sense inexhaustive or partial. Religious experience is said to yield immediate knowledge of what, with relation to the Objective of scientific knowledge, may be called the Beyond; of a spiritual environment more comprehensive than that of finite souls and of the physical cosmos as conceived by spiritualistic pluralism. Mystical experience, in particular, is asserted to overthrow the pretension of non-mystical states to be the only ultimate determinants of what we may believe. Such is the claim that we are now to examine.

We may perhaps take it that 'religion', as the word is generally used, is a collective name for specifically different kinds of experience. Provisionally, at any rate, we may refrain from committing ourselves to such views as that there is one sole religious emotion or sentiment entertained towards one sole kind of Object; one sole psychological source of religious experience; and one sole historical origination of religion in the human race. Of precise and restricted definitions of religion, there is a large number: some of them being mutually exclusive, and most of them but partial. If we would set out from common ground, it is necessary to be more general. It will scarcely be denied that religious experience consists of emotions, and sentiments or dispositions to emotion (one or many), that are responses to objects or Objects (actual, imaginal or ideal), as to the Real existence of which, cognition (whether belief or knowledge) is affirmed; and that such experiencings mould conduct and generally find expression in observances. Certainly in the developed form, such as the Christian, religion is a complex of sentiments, occasioning particular emotional responses. And the first question to be raised is, whether any one sentiment can be distinguished from others that are cognate or concomitant, as *sui generis* and uniquely constituting the universal essence of religion. On its affective side, religious experience, as commonly conceived, comprises such emotions or sentiments as reverence, awe, adoration, loyalty, love, joy; but none of these is peculiar to religion. To find in any of them an element that is distinctively and exclusively religious, we need to differentiate religious love, reverence, etc., from other kinds of love, reverence, etc. For that, it would seem sufficient to indicate the peculiarity of the Object toward which the religious emotion is a response. Filial love differs from parental love chiefly in virtue of difference between their Objects; and there would seem little room for doubt that religious sentiment contains whatever unique element it may have, in virtue of the uniqueness of the kind of Objects that elicit it. It is widely held that psychological analysis reveals no constituent of religious sentiment, no irreducible analyticum on its affective side, that is peculiar to it; but the opposite belief is also cherished, and has of late received definite expression in Prof. Otto's work, *Das Heilige*. This writer finds the uniquely religious ingredient to be 'numinous' valuation, which he regards as irreducible to other kinds of appreciation, such as of the sublime or of the ethical. Natural Objects were the original bearers of numinous value, exhibited in the notions of the clean and the unclean, worship of the dead, of animals, etc. Such things inspired an awe different from fear, and more akin to the sense of the uncanny. They were, accordingly, regarded as mysterious, or as if invaded by the Beyond, and endowed with majesty as well as with anthropomorphically conceived energies, so as to be at once daunting and fascinating. Such valuation, however transplanted in the course of mental developement from Object to Object, and however intertwined in process of time with ethical or other kinds of appreciation, constitutes the essence of religion throughout its evolution.

It might be questioned whether this numinous valuation and sentiment is after all wholly peculiar to religion, and religious experience is isolable, in virtue of it, from other kinds of experience; whether there is not some overlapping of the religiously uncanny, the religiously awesome and sublime, and the profane uncanny and sublime: but that is not an issue of first importance. Dr Otto's theory, which may be selected as perhaps the most definite, elaborate and impressive, instance of the class to which it belongs, goes on to assert that the numinous attitude is due to immediate apprehension of a numinous Object, over and above the natural thing that is the visible or tangible bearer of the original numinous value; of an Objective but unseen presence. Thus, in daemonic dread, there is evidence of acquaintance-knowledge, of a vague and obscure kind, with Deity. The theory joins hands with those which assert that if, in religious experience, there is a unique constituent or quality, it is ultimately constituted or determined by the unique Object that evokes religious affectiveness; and the point that is of epistemological import, is the assertion that numinous Objectivity or Reality is cognised with *immediacy* like that of sensatio, and as distinct from objectivity of the imaginal or the ideal order. A distinct faculty, not included in such as are contemplated in the psychology of natural knowledge, is thus affirmed; for valuation and emotion are not cognition of existents. Now, in sensatio, the particular *quale* of the impression is given; but there seems to be no corresponding or quasi-impressional *quale* presented, in alleged apprehension of the numinous Reality in the numinous phenomenon or thing. The numen is, in this respect, more comparable to the pure ego than to a sensible percept. And certainly the clearer conceptions of the numinous, characteristic of more highly developed religion, owe their definiteness to discursive thought. The vague original suggests the imaginal or ideal, rather than the underived such as we encounter in the concrete percept. Prof. Otto rightly observes that, in the God-consciousness asserted by Schleiermacher, God is really reached mediately, as cause of the feeling of dependence rather than Reality immediately 'felt'; but apprehension of numinous presence in phenomenal things, would seem to be similarly derivative and reflective. The numinous Real is indeterminate enough to enter equally well into a multitude of diverse mythologies and religions; it therefore seems to partake of the nature of the vague generic idea, rather than to be comparable with an underived and 'perceptual' object. The numinous is the germinal notion of spiritual environment or the Beyond; but its abstractness, qualitylessness, commonness to a variety of phenomena, etc., render precarious and apparently groundless, the assertion that it is apprehended in the concrete and with immediacy. What makes this pronouncement plausible or convincing to many, is that the alleged immediacy is discerned from the 'psychic' standpoint: while it is asserted from, and asserted as if discerned from, the 'psychological' (*i.e.* epistemological) standpoint. Save as made with clear and explicit discrimination between these points of view, affirmations of the immediacy of cognitive religious experience are worthless for epistemology. It can rightly be claimed that numinous cognition is (ψ) immediate; but this may merely mean that its subjects are unaware of its actual mediateness, as disclosed to reflection and analysis. *Prima facie*, at least, numinous apprehension does not suggest its (*ps*) immediacy; and the interpretation of it as possessing this kind of immediateness, seems to be both dogmatic and superfluous.

Again, though it may rightly be claimed that numinous and also highly developed, complex and comprehensive religious, experience, involves reference to the objective, it is generally overlooked that objectivity is not coextensive with Actuality or with Reality. The imaginal and the ideational are objective. And emotional attitude can be evoked by such objects as well as by the perceptual, the 'feelings' being as profound and intense in the one case as in the other. The numinous, or the spiritual environment to which religion is a response and an adaptation, the Beyond, the subtly interfused pervading presence in Nature, must be objective. But it is a further question, whether it is not conceptual; whether it is also Real; or only ideal, imaginal, or even illusory. The primitive 'sense' of the numinous, assumed to be a reading of Reality, may, pending further inquiry, be an interpretative or apperceptive in-reading of a derived notion. Originally an object of constructive imagination, evocative of affective states, the numinous may come to be regarded as Real, and to be taken for the cause of emotions excited otherwise. One can agree with Otto, that the numinous 'feeling' "indubitably has immediate and primary reference to an object". One can also endorse the conclusion of James, that "it is as if there were in the human consciousness *a sense of reality*, a feeling of *objective presence*, a *perception* of what we may call '*something there*', more deep and more general than any of the special and particular 'senses' by which the current psychology supposes existent realities to be originally revealed": provided that the words "as if" be taken as of first importance in his pronouncement. But if we insist, as we plainly ought, on the distinction between (ψ) and (*ps*) immediacy, and on the fact that the objective is inclusive of the imaginal, etc., as well as different from the Objective and the Real, we are at once compelled to suspend judgement as to whether this "feeling of reality", or feeling of a "numinous *object* objectively given", "must be posited as a primary immediate datum of consciousness".[1] We may believe in the Beyond, or in God, on less direct grounds reached by more circuitous paths; and *then* reasonably interpret numinous or religious experience in terms of the theistic concept and world-view: on the way back, so to say, as distinguished from the way out. But the short cuts of 'immediacy', often pursued since the downfall of rationalistic proofs, seem to owe their seductiveness and their appearance of being other than 'no thoroughfare', to the prevalence of the two confusions that have just been mentioned. It is affirmation of the Reality of what may be called the supernatural, that determines the religious quality of religious experience; but, as for religious experience of normal type, which may well spring from the root of the alogical 'numinous' as described by Otto, it is no psychological mandate, and no external control of empirically analysed empirical fact, that requires us to ascribe it to a unique soul-faculty such as apprehends, with (*ps*) immediacy, objects of another genus than the sensory and what the mind derives therefrom. Imaginal and ideal objects, equally with present actualities, can receive valuation, evoke strong emotion, and so mould conduct: provided only that *belief* in their Reality or Actuality is entertained.

2. MYSTICAL EXPERIENCE.

The beliefs, valuations and emotional attitudes that have been called numinous, and may be allowed to contain the germ of religion, are in some measure and in some form approximately common to mankind. And in general they can be entertained without special preparation of the mind for their reception. There are other kinds of religious experience confined to a minority of men and possible only, for the most part, when their minds have been brought into certain states; and for these experiences also, has been claimed an evidencing of direct cognition of the supernatural, the Real, the divine. Certain types of mystical experience are relevant to the present inquiry, because they are affirmed to involve reception of non-sensory 'impressions'; to yield truth unmediated by understanding, ideation, or normal reason: truth above reason, such as becomes comprehensible (when

[1] Otto, *Das Heilige*, E.Tr. (Harvey), p. 11, n.

comprehensible at all) only by translation into terms of imagery and ordinary reason. A brief study of the mystical will serve further to illustrate the importance, for epistemological inquiry (our sole interest), of distinguishing between the (ψ) standpoint of the rapt mystic, and the (ps) standpoint of a psychologist's exposition of the mystic's experience. Many writers, unalive to this crucial distinction, have taken the mystic too seriously as a contributor of new material for psychology and philosophy to assimilate: at least that conclusion is to be submitted, together with reasons on which it is based.

The most important kind of experience, among the many that are embraced by the generic term 'mystical', in so far as relation to the present inquiry is concerned, is that which is described as the last or highest stage of raptness attained through mystic contemplation. This is a process of selective concentration and concomitant abstraction of attention. It is not pursuit of introspection, but rather of 'introversion': dismissal of distracting sensible and motor perception, of imagery and discursive thought. The outer world and the empirical ego being hushed, a stillness is secured in which God may be 'heard'. The soul, to use another figure, is put to sleep; the natural eye of the soul is closed; waking-thought-process is in abeyance. Then only, the mystical experience *par excellence* emerges. In one aspect, this is ecstasy: there is no reception of sense-impression of the supraliminal kind, and often the body becomes cataleptic. There is no awareness, no (ψ) experience, of time-transition: a fact which von Hügel and others have erroneously identified with (ps) timelessness of mystical experience. There is no awareness of self: and this (ψ) selflessness has similarly been made the irrelevant ground of assertion, that the mystic becomes (ps) selfless. It is also one basis of the mystical metaphysic, according to which the subject becomes, in contemplation, absorbed into, or one with, God. The self or subject must, of course, be there to function in enjoyment of its raptness, and to *remember* it afterwards. The intermediary stages, at which visions, auditions, etc., often occur, having been passed, that of 'spiritual marriage', the only one with which we are at present concerned, is reached. The following citation of Pseudo-Dionysius, a *locus classicus* as to contemplation, may be reproduced from the article on Mysticism in Hastings' *Encyclopaedia of Religion and Ethics*:

"leave behind both thy senses and thy intellectual operations, and all things known by sense and intellect, and all things which are not and which are, and set thyself, as far as may be, to unite thyself in unknowing with Him who is above all being and knowledge; for by being purely free and absolute, out of thyself and all things, thou shalt be led up to the ray of the divine darkness, stripped of all and loosed of all". Observing that this 'darkness' is said, not only to denote cognition that from the point of view of normal experience is obscure, but also to include superlative light; and neglecting the insinuation, into this practical counsel, of the *via negativa*[1] and the metaphysic in which it issues, as not belonging to the essence of mysticism though its abstractiveness as a method of thought aptly parallels the eliminativeness of the mystical 'way': we may fix upon the relevant fact that contemplation, such as is here prescribed, issues in supranormal experience. The indubitable elements in this experience are (1) its exaltation; an inrush of vitalising energies, enhanced appreciations, enjoyment, bliss, peace, etc.; (2) intrusion of objective presentations, apparently as 'external' as those in normal perception of things; (3) the maximum of (ψ) certitude that these objects and affective states bespeak an enfolding presence; and that revelations of truth, glimpses of Reality, are obtained, that are not otherwise attainable. The only question of philosophical import, is one which writers on mysticism are apt to leave aside in their preoccupation with its psychological, biographical and practical interest. This is whether, as distinct from the (ψ)

---

[1] The *via negativa* is the abstractive method of reaching the concept of God. It negatives all positive characterisations supplied by human analogies, and has aptly been described as deification of the word 'not'. Everything that can be affirmed of the finite, must be denied of the Infinite One. Basilides, the gnostic, is said to have taught that we must not even call God ineffable, since that is to make an assertion about Him. Inherited by some early Christian Fathers from Philo, this method led them, as philosophers, to describe an Absolute, indeterminate as is pure being; while, as theologians, they of course spoke of God as if He were a personal Spirit. Having reached the highest abstraction and given it an apotheosis, Philo, gnostics, neoplatonists, etc., needed to invent powers, aeons, emanations, betwixt which there is philosophically nothing to choose, in order to appear to bridge the impassable gulf they had set up between the Infinite One and the finite many. Neoplatonism, in turn, was occasionally borrowed by later Fathers and schoolmen with tendencies to mysticism; hence one wing of mysticism within the Church became abstractionist and monistic.

certitude of the mystical experient, which is merely a matter of personal biography, there can be any (*ps*) certainty, for the psychologist, that the enfolding presence is Real; that the alleged revelations are true or valid of the existent; that a transcendent faculty, immediately apprehensive of the ontal, is exercised when normal functions of the mind have been put in abeyance. This question is significant for philosophy and needs to be discussed critically.

No account of the universe can be final, which leaves the mystical consciousness disregarded: its claims must be met. But they are not impartially and philosophically met, if they are taken at the mystic's own valuation of them; for he is seldom a psychologist or an epistemologist. As to his experiencings, *quâ* mental occurrences, and as to his convincedness or (ψ) certitude of their truth-claim, he can of course be trusted. Here he is "invulnerable" as he is harmless. But as to his assertion that his cognition is immediate, valid or certain; as for his interpretation of his experiencings, and his inference of their metaphysical implications: it behoves us, without disrespect, to pursue the method of doubt. That of course does not mean sceptical bias, but criticalness, in the sense of judicial sifting.

Confining ourselves as yet to the deliverances of the higher stages of contemplation or θεωρία, unaccompanied by 'psychic phenomena', we find that they may be divided into two classes. The one class consists of experiences that are described as ineffable. These defy expression or articulation, reduction, translation into terms of imagery or thought, even for the experient himself. In them the mystic knows 'he knows not what'; yet memory of them persists. As they are ineffable, not to say incommunicable, these experiences must ever remain occult as to their nature. They cannot, therefore, be amenable to description as deliverances of truth; the wrong word would seem to be employed to express what the experient should mean, when he claims for such experiences a revelation of supra-rational *truth*. Cognition of truth is not unanalysable or indescribable experience, nor an affective state. Nor is truth the existence of existents; it is a relation between two distinct kinds of entity: objects of some kind, and judgements *about* them that are valid *of* them. Where such intrinsic duality is absent, truth is an irrelevant predicate, a non-significant word. Knowledge of ineffable truth, is a contradiction in terms. If truth be correspondence of thought with Reality, there cannot be truth, whatever else there may be, where there is no thought.

The ineffable experience has often been compared, in respect of its alleged immediacy, with sensatio. Sensatio, however, is not truth, but non-conceptual apprehension of *idion*. It has been compared, again, to the intuitive intellection, in terms of which the divine experience is described; but it is neither intellection nor positing of its own data. And when we shift our inquiry to the data (or analytica), ignoring the fact that they require synthesis by some sort of forms, in order to yield truth or knowledge—for a bare datum-presentation evidences nothing but itself—we are told that these are immediate as sensa, but are certainly not sensa; and that they are equally 'touch with Reality'. Whereas the concept of the Real originates through intercommunication, or from the common standpoint, and for the purpose of coordinating the *idia* of sensible experience, it is precarious to assume that it must have relevance when transplanted to a context quite other: ideas, we have seen, are *necessarily* valid only of the percepts whence they have been actually distilled. However, having thus got our concept, and bearing in mind the precariousness of employing it elsewhere, we can investigate its problematic application to the mystical ineffabilities. And, in this connexion, it will be fitting to select for examination, as typical, an assertion of William James: whose sympathy with mysticism is beyond question, and, in this instance, seems to carry him into exaggeration.[1] "Mystical"

---

[1] *The Varieties of Religious Experience*, 1902, pp. 422–3.

It will be observed that the representations made, in this chapter, concerning mystical experience or, more pertinently speaking, as to the epistemological issues raised by such experience, are not the outcome of first-hand study of the writings of the mystics. I may be mistaken, but I do not think that such discussion as is here prosecuted, is thereby necessarily rendered superficial, or vitiated by lack of sympathy and relevant knowledge. In the first place, the mystics are not authorities on epistemology, the issue that is alone before us. And, further, the many concordant available accounts of mystical experience, which we owe to writers who have steeped themselves in the original literature and are in sympathy with mystics and their claims, even though the illustrative quotations they supply are often isolated from context, cannot collectively be misleading. It should today be as little necessary to ascertain, by first-hand study, the nature of mystical experience, before calling its alleged philosophical import in question, as to repeat for oneself Galileo's experiments, before venturing to hazard statements as to falling bodies. I assume, therefore, that I am talking about what has become common knowledge, be my conclusions or opinions

experiences are as direct perceptions of fact for those that have them as any sensations ever were for us. The records shew that even though the five senses be in abeyance in them, they are absolutely sensational in their epistemological quality...that is, they are face to face presentations of what seems immediately to exist". The word 'seems', at the end of this sentence, indeed gives away the case, in so far as relevance to our present inquiry (not necessarily James' own) is concerned; but we may let that pass. The issue is contained in the statement that the objective fundamenta of mystical 'truth above reason', are of the same epistemological nature or status as sensa; and in his previous words "our own more 'rational' beliefs are based on evidence exactly similar in nature to that which mystics quote for theirs". This, it must be submitted, is incorrect; unless, like the realist of a certain type, we identify the sensum with ultimate Reality, rather than with actuality of phenomenal status: and it has been found that the identification leads to difficulties. In any case, the sensum differs in epistemological status from the derived image and idea; and it is as yet an open question for us, whether the mystical data are not comparable with the latter, rather than with the former, kind of objects. There is another difference overlooked by James: viz. that sensa can be conceptualised into common Objects, while the mystical fundamenta, of the kind now under consideration, cannot. It must be concluded then that assertion of the *same* epistemological status for sensa and mystical data, goes too far. The most that these may have in common, is psychological objectivity. When we ask about their respective kinds of objectivity, we encounter differences between them; and the differences might be significant as are those between the impressional and the ideal, for the epistemological question of relation to Reality, were the mystical data not, in all other respects than bare objectivity, absolutely occult. It cannot be proved that the mystic's data have no relation to ultimate Reality; it can perhaps be shewn that there is no good reason for asserting that they have the relation which theistic mysticism claims, until theism be established.

There is no antecedent impossibility about there being other data or analytica than those of sense, and other modes of synthesis

as mistaken as they may be. If the epistemological claims, here weighed, be other than the mystics themselves put forward, then the mystics simply become irrelevant to this discussion.

than those by which our normal knowledge of the sensible world is acquired. But if there be mystical knowledge of the kind now under consideration, its whole *modus operandi* is inscrutable. Thus far, our only conclusion is, that though there well may be more in the universe than normal experience can understand or comprehend, the occult nature of the ineffable alleged revelations of mystical contemplation prevents their being safely included in the denotation of 'truth'. The experiences vouch nothing beyond their own occurrence; they are devoid of significance for 'knowledge', in any of the several senses of that word which have become established through reference to explorable contexts. Indeed, in the ineffable it is precarious to affirm objectivity at all: there is no (ψ) differentiation; and *(ps)*, it may be affectivity. Perhaps James' statements refer rather to experiences of the kind next to be considered.

The second class of experiences yielded as outcome of θεωρία, are those which are not ineffable, but admit in some measure, sometimes in full measure, of translation into terms of ordinary imagery and knowledge. Here we meet with deliverances whose truth-claims admit of being tested. The most general, and at the same time the most important, characteristics of experiences of this class, are that they bespeak to their subject an active presence, with which he is face to face and by which he is 'possessed', so that his attention is no longer under his voluntary control; and that, as to the Reality of this presence, he has the maximum of certitude.

As to the mystic's certitude, no more is to be said than has been said already. It is 'psychic' certitude. As such, it has no import for epistemology, science or philosophy, where the sole question is as to *(ps)* certainty. A witness in court, who can only assert '*I am sure* the accused is guilty', is of no use. When the mystic alleges grounds for the truth of his convictions, as in the case of the neoplatonist who expounds his insight in terms of an ontological theory, we can consider his utterances on their merits; then we are no longer dealing merely with his personal biography. All that we can gather at the outset, in the way of trustworthy evidence, is that, in his trance-state, it is *as if* he were grasped by a higher power, directly confronted with spiritual or ultimate Reality, one with God, and so forth. We shall later see that such experience as this, is not confined to contemplation-rapt mystics, and that its religious form presupposes normally acquired knowledge of theological doctrine. Meanwhile, we may bear in mind that (ψ) certitude, when examined from the (ps) point of view, generally consists in the mistaking of reading-in for reading-off; or of fact, *plus* interpretation thereof, for naked fact. Its immediacy is not necessarily more than unawareness, at the moment, as to the dependence of one's experience on previous conditionings, familiar suppositions, inferential complements. The (ps) indirectly apprehended, or mediately assigned, cause of an experience, is thus often wrongly included by the experient, at the (ψ) standpoint, in the object or state that *is* cognised by (ps) immediate acquaintance. The mystic hardly can cognise with (ps) immediacy, an efflux of spiritual energy from God or the One, and an influx thereof into himself; at any rate his claim to knowledge of that kind, is without vindication. All we can be sure of is, that he can become aware with immediateness of an increment to the intensity of his affective state, and such like changes. Causality is imperceptible; and whether his mental change is caused immanently from within himself, or transeuntly by external being, may not be a matter of immediate apprehension, but of interpretation in terms of previously acquired conceptual knowledge or hypothesis. The common confusion of mediate with immediate elements in experience, in which the mystic probably participates, is largely due to the fact that we have become adepts at reading-in—as the skilled pianist has become an adept at reading and performing difficult music—so that it appears to be done by us, so to speak, 'at sight'. And the confusion is fostered by the language which we cannot but use, but by which, as philosophers, we should not submit to be enslaved. When, as one lies in bed, one perceives a hooting noise and judges 'there's a motor', one does not sensorily perceive a car; one infers a car from past observations, in which hooting and car have repeatedly been conjoined. The sound of a detached hooter might have been heard, or even a good imitation of its noise, and the inference be wrong. Similarly, when the mystic believes he intuits God with sense-like immediacy, he is perhaps but causally interpreting his elation, peace, etc., by aid of a concept already to hand. For all he knows, his interpretation may be erroneous, his inference (seeming to him direct apprehension) illusory.

If then we cannot, without begging the question at issue,

positively repudiate the mystic's claim, and so must leave him invulnerable as to his private conviction, we can also leave him powerless to substantiate his claim. And we can indulge reasonable doubt as to his own interpretation of his experience, because another, a sufficient and a natural, explanation of it lies to hand. Further, however it be with the primary deliverance, as to direct intuition of the relatively (if not completely) uncharacterisable One or ultimate Reality: the natural explanation not only suffices, but is exclusively called for, in the case of mystical vision that issues in more specific and concrete theological formulation. We can then see plainly that alleged immediate 'reading off', is nothing but interpretative 'reading in', presupposing knowledge of a particular philosophical world-view or of a special system of ecclesiastical doctrine: and if this be so in one case, it is the more likely that it is so in all. Ignatius of Loyola, S. Theresa and other Christian mystics, when their spirits have been ravished, have been enabled to 'visualise' otherwise than by the eye, to 'see' otherwise than by understanding or reason, yet perhaps to perceive through some kind of imagery, the deep mystery of the Trinity, or in some way to comprehend how God can be three Persons. George Fox saw the mystery of the creation, and, like Adam, the naming of all creatures, in accordance with the non-evolutionary notion of their origination imbibed from the book of Genesis. S. Theresa, on one occasion, was given to see and understand in what wise the Virgin Mary had been assumed into heaven. As mystics have been given to see, sometimes, the manner of transpiring of events that presumably never transpired, their testimony as to other alleged revelations becomes suspect; certainly they have seen what they were by education predisposed to see. That God raises the rapt mystic's soul to 'union' with Himself; that certitude as to this, is such that God alone can give, and such like theological tenets, are "immediate" truths only to Christians or theists. They seem obviously to be interpretations, on lines familiar and consequently only 'psychically' immediate, of the affective states of rapture, etc., of the transcendence of the empirical self, of the (ψ) certitude, which alone are the elements common to experiences of the rapt. The various kinds of oriental mystic, the neoplatonic Christian, the anthropomorphically-minded Spanish saint, when severally expounding their mystic revelations, do so exclusively in terms of the doctrinal or metaphysical system in which they have respectively been brought up. In *The Varieties of Religious Experience*, whence the foregoing instances of mystical revelation have been cited, it is observed that, in so far as mystical experiences convergently point to metaphysical conclusions, these are optimism and monism. That is, of course, the natural issue of the experiences; the affective state of rapture and peace evokes the optimism, and the (ψ) selflessness suggests the monism. Any objective factor that defies expression, seems in this connexion to be a superfluity. As James further observes, it is the "overcoming of all the usual barriers between the individual and the Absolute [that] is the great mystic achievement". This overcoming, we have found reason to believe, is 'psychic' seeming. Indeed in the claim that it is 'psychologic' certainty—in its "great achievement"—mysticism over-reaches itself. For if "in mystic states we both become one with the Absolute and we become aware of our oneness",[1] do we not realise the impossible? 'One with' must mean numerical identity, else the mystic revelation is no unique deliverance, but only expression of the belief of common piety; and meaning that, mystical metaphysic belies itself. For the awareness of this 'oneness' is attributed to what cannot have awareness, if no longer an ego, even if it be other than a nonentity; and the awareness is the Absolute's, not the mystic's, if he has to become the Absolute, in order to acquire it. The mystic cannot have it both ways: if he knows the Absolute as an Other, he cannot be It; if he has become It, *he* cannot know it, as *he* has ceased to be. He can only claim his alleged awareness by playing fast and loose with words: to say nothing as to the difficulty of conceiving his alternating subsidence into the Absolute, and re-emergence from it with *memory* of his lapse. One who had not read the utterances of monistic mystics, would naturally suppose that they were victims of figurative or ambiguous phrases: 'one with', *e.g.* bears several meanings; and 'be as nothing' sounds

[1] W. James, *op. cit.* p. 419.

This type of mysticism, and that which is more dependent on use of the *via negativa* which leads to the conception of God as indeterminate Being or super-Absolute, represent the limit of abhorrence of the anthropic element in knowledge. In more reasonable schools, the 'union with God' is described rather in terms of a divine 'touching' and human response thereto. When it thus avoids superfluous extravagances, mysticism is less distinguishable from the personal religion of many who would not call themselves mystics.

so like 'be nothing', that rhetoric easily takes them as synonyms. But the classical exponents of absolutist mysticism evidently wish to be taken seriously when they propound their paradox, or rather contradiction, that an ego can at the same time be and not be. Boehme is quoted by James as saying "*I am nothing*, for all that I am is no more than an image of Being, and only God is to me I AM; and so, sitting down in my own Nothingness, I give glory to the eternal Being". An ego cannot be an image, and an image is not nothing; but how a nothing, of which (in the clause preceding) it has been expressly asserted that it *can do nothing*, can "give glory", this rhapsodical writer does not explain. Similar, if less rhetorical, passages are reproduced in most treatises on mystical experience, expressly asserting that the mystic's ego, when rapt, is not a part, nor even a mode, of the Absolute, but identically It: "absorbed in God (says Plotinus) he makes but one with Him, like a centre of a circle coinciding with another centre". In Hinduism, in neoplatonism and Christian mysticism imbued therewith, in romantic pantheism, and wherever absolute monism is already part of the socially inherited intellectual equipment of the mystic, the doctrine of union (numerical identity) with the One, passes for a revelation vouchsafed in mystic contemplation, though explicable enough as mediated to him by the reasoning-processes of metaphysicans, etc. In so far as *this* revelation, "the great achievement", is concerned, involving the paradox confessed for one and all by Boehme, there would seem to be nothing in the "eternal unanimity about mystical utterance" that ought, in the words of James, "to make a critic stop and think". The critic is not given occasion to hesitate, by revelations to the effect that a nothing can do something and at the same time not do it, or that a finite ego can at the same time be and not be: and he does well to call nonsense by its name.

The alleged unanimity of mystics as to the metaphysical trend of their experiences, requires large qualification, as was in part recognised by James.[1] But if such unanimity as there is, has been sufficiently accounted for by the affective factor and the 'psychic'

---

[1] This writer's lecture on mysticism has been selected almost exclusively for reference, because it comes to grips with the epistemological issue, which is wont to be passed over or confused. Also, its collection of original passages is more than ample for such borrowing as has here been necessary.

standpoint of mystical experience, it has become unnecessary to see in it a credential of truth or of direct contact with ultimate Reality. And when we pass to the deliverances of mystics as to the particular characterisation of the Object revealed, or as to whether absorption into the One occurs, diversity abounds.

One further general claim of the higher mysticism, bound up with those already discussed, calls now for consideration. This is the assertion that the specific 'faculty' involved in θεωρία, is a 'higher' faculty than those involved in ordinary knowledge. The mystic's preparation for θεωρία, as described, e.g. in the foregoing quotation from Pseudo-Dionysius, is evidently a method of stupe-faction of the normal self, a working up to a pathological state or a condition of enhanced suggestibility, a process having resemblance to hypnotisation and the means adopted nowadays for evoking the subliminal. Indeed, the mystic's trance or raptness is (ps) akin to states induced by other well-known methods, whether he would so class it or not. It is comparable with what is called the anaesthetic revelation, with the effects of hashish, and so forth. Anaesthetics, etc., cause some persons to entertain 'world-views' or to enter into 'cosmic consciousness'. As religious mystics have been given to behold how all things are contained in God, work together for good, or flow from the preordained divine counsels; so to persons under the influence of nitrous oxide, etc., are vouchsafed insights into "the deepest cosmic truth". Some patients continue to believe that they have then received genuine metaphysical revelations. And there is no antecedent reason for ruling out revelations thus mediated, as illusions, while taking those that are induced by the methods of the religious mystic, for veridical. There is little room for doubt that, in the one case as well as the other, the objective elements of the experiences are uprushes of the subliminal above the threshold. There appears to be much in common between mystic consciousness and hysteria or dissociated personality. And we have seen that, in those states, the subconscious and internal is apt to be taken by its experient for the external; that its revelations seem to come from elsewhere than from within the self. The intrusiveness of the objective factors, the suddenness with which raptness often supervenes, etc., do not call for 'external' causation. Psychologically explicable, in the sense of being reducible to the class of the abnormal, as to which we have a certain amount of natural knowledge, there is no psychological compulsion laid upon us, to see in the mystical visions the exercise of a unique higher faculty. It is another matter that they can be interpreted in terms of theistic or other metaphysical beliefs; but, of themselves, they cannot be said directly or exclusively to demand such causal explanation: as if explanation, in terms of proximate or natural causes, were obviously impossible. The supposed higher faculty is not empirically distinguishable from the partially understood subliminal functionings of the personality. Doubtless, resort to the mystical interpretation has sometimes been prompted by the ancient rationalistic dogma, that man has an intuitive reason that can read immediately the intelligible truths, a faculty which theology affirmed to be a spark of Deity, and religious mystics—especially of the neoplatonic type—found to hand and invoked. This, however, is afterthought read into mystical experience before it is "immediately" extracted therefrom.

Besides the kinds of mystical experience that have so far been examined, there is the class of 'psychic phenomena': visions, auditions, etc. These have been decried, by some of the classical exponents of mysticism, as beggarly elements: even suspected as possibly deceptions of the devil, though they are often concomitant with the lower stages of the process of contemplation. We may accept this ruling, while observing nevertheless that, as a matter of history, it is from such phenomena that the main contribution of mystical and prophetic insight to religion and theology, is derived. The higher raptness, apart from what is really brought *to* it from the sphere of ordinary knowledge, as interpretative means, has yielded little illumination or none; though its affective factor has done much to promote personal sanctity and practical devotion. Now the psychologically objective visions and voices, referred by their experients to the sphere of the epistemologically Objective, or of the Real, are assigned by psychologists to the imaginal, the hallucinatory and the pseudo-hallucinatory. They are pathological or, at least, abnormal. Some of the steps taken by the mystic to attain to the stillness of contemplation, such as rigorous fasting, concentration of attention by removal from its ordinary field, are comparable to those of anaesthetic treatment, crystal-gazing, hypnotisation and auto-suggestion, in respect of inducing psychic phenomena and uprushes of the subliminal. We may agree that what James calls medical materialism, though it convicts the mystical visionary of pathological condition, is irrelevant to the spiritual value of his experiences. That, however, is no guarantee of their Objectivity, of their causation by external Reality, of their being metaphysical or divine revelations: in other words, there is no evidence that stages preparatory to raptness involve divine agency. It has sometimes been contended that these visions and auditions are image-representations of intelligible or supra-intelligible truth, such as is vouchsafed in θεωρία; that though woven out of the residua of past sensory experience—including the subliminal—as the imaginal always is, they are none the less 'heavenly' visions and voices. But there seems to be no ground, in these experiences themselves and the methods pursued to induce them, for this supposition. In normal experience, intelligible truth is distilled out of perceptual cognition; it is, therefore, but fanciful to assume that, in mystical cognition, the reverse order is followed. And if the instrumental theory of illusory experience is untenable, and there is no reason to suppose that the effects of drugs, etc., is to open out new access to acquaintance with Reality; there is no psychological ground for the belief that the mystic's visions are veridical. Empirical psychology shews that the illuminations, which he regards as revelations imparted from without, *may* emanate from the subconscious deeps of his own personality; and that his (ψ) certitude, as to his interpretation of them, may be (*ps*) erroneous.

3. THE RELATION OF RELIGIOUS BELIEF TO NATURAL KNOWLEDGE.

It would seem, then, that religious experience in general, and mystical experience in particular, afford no reasons, as distinct from psychological causes, for doubting that all that can be called by the vague word 'knowledge', is dependent on sense and thought. The demurrer of religion, as to the sufficiency of the psychology and epistemology that reject its alleged unique data, cannot be rationally or reasonably sustained. Such immediate *rapport* between God and the human soul as theism asserts, cannot be discerned with (*ps*) immediacy, though it is not on that account asserted merely gratuitously; nor can any transcendent faculty, mediating such contact, be empirically traced.[1] What is called 'the truth of religion' or 'the validity of religious experience', cannot be established by the *ipse dixit* of that type of experience. If it is to be established, it must be as reasonable inference from discursive 'knowledge' about the world, human history, the soul with its faculties and capacities; and above all, from knowledge of the interconnexions between such items of knowledge. Thence alone are derived the notions of the numinous, the supersensible, the supernatural, and the theistic idea of God. Numinous things, or things evocative, in the first instance, of imaginal or ideal constructions, and then, interpreted supernaturally or religiously by the instrumentality of these constructed objects, evocative of religious response of the affective and other kinds, are Actual Objects, whether vehicles of the Beyond or not. But *the* numinous, the numen or God, as distinct from, though immanent in, such visible and tangible things, and as in touch with human souls, is not an object presented immediately and concretely, as is a percept, to any specific faculty of any individual in any state, normal or abnormal. Like anything between the generic image and the most abstract concept, the numen, God or the Absolute One, is an ideal Object, presupposing (in the order of knowledge) and derived from, the sensible and the introspectible. Whether it is more than a concept; whether it is a Real or Actual counterpart to the concept, which in itself is a non-Actual form or ideal frame: this can only be decided, for reasonable belief, by use of the discursive method and by comprehensive survey of 'knowledge'—from psychology and epistemology to theoretical physics, history and ethics. Knowledge of God, on this view, is in the same case with knowledge of the soul, of other selves, of and the Reality behind the sensible 'worlds' of individual experients.

[1] This is not dogmatically to deny that the mystic's claim is valid, but that he has no means of *knowing* it to be, any more than have we non-mystics. Subconscious or subliminal experience is generally derived from the supraliminal; but if experience be *rapport* with Real existents, there well may be such *rapport* that never does, perhaps never can, evidence itself to introspection, and that is not to be included in the 'lapsed' or retained. And among such Real existents, it is possible that God may be placed. But if there be such *underived* subliminal experience, its very inaccessibility to introspection, and its 'originality', prevent the possibility of knowledge about it, other than can be obtained discursively or inferentially.

Phrases such as 'immediate feeling of absolute dependence', or 'sense of the infinite', denote experiences that no one has had. The experiences they are intended to indicate, are only possible after theoretic world-knowledge has been elaborated out of the genuine immediacies. Schleiermacher himself teaches this, when he states that the 'intuitive feeling' arises on contemplation of a phenomenon as part of the Whole, and as exhibiting the infinite: and when he expounds the meaning of 'the Whole', he might almost be a rationalist or a deist, such as Tindal. What religious experience returns enriched with, from its laborious ascent to the perfected theistic concept and the theistic view of the world, may legitimately be used for re-interpretation of the data from which it started; but it was not known to be present in the data, or the experience, at the start. On the other hand, there well may have been *rapport* between man and God, or rather a touching of man by God, before man had religious experience, or any notion of the supernatural, and any belief in the daemonic or divine, wherewith to constitute his surmises as to the unseen, and his affective states, uniquely religious. Such *rapport* would not be religion, till it was what is called 'conscious' rapport; and (ψ) *rapport* is not necessarily (*ps*), or Real, *rapport*: else there would be no mythology to contrast with ethical theism. It is thus necessary to distinguish clearly between experience, as it is for its experiencing subject, and the exposition of such experience, in terms of knowledge or belief that subsequent learning and reflection have made accessible. It is, perhaps, largely through the confounding of these, or to committing 'the psychologist's fallacy', that what may be called the rationalistic and the immediatist theories of religious experience, have been engendered. The empirical method of genetic and analytic psychology, and the *ordo cognoscendi*, lead to the conclusion that religious experience owes its uniqueness to the interpretative concept, by means of which, experiences, that otherwise are not religious in virtue either of their Objective reference or of their affective response, become coordinated, explained, and endowed with a supernatural aspect: clothed upon with which, they now evoke unique emotional reactions. He who would look upon parts of his own mental life as religious experience, or as intercommunion with the Divine Being, must attribute the peculiarity of that experience, in virtue of which it is differentiated,

as religious, from other kinds resolvable into the same constituents, to the fact that it is pervaded and coloured by the concept of God, and by belief that He is. But in order that his claim,
thus to interpret his experience as religious, be reasonable, he
must have reasons for entertaining the idea of God at all; and
reasons for his assurance that this idea, unlike some of his ideas,
has its Real counterpart in an Actual Being. Such reasons are
not obtainable from (ψ) certitudes and immediacies, which are
causes rather than reasons, though miscalled reasons which "the
heart has"; they can only be derived from comprehensive 'knowledge'. They must be brought to the (ψ) immediacies, before these
can be validated as (ps) truths. He that would come to God, must
first believe that He is: revealed religion presupposes natural
religion of some kind, if presupposition here be logical, not
biographical. The diversity of developed and organised religions,
is due to diversity of intellectual presuppositions. Distinctively
Christian religiousness is determined by distinctive Christian
doctrine; Christianity is neither a doctrine nor a life, but a life
coloured by a doctrine. Christian theology is often said to be the
outcome, as an afterthought, of Christian experience; the Church's
doctrine, to have followed upon its faith. But it is all a question
of what particular stage, of a continuous developement, we would
isolate for consideration. That the Chalcedonian formulation of
dogma, as to the Person of Christ, presupposes some Christian
belief and experience, goes without saying; but the religious experience of S. Paul the Christian Apostle, differed from that of Paul the
Rabbi, in virtue of his new theological convictions as to the Person
of Christ: relatively undeveloped or indefinite as these may have
been, at the moment of his conversion. The faith and experience
which doctrine, at any phase of its developement, *pre*supposes, is
never *precisely* the same faith and experience as that which the
increment of definition, or developement, renders possible; it has
its intellectual presuppositions, but they are not identical with
those of the newer experience. And so on, backwards to the first
origination of religious experience. The 'hen and egg' paradox,
that has been insinuated into argumentation against the dependence of religious experience on its theological or conceptual
conditioning, is irrelevant to a case of continuous growth of
cognitive presupposition and affective response, which interact on

each other as each passes out of one stage into another. There is little reason to doubt that mankind believed in the unseen, and had some 'sense of the mysterious', before they possessed religion, in any definable sense. Here lay to hand a vague notion which, treated with a little constructive imagination such as is involved in anthropomorphism, could yield 'the numinous', or the distinctly religious concept. Image or idea, constructed out of partial images derived from percepts of things and of self, and then read into particular things, endowing them with attributes evocative of *peculiar* valuation or emotional response, would in this case be the primitive equivalent to the theological concept that gives religious colour to the experience of monotheist or Christian. Thus, from last stage to first in the developement of religion, we can account for the uniqueness of its affective side, in terms of the theological concept or image, as the case may be, in the Real counterpart to which, the religious experient believes; and at every stage, the 'object' of religious experience can be said to be derived by the soul from its knowledge of self, humanity and natural world.[1] The psychology of religious experience, and the epistemology of religious belief, like science of the physical world, can be expounded "atheously"; indeed, so long as the *ordo cognoscendi* is pursued faithfully, exposition *must be* atheous. They can, however, be re-expounded theistically and according to the *ordo essendi*, when, by the more comprehensive philosophical study of Nature and man, and our 'knowledge' as to both, the theistic world-view shall have been established. That argument, however, relies on other data than those of religious experiences, and on other sciences than the psychology thereof. "The fertile

[1] As to the last stage referred to above, it should be observed that, though the developed and refined idea of God is "no combination, arbitrary or otherwise", of the ideas of other experienced objects; and though, in a religious experience (*regarded from the 'psychic' standpoint*), there can be "no thought" of any such combination made by us, "hypothetical" or other, of "objects of experience, however magnified": still, the idea of an infinite or a perfect spirit requires, to account for its origination, appeal to no other process than that of idealisation, by which the ideas of infinity and perfectness are obtained in the sphere of mathematics. The phrases that here have been given inverted commas, are quoted from J. Cook Wilson's *Statement and Inference*, II. 863, where what purports to be an ontological argument based on religious experience, is presented. The whole passage is an apt illustration of the unconscious confounding, by the best of philosophical and theological writers, of objectivity with Reality, (ps) with (ψ) standpoint, efficacious certitude with logical certainty.

bathos of experience", to use a phrase of Kant's, is a source of absurd superstition, as we have seen, as well as of reasonable belief: the irresistibility of private conviction is not always a guarantee of its truth.

As some of the distinctions that it has been found necessary to draw, are not wont to be drawn, and may at first seem somewhat subtle, it may be well, at this stage, to press their importance by indicating the main consequences to which they seem to point. No one doubts the actuality of religious experiences; they are psychical occurrences. But their mere occurrence does not vouch for any causal explanation, or other kind of interpretation, that their experient may put upon them. A belief is rendered true, not by its occurrence. accompanied by (ψ) certitude, but by its accord with Actuality or Reality, with fact which may be (ps) outside the occurrence or the believer's experience. Illusions are as actual occurrences as percepts; and psychology of experience, $qu\hat{a}$ experiencings, has nothing to do with the validity of their truth-claims. Again, no one doubts that religious experience has its objective constituent; there is no affectivity or emotion that is not objectively evoked. But it is a further question, whether the object, evocative of religious sentiment, is quasi-impressional in respect of underivedness, or is imaginal; resurgent, subliminal residuum; ideal or conceptual. If it be of any of the latter kinds, it is yet a further question, whether to it there is a counterpart that is Real, or existent otherwise than in the sense that the idea of a line without breadth, exists. And this farthest question, the one that is of fundamental import for theology and philosophy, cannot be decided by appeal to immediacy: (ψ) immediacy is irrelevant, and (ps) immediacy is not guaranteed by religious experiencings alone. When the Christian communes with God, his actual experience consists of consolations, upliftings, 'feelings' of peace and joy, bracing of will and so forth. It does not necessarily include apprehension of the divine causation of those states, nor face-to-face vision of their alleged cause: "no man hath seen God at any time". When the Christian affirms that Christ has passed into his life, or that he has immediate sense of the presence of the indwelling Christ, he is obviously superimposing interpretation upon his (ps) immediate experiences. He would not interpret his genuinely immediate experiences of uplift, etc., in that way, had Christ not been preached to him, and had not he been previously convinced that Jesus lives, that Christ can now 'indwell'—which are theological dogmas not fashioned by himself. Nor, again, is the question of the Reality of the Object of religious experience to be settled, as many seem to think, by appeal to the spiritual value and efficacy of the experience. For we know that purely ideal Objects, when *believed to be Real*, can evoke emotional response that issues in heroic action, moral earnestness, fervour in business, and so forth. It is the *idea* of the ideal woman, which a youth sometimes mistakenly reads into a worthless person whom he loves, that then may raise him from a characterless being into a chastened, strenuous and high-minded individuality. The value of belief in an Object, is no universal criterion of the truth of the belief, or of the Reality of the Object. Some say that religion is not concerned with truth or falsehood: religious experience *is* religion, and the whole of it. That is *prima facie* the import of Bradley's statement that "the man who demands a reality more solid than that of the religious consciousness seeks he knows not what". But many people who would fain count themselves religious, believe that their experience authorises them to entertain a view as to the nature of the universe such as, *e.g.*, that which is easily read between the lines of the Sermon on the Mount; while their religious experience would be wholly inhibited, if they were deprived of reasonable basis for such a view. And, put quite generally, there would seem to be no justification, in reason, for the interpretative and cognitive element, in virtue of which an individual's emotions, etc., are constituted religious, unless that element is supplied by what passes for knowledge and, strictly speaking, is well-grounded probable belief, derived from study of world, man and self.

On the other hand, it does not follow that if the psychology of religious experience must be atheous, it implies atheism: as certain exponents of that science seem to inculcate. Psychological explanation of religious experience does not exclude theistic reinterpretation. What psychology cannot find, may yet be there. Proximate causes are no more exclusive of divine agency, in the psychical, than they are in the physical, realm. Let it be understood, then, that the sole concern of the foregoing argumentation is to shew that the cognitive element in religious experience, which the emotional aspect presupposes, cannot be proved veridical by a psychological examination of that experience alone. Whether that element can be regarded as belonging to knowledge, and what 'knowledge' will then precisely mean, are further questions for future consideration. Meanwhile, the *ordo cognoscendi* is pursued, and exposition must proceed solely in terms of the *ratio cognoscendi*. Until that kind of inquiry shall have issued in knowledge as to the *ratio essendi*, the latter *ratio* cannot be invoked without dogmatism. Resort beforehand to the *ordo essendi* would involve the psychologist's fallacy.

Extraction of theological doctrine out of religious experience, supposed to be devoid of any dogmatic ingredient or to presuppose no theological concept of any kind, is an endeavour that has taken various forms, some of which have been discussed by the way. It has here been maintained that, in so far as the beginning of religious experience, whether in the race or in successive individuals, is in question, the endeavour must be vain. And the ground on which this opinion is based, is that religious experience is constituted religious by the permeating influence of some prior 'theological' notion or concept, derived from experience of wider kind than the religious itself. Religious experience, from the numinous of the ancient Semite to that of the Christian mystic, presupposes belief as to the Object, association of which with natural Objects, etc., causes emotional response to them to be *sui generis*. It is this cognitive element, originally anthropomorphic interpretativeness, that mediates religious experience, and without which no single experience is religious.

If this be so, it cannot be argued that theological dogma gains authority, comparable to that of a scientific theory, through successfully expressing, relating and accounting for the experiences of the religious.[1] This it needs must do, if it mediates, conditions or causes the religiousness of the experiences; but the experiences, *quâ* religious, are not independent of it, as should be the case in order that this plea be admissible. The likening of religious doctrine, supposedly derivable from religious experience, to scientific generalisation, in respect of authoritativeness, suggests the

---

[1] I differ here from Mr Spens who has presented in his *Belief and Practice* an argument to this effect.

desirability of stating clearly the differences between these two kinds of product.

Science and religion differ firstly as to their data. Both set out from percepts and the common-sense organisation thereof; both, therefore, involve anthropic interpretativeness and conceptual artifacts. Subjective activities and beliefs are brought into play in science, even before observation gives place to induction. But religious experience seems to be conditioned, as to both its existence and its distinctive nature, by antecedent belief, over and above all such as is indispensable for knowledge of the physical. Religion seems to have no known quasi-impressional data, or rather analytica within its data, in addition to the impressional; while the impressional, or the perceptual, is rather datum *for* religious experience than datum *of* it. The percepts, whence both science and religion ultimately set out, are data for science, or at least are sub-data for the Actual data of common knowledge; but they are not as yet religious data. They only become religious, or numinous, in virtue of the reading into them of the religiously interpretative or theological conception. Thus, the data of religion contain not only the postulatory elements common to scientific data, but more in addition to them.

Science and religion differ, further, in respect of the kind of 'verification' which their respective postulations receive. In science, verification consists in appeal to the external control of percepts; the results by which religious postulation is pragmatically justified, are, on the other hand, concerned with valuation rather than with existential knowledge. Lastly, the religious postulates are not so inevitable, at any rate *prima facie*, as those of physical knowledge: and they involve a further venture of faith. Thus, in spite of the facts that religion and science proceed from a common root, and are alike in certain respects, there are important differences between them. The objective determination of religious experience needs, unlike the impressional core of scientific knowledge, to be shewn to be other than imaginal or ideal. This, indeed, is the fundamental task of philosophical theology. It shall be undertaken in another volume, to which this may be regarded as preparatory.

CHAPTER XIII

The Nature and Limitations of Scientific Knowledge.

1. This inquiry into the capacities and faculties of the human soul, prosecuted with a view to subsequent discussion of the reasonable interpretation of the world and our knowledge thereof, now arrives at its final stage: viz. examination of the scope and limitations of our scientific knowledge of the world, which is accounted knowledge (of Actuality) *par excellence*, and an orientation of science with reference to other departments of knowledge. The nature of scientific method, in so far as it consists in inductive logic, has already been ascertained; but there are other aspects as to which something needs to be said.

It is by its method, rather than its subject-matter, that science is characterised: nowadays we take any subject, that is more or less amenable to this method, to be a science. Half a century ago, it was taught that the scientific method is the sole means of approach to the whole realm of possible knowledge; that there were no reasonably propounded questions that science could not reasonably hope to answer; no problems worth discussing, to which its method was inapplicable. Such belief is less widely held today. Since many men of science became their own epistemologists, science has been more modest. This is so in Britain, although few of our leading *savants* have taken share in the "almost exaggerated" criticism, as Boltzmann some years ago called it, which the method of scientific investigation has received in France and Germany; although the British Association has no Section for what may be called the philosophy of the sciences, and no scientific periodical analogous to the *Annalen der Naturphilosophie* is current in this country; and although in our Universities (thus differing from the Sorbonne and Vienna) science is taught without relation to its general history, and (as is perhaps not generally the case in Germany) with severe neglect of relevant philosophical 'disciplines'. We teach our students of natural science to calibrate the instruments they will manually use, but do not encourage critical examination of the thought-instrument, or the knowledge-machinery, that is also provided for them ready-made. Thus taught to view their science wholly from within, and not at all from without, individuals are left to take their own precautions against developing a tendency to insularity. They will inevitably make use of their learning as to the physical world, or as to such aspects of it as science deals with, as foundation for intellectual superstructure, when they become increasingly confronted with problems not wholly contained within even the wide domain of science, yet of perennial human interest; and a liberal education based on natural science, than which there is perhaps no better foundation, should include some teaching as to the place of science within the whole of knowledge. Science might be used, in this connexion, by way of a stimulant, rather than by way of an anaesthetic. But, taught apart from its 'higher criticism', it should tend to foster a kind of obscurantism, or misplaced confidence that no critical problems exist, and so engender superstition.

Without indulging further in reflection on traditional methods of education, one may insist that, in general, the nature and scope of science will inevitably be misconceived, unless as much regard is payed to its limitations and bounds as is wont to be bestowed upon its achievements and its prestige. As Kant taught, the understanding, as occupied with empirical exercises and the pursuits to which science restricts itself, not reflecting on the sources of its cognition, may exercise its functions successfully: but, one thing it is quite unable to do, viz. determine bounds that limit its employment, and ascertain what lies within and without its sphere.

2. To begin at the beginning, we may inquire into the nature of Fact. Science accepts, as its data, 'facts' as they are organised at the level of common-sense experience. Not being epistemology, science asks no question about the constitution of such facts: which include not only phenomena, events and things, but also truths about them. The implicit theory of knowledge with which science actually works, at least at its lower stages, is consequently an uncritical or unsifted realism. Etymologically, 'fact' connotes something 'done', as contrasted with something supposed; and the implication is, that what is done, is in no part done by our minds, but exclusively by the Objective or Real. The reading of fact by common Experience, is assumed to be as purely a reading

off of what is 'done', as is the sensatio of individual experience: the whole of the fact, not merely the sensory kernel in it, is taken to be given, not mind-made. This common-sense view was eloquently expressed in words which Dr Johnson quotes from Bishop South: "matter of fact breaks out and blazes with too great an evidence to be denied". Further, phenomenal Nature is commonly regarded as a storehouse of ready-made facts, awaiting science's observation and systematising. If there be error as well as truth in this implicit epistemology of elementary science, the error in no way affects science; but it becomes the salient matter, when from physics we pass to metaphysical discussions.

Simple fact is not the only kind of grist supplied to the mill of science. Science has been described as "systematised common sense"; and common sense consists of more than unsystematised brute facts. It contains a complex apparatus of thought, expressive of a way of thinking that is not so much logically or philosophically necessary, as practically convenient; but which nevertheless must stand in some relation to the truth. The facts, in other words, are already crudely organised by a prescientific metaphysic, embodying what is loosely called 'instinctive' belief, and comparable to the unpremeditated art of Shelley's skylark. All this is taken over, in the gross, by the science that is an outgrowth of common sense, to be revised in detail as occasion calls. It escapes notice, for the same reason as does the air we breathe; it pervades the very language we have fashioned for the expression of our thought. We receive it ready-made, unquestioningly and unknowingly, before we begin to think for ourselves, and so are socially coerced to proceed in accordance with preconceived notions, and to see what we have been taught must be there. As if anticipating the slowness of progress in constructive and critical philosophy, and providing against failure of social order from lack of a comprehensive and consistent theory of knowledge and of Actuality, Nature (as Hume and Schiller observed) supplied man with 'instinctive' or inevitable beliefs. More correctly speaking, man supplied himself with an articulated Experience. There is a sense in which man could not "first live, and then philosophise": to survive at all, was to philosophise after a fashion. Language, in its word-roots and its spatial metaphors, evidences its developement under the influence of attention to the external world; and primitive man would not be curious about Nature for its own sake, but about its coexistences and sequences involved in successful hunting, and so forth. Shaped for practical needs, language is a tool, an artistic rather than a scientific thing; and the concepts and theories now permanently embodied in language, served the purpose of social intercommunion none the less effectually, for that their underlying analogies were sometimes superficial, partial or fanciful. For this very reason, words are treacherous to the sophisticated philosopher. Certain epistemological problems now admit, only with great care and difficulty, of being stated, if indeed they can be properly stated before they have been solved: so deeply engrained are dualism, realism, etc., in our ordinary speech and thought, which we needs must carry with us into science and philosophy.

The intimate connexion, genetic and epistemological, between science and common sense, is an important fact to be reckoned with, when we pass from physical generalisations to critical and comprehensive philosophy. The province of common sense is that of the practical life; and there it can scarcely go wrong, because it was framed to suit that sphere, and has been tested by time and by countless numbers. But speculative interests, such as are pursued by philosophers, are beyond its province and jurisdiction: whenever such questions are concerned, common sense cannot be taken at its face-value. Similarly, science is trustworthy as a departmental study, prescribed by certain presuppositions and conventions: but when these are transcended, its authoritative dictation ends. That science takes certain things for granted, is of no consequence, so long as she confines herself to her own business; but inherited theories, concerning matters beyond her proper sphere, are not to be taken at science's private valuation of them, when we would pass from phenomenal knowledge to cosmic ontology. The inherited assumptions and self-imposed postulates may then beg the precise issue. Science, like common sense, would fain use the word 'fact', thereby indicating what is bedrock, to denote what we observe and in no wise make; but we have already found it hard to ascertain where making, or subjective activity, stops. As Hume saw, no sooner do we get from the sense-particulars of individual experience, which are subjectless 'propositions' rather than judgements, to what common sense and science *call* 'matter of fact', than we also get to uncertainty. *Positum* is then overlaid with *suppositum*: fact is made Fact by fiction; and if the fiction is fact too, the 'verification' of it is practical certitude. The solid rock of fact, to put the matter the other way round, dissolves into the shifting sands of sense, in so far as postulatory ideas are excluded. In short, Nature, as commonly before our minds, is not natural rock, but rather a concrete in which the cement is mainly human assimilativeness. To common sense which conceives otherwise of Nature, and to science which in this respect is but a refinement of common sense, philosophy must be critical, before using them constructively. To quote from a satire by the author of *Hudibras*,

> It is the noblest act of human reason
> To free itself from slavish prepossession,
> Assume the legal right to disengage
> From all it had contracted under age,
> And not its ingenuity and wit
> To all it was imbued with first submit.

3. The first prepossessions of common sense, which philosophy needs to cast off, are those that have been indicated with regard to fact. Facts of common or conceptual Experience, are not data as 'pure' as are the sensa of individual experience. Our Facts are partly theory; Nature, as commonly conceived, is founded on our act as well as on objective fact. And this accounts for two eliminations performed by science, in virtue of which it is constituted a kind of 'knowledge' distinct from other knowledges. It abstracts from the subjects knowing, and from the subjective factors involved in all knowing, regarding its Objects as if purely objective and as independent of all subjects, as well as of any: a useful device, but philosophically a fiction. Further, in proceeding to generalisations and laws it confines itself exclusively, and of necessity, to the 'repeatable'; which involves elimination or ignoring of whatever there may be of idiosyncracy and of the *einmalig*. The common and the repeatable are necessarily in some degree abstract; whence it follows that science isolates itself from history, and that the Nature which it studies is a skeleton or a diagram, as compared with the Nature constituted by the presenta-

tional continua of experients, and by the behaviour and inter-actions of the world's Real members.

As to the former of these self-limitations, the elimination of the subjective, something has been said on an earlier occasion. For the purposes of science, the subjective contributions in Objects and Objective knowledge can be left out of account. Present everywhere, they become practically as if present nowhere, and negligible. Hence the abject selflessness of science. But there is difference between unheeding the atmosphere we continually breathe, and dispensing with it; also, between an empty room and a vacuum. Science is at liberty to make the rules of its own procedure, to define Objects and Facts as it pleases, to ignore whatever conditionings and factors it likes; but its rules will not be applicable to the different games of psychology and philosophy. The convention, to deal with phenomena as if they were *per se*, because the subjective side of phenomenality can, for a specific pursuit, be neglected, is as harmless as it is essential to science; when taken for a dogma, it leads to an *impasse*. Hence 'psycho-logy without a subject', the naturalistic theory of conscious automatism, and scientific materialism; also the newer doctrine, that the world's diversity is subjectively fashioned out of nothing, inasmuch as the Real world is but identical, immutable, unpro-vocative mass-particles or absolute space-time.

The latter of the eliminations above mentioned, calls for fuller notice. It characterises science by indicating its demarcation from what may broadly and technically be called history, and illustrates the selectiveness and departmentality of scientific knowledge, which presently must receive more general treatment.

The basis of what is here called the historical, is the *posita* that constitute the primary actuality of individual experience. As 'complicated' into percepts proper, these *posita* yield concrete particulars, *idia*, in part determined by the individual's peculiar point of view, idiosyncracies, etc., and which are unique. It is in virtue of these *idia* being the fundamenta of common Objects, and of their being read by each of us singly into the conceptual framework of categories, etc., *i.e.* into the things and phenomena of common Experience or science, that the latter constructions, with their *supposita*, have connexion with primary actuality, have any derived Actuality, and have come to be commonly called

perceptual. The *posita* and *idia* are of course the ultimate foundations of science and determinative of our Actual world, as distinct
from all possible, or abstractly conceivable, worlds. But, having
once been built upon them, science deals with them, as such, no
longer; its own data, received and not made by it, are conceptual
constructions. As these are refined, the element of *suppositum*, as
distinct from that of *positum*, becomes increasingly dominant;
indeed, relations, rather than their *relata*, are constitutive of scientific knowledge. It is true, of course, that in studying their
relations, we get knowledge about the *relata*; but, nevertheless,
common sense and science may be said largely to replace actuality
and the historical by the conceptual and rational. Indeed the
ideal, but never completely attainable, goal of rational science, as
of rationalistic philosophy, is to dispense with sensory *posita*,
idia, etc., the concrete and historical, and to supersede that realm
by one that is rational: the real by the Real. The unattainableness
of this goal or desideratum is confessed in the indispensableness,
to science, of experimental and observational procedure. The world,
as an assemblage of *posita* with relations, is evidently rationalisable
or rationally knowable in part; it cannot be rational through and
through, because of the alogical, the simply posited foundations,
the relations between which, alone, admit of logical treatment by
the understanding.

This alogical element in the world is of philosophical import,
and its alogicality shall therefore be more fully discussed. Though
in one sense all science is determined by it, and is knowledge about
it, in another sense there neither is, nor can be, science of it. For
the *posita*, that are determinative of our knowledge of Actuality,
are ultimate: happenings that just are, prior to all logic and
knowledge. No reason, let alone *a priori* reason, can be assigned
for their being what they are. When Leibniz assigned a sufficient
reason for the contingent, its resulting deducibility was only
possible from the experience of the divine *Positor*, not from human
experience. To us the particular determinateness of the posited
is occult, for ever inexplicable and incomprehensible. If we had
minds of the order of that of the Laplacean calculator, and could
predict that a given individual, at a given time and place, would
receive on his retina ethereal waves of a specific wave-length,
we could not predict—apart from our sensory acquaintance, or

a priori—that he would perceive the colour-quality red or blue. Qualitative essence, again, is not deducible from idea or form, because not contained therein. We cannot, by piling up any finite number of universals, produce one particular; nor from any number of propositions extract one *positum*. For science to 'describe' the historical event exhaustively, as Laplace's calculator might describe certain aspects of it, it would need an indefinite number of equations with indefinite numbers of terms; it would have to supply the *whole* account of every world-state, and so pass from science to history. The alogical, then, is so, in virtue of its irreducibility, of its non-deducibility, of its incapacity to be included without remainder in the general, of the impossibility of its being assigned a place in a scheme of laws: it is an irrational surd. It is further non-rational, or alogical, in that its order and connexions are not those, and not like those, of thought. The world is irreversible, or rather, hitherto unreversed; that of scientific thought is not. Brute facts are, in the first instance, not predictable; it is only after the event of acquaintance with some of them, that science can in that way be wise about others. The relation of *positum* to *positum*, and indeed of Fact to Fact, is not that of logical implication: the *rapport* of cause and effect, whatever it be, is not identical with the relation of ground and consequence. Thus there never can be a rational science of the world, that is adequate and exhaustive. There are things, or rather aspects of all things, that "do almost mock the grasp of thought";[1] there is no thought that "pierces this dim universe like light". Sense is not obscure thought, if that mean that the apparent brutality of fact is due but to our indolence or intellectual limitations. The alogical core of the world is not a residuum of haze, that science, when ideally perfected, will have dissipated. Psychology here is decisive; and rationalistic philosophy has often, in spite of its own pretensions, tacitly endorsed psychology's decision. Plato did so when, in the Timaeus, he was in earnest with his ὕλη; Leibniz, when he invoked finitude and imperfection. Hegel was aware that Nature has to be regarded as a kind of Bacchantic dance; he did not deem the particular and the contingent to be deducible, but taught that the alogical of this sort can find place in a rational world. So it can and does; but then 'rational' no

---

[1] Dante, *Purgatorio*, xxix.

longer means what the extremer rationalist would have it mean. The alogical will not some day be made rational.

But there is another side to the shield. The alogical is not so much against law, as "without law". And, with all deference to science, there is knowledge, though perhaps no scientific knowledge, where law is not traceable. The alogical is not unknowable, in the broadest sense of that elastic word; for we have acquaintance with it. It may pass our understanding and be beyond or above reason, in the sense of being logically, intellectually or rationally incomprehensible. But it is not irrational in the sense of nonsensical. It is not meaningless; it can be 'understood' or assimilated by means of sympathetic *rapport*; we can 'come to an understanding' *with* it. It is explicable teleologically; it is not 'unreasonable' in respect of being functionless, or in that we can make nothing of it, or as being devoid of interest or value. The surd mingles with the rational, serves purposes of rational beings, and indeed redeems our world from the unreasonableness that would characterise it, if it were purely rational.[1] It takes all sorts, we say, to make a world; and it takes a saving tincture of the non-rational to make a reasonable world. It is even possible that the alogical may have revelation-value, so long as revelation is more generously conceived than as imparting of cut and dried existential dogma. Science and philosophy have been wont to fashion conceptions of ultimate Reality with a view to accounting for the world's structure, and the relations between its parts or supposed constituents; and to disparage appearance, in favour of some essential Reality. But 'essential' has no meaning, save in reference to some interest or end. Aspects, essential for science, need not be of prime essentiality for other interests and ends. It may be that the sole function of the noumenal is to support the phenomenal, or to appear. If so, as Lotze said, "the blossoming in consciousness of these effects of things is unspeakably more valuable than anything which may take place between them". Thus Nature's conjoinings, when not analogous to logical linkages, are other

---

[1] A rational world, for science, would be one whose constituents are immutable individuals, or rather 'atoms' with no individuality or no 'insides', no activity, no *rapport*; a world in which there was nothing emergent or new under the sun, no change but of configuration. Such a world would be logically calculable: and equally purposeless or meaningless—a world of 'unreason'.

than chaotic, baffling or stultifying, to beings which, besides the faculty of thought, possess the capacity to feel; to value, and to 'be on terms with' other existents.

It is obvious that the ultimately Real worlds conceived by philosophers, like that sought after by realistic scientific theorists, owe their difference from the Actual and historical world of alogical positings, their lack of colour, variety and activity, to the demands of rational knowability and the exigencies of logic. Change is logically unmanageable: so pluralists replace it by substitution, and monists call it appearance. The Real must be immutable, otherwise Reality would be incomprehensible: hence science's conservation-principles, and its unchanging substrata, from matter to space-time. Logic, again, can only deal with the discrete and the self-identical: hence the logistician's terms and science's atoms, from miniature billiard-balls to electrons or ethereal vortices. *Without* diversity in the phenomenal or Actual, there would be no science and no call for any: *with* diversity, there can be no purely, or wholly, rational science. The world, or the Reality behind it, has been conceived as it *must* be conceived *if* it is to be pervious to thought; but that it must be as it is thus conceived to be, is groundless dogma, assignable only to the pride and prejudice of human intellect. And what is perhaps offensive to this pride, and odious to this prejudice, must, in the interests of psychological truth, be spoken: viz. that the demands of thought, and of what is called disinterested science or non-anthropomorphic philosophy, are dictated by human interests. But, of that, more shall be said in connexion with the next main topic of this chapter.

Meanwhile, we may observe that primary actuality, the only foundation of knowledge as to Reality, is change; while if the Real were the immutable, primary actuality could not be forthcoming. Experience is change and is experience of change. If change be said to be appearance, it is not thereby abolished; for appearance is change. The immutable cannot play any part in producing or accounting for change; it cannot therefore appear. And if subjects, to whom the appearance appears, produce it without provocation on the part of the Real, they must create it *ex nihilo* or, like Leibniz's monads, spin it all by immanent causation out of themselves: and then *they* cannot be Real, because they suffer change.

Whatever may have to be said of conceptual time, and as to whether any variety of it is Real, or is but economic fiction, perceptual time is as actual as experience or change. And this reference to time mediates the transition from the alogical, that has so far been under consideration, to the 'historical', which shares in the alogical but involves something more. The essence of the meaning of this word, which has been more or less a technical term since Rickert's *Die Grenzen der naturwissenschaftlichen Begriffsbildung*, is uniqueness or the once-occurring (*einmalig*). History is what does not, and cannot, repeat itself;[1] it is knowledge of the 'unrepeatable', even in the figurative sense in which science is said to be knowledge only of the 'repeatable': *i.e.* of what is so like something numerically other, as, for the purposes of science, to admit of treatment as if it were identical or literally the same again. Everything that happens, or is concretely actual, is thus historical: *die Natur ist nur einmal da*. But science cares nothing about a unique and once-occurring event, once it has observed it. Facts are of interest to science, only as cases of a law, as members of a class: the respects in which a fact is unique are disregarded, and science is only 'of the general'. History is of individuals, science is of units; history is of the concrete, while the Objects of science are conceptual types. Human history is of the actions of individuals, not merely as peculiar, but as influenced by interest and worth; and events receive attention, not in respect of similarities with others, but in proportion to their significance. To the historian, an event may be of 'historical moment' while, to the student of science or philosophy, it may be 'but of historical interest'. History, as ordinarily conceived, uses sociological, philological and other generalisations: it may even generalise for itself. But it is no more identifiable with these its

---

[1] If Rankine's theory, that the ether has bounds, be true, and if the ether be not absorbent of luminiferous waves in it, undulations should be reflected back from the bounds and reconcentrated into foci. We might then see the events of the remote past. On the same hypothesis, the rays thus focussed would again diverge, to be reflected back from the opposite direction, so that history would not only repeat itself, but go on repeating itself, the past being re-pre*sent*ed or re-*present*ed in cycles. Again, when aeronauts shall have perfected their craft so as to exceed the velocity of light, they will overtake luminiferous waves set up on this earth, and read history backwards. But as yet our world is not so lenient to historians. And if it become so, the repetition will be but figurative. The veteran of Agincourt might again be seen receiving his wounds of Crispin's day, but he would not then be receiving them again.

tools, than is physics with the pure geometry which it applies. Like geological science, again, history seeks unobservable causes: but it seeks them as efficient agents, not as antecedents, or as equals to their effects. Science *makes* repeatables out of the historical and unrepeatable by abstraction, setting up concepts in the place of percepts. This necessary process is, unfortunately, also the first *mauvais pas* in the direction of vicious abstractionism.

The domain of natural science, already differentiated from theory of knowledge, etc., and from pure sciences, can now be assigned another bound. History may be knowledge, though it is not science; and though it is concerned essentially with the alogical and the once-occurring, it is no more a chronological inventory than natural science is a catalogue of facts. History co-ordinates, as does science. But whereas science co-ordinates according to law and in the interest of thought, history chiefly does so according to value of some kind. History never has enough data for completeness; science is largely what it is, because on its hands lie indefinitely more data than it can cope with and 'reduce'. Science is not concerned with values, import, significance, save such as constitute its own peculiar interest. But import and value are as much aspects of Actuality as are structural relations, and may be as much evinced in the unrepeatable and unique as in the common and the timeless. In the house of 'knowledge' there are several mansions; science occupies but one, and while science itself is by no means non-interpretative, it leaves room for interpretation of other kind.

4. Science is "common sense systematised": and we may now consider its systematisation. "Science is made with facts as a house is made with bricks; but an accumulation of facts is no more a science than a heap of bricks is a house."[1] But 'systematisation' requires to be particularised, before it defines science with any precision. Facts can be systematised without yielding science. The Linnaean classification of plants is probably now accounted an unscientific, or at least an imperfectly scientific, system. Alchemy, the 'science' of Empedocles, and magic, are systems. Magic, "so far from being an unorganised collection of bizarre superstitions, has every claim to the title of a logical intellectual system based upon fundamental principles, to repudiate which

[1] H. Poincaré, *La Science et l'Hypothèse*, 6me mille, p. 168.

would be at the same time to repudiate science".[1] As Dr Nunn says, systematisations of the non-scientific kind may not differ *formally* from the admittedly scientific. It is its *kind* of systematising that is determinative of science and gives the fruitfulness lacking to magic, etc. And as to what constitutes the essence of scientific system, opinions have differed. Hamilton regarded science as "knowledge of effects as dependent on their causes"; Helmholtz[2] would judge of the progress of physical science by its success in acquiring knowledge of a causative connexion embracing all phenomena, and taught that scientific knowledge only begins when the laws and causes are unveiled; more recently Prof. Gotch endorsed the view, as to the generality of which it is not necessary to multiply evidences, that "science is the causative arrangement of phenomena".[3] As, however, there are classificatory sciences or portions of sciences, and as in more highly developed sciences the causal notion is replaced by another, this description of science, in terms of causative systematisation alone, must be taken as but approximate. More obviously inadequate and narrow are those which confine the functions of science to co-ordination in terms of mechanical laws, atomistic concepts, and so forth. Inadequate also, because not narrow enough, is the recent type of description in terms of general law alone; though certainly the ideal of science is knowledge in which every item shall have its place, in virtue of universal and necessary laws. The one law that underlies particular laws, viz. that wont to be called the law of uniformity, has again been singled out as sufficient to characterise scientific systematisation, as by Poinsot: "Nous ne connaissons en toute lumière qu'une seule loi, c'est de la constance et de l'uniformité. C'est à cette idée simple que nous cherchons à réduire toutes les autres et c'est uniquement de cette réduction que consiste pour nous la science".[4] This is doubtless the fundamental postulate underlying scientific procedure; but it is the condition of the possibility of empirical laws, rather than the source whence they are deduced, or by which they are all subsumed. It therefore cannot afford exhaustive characterisation of science.

[1] Frazer, *The Golden Bough*, cited by Nunn, *The Aim and Achievements of Sci. Method*, p. 49.
[2] *Popular Science Lectures*, I. 327 and II.
[3] *Lectures on Sci. Method*, ed. Strong, p. 28.
[4] *Eléments de Statique*, 1861, p. 239.

The co-ordination of facts which constitutes science, is not more than roughly defined by any of the foregoing descriptions. It must now be urged that a perfect characterisation is impossible, that does not take into account the *aim* of science. It is the end that prescribes the means. As a construction of the human mind, science must serve a purpose and be directed by an interest; and we may inquire what end, or ends, are in view, when facts are marshalled by science. Here again various answers are forthcoming. Some are content to say that the aim of science is "to render intelligible, phenomena perceived by the senses"; some, desirous of rather more precision, affirm that it is to 'explain' by reducing the unknown to a case of the known, the obscure or strange to the familiar; others, that it is in no way to explain, but to 'describe how' things behave, and then the interest assigned is usually that of economy of thought. Thus physics, according to Mach, is "experience arranged in economical order"; its ideal is a complete synoptical inventory of fact, from which all speculative (metaphysical) elements are eliminated and in which it matters not what concepts are used, so long as they are time-saving. Elsewhere, however, Mach defines the aim of science to be "the representation of facts in thought, either for practical ends or for removing intellectual discomfort": from which we should gather that he recognises other functions than that of simple description, and the removal of discomfort, of kinds over and above that of the tedium of recurrent observation and discursive thinking.[1] Indeed, while he holds the chief aim of science to be the replacement of "experience" by the shortest intellectual operations, he plainly believes, like his predecessors Comte and Mill, that science is constructed with a view to prevision of events and to action. Mach admits, lastly, that one aim of scientific research is "the adaptation of thought to facts";[2] and that involves more than a perfect mnemonic system, if it does not presuppose an element of 'explanation' which the technical term 'description' was invented to repudiate. Brevity for brevity's sake, then, is confessed not to be the whole of science's aim. And indeed, apart

[1] See, on the one hand, his *Popular Science Lectures*, E.T. 3rd ed. pp. 197, 207, etc., and his *Wärmelehre*: on the other, *Contributions to the analysis of Sensations*, E.T. 1896, p. 153.

[2] *Contributions to the analysis of Sensations*, p. 156.

from Mach's particular teaching, the most economical description may not always coincide with the most perfect adaptation of thought to fact, whether in respect of suggestiveness or of ministration to prevision and action: there is no antecedent reason why it should.

Another view has been more recently presented, according to which science seeks to supply rules for action: "une règle d'action qui réussit", in Poincaré's words. Bergson has maintained that science, however speculative be its form, and however disinterested its immediate ends, is ultimately concerned with practical utility, or control of Nature; and that, with this purpose in view, it distorts the truth given in immediate experience. It seems to be implied that science, considered as a product, is vitiated knowledge; but it is perhaps overlooked that science professes to be knowledge about the Objective, and that any common knowledge of the objective is impossible without what is, rightly or wrongly, spoken of as vitiation. This kind of pragmatism does not do justice to the intellectual or theoretical aspect of science, through one-sided insistence on the service of science to human action. Moreover, aim at the control of Nature does not differentiate science from magic.

Prediction of events, again, has sometimes been exalted from a subsidiary or collateral purpose into the most characteristic, if not the sole, end of science. But Comte's saying, *savoir pour prévoir, afin de pourvoir*, puts things in the proper order of fundamentality, as conceived in the French school represented by Laplace. Prescience is but a consequence of the *savoir* which would grasp in a single formula all the past and the future of the world's course.

Simple or economical description, could simplifying be carried to its ideal limit, would become unification; and unification has in turn been regarded as the aim of systematic science. "Le vrai, le seul but, c'est l'unité", Poincaré affirms in *La Science et l'Hypothèse*. But economical description of particular groups of facts might prove incompatible with unification of all groups; the two ideals might refuse to coalesce, and might even prove irreconcilable.

If there be any one purpose more fundamental or more comprehensive than others, it is that which has been singled out by

Dr Nunn. "The *differentia* of science, as a conative process whose aim is to render the Objective intelligible", he says, "is the presence of no motive except the *desire* to render it intelligible—particularly in its quantitative determinations. No philosophical leanings, not even the desire of power over Nature for which Bacon was willing to be her minister, can be admitted beyond the 'margin' of the apperceptive area in which the Objective facts are central. The scientific attitude is essentially that of the *savants* who, drinking to the next great discovery, coupled with their toast the hope that it might never be of use to anybody."[1] As this writer further remarks, science seeks to explain, or render intelligible, in a special way. It would satisfy the rational understanding rather than the teleological reason; it arranges the primary facts in an apperceptive system, *i.e.* under concepts drawn from other contexts of experience or by means of secondary constructions, the uniqueness of which lies in the condition that they must be capable of leading to other determinations of the world, or from the known to the unknown. Apart from this provision, that systematisation must serve to extend the sphere of knowledge, in the sense in which science 'knows', freedom of choice is left as to the concepts to be used; and though at the same time causal connexion, economical description, prescience, practical ministration, unification, etc., may be attained, these are but collateral and more or less accidental results, constituting criteria, rather than the essence, of scientific knowledge.

Of subsidiary characteristics of science, none perhaps comes nearer to essentiality, in the sense of indispensableness, than the verifiability that has previously been discussed. Any sphere of presumptive knowledge that claims exemption from the need of empirical verification, thereby denies its claim to be a science. "When there is no possibility of verifying any assumptions of theory by phenomena, the sphere of investigation ceases, and the sphere of speculation and subjective thought-creation begins."[2]

Science firmly believes that *le monde ne saurait être deviné.* It is precisely on that account that science has, from the first chapter of this book onwards, been regarded as, after psychology and theory of knowledge, a necessary propaedeutic to philosophy

---

[1] *Op. cit.,* p. 59.
[2] Riehl, *Introduction to the theory of science and metaphysics,* 1894, p. 101.

and theology. It is in virtue of invoking science *after* prosecuting the epistemological excursus which science itself is not concerned to make, or of following a different direction of departure from the facts of common sense, that philosophy differentiates itself from science, and has other rôles to play than that of *scientia scientiarum*.

5. If science is characterised by a specific aim or aims; if its way of making phenomena intelligible by systematisation, be but one way of making them so; and if it makes them intelligible in but one sense among others, its procedure must be essentially selective and eliminative. This selectiveness, relating science with art, involving self-limitation and indicating bounds, shall be our next topic.

We may begin by observing the necessity, laid upon science, to be selective. A complete description of the external world, taking The World to be what is conceptualised out of the worlds many—the presentational continua—of individual subjects, would require not only a catalogue of the things in it, but also a statement of all their qualities and relations. This is an impossibility; for the world contains more than science can manipulate. Were it possible, what would emerge would not be science, but history; not a system, but an inventory. The following words of W. James seem to refer to the worlds just now distinguished from The World, as well as to it, but are in consequence perhaps the more, rather than the less, pertinent in this connexion:

The mind, in short, works on the data it receives, very much as a sculptor works on his block of stone. In a sense the statue stood there from eternity. But there were a thousand different ones beside it, and the sculptor alone is to thank for having extricated this one from the rest. . . . The world *we* feel and live in will be that which our ancestors and we, by slowly cumulative strokes of choice, have extricated. . ., like sculptors, by simply rejecting certain portions of the given stuff. . . . My world is but one in a million alike imbedded, alike real to those who may abstract them.[1]

Making a different use of James' imagery, we may remind ourselves that what science, as distinguished from individual experience, carves from, is not the hard rock of positive fact. It is in vain that the realist twits the man of unsophisticated common sense with the remark, that it is an easy and a logically contemptible

[1] *Principles of Psychology*, 1. 288–9.

matter to shape a brain-spun world, nearer to the heart's desire, than to construct that of positive and disinterested science: for there is, as we have already seen, no positive science; and there is no 'disinterested' science, as we shall presently find, that has not some interest. The logico-realist would exchange common-sense symbolism for logical or mathematical functions, etc. But this is no less symbolism, if of another sort; and it perhaps gets no nearer to photography of bare fact, assuming that such fact there be. However, the point now before us is not the suppositional nature of the conceptual instruments requisite for any systematisation, but the fact that the chaos of *idia*, and of the concrete and *einmalig*, is scientifically unmanageable without abstraction and elimination. This is no defect of science, though a limitation. And it is none the less a limitation for being a self-limitation. Science needs to eliminate what *for it* is irrelevant, in order to cope with what *for it* is relevant. The limitation only passes into defect, or becomes vicious, when what has been omitted as irrelevant is denied to have been there; then unscientific philosophical theories are generated.

Elimination involves selection. And in selecting, science—without ceasing to be science: nay, rather in becoming scientific—takes on the nature of art. It becomes the art of 'knowing'. *L'art*, said Delacroix, *c'est l'exagération à propos*. In the particular case of science, however, art consists rather in exclusive attention *à propos*, than in exaggeration of emphasis. We may also recall in this connexion, and in coupling, the observations that style consists in elimination, and that style is the man. The man, the anthropic element pervading science, is to receive further attention later; meanwhile, it will not be pointless to institute comparison between the pursuits of the artists who construct knowledge of Nature, and of those who paint Nature. To both, Nature is a chaos indiscriminately clamouring for attention; and both would be confronted with the unmanageable, had they not established habits of inattention. None of us attends equally to all that is presented: that way madness lies. And inattention is selective attention. Berenson compares the product of art to a garden cut off from Nature; which, even in its least chaotic state, has more resemblance to a freakish and whirlingly fantastical Temptation of St Anthony by Bosch, than to such compositions as those of

Duccio or Raphael.[1] Typical, within the realm of painting, of the physicist in the realm of science, stands Giotto, who sacrifices distracting detail in order to secure masterly sweep of line and dramatic concentration. Giotto, to quote Berenson again,[2] "with the simplest means, with almost rudimentary light and shade, and functional line, contrives to render, out of all the possible variations of light and shade that a given figure may have, only those that we must isolate for special attention when we are actually realising it". Science similarly simplifies, that Nature may speak more plainly. She adopts the epic or monumental style of Giotto; not that of van Eyck and other early Flemings, marked by fidelity to the veriest minutiae, sometimes piled up with distracting multiplicity. Giotto painted types rather than individuals; pursued economy as well as generalisation; and in his pre-eminent instrument—line—made use of one of pictorial art's great conventions. In all these respects, his method resembles that of science. So also, in another way, does that of Velasquez or Chardin, whose greatness lay, not in the accuracy with which they seized fact, as the petty 'realists' in painting and literature may do, but in revealing beauty by the selecting and handling of their facts: a beauty analogous to that of some scientific theories and correlations. Science, by the way, would profess to eschew the subjectivity of a Mantegna, painting rock-scenery according to his curious predilection, or of a Bellini, representing Nature as in sympathy with man; but, as to science's disinterestedness, something shall be said later.

Turning to another art, we may recall Dr Johnson's description of poetry: "poetry pleases by exhibiting an idea more grateful to the mind than things themselves afford. This effect proceeds from the display of those parts of Nature which attract, and the concealment of those which repel, the imagination". Science similarly selects and substitutes. She selects what lends itself to measure and number, concealing what cannot be so treated; and presents ideas or concepts amenable to such treatment, in lieu of the only concretely presented Nature, that of individual experiences. Indeed we can only describe perceptual Nature by idealising it, after the manner of the poets within Johnson's

---

[1] *The Italian Painters of the Renaissance*, p. 58.
[2] *The Florentine Painters of the Renaissance*, p. 15.

purview. Numbers, as well as mechanical models, are constructed concepts; law and uniformity are idealisations. In what degree science approaches the art of literary fiction, in its imaginative construction, is a question for future inquiry; but it may be remarked here that the statement, that 'science gets away from Actuality', made without qualification, is misleading. Science does so and does not; or, to speak plainly, when it does, it is largely with the purpose and the result of returning enriched with insight into Actuality, even if some aspects thereof are ignored.

If science may be called an art, in virtue of its selectiveness, and may be personified as an artist, she is comparable with a Rousseau rather than a Corot. She regards Nature, that is to say, as entirely independent of the self of the physicist, and out of relation to him, paying no heed how Nature impresses observers. This profession is indeed a deliverance of science from the (ψ) standpoint. Whether it is true from the (ps) point of view, or whether science is not temperamental in another sense than that in which Corot is called a temperamental painter, brings us to the question of science's alleged disinterestedness.

Sometimes a characteristic of science is included in this disinterestedness, which is more properly called uninterestedness, or indifference. Science studies the world's structure and order, not its relation to human wishes and aspirations; it is not concerned with interpretation in terms of value, of final cause, of meaning, or of God. It does not find and assert the world to be meaningless or Godless, nor decry inquiry into such matters, as futile; it merely disavows interest in them, as none of its business. That affective-volitional attitudes are evoked by the Objects which science studies, is as much a fact for investigation, as that they have such and such constitutions and relations; and our valuations of things depend on what evokes feeling, etc., as well as on subjects and the feeling-attitudes, etc., evoked from them. In leaving such considerations aside, science but confesses her departmentality. To avoid all questions as to value, is not obviously a prime condition of a valuable world-philosophy, however essential to the pursuit of science, as contrasted with comprehensive philosophy.

Science is more properly called disinterested when, not its inattention to values, is meant, but its impartiality, or the fact that science is devoid of the subjective bias that is wont to warp many kinds of human judgement. It is unmotived by desire to impose certain human values on the world, in lieu of physical relations; and, while pursuing its own business, works uninfluenced by the needs of the heart. It does not decide the orbits of planets to be circular, because the circle is the most perfect figure. Its conclusions are not affected by human fears, hopes or wishes. Its disinterestedness, in this sense, goes without saying.

But it is only relative. At bottom, this disinterestedness involves another interest. The fact escapes notice, so long as we acquiesce in the claim that science yields knowledge of things as they Really are, independently not only of our feelings, but of our perceiving. It has previously been argued that no such knowledge is known to be forthcoming. The cognitive and the practical sides of mentality are not actually separable. There are no objects but what are subjectively apprehended, and no Objects that are not Subjectively constructed and largely supposed. And there is no synthetic cognitive process uncaused by interest. We take up, indeed, what we find and 'is there'; but, after the first stage of cognition, we do not take up what is uninteresting, nor retain and assimilate it. Nor do we find unless we seek, nor seek unless we desire. Cognition is partly interpretation, induction is partly faith or hope, axioms are postulates, and most scientific concepts are fashioned *ad hoc*. The rationalistic trend, historically evident in science, is largely expression of pride of intellect; and it has had distorting effects, comparable to those of " pride of life " in practical affairs. But it is enough, in order to convict science of interestedness, to refer to its selectiveness, which can never be other than interest-determined. What is selected as essential, is essential in no other sense than for the peculiar and inalienable interest of science. Roughly speaking, science's 'essential' is the measurable. This is no more Real than the non-measurable: from another point of view than that of science, it may be insignificant. Whether we assert or deny such statements, we utter value-judgements presupposing interest.

Here an anticipated objection may be met. Granted, it may be said, that intellectual seeking originates in interest, as in the case of Mayer's discovery of the principle of energy, ensuing on the fact that he "vividly felt the need of it"; are not the findings, when found, entirely independent of interest, and simply true to fact? Is not all that is said above, therefore, irrelevant? Not so, it may be replied; unless again we acquiesce in the claim that science is 'positive' knowledge. Did Mayer, to return to our instance, discover what is Really there? His principle may have passed for science; but how far Nature corresponds to the principle that satisfied his need, is still an open question. Mach has remarked that the substantial notion of the principle of energy, like Black's material conception of heat, has its limits in facts, beyond which it can only be artificially retained. To generalise: pragmatic verification is never logical certification, though for practical life the two are equivalent. Science, such as falls short of logical certification, must be need-fulfilling or interest-satisfying supposition, subject to revision and supersession. Science is not merely classificatory and formally logical; nor can the claim, made by some logicians on its behalf, that it uses a purely theoretic and "trans-anthropological" (*sic*) principle of selection and synthesis, be admitted. "That the application of this principle in the empirical pursuit of Natural Science is determined partly by human needs and interests, concerns only the direction and sphere of the inquiry", we are told, "not its scientific procedure".[1] If scientific procedure were formally logical, science would be disinterested. But many of its essential concepts are selectively fashioned for specific purposes: the wish is father to the thought, and the thought cannot wholly break with its paternal home. The gratuitous leap from the individual to the over-social or absolute, that has already been criticised in several contexts, is dictated by interest. The "trans-anthropological" finished product of thought, that alone meets the eye when the scaffolding, by means of which it was constructed, has been pulled down, is mistaken for the heaven-descended, only in consequence of a very human *Willkürlichkeit* that is impatient of reminders as to such things as human *tempo*, embodiment, limitations compelling discursiveness of thought, inalienable conditionings of our categories, of our weighings and measurings, of our very 'understanding'.

Assertions have occurred in foregoing paragraphs, concerning concepts, that must now receive justification. Scientific concepts have sometimes been taken as if they were all on a par, in respect of both origin and validity: whence have arisen mistakes as to

[1] Windelband in *Encyclopaedia of the Philos. Sciences*, vol. i., *Logic*, pp. 48–9.

the nature of scientific 'knowledge'. To indicate the differences between concepts of various kinds, will throw further light on the selective and artistic aspect of science.

(a) There are concepts, of relations and classes, that are *directly educed* from fundamenta. Their function is economical co-ordination: they make the manifold intelligible, in the sense of comprehensible. Although indispensable to thought, they are but instruments of thought. Useful for making parts, particular aspects, etc., manageable, they are inadequate to the whole, and inexhaustive of the individual. As

> The flowering moments of the mind
> Drop half their petals in our speech,

so do the relatively concrete Actualities, with which science is first confronted, drop half their qualities in our classificatory thought. Class-concepts are rigid and static, while actuality is fluid and fluent; discrete, while becoming is continuous. The limitations of rough tools for fine work, as of fine tools for rough work, need to be borne in mind, when these concepts are put to use. When they are hypostatised before used, they do not minister to science. It conduces to scientific knowledge, to abstract the mass which material bodies *have*, from their other properties: it conduces to no scientific end, to say that bodies *are* masses, even if, for the purpose in hand, they may be treated as if they were such mathematical fictions.

If science had need of none but formal conceptions, such as class-concepts, science might be as positive as the positivists took it to be.

(b) But the formation of scientific concepts is not guided by the exigencies of logic and mathematics alone. Concepts enter into scientific knowledge, that are selected according to no fixed rules. Without using the 'real' categories, the irreducible minimum of the anthropic element in science, science would find nothing to describe. These may be alogical, the outcome of understanding, in the sense of 'being on terms with' things, but they are as yet indispensable, and represent the best we can do. And with their introduction, logical validity is exchanged for relevance, logical certification for presumptive evidence; 'subsistence in' is replaced by 'usefulness for'.

(c) There are concepts more obviously devised *ad hoc*, and for satisfaction of interest, such as those of non-presented things, imaginal models. These are sometimes called *Hülfsbegriffe*; sometimes, fictions. Suggested by the perceptual, and fashioned after analogy therewith, they are not percepts. They are 'possible' percepts, in the sense that they are conceivable; whether in the sense that, given certain conditions such as finer sensibility, they would be perceived, and therefore are Actual, we have no means of knowing, though we may have sanguine belief based on strong evidence of the presumptive kind. Atoms, α- and β-particles, etc., belong to this class. And the fact that many and varied phenomena are co-ordinated and explained by their means, coerces some to believe that these constructed *supposita*—for they are neither educed nor deduced—are Real; though other physicists are content to say that Nature behaves *as if* she were constituted by such entities. Scientific concepts of this kind may successfully 'resume' many facts, yet after all may need to be supplemented, revised or abandoned. Indeed, theoretical physics has never yet continued long in one stay; and if it did, there is no way from assimilative and constructive imagination to knowledge that their envisaged entities are Actual, nor from analogies to identities. Moreover, concepts that have been found to be wrongly 'read in', sometimes continue to serve scientific ends, as coordinative and suggestive symbolism. Science only requires that a concept of this class, in order to render facts scientifically comprehensible, should be evoked by them and suffered by them, though borrowed from another context. The comprehensibility effected by *Hülfsmittel*, is always comprehensibility for the human mind with human interests. And these conceptual means may be equally useful, and even essential in science, while differing greatly in 'realisableness' or in respect of imitating Actuality: the valency-bonds of the chemist will perhaps generally be taken to say what they mean, but not to mean what they say.

(d) Lastly, science has use for the concept of what is conceivable yet not experienceable, or the concept that contains no element of imagery or sensory symbolism: *e.g.* that of entropy.

If this discrimination between kinds of concepts be necessary and significant, it should also be observed that its lines of demarcation are, as usual, too hard. Thus the classificatory concepts actually used in science, do not all fall within the division that was first mentioned. This is because the aim of scientific classification is not the same as that of the curator of a museum. It is, rather, to make classes, such that natural laws shall be found to be valid of them, and is therefore guided by theory. This often involves construction of ideas *ad hoc*. Galileo's idea of acceleration is of such nature, though usually it is assigned company with the directly educed concepts, such as those of likeness and number. Types, above distinguished, actually overlap. Indeed classification is selective and, though never arbitrary, has reference to interest. Classes are constructed to yield laws; and laws are scientifically useful, largely because of the excellence of the classification that they yield. If there be circularity here, the fact will be assimilable with the outcome of our examination of induction, as well as with what has been submitted, in the present chapter, concerning science as an art subserving an interest.

It remains to be observed that the selectiveness of science begins further back than at the level on which it has so far been discussed. If our science of the world, at its first stage, is what it is, because our impressional *idia*, collectively, are what they are, our theoretical physics, or science at its highest stage of developement, is what it is, partly on account of selective interest evinced in the setting up of a hegemony of one or more senses, and in endowing their deliverances with superior importance. Subjective necessity is the mother of the invention of this device for making perceptual experience scientifically intelligible; consequently the tendency of science to issue in mechanism has psychological motivation.

There is reason to believe that our specific senses are differentiated out of one. Speaking in terms of phenomenalism, the differentiation will not be in the ontal (ω-Objects), but in our apparatus for apprehending. It has been controlled, of course, by our environment; hence there is antecedent probability that all sensa are equally relevant and revealing: that in them there are no "degrees of reality", *i.e.* different removes of phenomenality. The differentiation, in so far as relative specialisation of any particular sense is involved, is also conditioned by contingent human needs and circumstance: it was different, *e.g.* in Fenimore Cooper and the Indians of whom he wrote. There is, then, no psychological justification for the hegemony set up by science; it is an epistemological device: and in so far as it is not due to the needs of life, it is an arbitrary convention. Nature was perhaps not created in order to be, before all else, easily calculable: the conceptual frame of Nature, fashioned by science with a view to make her calculable, is the outcome of teleological adaptation to science's valuations. Psychologically, all sensa are on a par; and we may ask, with Browning,

> Why distrust the evidence
> Of each soon-satisfied and healthy sense?

Common sense and science have, however, distinguished between sensa, regarding some as secondary, or as phenomenal effects of others, that are deemed primary and are taken to be non-phenomenal presentations of the Real.

For the view that extension and impenetrability are primary qualities, while colour and scent are secondary, various reasons have been assigned, some being plainly insufficient. Thus, it has been urged that the primary are presented to several senses, or that their Reality is established by multiple witness; but unless the witnesses differ in character from those that testify only to the secondary qualities, there is no good reason to put greater confidence in them. Moreover, impenetrability is sensed by touch alone. Another argument for the superior status of primary qualities, or such as are apprehended by touch, is that touch is the one sense that knows no illusion. Sight, though it takes precedence in scientific observation, often suffers illusion, and so is not to be trusted to give more than appearance. Whether the sense of touch ever suffers illusion, seems to be disputable; but as to its mediating cognition of Reality, so that the Real is the tangible, it is more important to insist on the fact, that it would make no difference to science if the tactual sense mediated but appearance. Had we an electric sense, as perhaps some fishes have, it would perhaps be easier, as well as in accord with recent tendencies in theoretical physics, to make electricity the essence of substantiality or Reality, and to regard tangible matter as appearance. However, touch has from early times been taken for the sense that apprehends the substantial: witness the psychology of Democritus and the figure of speech, 'the mind *grasps*'

The psychological genesis of this belief was described in an earlier chapter. There we found the true explanation of the primacy of the tactual, and consequently of the prejudice in favour of contact-action in physical theory. It is part of our anthropism. A philosophical dog would perhaps argue, as Mr Bradley says his dog did, that whatever exists, smells: that what does not smell, is unreal. Such a dog would reduce colours, etc., to smells beyond his range of sensibility, but possibly discernible by dogs more highly gifted in respect of nasal sensitiveness; he would work with a corpuscular theory of light and an olfactory theory of matter. With us, smells do not happen to be adapted to ideal revival in serial succession, as are sights and sounds. Nor can our noses analyse odours, as a dog's nose seems to do; by the time we have reached middle age, the small part of the brain allocated to smell shews atrophy, while that allotted to vision is relatively large. It is all a matter of contingency and evolutionary process. Had we been required, in the struggle for existence, to develope our ears to an indefinitely higher degree of sensitiveness and delicacy, Laplace would perhaps have expounded the music of the spheres instead of a *mécanique céleste*. The theory of sound would have been the basis of our physics. Length of rods and strings would be measured by the notes emitted by them when made to vibrate, and rule-of-three sums could be explained by reference to harmony; temperature and chemical composition would be ascertained in terms of telephonic records of electrical resistance; a violin would be a kind of calculating-machine. However, we have been otherwise determined in arriving at our proportionate susceptibilities; we happen to have become more delicate and discriminating in respect of touch and sight, there being in those kinds of sensatio more variation corresponding to a given variation in stimulus. We have *become* almost incapable of representing phenomena in terms of other sensa, and familiarity dictates what shall be primary.

But other reasons for the primariness of primary qualities remain to be mentioned. One is that the properties of matter revealed by touch, especially, are universal, while scent may be absent, and colour may vary according to conditions. But such universality does not imply higher ontological rank; ubiquity or geographical distribution is irrelevant in that connexion. Again, it is claimed that primary qualities are commensurable, allow of comparison, of measurement or correlation with numbers, and so are calculable. This no doubt gratifies our desire for simplicity, and our capacity to work sums. But when, because movements are the changes that can be most easily measured and computed, we select movement as typical of all kinds of change, and would reduce all change to cases of it, we do but mistake analogy for identity. Lastly, we may recall the Cartesian emphasis on the clear and distinct, curiously applied to the matter before us. When we see a body, "we know", says Descartes,[1] "its property of figure with far greater clearness than its colour". "To say we experience colours in objects", he continues, "is in reality equivalent to saying we perceive something in objects and are yet ignorant of what it is, except as that which determines in us a certain highly vivid and clear sensation, which we call the sensation of colours". Here Descartes seems to replace 'acquaintance', at which level colour is at least as clear as figure, by 'knowledge about', in which the causal theory of secondary qualities is merely assumed. Extension and motion are qualities, as much as is colour. They are taken to denote the essence of things, only because they lend themselves to measurement, etc.; but that may no more exhaust the significance of Nature than the counting of the words in a poem reveals what the poem is.

Perhaps it is now plain that different qualities can no more be 'reduced' to one kind, than they can be eliminated from the world that science seeks to rationalise. When science tries, in its description of Nature, to rise above qualitative differences, and regards its theoretical work as incomplete till this is done, or until it can be seen analytically how a quality comes about from some combination of the quantitative or the less markedly qualitative, science may be said to have an axe to grind. Sensa are not constituted by relations; description is not apprehension; the concrete becomes no less concrete, for being conceptually describable. Science passes into a kind of 'philosophy of the *als ob*', treating Nature *as if* qualities were Really quantitative variations of the homogeneous; which, of course, they cannot be. The qualitative, *e.g.* colours and sounds, may have quantitative aspects: everything of that kind has quantitative relations, but there is nothing that

[1] *The Principles of Philosophy*, i. §§ 69–70.

consists of them. Nevertheless, it is asserted that physics "reduces" sensible qualities to one only, or to the quantitative; so we may ask what 'reduction' means. Sometimes 'reducibility to' seems to be taken to be 'identity with'; as in the case of 'heat is a mode of motion'. But if 'heat' mean warmth-sensum, that *is* not corpuscular motion, however related it may be thereto. If one could observe the increase of velocity in the molecules of a body becoming hot, the experience would not be identical with that of a growing warmth in one's skin, even if the body were one's own body. So it is more usual to find 'reducible to' interpreted as 'caused by'. Then the qualitative diversity is not resolved, but only shifted from the material to the mental, or from the Objective to the objective. Lastly, reduction may consist in what were better called traduction or translation. One quality then stands for, or represents, another. Which is prototype, and which ectype, will be matter of convention; and representation will not be copying. Knowledge may thereby be promoted, but it will not be made adequate or exhaustive. Science culminates in a description of the conceptual world, in which no account is taken of a large proportion of the essence, or the possible significance, of the concrete fundamenta whence the conceptual framework has been derived. Its departmentality is self-confessed.

Thus far, only specific instances of the limitation of the scope and aim of scientific knowledge, have been discussed. These may now be recapitulated and assigned their place in a completer survey.

6. Limitations are not to be confounded with defects; and to point out those which beset scientific knowledge, is not to disparage science. Science is none the less genuine knowledge (knowledge being what, in previous chapters, it has been empirically found to be), for being limited; and none the less limited, for being genuine. Discernment of its limitations is essential for a true understanding of what lies within them, as well as for any reasonable surmise as to the Beyond, which its limitations may suggest. The frame of a picture may seem, to the average beholder, a mere limit and a hindrance to wider vision: to the painter, it is the condition, and a determinant, of what he puts upon his canvas. Neglect of science's limitations has in the past been responsible for pseudo-science and pseudo-philosophy—even pseudo-theo-

logy: for anti-intellectualism, or irrationalism, and for overweening dogmatism. And theology, concerned with the Beyond as to which it claims reasonable belief, is not nowadays content, so to isolate itself from science as to stand to it in negative relations alone. At one time the religious could look upon science as if it were a black art; and, nearer to our own day, there were representatives of science who would grant to religious faith only the realm of nescience in which to expatiate. Today theology has no concern with doctrine of a double truth, as if what is true in its sphere could well be false in that of science; with a system of bookkeeping by double entry, with water-tight compartments, or with mutual irrelevancy. It is perhaps equally impatient of compromise, accommodation, and reconciliation. Without servility, it would establish positive relationships with science. It would find the unifying bond, in Reason: the *differentia*, in diversity of operations on the same data. At least this is how theology is here conceived, whatever different estimations of its nature and attitude may obtain elsewhere. Hence theology's interest in science's limitations. Conscious of her own, she yet indulges the hope that her research may prove supplementary to that of delimited science.

To begin at the beginning, we may remind ourselves once more that, while it is only what may be called the *core* of science's data that is impressional, the impressional is the sole basis of scientific knowledge of Actuality. *If* there be any other 'first touch' with ontal Reality than the sensory, science is *ipso facto* not only limited to what is not beyond, but also bounded by what is beyond. Rationalism has sought to transcend this limit by alleging thought-given Realities; religion, by alleging direct experience of the Objective otherwise than through sensibility or thought. It has been argued already that, *if* there be contact with Reality in either of these transcendent ways, science of any kind and philosophy do not *know* of it. It is not, then, at this initial stage, that the Beyond can be asserted by one who is constrained to reject the epistemological claims of rationalism, or those of religious experience belonging to the alleged 'immediate' kind.

In the number, nature and prescribed range of our senses, limits are imposed on these inlets of possible impression. Interpreted in terms of the theory of knowledge that, in an earlier chapter, commended itself as alone fact-satisfying, this means that there is more of possible experience than is actualised, more possibility of *rapport*, and apparently even more actual *rapport*, than we have introspection of, and knowledge about.[1] But this involves limitation rather for aesthetic than for scientific apprehension; the Beyond, of which we thus get an inkling, is not of different order from the Within, nor perhaps would acquaintance with it serve to enlarge the borders of science.

We first meet with limitations, that are of philosophical moment, when science deliberately excludes from its field the pursuits known respectively as history and epistemology. Here are departments of possible knowledge that are not science, but are of highest import for philosophy. The alogical, which science increasingly ignores, and replaces by the conceptual when from experiment and verification it passes to theory, calls for exercise of Reason, as distinct from formal rationality, for teleological explanation and 'understanding', and evokes considerations as to value. If science be said to strain out this element as non-essential, it is nevertheless in what is then relegated to the accidental, that, for the most part, our life consists; for we live and move and have our being in it, and reasonableness consists largely in coming to an understanding with it. Moreover, the alogical is not merely determinative, as *positum*, of science's data and concepts; the knowing-process, we have found, in virtue of which the data are forthcoming, involves uneliminable 'real' categories which are not 'rational', but interpretative. In insisting on this truth, which is so apt to be overlooked, philosophy and theology would not offensively fling a *tu quoque* at science, deserved as it would be if science persisted in arrogating to itself the epithet 'positive', but would rather

---

[1] In virtue of our knowledge as to the subconscious, etc., we may compare the soul to a living wind-swept lute, receptive of influences and responsive to them by vibrating, but not hearing the vibrations. The soul may have but very partial knowledge as to its own contacts, doing and undergoing more than it can be aware of. It is conceivable that overtones, beyond the range of our audibility, may help to determine the *timbre* of notes that we hear, and that non-introspectible phases of soul-life tell on the phases that are manifested. Perhaps this is why "we feel that we are greater than we know"? It has already been suggested, and it may be remarked again in this connexion, that the mystic possibly has 'glimpses' of the Beyond, though he cannot epistemologically establish his claim to mystical knowledge.

As for the present state of science with regard to physiology of the senses and sensation, we shall be wise, perhaps, to entertain the possibility that it is but similar to that of chemistry before Lavoisier.

establish brotherly relations in virtue of a common humanity or anthropism, and by division of labour to a common end. There is more than one sort of intelligibility. And though neither kind is possible at all, without some tincture of the other, either may be preferentially pursued, legitimately and fruitfully, with a view to the final adjustment and comprehension of both. Science has enough to occupy it, if it abstract from subjects and the subjective, even though it thereby ignores the larger part of its every fact; but its partiality warrants no claim to disinterestedness. It may concentrate on the problem of the world's structure, using such assumptions and postulates as are necessary, such faith or belief as is indispensable, such conventions as are expedient; and that, without disparagement of investigations for which structure becomes of secondary importance. For theology, other utterances of things become of paramount significance, and science's postulations may be pernicious and question-begging. In that science is not epistemology, and makes no epistemological regress for itself, it is, from the more comprehensive view of philosophy, relatively superficial. This is no defect in science, but it is a severe limitation, of which account must be taken when the relation of science to the whole of knowledge is concerned. There can be no science, in the specialised sense of the word, of the principles of science that are due to constructive art; the only critical science of them, is the epistemology that is not natural science.

Further, if the phenomena studied by science be appearances of the Real to subjects, science can only know the phenomenal or, more correctly speaking, know the Real through and as the phenomenal. It is precluded from making statements, positive or negative, as to the ontal, and from claiming absolute knowledge or non-phenomenal knowledge of the absolute. If there be any such metaphysical knowledge, it will constitute another of science's bounds; whether or not there be such knowledge, science here knows another limit. Boutroux has said that though science no longer aspires to absolute knowledge, she does not thereby "recognise" the existence of another realm, in which religion can freely expatiate; which is true. But when he adds that science "warns off" from any region inaccessible to herself, either he misrepresents the situation, or he claims for science, as a prerogative, what must be called intolerance. If "every attempt to interpret her ignorance, as well as her certainty, arouses her suspicion", she may be said to stand in need of psychotherapy. The limitations of her knowledge, and the antecedent possibility of room beyond them for reasonable beliefs, are plain enough; indeed she may be said to stand in need, rather, of deliverance from her friends.

Lastly, science knows nothing as to absolute beginnings—she has a cosmology, but no cosmogony; nothing as to the end of the world or the destiny of the soul—she has no eschatology; nothing as to the world as a whole, the universe or Nature—about which not a single *scientific* statement is forthcoming.

But more significant than all these specific limitations, is the nature and constitution of scientific 'knowledge' itself. It is not positive or apodeictic; not necessary, universal or unconditional; not adequate or exhaustive. Its verification is pragmatic, not logical: the probability that is its guide, is not mathematical but, at least in part, psychological; as also is the certitude that needs must play the rôle of certainty. For all its rationality, it is but reasonable; for all its self-constituted realism and positivism, the very Objects, as to which it is realistic and positivistic, are but derived or constructed interpretations of the one and only kind of *positum* or primary actuality; and to what extent our sub-jectivity, the *modus recipientis*, conditions even that, is scientifically unknowable. Not a single item of genuinely scientific 'know-ledge' would need to be disputed, if the Real world were proved to be purely spiritual and primarily a realm of ends. It does not appear, if the foregoing statements be soundly based, that science is in any position to warn off from other kinds of interpretative assimilation—which is the only meaning that 'knowledge' can bear, if it is to have denotation—such as shift the emphasis to aspects of Nature which she herself disregards. It is not so much to the point, that her own house is glassy enough to make stone-throwing inexpedient, as that science and theism spring from a common root. In a future volume it shall be inquired, whether theistic theology be not a reasonable continuation, by extrapola-tion or through points representing new observations, of the curve of 'knowledge' that science has constructed.

APPENDIX

Note A. *The attempted repudiation of consciousness.*

The recent phase of the effort to get rid of the concept of consciousness, seems to have been initiated by Prof. W. James. That psychologist—who was also a rhetorician—propounded, in the title of an essay, the question 'Does consciousness exist?' and suggested a negative answer. He would have expressed what he meant, had he asked whether a substantial ego exists, and whether thoughts consist of mental stuff, or of a neutral stuff devised by himself. He did not doubt the function of knowing; so he was not rejecting consciousness, in the sense in which the word has been adopted in Chap. II of this book. True, he asserted thinking to be identical with breathing: "I am as confident as I am of anything that, in myself, the stream of thinking (which I recognise emphatically as a phenomenon) is only a careless name for what, when scrutinised, reveals itself to consist chiefly in the stream of my breathing" (*Essays in Radical Empiricism*, p. 36). But the context shews that, even in this passage, it is not a unique function that he is anathematising, but only the permanent ego; his prejudice against which, led him into the error of taking it for the ghost of the quasi-material soul, believed to have perished in the downfall of the old rational psychology. This unique functioning, which is all that orthodoxy asserts as known fact, is distinguished from the properties of physical things, as clearly as common sense could wish, by such words as "confident", "reveals itself", etc.; so that if he had meant to obliterate the distinction, James would have asserted and denied it 'in the same breath'. But he did teach that awareness of breathing is the same breathing over again, in another "context" or "grouping"; that both are constituted by the same "neutral stuff", which is subject or object, accordingly as "it is taken" in one or another "context of associates".

Now psychology, as a science, has no concern with neutral or other sorts of stuff; it only asks, before the subject is relegated to the heap of antiquated and superfluous notions, whether taking things in a context does not presuppose the presence of the agent whose expulsion is desired. It was by hinting that this is not the case, that, apart from his metaphysical speculation, James prepared the way for the repudiation of acts of consciousness, in which he himself retained some sort of belief. His notion of contexts found favour with later writers. But they, like their master, are "sagely unanalytic" as to this vague term. James could only hint at its meaning, by analogies presupposing the received analysis of experience into a duality, and he overlooked the tacit retention of the subject which his phrase "taken in a group of associates" involved. His school has not so much as presented a case for the abolition of awareness, until it has shewn how 'contexts' differ from spatio-temporal collocations, in which things do not 'take' themselves; and in what 'taking' exactly consists. This lack of explicitness is not made good, when consciousness is said to be a case of irritability or nervous response of organism to situation. It remains the same irreducible and unique functioning, and becomes no other, when called an instance of response or of behaviour; its uniqueness, the only relevant consideration, is then merely shelved. What needs to be accounted for, is the world of difference between the 'sensitiveness' of the Mimosa-leaf, which folds up when touched, and the sensibility of an organism that feels or even knows what touches it, as well as moves when touched. Writers, whose verbal trifling with the unique *quale* of the conscious consists in invoking the nervous system, abstain from explaining how, without 'feeling', over and above irritability, we could have associated sensibility with a nervous system; or how some of us have got the belief that we are conscious *of* breathing, and that breathing is not consciousness. They resort to figurative obfuscation where precision is vital: "thought is the labile interplay of motor settings", the contents of consciousness are "a cross-section of things" or "a projection" of things upon some "plane". These metaphors and quasi-entities, like their prototype "contexts", effect nothing, unless clandestine retention of the overtly renounced.

Other disbelievers in any act or state of awareness, have indeed presented their doctrine without the veil of allegorical obscurity. With engaging downrightness, they have hazarded the stark denial of any difference between sensum and sensatio, seeming to give the lie direct or indirect to the law of contradiction in the assertion "there are things heard and seen, but there is no seeing or hearing". Consciousness, according to one group of behaviourists, consists not even in nervous response to things: it is the things themselves, and no more. Thus a writer is cited with approval by Mr Russell (*The Analysis of Mind*, p. 143) as suggesting that, if the realist try the experiment of conceiving perceptions [percepta?] as purely natural events, not as cases of apprehension [perceptio?], he will be surprised to see how little he misses. If 'little' be here the all-significant word, this sentence is redeemed. It then finds a parallel in the candid confession of Dr Ward, that presentationism "accounts for nine-tenths" of the fact: but whereas orthodoxy would here apply the text "the little less, and what worlds away", behaviourism often evinces that by 'little', it would mean 'nothing'. Thus it reaches its paradoxical conclusion, that 'x is' and 'x appears' (to S), are identical propositions; so that to observe a thunder-storm, it would seem, is to be one. If this climax be not a *reductio ad absurdum*, perhaps its consequences will be found to yield one. How is it, we may ask, that in a world in which *ex hypothesi* there can be no seeming, there is nevertheless error, such as the traditional psychology? So long as "things are not what they seem", further enterprise in "simplifying" psychology is required by behaviourism, and an explanation of seeming, as something other than consciousness over again, is due. It is difficult to see how this explanation can be offered, without recantation of the paradox to which the extremer school has rushed. But until some better device than that of identifying error of opinion with opposition between physical forces (which has seriously been suggested), is forthcoming, we may fairly conclude that nothing has been made plainer, save that we cannot even talk nonsense about states of consciousness, without presupposing their actuality and uniqueness: that in advancing to its *ne plus ultra*, scepticism has achieved naught but suicide.

Note B. *Analysis.*

Analytical psychology is not concerned with such analysis as may be possible within the immediate experience of a subject, while that experience is simply transpiring or being 'enjoyed', and is not being reflected upon. Such relatively slight analysis as may be forthcoming from the standpoint indicated, has been distinguished by the name 'psychical' (see p. 46). It is only alluded to here, because of the importance of distinguishing from it the examination of experiences, from the standpoint of reflection on the part of a psychological observer. It is analysis of the latter kind, issuing in common scientific knowledge, that is pursued in analytical psychology; and such analysis needs to be distinguished from other processes unfortunately called by the same name, and from yet others apt to be confounded with it.

1. It is not actual separation into perceptual parts, *i.e.* partition, as when sulphur and iron, in a mixture or aggregate, are isolated by use of a magnet or by solvents, or when a compound such as water is decomposed by an electric current into oxygen and hydrogen. These processes yield more data, two things instead of one, which can be recombined. And such partition takes into account the relations subsisting between the constituents, exhibiting that the compound is a synthesis, rather than an aggregate or mechanical whole: so providing for reconstruction. In this sense, a watch can be analysed by taking it to pieces, but not by grinding it to powder. There are wholes that cannot adequately be described as consisting of separable parts, in that as wholes, their properties are not identical with the sum of the properties of all the parts; the self, we shall see, is such a whole.

Again, a note may be resolved into its constituent tones, rendered separately audible. But something quite different is meant, when we say a note can be analysed into pitch, loudness and timbre, none of which can be detected without the others. It is analysis in this sense, that is pursued by the psychologist. No separation, as in chemical analysis is effected; but conceptual distinctions, counterparts of no separate actualities, are set up. Thus in a given momentary experience or psychosis, we may distinguish the irreducible constituents of attention, feeling and conation, though no subject ever has a feeling without attending to some presentation; and an emotion can be analysed into distinguishable factors that no more exist in isolation than do the north and south poles of a magnet.

2. Analysis is not abstraction, though psychological analysis is akin to resolution of a sound. Abstraction is *attending to* one distinguishable or conceptually isolable factor; concentrating on one, and ignoring others while leaving them there. Useful enough when its limitations and approximateness are recognised, it becomes a vicious method when these are transcended or forgotten. From the one property abstracted, the rest, from which it has been abstracted, cannot be got back or deduced. Spinoza's substance is easily reached by abstraction from the world of common sense; but his deduction of the finite world from it, is the classic example of rationalistic conjuring. What has been left out is, of course, no longer in. The ultimate or most general concept is the emptiest. And though an abstracted analyticum may be all that matters for a specific purpose, other qualities being irrelevant, it no longer exhausts the significance of the whole. Moreover, the re-synthesis of abstractions yields but an abstraction. If mass, length and time be abstractions, so-called bodies, describable solely in terms of these dimensions, will not be actualities of experience. Abstraction, unlike partition, does not increase our data, but expunges them.

3. Psychology being a science of the actual, the analysis which it prosecutes is not guided by metaphysical presupposition, such as that logic must apply without remainder to mental phenomena, and the mind be therefore resolvable into discrete terms, such as logic can deal with. This is to take the kingdom of actuality by logical violence, and to mistake an empirical for a pure science. Analytical psychology, faithful to the empirical method, must derive its conceptual analytica straight from experience of the perceptual kind, not indirectly by constructive imagination and arbitrary fiction. On this ground must be pronounced devoid of relevance or fruitfulness, the approach to psychology, nowadays common, that may be called the logistic. This method, imitative of the mathematical, sets out from invented concepts such as 'sensibles' (unsensed) or pure data, which have place only in a pure science, in order that its 'analytica' may be amenable to logic of the discrete. Such exercises of ingenuity can contribute to science of actuality, no more than do elegant compositions in Latin verse; and the number of such possible ventures, of equal because of zero value, is as indefinite as that of possible translations of a sonnet. They are wrongly called 'analytical'. In order that any analysis be scientifically useful, it is necessary, before all things, that the analytica reached admit of re-synthesis, so that the analysis can be tested; else it may leave out—as is often the case—what is psychologically most significant. If, as in sensationism, the so-called analytica will not admit of re-synthesis, the analysis is as unverified as it was unfounded; and much that

has been offered as analysis, rejoices in both these characteristics. It should be called by another name.

Actual analysis can never be known to be ultimate, though the analytica we reach may be irreducible by us; and the simples we arrive at, can never be asserted to exist in isolation or to be prior, in order of time, to the complexes in which they are discovered. Nor can actual analysis ever be wholly replaced by that of the logico-mathematical kind. If space be analysed into points, and time into instants, the point must still have spatial, and the instant, temporal, *quale*; else neither analysis excludes the other. There is something in space (as relevant to spatial perception) which has no counterpart in the mathematical continuum. The realist, again, is apt to forget that though, as he contends, where the mind can distinguish objects there must be objects to distinguish, these objects are not necessarily actual, but possibly only ideal. In order to be valid as well as logically possible, analysis must discover, not merely invent or create.

Note C. *Actuality, Reality, Existence, Being.*

ACTUALITY.

Of this series of philosophical terms, the one that *in ordine cognoscendi* is primary, is 'actuality', in the sense that has been conventionally assigned to it on most occasions on which it has here been used. It then denotes the perceptual proper, the concrete fundamenta of all common knowledge; and the perceptual especially as distinguished from the imaginal and the ideal, which are also objective but lack impressional core.

This is not the meaning of 'actuality', as the term is generally used. When we speak of the actual world, we usually refer to the so-called perceptual, the Objective rather than the objective, the phenomenal which (or, as some would have it, the knowledge of which) is elaborated out of the objective by means of explicated categories, and at the common standpoint. Using the device already adopted in cognate connexions, we may call this Actuality. But in so bowing to custom, it is well to recognise that we are applying one name to profoundly different things, viz. individual and trans-subjective experience, respectively. In both actuality and Actuality, nevertheless, there will be elements cognised by sense; and both terms will bespeak antithesis with the imaginal. For though the Actual world (or our knowledge of it, as the case may be) is conceptual, concepts without percepts (proper) are empty, and of themselves yield no knowledge of Actuality. Knowability through sense-impression, is thus the one fixed and essential characteristic of what, historically, has been denoted by 'Actuality'. Thence is derived the contrast of the Actual with the potential or the possible; also, in virtue of the notion of efficient causation, the reference to action, which 'Actual' (*wirklich*) suggests, and the especial applicability of the term to movements and phenomenal events. As thus defined, 'the Actual' is no synonym for 'the existent'; for there may be existents unknowable through the instrumentality of sense. Indeed, once transition, under cover of one name, is made from the actual to the Actual, it is hard to find a logical halting-place at which we may cease to bestow the predicate 'Actual' on the successive conceptual removes from the perceptual, such, *e.g.* as the sun, the trilobite, the molecule, the electron, space-time. The word 'Actual' can now hardly be avoided; but we may keep our eyes open to its indefiniteness. To introduce definiteness into established philosophical terminology, would involve revolution rather than reform.

REALITY.

'Reality' is much more ambiguous than 'Actuality': it is therefore perhaps the most "blessed" word in the philosophical vocabulary. Both "fool and advanced thinker" use it as if it had one meaning immediately discernible by everyone; whereas the signification that it may on occasion possess, is determined by a writer's convention: and that is not always invariable. Sometimes the word is scarcely more than a vent for emotion. The following instances of its variable meaning, are but a selection.

1. With the British empiricists and sensationists, the real is the impressional, or the concrete perceptual of individual experience, which crude realism erroneously identifies with the Objective. This reality is what is denoted by 'actuality', as above defined. It is the more nearly approached, the less there is of the conceptual, of the thought-element, in knowledge.

2. 'Real' denotes what has here been called the Actual: the phenomenal of Kant, the physical Objects of common sense and of molar or macroscopic science: what is thought or supposed to be 'there' for all, and more or less abidingly, or independently of the sporadic percepts of individuals, which are taken to be copies or appearances or effects, of it.

3. 'Reality' refers only to ultimate reality, or the ontal, which lies behind, so to say, the Real in sense (2). The Real is now the noumenal that co-operates with us in producing the phenomenal. 'Reality' denotes the unknowable things *per se* for a Kantian, the monads for a Leibnizian, the electrons, ether, etc., for the realistic physicist, space-time 'structure' for some of the school of Einstein, human souls and acts of God for the Berkeleyan: and so forth.

4. The real is the noumenal, in quite other senses than that of Kant: the 'intelligible' as the archetypal, the Ideal of Plato, the universal *ante rem*, the rational. The word then denotes numbers, concepts, relations, laws, an eternal *prius* of 'the valid', hypostatised into the existent, and to which any determinate being must conform, in order to be. It excludes the actual and the Actual, as illusion or non-being—whatever those terms then may 'mean'.

5. Hence, often, the real has been defined as the immutable.

6. Overlapping some of these meanings, are those of 'independent of experience' and 'self-subsistent': 'experience' now meaning sense, now reason, now both.

7. When contrast with the imaginal or the illusory is the core of the meaning of 'reality', some define it, not merely in respect of impressional content, but also with explicit reference to human interest, and in terms of fulfilment of expectation, demands of will, etc.: as what has to be reckoned with, or what makes a difference to conduct.

8. When the real is defined as the self-consistent, it is perhaps meant that what is regarded as real on other grounds, or in some other sense, necessarily possesses also self-consistency. If not a tautology, this definition gives expression to a dogmatic prejudice or to an anthropic need.

9. Perhaps the notion that 'real' has any intrinsic meaning, enabling it to be applied, without preliminary definition, to this and not to that, is due to implicit mingling of significance, derived from the sphere of value, with ontological import. Thus arises a hybrid conception and a logical monstrosity. A tinge of pragmatism (7), or the notion that 'real', whatever else it stands for, must somehow denote what is important *for us*, then colours the rationalistic transparencies, presented in some of the other definitions; and the conception of 'degrees of reality' emerges. There are conceivably degrees of adequacy with which the real, in some of the senses mentioned above, may be apprehended—degrees of phenomenality; and we know of degrees of correctness or erroneousness in beliefs: but to speak of degrees of reality, implies that some criterion of gradation in reality has been found, and some principle according to which degrees ought to be assigned. Our ethical ideals, however, tell us nothing about the universe regarded ontologically, save that it contains beings who evaluate, and that the world is more or less instrumental to the realisation of particular values. That the universe will finally satisfy human aspirations, is ontologically unknown; and to define a concept, presumably of ontological import, in terms of human hope, seems an incongruity.

The word 'real' cries for expunging, as it is a source of little else than confusion. It shall here be avoided so far as possible; whenever it needs must be adopted, it is hoped that the specific meaning it is intended to bear will be sufficiently indicated in the context, and that, for the most part, the distinctive usage of 'real' and 'Real' will serve this purpose.

EXISTENCE.

The source of the abstract notion of existence, is the issue of perception in the existential judgement of perception. Unless there were change in the individual's field of presentation, no judgement as to the existence of anything could arise. At the hypothetically distinguishable lowest level of purely individual experience, *esse* is *percipi*; at the level of common and explicitly conceptualised experience, to exist is primarily to 'stand out', or be Objective, in common space and time. If that were all that common sense and philosophy had agreed to refer to, in predicating existence, the meaning of the term would have remained definite. But of course this was impossible. Our thoughts 'stand out', though not in space, over-against us; and existence is therefore affirmed of them, as also of things conceived and never perceived—such as the back of the moon, the soul, etc., because they must be supposed to exist, in order to account for, and to systematise, the knowledge of what we do perceive. In ideation, we abstract the 'what' from the 'that'; and in parting company with the matter of the percept, we are apt to bestow its form where, for all we know, there is no matter. And such abstraction, once started, knows no end. The existent being wider than the known actual, and even than the Actual, any characteristic, by which the existent can then be described, is no longer forthcoming. Hence, on the one hand, the doctrine that existence is an ultimate and indefinable concept, whose denotation—or a fragment of it—can only be ostensively indicated; on the other hand, Bain's view that the word 'existent' is a redundancy, meaning nothing beyond what may be called the 'position' of actual things and attributes. 'I exist', according to Bain, is an elliptical expression for 'I am something'; and as Hume and Kant argued, to take existence for an independent attribute of an idea, over and above those involved in the 'what', is the fallacy of the ontological argument and of ontologism in general.

To define existence in terms of space and time, however useful it might be as a verbal convention, is said to be arbitrary, in that it involves assumption that space and time 'are', apart from things in space and time. That charge is perhaps an exaggeration: no more need be implied than that, what we agree to call existent, shall have spatial and temporal relations, neither terms nor relations being before or after other, in any sense. But even so, we need a word for entities, such as the psychical, which stand out in time only; and there may *be* entities that stand in relations among which time is not included. To exist, and to be, are so commonly identified that, conventionally to assign them different meanings determined by reference to space or time, would prove an insufferable artifice. We must continue to attribute existence, and not merely being (as something different) to supersensible, and possibly timeless, entities, *e.g.* the soul and God. So long as substantival or characterisable entities are in question, that which has determinate being can hardly be denied existence. Perhaps the only use to which such a differentiation of being and existence could be put, with advantage, is to distinguish the abstract idea, *e.g.* of a circle, as having being (when attended to as object), from the existent or actual circular body-surface.

But besides the substantival—from which is here excluded the universal, though it receives an abstract noun for its name, such as beauty which only 'exists' in the sense that beautiful things exist—there is the realm of the adjectival and relational. In this connexion, the term 'subsistence' might be put to use, notwithstanding its recent spoiling by arbitrary appropriation. It might be applied to 'the valid', *i.e.* to relations that have not the same existence-marks as terms, but which *are*, or subsist between terms. Within the sphere of actuality, terms can no more exist without relations, than relations can subsist apart from terms; though, in thought, the two are separable or distinguishable. Abstracted from terms or *res*, relations and universals are admittedly timeless, so that subsistence might be predicated of them by those who prefer to reserve 'existent' for what is 'in time'.

BEING.

Being is certainly indefinable, as is existence, when not coextensive with actuality: not merely because, like redness, being is ultimate; but because it is a contentless abstraction. Pure or indeterminate being is not distinguishable, by any assignable character, from nonentity. In order to be, or even to be conceived, an entity must be this and not that. And it serves no purpose to attribute being to the round square, or to distinguish "whatever can be mentioned", as 'entities', from existents. There could then "be" no nonentity. But if we once allow that a concept may *be* (before the mind) and yet be *of* a nonentity, we cannot but invoke the notion of existence, as distinct from that of being. Perhaps the only use of such inquiry as this, which is apt to end in logic-chopping, is to indicate the treacherous ambiguity of our word 'concept'. There may *be* concepts that have no existing counterparts; the 'entity' conceived, or supposed, may not be an existent; and if it be not, it does not seem fitting to speak of it as an 'entity', but rather as a nonentity.

It is now easy to understand why some metaphysicians, *e.g.* Lotze, in endeavouring to specify the characterisations which must be possessed by any entity, in order that it may have (1) determinate being and (2) existence, other than as an idea-form in this or that person's mind, have gone too far and have read into their definitions the findings of their own systems of philosophy. It is but recoil from empty abstractions or merely verbal entities; and recoil seldom knows where to stop. Indeed, how much of the richness of content of actual things can be dispensed with, while something determinate and existent is left, is not an easy matter to decide. However, in order to be philosophical, it is not necessary to meet trouble half way, nor to court it when no purpose will be served; and, perhaps, to attempt to define the marks of the existent, when supposition of it is but conceptually constructed, and it is neither concretely presented nor inferred from presentations, is to do the one or the other.

In conclusion, attention may be called to the ambiguity of the word 'is'. It may assert (1) existence or being, (2) identity—*e.g.* paste is flour and water, (3) (as copula) the relation of predication—grass is green. There is also a figurative use, in which 'to be' stands for 'imply', or some such word:

as in "to be good is to be happy". Unfortunately this is not always confined to colloquial occasions or to poetry, but replaces one or other of the
stricter uses of 'is', when a loose thinker undertakes to write science.

Note D. *Multiple Personality*.

Of the classic cases of divided personality, two may be selected for brief
notice, that are of peculiar interest to general psychology. The first is that
of Mr Hanna, to which a work has been devoted by Boris Sidis. Mr Hanna,
when 24 years of age, in consequence of an accident lost all his acquired
experience and reverted, roughly speaking, to the infantile stage of mentality.
His sensory organs remained unimpaired, but he could not discriminate or
perceive 'things', nor control his movements. Though there was complete
amnesia of his past experience, its traces nevertheless persisted subliminally;
for the form (so to say) or the *dispositio* of his previous knowledge remained,
in that he learned again more quickly than would an infant. In dreams, and
under hypnotic treatment, he gained glimpses of his old life, but without
awareness that it was his. He acquired a second personality in substitution
for his first. In course of time, this second personality began to alternate,
for brief periods, with the earlier; then came awareness of both, but no more
ability on his part to unify them, than if they had been manifestations of two
separate individuals.

A much more complicated case is that of "Miss Beauchamp", on which
a most interesting book has been written by Morton Prince. The lady
first known, as patient, to Dr Morton Prince, may be referred to as personality B_1. When she was hypnotised, an artificially produced personality,
B_2, emerged. B_1 knew nothing of B_2, but B_2 professed to know B_1's mind,
and spoke of her as 'I'. In course of time, recovery from the hypnotic trance
reinstated, instead of B_1 (the lady-like and resigned "Miss Beauchamp"),
a quite different personality, B_3 or "Sally". This was a mischievous creature
who despised B_1, spoke of her as 'she', and annoyed her with practical jokes.
B_3 alternated with B_1, but was sometimes coexistent with her and also with
B_4—a later revealed 'person' who emerged suddenly, and appeared ignorant
of both B_1 and B_3. Sally, though first appearing to the doctor after hypnosis
of B_1, was not (like B_2) a product of hypnotic treatment, but had alternated
with B_1 from early childhood. She claimed to know about B_2, and to know
directly B_1's thoughts. This latter claim seems to have been due to illusion;
Sally's word is not always to be trusted, and in such a matter as this, the most
truthful of beings, destitute of psychological education, can be in error.
B_3 gradually grew more distinct from B_1, in consequence of successive shocks,
and partly, perhaps, in consequence of hypnotic treatment. Her alleged
intuition of B_1's experience, can be accounted for partly by the insight
mediated through dreams, marginal attention, etc., and partly by the common

illusion of memory, which leads to belief that another person's experience was our own. Her handwriting was the same as that of B_1; but she was not in command of Miss Beauchamp's knowledge of French. She could hypnotise B_1 and make her tell repugnant lies: the two personalities could have struggles of will, and so furnish an instance of co-consciousness, as well as of alternation. When B_3 was hypnotised, suggestions, given to her, influenced B_1 as if they had been given to B_2—another of the numerous proofs that B_1 and B_3 were connected.

B_4, when hypnotised, evinced memories belonging to B_1; and these two had dreams in common, each of them calling the dream her own. B_3 knew of B_4's dreams, but nothing as to her waking mind; and B_4 was disintegrable, apparently without limit.

So much for the dissociation of Miss Beauchamp: it is not necessary to go into further complexities of this remarkable case. But the re-integration, effected by the skill of Dr Morton Prince, is significant. It was a tragic and pathetic, if a happy, end to the drama. B_1 and B_4 were fused by suggestion; and when their fusion approached completeness, B_1 became the dominant personality, while Sally was banished to the subliminal region. As both B_4 and B_3 resented and opposed this fusion, it was not accomplished for some time. B_4 made use of pre-suggestion, and prevented her hypnotic self from accepting the doctor's suggestion; it was only when he almost forcibly overcame this resistance, that B_4 was absorbed. If Sally was banished to the subliminal limbo, "Miss Beauchamp" was made whole. B_3 and B_4 were evidently offshoots from B_1, as experience-masses not capable of fathoming or fully analysing themselves. They had been synthesised respectively by one ego and were resolved into one normal personality, in so far as "Miss Beauchamp" could be normal.

Note E. *Relations.*

The word 'relation' is as ambiguous as most terms in our language that have psychological or philosophical meaning, serving for all the words *Beziehung, Verhältniss* and *rapport*. It is used indiscriminately of relations, presumably due to the intrinsic and inalienable natures of things—such as resemblance, degrees in quality, etc.—sometimes called necessary or ideal or *a priori*, and giving rise to mathematical and logical knowledge, characterised by certainty; of relations, not compacted by implication or by intrinsic nature, but due to Nature's contingency and alogical conjoining—such as situation in place, time, and causal sequence—in which case, a relation will often be an actual process or activity; of factitious relations, such as are involved in correlating things with numbers in counting, as distinguished from real relations, such as that between a father and his son.

A relation is a characterisation or predicate of an object, viewed as belonging to it when considered with reference to others: or rather, a predicate having reference to a plurality, and so denoting subsistence 'between'. (If numerical identity be a relation, a thing can have at least one relation to itself.) Thus a relation differs from a quality denoted by an adjective, which is a character viewed as belonging to the thing, apart from reference to, or in abstraction from, other things. Frequently a concept can be substituted for a relation, for purposes of diction. Thus the fact that A is the father of B $(A.r.B)$, can be expressed by saying that A has the attribute of 'paternity-to-B' (rB being now an adjective); and if we eliminate reference to B in particular, A can be described by the concept 'father'. In this way many concepts have arisen, that may be called relative, by way of distinguishing between them and such as may be called intrinsic. But not all relations can so be transformed into adjectival concepts: we do not similarly speak of x as equal, or having equality. Of course, A can no more have paternity, without being father of some particular individual, than x can have equality, without being equal to some particular thing. Evidently we are here concerned with a mere linguistic artifice, having no philosophical import. But, by means of such a verbal trick, traditional logic sought to resolve all judgements of relation into judgements of simple predication, of the type S is P; and by means of such logic, plausibility has been secured for philosophical systems. Monism would regard a relation between x and y, as an attribute of the complex x, y, and ultimately as an attribute of the 'whole of Reality' or of The Absolute. Such theory, as Mr Bertrand Russell has pointed out, cannot explain the 'difference of sense' in relations, of a certain type (the asymmetric), between the same two terms: e.g. if $x > y$ mean nothing about x or y, but only something about the couple as such; or if it mean that the universe contains diversity of magnitude: that meaning would not be affected by whether x or y be the greater, and so could not account for the particular fact. Pluralism of the Leibnizian kind, in this respect meets its extreme, in regarding relations as adjectives; though, for it, they are qualities inherent in the monads severally. Lastly, recent logistic realism has gone to the opposite limit of discarding the substance-attribute conception altogether, and basing itself on the grammar which would recognise only terms and relations. It then profits by the ambiguity of the word 'relations'.

Hence has arisen a controversy as to whether relations are internal or external. This controversy is irrelevant to philosophy of the Actual; for the polemic of the adherents of the external theory is ultimately based on the assumption of terms without natures—i.e. indeterminate beings—absolute simples, and so forth, which are fictious of "analysis"—i.e. of abstraction. Within the sphere of Actuality, there can be no talk of a relation such as similarity between two terms, unless the similarity be in respect of some specific quality; unless the relation of likeness between, say, a buttercup and a dandelion, is constituted by their both being yellow, or the relation of difference between a poppy and a daisy, is constituted by the one being white and the other, red. Qualitative difference cannot exist, unless there are qualities: or unless the relation is internal, in the sense of being grounded on the intrinsic. The spatial relation, denoted by 'to the right of', is not so directly grounded in the things related, and can be reversed, without affecting their natures; still, there could be no talk of leftness or rightness, unless both the things had the quality of spatial extension. Numerical diversity, or otherness, is one—perhaps the only—relation that is not internal, so far as Actualities are concerned. Moreover, if there are terms in the Actual world, they are not the immutabilities which logistic philosophy demands; it is only, however, when they are misconstrued as such, that the doctrine of the internality of relations can be accused of issuing in absolute monism. Logic is applicable to changing Actuality (and Actuality *is* change, whatever Reality may be) only in so far as, within the flux, things and relations change sufficiently slowly, in relation to human *tempo* and time-span, that they may be *treated*, with practical advantage, *as if* they were logical Objects. Such applicability knows severe limitations, the neglect of which has engendered much futile ingenuity. The partial applicability of logic to Actuality, progressively correctible and extensible by understanding, bent on seeking, selecting and retaining the 'rational' alone, is to be discussed in the chapter evocative of this Note. Science makes its categories fit its 'things', and uses words as verbal type that is but of sufficient durability to record supersedible thought; pure logic stereotypes its words, and, when posing as philosophy, can only clip facts into applicability to them.

Note F. *The meanings of 'Intuition'.*

In the phrase 'forms of intuition', and in other connexions, 'intuition' means sensible perception, whether perception (proper) of object, or (so-called) perception of Object and of external world. Such intuition involves the notion of putting together, of synthesis issuing in synopsis, or seeing as one; of conspection, as distinguished from inspection or simply apprehending. Perception is (ψ) immediate and simple, (ps) mediate and complex.

'Intuition', however, is also used in senses in which (1) contrast with sensibility is involved and (2) immediacy, whether (ψ) or (ps) or both, rather than *con*spection, becomes the essential feature of the apprehension indicated. Thus, rationalistic intuitionalists have claimed that there is cognition independent of sensory experience, whether by means of innate ideas or otherwise, (ps) immediate and simple as sensatio. When the great difference between (ps) and (ψ) immediacy, and the corresponding difference between subjective certitude (a mental state) and logical certainty (Objective implication between propositions), escape recognition, intuition is often claimed for apprehension which (ps) involves processes of reasoning rapidly performed and unknown to oneself, or apprehension presupposing opinions to which familiarity has imparted the semblance of 'self-evidence'. The 'felt certitude' that may accompany erroneous belief, is in such cases the cause of their being called intuitions.

There is, however, cognition, other than sensatio, that is (ps) immediate and certain, as well as (ψ) immediate and accompanied by 'feeling' of certitude. This is the apprehension of certain relations, or objects of higher order, such as likeness and difference. It bespeaks an activity distinguishable from sensatio, depends on sensa solely for the supply of its fundamenta, and issues in judgement as certain as the judgement of perception. This genuine intuition seems also to include explicit apprehension of universals, and what is called intuitive induction. It then underlies all principles of logical inference, and yields the self-evident axioms on which logic and mathematics are based. Its certainty is not mediated by enumeration of all instances; one instance is sufficient. It applies equally to impressional, imaginal and ideal data.

Intuitive induction is further discussed in Chap. xi and Note L.

Note G. *Comparison.*

It has been observed before that no hard lines, such as are suggested by our concepts of sense and understanding, exist in actual experience: in sensatio or sense-knowledge there is already implicit, what, as explicated, is thought. An instance of this truth is afforded in the fact that explicit, or consciously logical, comparison presupposes, and is preceded by, what has been called anoetic, or more aptly, hyponoetic, apprehension of likeness and difference. In the case of complex presentations, we can by analysis find common and peculiar elements, while, in virtue of the discovery, we can establish resemblance and difference. In the case of (ψ) simple presentations, this is impossible, yet we immediately apprehend such relations. We discern closer resemblance between red and orange, than between red and yellow, before we have learned that orange can be got by mixing red and yellow pigments, or that orange comes between the other two colours in the spectrum. This seems explicable, only in terms of attention-movement: the detection of closer and more distant resemblance, is a hyponoetic apprehension of relation, involving continuity and change, in which the universal (or rather 'first universal') colour, is given and not reached by abstraction; and in which less and more of change, respectively, are experienced in the transitions of attention. But however this may be, it is certain that hyponoetic comparison exists, where as yet there is no comparison proper. Such vague awareness is not sense-impression or primary presentation, as that is artificially abstracted in thought, with its discrete and definite concepts. Likeness between impressions a and b, is neither a nor b nor a third impression, but an object of higher order, the apprehension of which involves an innate faculty of the subject, the germ of thought. On the other hand, such innate faculty could never function, were there not objective occasioning. If we may say 'no comparison, no thought', we may equally say 'no sensatio, no comparison'. There is no direct reasoning from particulars to particulars; there is also no reasoning without particulars and even sense-particulars, in the first instance: though in actual experience there are no particulars, in the sense of unrelated terms, such as pure logic contemplates. It is going too far to assert, as some have done, that all consciousness is consciousness of difference; but there is much truth, at the noetic level, in the saying of Mill, that "a thing is only seen to be what it is by contrast with what it is not". If there were no diversity in presentation, if there were only absolute diversity or disparateness, or if there were no uniformity in repetition of presentations, there could be no comparison and no thought-knowledge; no description, not to speak of explanation, however much of innate capacity, for comparing and thinking, human subjects possessed.

If hyponoetic comparison be involved in all recognition, explicit comparison is involved in all intersubjective communication and in conception. Not only science, but all common thought, may be said to arise from discovery of likeness in difference. Comparison is the

Dread opener of the mysterious doors
Leading to universal knowledge.

For classification is the beginning, and likeness behind difference is the goal, of science. The individual reveals the class, and the class reveals more of the individual: whence logic, inductive and deductive: coordination and generalisation. Comparison in the field of the imaginal, and discernment of similarities such as escape the general eye, which are matters of association of ideas rather than of formally logical operations performable by anybody, are the processes in which the discoveries of the genius are made. Analogy, which plays so important a rôle in many sciences, consists in discovering some resemblances, and then expecting and seeking for, or supposing, others. Measurement, or quantitative comparison, is the basis of 'exact science', though comparison need not be quantitative to yield science: qualities, as intensive magnitudes, cannot be measured or correlated with numbers, though some can be correlated with extensive magnitudes. In theoretical physics we conceive, as like, what we perceive as different: and proceed analogically, in assuming that the same grouping of particulars under general concepts, that is warranted by knowledge of a part of the world and its history, holds throughout, or in regions where we cannot observe. Thus, science contains vastly more than the reading-off of formal relations between perceptual data; but the only point with which we are at present concerned, is that establishment of relations by comparison constitutes the first step to science.

Note H. *Logic*.

1. The traditional or Aristotelian logic is not one science, but a medley of grammar, metaphysics, etc., together with what may properly be called formal logic. In so far as it involves theory of definition, predicables, substance and attribute, it contains doctrine which is not exact science characterised by certainty. From the time of Descartes, effort was made to isolate its purely logical element, and the other ingredients have been handed over to epistemology, methodology, etc. Thus emptied of implication of the 'real categories' and epistemic or psychological considerations, and so becoming formal and normative, logic ceases to deal with thought, as a process of thinking, and as involving matter. It confines itself to the manipulation of thought, as a product, or of "thought, as thought". It then gives laws of correct ratiocination—one particular species of thinking—and classifies fallacies: it tells how to deduce necessary conclusions from assumed premisses, but nothing as to the truth or falsity of the premisses. The old formal logic is chargeable with narrowness within its own domain, *i.e.* as purporting to supply the ideal for future thinking. In the first place, it resolves all concepts into substantive concepts; a quality or a relation, as subject of a proposition, receives a substantival name, and is grammatically reified into a thing with attributes. The type of all propositions is, consequently, S is P. This implies that all relations are dyadic: which makes some kinds of erroneous judgement inexplicable, and also obscures the difference, in form, of particular and universal propositions. Further, the grammatical device just mentioned (parent of both realism and nominalism), causes obliteration of the difference between the relation of member to class, and the relation of part to whole. Concepts, for formal logic, are all alike, because no difference between them is recognised, other than those affecting their relations as terms in a proposition: all predicables or categories they may involve, are ignored, except that of whole and part, qualitatively considered. Grammar confers on such logic a subtilty and clearness, which is deceptive through its insularity. Implication becomes a relation of class-concepts alone, whereas it holds between relations also; and judgement becomes not merely comparison, but comparison in one respect alone—inclusion or non-inclusion. Thought is made consistent, through abstraction from matter and objects of higher order; and logic tends to become extensional only. Logic, in order to be formal, needs to isolate itself severely from epistemology, or psychology, and so becomes a pure science. Lastly, syllogistic procedure, and elimination of the middle term, do not exhaust elimination and inference.

2. The only element, in the old mixed logic descended from Aristotle, that can yield certainty, because alone dealing with formal relations, is quasi-mathematical. It owes its clearness to spatial analogies, such as are

involved in the notions of inclusion, opposition, conversion, etc. Its concepts are geometrical, but its processes algebraical. As geometrically derived ideas can only serve extensional or denotational logic, intensional logic requires algebraic formulation. But the algebra in question needs to be of peculiar kind, to accommodate itself to the difference between the direct procedure from ground to consequence, which is definite, and the inverse procedure from consequence to ground, which is indefinite. This formal ingredient of the old science was developed into the symbolic logic of Boole and others, also called algarithmic, though it is a non-numerical algebra. A calculus dealing with properties of relations expressible in terms of logical constants, it is concerned with computation, not with thinking; it is mathematical, not normative

3. Of the same algarithmical type is the new logic, or logistic, developed by Russell and Whitehead. This professes to be a science of what are called 'entities', or objects that are "neither physical nor mental"—propositions, terms, relations, classes, etc.—and to deal with the truth and the implication of propositions. Its entities are largely identifiable with what have here been called objects of higher order, and concepts; but the new logic considers them in abstraction from the contexts, grammatical and scientific, in which they have been suggested. The fundamental entity is the 'proposition'. This is not the verbal expression of a judgement. It is an entity "existing" in its own right, so to say, independently of whether it is asserted; and within which, entities, such as terms and relations, "occur". It is described as whatever is true or false, *i.e.* significant. The notion of truth arose in connexion with beliefs or judgements, and thence was applied to propositions, in the old sense of the word; but the new logic professes to be entirely unconnected with the psychological and epistemological: indeed it is claimed for it that it is a pure science, indifferent to whether its laws apply to Actuality. Inconsistently enough, it is also claimed for it that its entities "determine the actual world", that it is a science prior to theory of knowledge, and cannot be ignored by a philosopher who would be other than an amateur. Indeed, without such inconsistency, it is hard to account for the notion of truth being taken over from the sphere of correspondence with Actuality. However, it is in terms of truth that a proposition is defined; and it is admitted that, in truth and falsity, we come upon what is metaphysical or metalogical. The methods of demonstration which this logic sanctions, are transitions from premisses to conclusions, permitted by the laws of the calculus; they have nothing to do with evidence, intuition, etc., but only with implication: and the logical laws made use of are, of course, not premisses. Hence 'truth', in the new logic, can only mean what it does in mathematics; *if p* is true, then q is true: truth, not in the sense of validity of the Actual, but in the sense of being a necessary consequence of a supposition. The primary propositions (principles) used, cannot be demonstrated; they are simply adopted

as axioms, though they turn out on examination to be conventions or postulates. In these the whole theory is contained; and deduction from them
establishes no truth, in the usual sense of the term. Logical proof, in other
words, presupposes alogical assumptions. Moreover, there is no one *a priori*
and absolute set of fundamental notions or principles, from which a deductive
system, of this kind, can set out: the ultimate indefinables of any one such
system are posited, created, selected and adopted. *We* decide what shall be
taken for axioms. Thus the epistemic element, rigorously extruded from
so much of the new logic as appears above ground, permeates its subterranean
foundations. Primary definitions, and indefinables, are a matter of free choice,
when they are not empirically derived; and "truth", in the last resort, is
what we are pleased to accept, *i.e.* convention.

Logistic is of no more import, for philosophy, than any other instrumental
science, such as mathematics; but it calls for some attention here because,
like the scientific theory of relativity, it has been exploited in the interests
of various kinds of philosophy. It may be instructive to observe some of the
applications to which, according to predilection, it has been put. When
assumed capable of being applied to Actuality, it lends itself to the rationalist,
who, rightly holding that there can be no knowledge through sense apart
from thought, proceeds to assert that any law, for thought, must impose itself
on all Reality that we can know, imagine or conceive; since to allow that
the self-contradictory exists, is to inhibit all inference. In the first place,
there may be Reality that is not knowable, imaginable or conceivable. Further,
if logic and laws of thought be not the whole of the apparatus used in knowing,
Reality or Actuality may be knowable, without being characterised by the
formal relations alone, to which laws of thought have reference. Yet again,
it is but unnecessary assumption that logic *must* apply, or that it applies
without remainder, to the Actual world; certainly the world is not known
by logical inference alone, and it contains much that is not amenable to
logic. That consistency with laws of thought, such as alone are within the
province of formal logic, is the prime attribute of Reality, whatever Reality be,
is a supposition that satisfies the craving for formally logical intelligibility;
but that craving is, as much as any other wish or 'sentimental pose', a matter
of alogical conation, not of logical necessitation and pure intellection.

The forthcomingness of the logic that has here been called 'logistic', has
been regarded by one of its expounders, Windelband, as indicating the subsistence of the 'valid in itself': not indeed as Actual and separate; yet as
determinative, not only of knowledge, but also of existence. From this it is
but a step to the eternal prius of law: to relations and propositions that wait
for things to enter into them, or tally with them. Royce was similarly imbued with the belief, that the world is ordered according to the findings of the
new logic, which he regarded as a "science of order", predetermining scientific
methodology. He maintained that significance, or having either truth or

falsity, characteristic of the proposition, implied that fact or Actuality has the determinate constitution that logistic assigns to its terms, etc.; and that invention of order-forms is also discovery. But he preferred idealism to realism, teleology to ungrounded coincidence; and he represents the debouch of logistic into voluntarism or pragmatism. Speaking of the 'individual' as a logical indefinable, he emphasises that, for logical purposes, an individual is what we propose to regard as one, and that this involves an attitude of will: we postulate, not find. To do so, he adds, is neither arbitrary nor necessary, save as requisite for reasoning; but, to be reasonable, is to conceive of order-systems, real or ideal, so that the individual, as postulate of all definition, becomes an absolute logical need.[1] We may ignore the confounding, here, of the conative and the cognitive, the reasonable and the rational, and the inflation of the pragmatic into the absolute; but Royce, as logistician, testifies to the inevitableness of a pragmatic foundation, for logic such as professes to renounce epistemology.

The New Realism, of British origin, is perhaps not a welcomer of logistic as a godsend, but rather parent of it. It is chiefly on account of the emergence of this philosophy, that the logic possesses interest for the present-day philosopher. Realism is not content to see, in the 'entities' of logistic, objects which, like the series of links between image and abstract idea, psychology endows with 'existence', only when they are fashioned, abstracted, or supposed, by minds. It prefers to regard them as independent of subjective activity, and as if they lived and moved, much as common sense believes 'things' to behave.[2] Unable to assert their Actuality, save as *in rebus*, it promotes them to 'existence' or 'subsistence', concealing their bloodless 'substantiality' and *quasi*-Actuality, by use of the mild and mysterious term 'entity'. Logical realism—or logical pluralism, as it tends to become in respect of its essence—may be described as logistic applied to Actuality. Apart from its veneration for the abstract, it contains a vein of rationalism. This is revealed in the tacit demand that Actuality or Reality must admit of, and shall receive, rational, *i.e.* logistical, description. Logic can only deal with discrete terms, wherefore Actuality must be "analysed" into discrete terms; and if such analytica cannot be found, they must be invented. Psychology,

---

[1] *Encyclopaedia of the Philos. Sciences*, vol. i., *Logic*, p. 107.

[2] The word 'independent', interpreted in terms of the dictum that experiencing makes no difference to the facts, brings up an essential tenet of the new realism and of American neo-realism. Prof. Perry has enumerated the several relations that are comprised under the name of dependence, and finds that the experience-relation, between subject and object, does not fall among them. As his types are all relations between Object and Object, that between object and subject, which is unique, is simply ruled out, through a definition determined by no universal criterion. If non-dependence, of fact on experience, means that into fact there enters no subjective discrimination, selection, unification, nor any synthetic functioning of understanding, instances of 'fact' are surely called for.

as we have seen, has lately been treated from this standpoint instead of from its own. But the treatment does not yield science, unless it be another pure science of entities created by the imagination; certainly not empirical science of the Actual world.

Lastly, in Coutourat we may see the new logic, when assuming the rôle of philosophy, issue in scepticism. Referring to its indefinables and inde-monstrables, this writer observes that the objective and whole truth seems to have the form of a vicious circle. [It will be found later that inductive logic is in the same plight.] Going back from premiss to premiss, says Coutourat, we come to primary propositions, indemonstrable but admitted as axioms. In these the whole theory is contained; but it is not logical truth. Logical deduction establishes no truth whatever: that is lodged, if anywhere, in the axioms. Proof of truth involves 'logical principles' which cannot be proved. At bottom logic is alogical.

Thus, when science drops the real categories of common sense, and logic keeps itself unspotted from the 'epistemic' or psychological study of thinking and knowing, neither gets any nearer to the rationalistic ideal of knowledge concerning Actuality. Once more we find we are shut up to anthropic interpretation, which is all that knowledge can be, so long as we know but in part and "see through a glass darkly".

The new, mathematical and non-normative, logic owes its quality to its professed dealing with thought, as product; or rather with entities thought about, in isolation from the thinking-process. It does not prescribe 'if we are to think this, then we must think that'; but 'if this is true, that is true'. Since Kant, we have been made alive to the difference between 'the thing must be so' and '*we* cannot conceive [imagine?] it being otherwise'; in other words, inconceivability of the opposite is a criterion of belief, not of truth. Laws of thought are not the same as laws of things, for things may decline to be thought. The new logic will have no connexion with laws of thought, *i.e.* of thinking. Its attitude to things is not easy to ascertain; but it is clear that its laws are laws of 'entities'. Inference is said to be direct apprehension of implication, in which the mind is as passive as it is commonly supposed to be in sensation; and implication is declared to be an indefinable relation between propositions. If we approach implication from inference, logic from epistemology, it may be maintained, as by Mr Johnson, that implication *can* be defined—as potential inferability; in fact its alleged indefinability, like that of 'good' commented upon in an earlier chapter, is consequent on logistic abstractiveness. Mr Johnson contends that logic cannot be treated, without reference to what he calls its epistemic side, *i.e.* the relation of a proposition to the thinker as well as to the 'fact', the latter relation being one of accordance, not of identity. Truth and falsity cannot be understood without reference to subjective attitudes, he maintains; and we have already seen that logic, of the more abstract kind, has to admit that, from its own point of view, truth and falsity are metalogical though fundamental.

That a proposition is false, means that anyone's assertion of it would be erroneous; and truth is primarily relevant only to beliefs or judgements, not to propositions. The epistemic element can be eliminated from the finished products, as in logic generally; but it is a mistake to suppose it eliminable from the earlier stages, with which the later have continuity. This is what is done, when truth is said to apply to the 'objects' of beliefs, not to beliefs, and logic is regarded as a science of the nature and relations of propositions, pursuable in complete abstraction from psychological inquiry as to the knowledge, or knowing, of them. It then becomes a pure science like rational dynamics, and its applicability to Actual things is precarious. There are indefinables that are such because they are ultimate, *e.g.* consciousness and activity, as well as the fundamental concepts of logic; and they are none the less intelligible for being indefinable. But it is gratuitous to swell the number of indefinables by abstracting notions from the context, *connexion with which, bestows on them all their significance.* We then achieve but a logic which cannot be applied, or be of instrumental value. Indeed formal logic, throughout its history, has had suspiciously close affinity with nominalism.

4. The name 'logic' has been bestowed on other pursuits than those of the formal and computational kind: pursuits in which thinking, as process, and content, as well as form, of thought, receive consideration. Epistemology, or the investigation of the origin, nature, and validity of knowledge, is sometimes called higher logic. Hegel's logic is metaphysic of Reality conceived as dialectic process. Kant's transcendental logic arose in the distinction of form and function. The products of thinking are, in formal logic, emptied of their content; but the functions of thinking cannot so be emptied. Hence there is room for a transcendental or functional logic of the living thought that is presupposed by the dead forms of formalism. Epistemology is an apter name for it.

Note J. *Causality.*

1. EFFICIENT ACTION.

The original meaning of causation is efficient action. This notion is derived from individual experience within which there is, strictly speaking, no causality, in the senses which science substitutes for that of efficiency: such as regularity of succession of like consequents on like antecedents, or logical 'function'. Within this psychical sphere, the notion of efficiency may be said to be indispensable; without it, the uniqueness of selves and the contingency of their psychoses would be inexplicable. Subjective activity may be a source of mythology, when physical Objects and thinghood are interpreted in terms of it; but it cannot itself be myth, else forthcoming facts could not be forthcoming. The only existents we can claim to *know* to be efficient, are subjects possessed of conatus or of volition.

In so far as efficiency is nowadays attributed by common sense to inanimate things, somewhat of primitive anthropomorphism is dropped. Things are supposed to interact, and earlier physical events to determine, condition or compel later events; but feeling and motivation, effort and muscular sensatio, such as we experience as agents and patients, are not ascribed to them. Anthropomorphism, at least in the form of explanation in terms of the familiar, lingers in physicists who can countenance none but contact-action, pushes and pulls; but generally, all that is retained, in the notion of efficient causation, is priority of a certain stretch of process, called cause, to another stretch, called effect; and transeunt influence, of some undefined kind. Even thus purged, the interpretative notion of cause is but precariously applicable to physical Objects and events; though it may re-emerge, as an inevitable form of thought, if from phenomenal science we pass to metaphysic. In the first place, the activity and compulsion read into things are imperceptible; as Glanvil observed earlier than Hume, "causality itself is insensible". Further, the sequence of one phenomenon *C* on another *B*, does not find explanation solely in the ascription of efficiency to *B*; the emergence of both *C* and *B* may be due to the energising of an *A*, to the universe as a whole, or to God.

For such reasons, the idea of efficient cause is useless to advanced science. It becomes even objectionable when science, such as would fain be 'positive', regards itself as able to dispense with anthropic interpretation altogether. It is not cast out of anything but scientific description, in consequence of being dispensed with when science strives after mechanical interpretation: efficiency in things is compatible with their amenability to mechanical description. Indeed, the assertion of efficiency does not imply either the causal law (uniformity) or the causal principle. As *causa eminens*, to use obsolete language, an agent may have no likeness to that on which it acts, or to the effect produced; creative fiat or efficiency may conceivably—*i.e.* before observation—be supposed to produce anything whatever, and that without any invariableness. But if efficiency be banished from the physical and phenomenal, a sufficient reason for the order and connexion of things, as to which something *is* known if anything be known, and which is the pre-condition of there being science of any sort, may be demanded. Not indeed from science; it is none of her business: but from philosophy. Philosophy, having discarded efficiency analogous to our own, has been at a loss for an idea of Actual nexus or of necessitation between things, by which to replace the anthropic notion of compulsion; at least none has emerged that commands general acceptance. If we retain our common-sense pluralism, the source of all our trouble in connexion with the causal problem, our one hope seems to lie in the conception of substance-cause or continuant. If we exchange our pluralism for an ultimate monism, we may replace transeunt action between the many, by immanent causation within the One. But, assuming provisionally that such metaphysic is facile, we may note that philosophy needs to find some concept intermediate between cause, as force or effectuation of the anthropic kind, and cause, as logical *ratio*, which is not cause at all. Descriptive science sometimes, at its higher levels, proceeds on the tacit supposition (methodologically, not dogmatically entertained) that cause, when it stands for anything more than temporal antecedent, is ground; and that transeunt action is but implication. Yet there would be no ideas and propositions for logic to connect, were there not Actual things in Actual *rapport* of some kind. Things cannot be sublimated into ideas, which have quite another kind of 'existence'; nor *rapport* into implication. The logical apparatus of science, which seems to dispense with the notion of cause proper, presupposes causation of some sort, however dissimilar it be to conative efficiency. It may be observed, moreover, that it is the element of efficiency in the old causal notion, that chiefly gave it its fruitfulness in the past, when *rerum cognoscere causas* might have been science's motto. From it are derived the assertions, that the relation of cause to effect is non-reciprocal, and that cause (as more or less of a process) precedes effect: which tally with the irreversibility of the Actual world, but not with all scientific descriptive formulae. It also accounts for evolution being epigenesis.

So long as efficiency is regarded as the essence of causation, the only Actualities that can be called causes, are substances or continuants. Causation will not be a relation between states, as such, though the effect produced, on occasion, by one substance in commerce with others, will depend on the states of all. Hence, when causality is regarded as a relation between events or phases of processes, it is inevitable that some arbitrariness is involved in selecting what stretch of each continuous historical process, causative and effectuated, and what aspects thereof, are to be taken into account. Thus arises the crop of old puzzles that have made the causal problem confused and confusing: whether cause and effect are successive or simultaneous, whether a cause in the past operates in the present, and so on. By adopting different degrees of preciseness in determining how much of one process shall be called cause, and how much of another shall be called effect, we can establish the doctrine of plurality of causes, or that of plurality of effects; several causal paradoxes have been thus engendered. Similarly, the contrast between what is miscalled 'immanent', and might be called 'internal', causality, when a complex system rather than a simple substance is in question, is often non-essential, and but the outcome of distribution of our attention. In a system composed of parts, a change that is 'immanent' or internal to the closed system, may be transeunt to the parts; and while expressions such as 'persisting in the same state' and 'behaving according to its own nature', are based on assumption of isolated systems, the only warrant that a given system is isolated, is that observation has not furnished evidence of the influence of external forces on it.

Again, if the only efficient causes we know, are subjects, so also the only final causes are subjects willing. To speak of volitions (abstracted from agents) of ideas and ends, as final causes, is to eject our own activity into entities that cannot have it. An idea, representing the end to be attained, does not suffice for the attainment; else every wish should be fulfilled. The only efficient and final causes we can claim as yet to know, are substantial causes; and these are internal forces, not external, whether purposive or merely impulsive. We are authorised to eject efficiency only into things such as, by their behaviour, suggest possession, in some degree, of the life and individuality pertaining to ourselves. Inanimate things do not suggest such spontaneity, at least at the level of interpretation, or of experience-organisation, represented by science. But this verdict may be reversed, when from physics and the phenomenal we pass to metaphysics and the ontal: inertia in matter may admit of translation into terms of conation in the spiritual. Indeed it would seem that it is only in the language of metaphysic, of some particular kind, that the idea of causality, as involving Actual necessitation, can admit of definite statement. In that of science, cause seems to be as shifting a convention as ether has been. Setting out originally from the anthropic notion, then using it only as metaphor, science has finally become silent as to the *modus operandi* involved in that Actual connectedness of things, which its own existence presupposes. Science talks only of causal laws, the causal principle, uniformity, conservation, and so forth: in relation to which topics, cause itself receives various *ad hoc* definitions. At some of these we must presently glance; but discussion of them requires prior consideration of the causal law and the causal principle.

2. THE CAUSAL PRINCIPLE.

There is no accepted convention as to usage of the phrases 'the causal principle' and 'the causal law': here they shall be applied respectively to the assertions, that every effect has a cause, and that like causes produce like effects.

The causal principle, as thus distinguished, does not imply that effect resembles cause, or is equal to it; nor that the concept of the nature of the effect is involved in the concept of the nature of its cause; nor, again, that like causes produce like effects, or that efficiency is characterised by invariability of outcome. Conversely, invariable or unvarying sequence does not logically imply efficiency in the antecedent; it only demands sufficient reason in the Actual, rather than the logical, sense: whether in terms of substance-activity, pre-established harmony, *coutume de Dieu*, or what not. Further, the causal principle does not say what it would denote by a cause, but leaves it open to interpretation, as particular agent or event, state or attribute, or as a plurality varying in comprehensiveness, from one or a few specified antecedents, to the sum of conditions, even to a state or states of the universe. Mill used the phrase 'sum of conditions', though he really only refines the common-sense isolation of the obviously relevant, or significant, antecedents. Indeed, science cannot work with the definition of cause, as the whole of the antecedents; for the sum of them can hardly recur: as Mach says, *Die Natur ist nur einmal da*. Science can but invoke the observably relevant, and cannot rule out, with absolute security, the as yet non-observably relevant, as irrelevant. On the other hand, if causes are to be 'repeatable', so that we can speak of 'same causes', it becomes a question, what shall be called an event: the event must be sufficiently abstract, as compared with the concrete, the historical or once-occurring, in order to recur. Indeed, when the causal principle is made logically precise, it becomes practically useless. Rejection of efficiency, and concentration on time-relations and regularity, was an exchange of one kind of obscurity or mystery for another; while regularity is an importation from the causal law, foreign to the causal principle, as such. If particular causal laws are to be regarded as instances of the causal principle, and if they refer to antecedents and consequents capable of recurring, then cause and effect become names for, or concepts of, groups of abstract characteristics; and we have to assume, among other things, that an event can be exhaustively and uniquely described by a finite number of its abstract characters.[1] We are then well on the way to the conception of cause as *ratio*, and have strained out of Actuality the alogical or historical element, in virtue of which it is Actual.

The causal principle, in itself, is capable of adaptation to various notions of cause, such as that involved in the theory of efficiency, that of occasionalism, or that of rationalism which uses cause in the sense of logical ground. It has consequently been identified with the principle of sufficient reason, elastic enough to include both Actual connexion and logical implication; and this, in turn, has sometimes been regarded as an *a priori* axiom and a condition of experience. It must rather be pronounced to be an anthropic postulate. *Ex nihilo nihil fit*, like the principle of 'the inconceivability of the opposite', is a criterion of believing, not of truth. It is only *a priori*, in the sense that any supposition may be called so; it is only to be applied where experience authorises; it is 'sufficient', in the sense of satisfying a human need. And the same must perhaps be said, eventually, of principles invoked in order to assimilate the determination of successive phases of the course of Nature to logical necessitation.

[1] See Dr Broad's Article in *Mind*, N.S. No. 113, p. 40.

3. SUBSTITUTES FOR EFFICIENT PROXIMATE CAUSE.

When transeunt action in the physical world began to appear incomprehensible, various attempts were successively made to dispense with the notion. In one class of such endeavours, the idea of efficiency was still invoked.

(a) The occasionalists, on passing from their original problem of mind and body to causation in general, taught that there are no proximate causes. They ascribed all efficient causation to God alone, Who, on the occurrence of what had been called a cause, produced the event called effect. Thus cause became occasion. Secondary causes were later regarded, by Berkeley, as but signs; and thus a kind of occasionalism was reached, by a route somewhat different from that of Geulincx or Malebranche. The doctrine of the Cartesians being one of incessant miracle or creation, Leibniz substituted for it a theory of pre-established harmony, involving but one initial miracle, but equally dispensing with transeunt causation. If descriptionist science and recent logistic professed to be philosophy, we should need to account them also as types of occasionalism, and to see in causation, as understood by them, an altar to the unknown God, groundless coincidence.

(b) Hume's criticism of the causal concept issued in apparent reduction of a 'real' category to formal categories: for, in so far as causality subsists between 'objects', he declared it to be a 'philosophical relation'. In so far as causality is a 'natural relation', between our thought and things, it expressed, for him, but a mental propensity, an association of ideas. Contiguity in space, succession in time, constancy of recurrence of like consequents after like antecedents: these alone are observable and Objective. Efficiency or power, and necessary connexion, either logical or Actual, are not. These he regarded, therefore, as subjective interpretations, ideas not derived from the impressional and having no assured counterpart in Actuality.

This doctrine has become widely accepted, though Hume's own conception, as to what is the nature of the subjective element that he disclosed, is wide of the truth. He failed, for all his shrewdness, to see that the habit of association, to which he appealed, doubly invokes, in the mental sphere, the very causal determination that he sought to eliminate from causation in the non-mental sphere: any impression of the nexus being as wanting, in the one sphere, as in the other.

Hume was not concerned to deny necessary connexion between his 'objects'; there hardly was need to do so, after the notion of substance had been discarded. He was concerned to point out its non-observableness, in respect of immediacy, and therein its difference from relations such as sequence, conjunction and resemblance. Nor did he doubt that causal reasoning is *de facto* certain, and that to use it, is to proceed as Nature requires of us. He thus implicitly recognised that the causal notion is thrust upon us, if mediately, and that Actuality is tolerant of our 'reading' of it 'in'. But in accordance with the dangerous maxim 'seeing is believing', he distrusted it because it is not directly read off from the impressional. The reading-in is a process, he taught, that reason cannot justify. That too may be granted: if by 'reason' is meant use of but his "philosophical" relations, or the formal categories of what Kant called understanding. But to deny that causal reasoning is not, in this narrow sense, 'rational', lands no one but the rationalist in philosophical scepticism. Hume was thus rationalist in empiricist's clothing. It does not seem to have occurred to Hume, the philosophical inquirer, as distinct from Hume, the common-sense agent, that constant conjunction must have some ground in the nature of 'objects', if our subjective interpretations are valid of them: that if Nature honours our interpretation, that interpretation cannot be wholly or purely subjective fancy. So he failed to discern that, though reference to determination or causal nexus may be avoided in exposition of the achieved results of science, every experimental and inductive process presupposes, however non-observable, a stable nexus in 'objects' *as well as* some connexion of our ideas in respect of association. He blinded himself somewhat by equivocal usage of terms such as 'objects', 'mind', 'determination'; also by inconsistencies: *e.g.* in endowing 'objects' with identity, but not with causality, after teaching that inferences as to identity depend on causal inferences. Also Hume was far from the truth, in asserting that "multiplicity of resembling instances... constitutes the very essence of power of connexion, and is the source from which the idea of it arises".[1] That was to confound the concepts of efficiency and regularity, the causal principle with the causal law. These have no logical connexion. But it would seem that many cases of uniform sequence must have a metaphysical ground in determination, whether that be conceived as efficiency or otherwise.

4. THE CAUSAL LAW.

The causal law, which may be identified with the principle of uniformity, asserts that like causes produce like effects: or rather, that like antecedents are followed by like consequents. Over and above the difficulties involved in making precise the denotation of cause and effect, antecedent and consequent, this law encounters a further difficulty: that of determining what shall be meant by 'like', before it can attain a form that is logically precise and practically useful. Causes, as events or phases in continuous process, must not only be abstract, to be repeatable; they must also be like, and like only in certain respects deemed relevant or essential. Thus, selection *ad hoc* is involved in their isolation; and a limit needs to be fixed to retrogression along the course of antecedence. The more of irrelevant difference is eliminated from Actualities, the more attenuated become the abstract causes

---

[1] *Treatise of Human Nature*, Book i, iii, § 14.

and effects. When the causal law takes the particular form of the principle of conservation of energy, these are respectively made, or conceived as, like, by being despoiled of all quality: change being treated as if it were change of motion alone. Likeness then becomes qualitative identity, difference being confined to spatio-temporal relations; and, quantitatively, *causa aequat effectum*. Repetition is then but hypothetical, and the causal law assumes the form: if there were like causes there would be like effects. We have passed, in fact, to a pure science that is but tentatively and partially applicable to Nature as Actual, exhaustively and categorically applicable only to Nature as a conceptual artifact and diagram, or possibly as a skeleton of the world of qualitative diversity.

It is often represented that regularity of succession, of like consequents on like antecedents, is all that causation is, because, in connexion with causation and causal laws, it is all that science needs to concern itself with; inasmuch as science seeks but descriptive laws, not explanations. In so far as exposition of achieved results is concerned, this is true: equations replace quasi-metaphysical statements; force means rate of change of momentum, nothing more; and so on. But in its process of achieving these results, whether in experimentation or in applying inductive logic, science actually presupposes much more. And when Hume eliminated necessary connexion or determination, in general, as well as power or efficiency, in particular, from the causal concept, he demolished the foundation on which all science is built. Sequence and likeness do not suffice for scientific research and prediction. That like events, such as thunder-claps, follow like events, such as lightning-flashes, may be the only observable relation between them, on the surface; it is not, on that account, the only relation that science needs to suppose. If it were, there should be no reason why thunder should follow lightning, and none why thunder should not be followed by earthquake. Science somehow knows better. She works, and inevitably must work, with implicit belief in the *conditio sine qua non*. Were there no Actual necessitation, of some kind, between successive stages of the course of physical Nature; were the world one in which anything could succeed upon anything: there would be neither cosmos nor science. Night always follows day; but if day be antecedent, it is not cause or necessary condition of night. On the other hand, if the sun be the source of daylight and the earth revolve on its axis, the sequence of night on day, in our part of the globe, is as much an Actual necessity as that 'light is not darkness' is a logical necessity; and it is as idle to ignore the necessitation in the one case, as it is in the other. Whether the sequence is unconditionally invari*able*, is another question, involving another sense of 'necessity': but, determinate physical relations continuing as they are, the sequence is invariable as well as unvarying. We may renounce the notion that there are necessary laws prior to Actuality, to which anything Actual must conform; but once there is a world of determinate beings with specific natures, as distinct from any others possibly conceivable, the potencies of things are limited. Such and such interactions and relations are actualised, and not others; laws describe what these are. We can only know what is within the ken of human experience, and can only explore the conditioning of what has obtained up to date. But, within a certain stretch of time, certain uniformities have as a matter of fact prevailed, and there must be some sufficient ground for such regularity as has been observed. The rationalist's absolute and timeless truths, to which all sensible happenings must conform, may well be fond fancies; and the empiricist, such as Mill, has no right to his invariables and unconditionals. Moreover, when we come to examine induction, with which the causal law or principle of uniformity is bound up, we shall find that it ultimately rests on alogical postulation. There is no escape from the anthropic, refine our notion of cause how we may. Bain seems unintentionally to abandon the logical certainty claimed by Mill, for the subjective certitude with which Hume said we must rest content, when he remarks that "such well-established scientific inductions as the law of gravitation and the law of causation render wholly *incredible* any assertion that contradicts them".[1]

So hard does the notion of transeunt action die, in science, that though *vis insita* has long been discarded, and *vis impressa* has come to be regarded as a superfluous metaphysical notion, 'transference of energy' is still an orthodox expression. Again, though antecedents are all that disciples of Hume ought to allow themselves to recognise, we find Mill using the phrase 'sum total of *conditions*'.

5. SUBSTITUTES FOR EFFICIENT CAUSE (*continued*).

(c) *Cause as condition.* When the sum of conditions is broadened into the whole of Reality, or into a state of the whole universe at a specific moment, the phrase becomes but verbiage for which science, ever on the look-out for particular conditions of particular phenomena or isolable phases, has no use. But cause, in the sense of Actual *conditio sine qua non* of effect, or of determinant—whether or not efficient producer—is certainly at the back of the mind of every scientific investigator until, wise after the event, he comes to represent his results in the form of equations, from which all reference to conditioning is left out. And, more important than that this notion is psychologically a precondition of the intellectual activities of scientific investigators, or that Mill and others felt the need to try to rehabilitate it by empirical procedure such as never could yield it, is the fact that the very existence of such science as we have, would be inexplicable, without its being valid. Transeunt activity and efficiency, conceived in terms of muscular action, etc., may be eliminated from the concept of causation;

---

[1] *Inductive Logic*, p. 149. The italics are not Bain's.

but not determination. Temporal succession is not enough. Nor, when we pass from the causal principle to the causal law, is constancy of conjunction of the like, a sufficient basis for what are called causal inferences. Such conjunction is not always causal; therefore causality is something more. And constancy of conjunction implies, if not causation according to any forthcoming conception of it, yet a sufficient ground somewhere and of some sort. Science is not concerned to investigate, or to profess any opinion, as to what this ground may be; but were there no such ground, there could be no science. It may be that the dismembering of the world into things, or applying to the physical the same kind of pluralistic interpretation that the psychical realm positively requires, is the prior fiction that has necessitated resort to the secondary fiction of interaction and determination between such supposed things: so that the law of inverse squares, *e.g.* is a law concerning unreal or fictitious entities. But, even so, the dependence of subsequent phases of the world-process, conceived as monistically as science or philosophy pleases, on earlier phases, is established fact, for which philosophy needs to account. And causal nexus is not made any the more comprehensible or dispensable, when we conceive it as immanent, instead of transeunt. A 'real' category of some kind, over and above the formal categories of succession, likeness, etc., is requisite. And such a category, or functioning of the understanding, cannot be a *causa cognoscendi* or be psychologically effectual, unless there correspond to it, in some sense, a *causa fiendi* in the Objective and Actual.

We may now pursue further the inquiry as to how this bond of determination or necessitation, which Hume failed to explain away, has been, and should be, conceived. Historically important is the rationalistic interpretation, against which Hume's philosophy of causation was largely a reaction.

(d) *Cause as logical ground.* The rationalist of the early modern period was often unconsciously steeped in scholasticism: Descartes, when reclothing his doubt-denuded soul with mental habiliments, filched from a medieval wardrobe. According to a view handed down from antiquity, and framed in the times of relative ignorance, efficient causes were supposed to be knowable from analysis of the essential nature of their effects, and effects to be deducible from the definition of their causes. Such a view suited a rationalistic theory of knowledge. For the rationalist could not be content with the empiric fact, that such and such an effect followed upon such and such a cause. He wanted to find, not merely some connexion between the cause and its effect, that should make the production of a particular effect an Actual necessity; but also something in the nature of the cause, from which it should logically follow that the effect must ensue. Then alone could science, or necessary knowledge not waiting on sensible observation, be possible. Efficiency must be made intelligible: nay, must be intelligible in order to be. Geulincx explicitly maintained that we can do nothing, without knowledge of how the doing is performed; and, as to causation in general, it was assumed that whatever is produced, must be produced clearly and distinctly. Things must happen in accordance with the need and the capacity of our minds, working with formal categories and logical relations alone, to conceive their happening. The rationalist, in fact, made, not man, but man in the sole aspect of a logical machine, the measure of the universe.

So long as a concept, as abstract frame 'existing' apart only when thought of, or as idea, is distinguished from the thing or Actual filling, *of* which the concept is a concept or an ideal frame, the order and connexion of ideas may be analogous or parallel to the order and connexion of things; and implication between ideas, or propositions, may tally with interactions between existents: there will not, however, be identity between the two orders and connexions. But concepts-of-things and things-conceived-of being confounded, the causal connexion would be identified with the logical. Such was the case in Spinoza's philosophy; consequently he could teach that *aliquid efficitur ab aliqua re* means *aliquid sequitur ex ejus definitione*. Causality was thus reduced to logical implication: actual *rapport* and determination were found superfluous, and temporal relations should be irrelevant.

The work of Hume and Kant has made it plain that the causal relation is not analytic but synthetic, not logical but Actual, if it be Objective at all. The ultimate principles involved in logical grounding, are those of identity and contradiction. These do not apply, however, to change, in connexion with which the causal concept is chiefly evoked. In 'what is, is', there is no denial that 'what was, is not'. From the bare notion of causality alone, however interpreted, can never be deduced the particular nature of the effect in which causal process will issue. In order to deduce historical particulars, scientific generalisation would need to be replaced by exhaustive history of the universe, of infinite complexity, because unique individuals cannot be described in general terms. Sensible, or else introspective, experience, in other words, is an essential condition of any causal proposition.

It has also become plain that definitions and concepts are not things, and that logical relations do not subsist between things, but only between propositions about things. Nevertheless the tendency to speak as if these distinctions could be obliterated, still persists. We are told that two configurations of the world, at any two moments, "imply" the configuration at any other moment, and even that some events "imply" others. But there is nothing in the chemist's concept of arsenic, to enable us to deduce that consumption of arsenic is followed by death; knowledge that arsenic is deadly, can only be had through sensible experience, observation on men as well as on arsenic. The causal relation, in this as in all cases, is quite different from any relation subsisting between concepts or propositions; moreover, propositions, for logical relation, are only forthcoming after observation of brute fact, and perhaps a considerable amount of its context. Concepts only 'imply' concepts when, to speak more correctly, propositions (generally established by induction) imply propositions; and it is only after observation and induction, that events exhibit Actual connexions having the semblance of identity with relations between concepts or propositions. The rationalistic identification of *causa* with *ratio*, then, may be dismissed, in that it confounds concepts with things, logical implication of propositions with Actual determination between events; and because it ignores the temporal relation between causes and their effects, which, in a non-reversible world, is part of the very essence of the causal relation. Non-reversibility plainly implies that there is more, in causation, than equations take account of. Hume's empiricism, on the other hand, in exclusively emphasising the temporal relation of constant succession, equally fails to give us a formal category in place of a 'real' category, because there are relations of constant succession that do not call, in science, for causal interpretation. Direction of natural process is as important as equivalence between its phases; and the temporal relation, which admits of refinement by way of continuity and intermediates, but never of being refined away, is as essential as that of apparently 'rational' connexion. Actual determination still survives both these kinds of attack.

(e) *Causality as connexion according to law.* The fact just stated, is recognised when causality is regarded as connexion according to law; though, once again, the description will be found to be too general. Connexion according to law is said to suffice for science's predictiveness; and the postulate expresses our persistent demand for intelligibility in the world.

Laws are not agents, nor are they subsistents apart from the things which 'obey' them; they are statements as to how things behave. Were there no relatively settled order of Nature and no Actual determination of phase by phase, or of phase by whole, there could be no particular laws and no general 'reign of law'. Thus the phrase 'connexion according to law' either implicitly asserts causal determination, or else is a *suppressio veri*. The suppression is harmless enough in science, aware of its self-imposed limitations; in philosophy it would be obliquity and evasion. In Lagrangian mechanics, we may keep but the threads of connexion, ignoring individual substances; in metaphysics of Nature, connexions, without ground in *connexa*, are nonentities. But connexion according to law is a wider conception than that of causal nexus, in that it makes no reference to the time-order; which is essentially involved in causation, in any sense in which science can invoke it: determination in natural process is one-directional. The relation of cause to effect is but a particular species of the many-one relation between variables and function, and consequently the causal principle does not mean simply that phenomena are related according to law. Again, if causality is made more precise by being identified with 'functionality', an effect can only be treated as a 'function' of the conditions, and causality can only be regarded as invariable relation, when effect and conditions can be measured or correlated with numbers. Also the resolution of isolable events, to which cruder conceptions of cause and effect apply, into phases of continuous process, is possible only in mechanics, not in all physical sciences. In these respects, the logistic substitute for causality gains its precision at the cost of adequacy; while it rests, as much as does any cruder conception, on postulation.

'Determination', such as is involved in the more general conception of the 'deterministic system', is said to have but purely logical significance; and, as with any other principle of a pure science, its application to the empirical is hypothetical. But it is more important to observe that it is too general to be of import for science of the Actual. It does not involve one-directional determination of future by past; it does not even involve uniformity.[1] The functions in question are assumed to be 'analytic';[2] and for any values of the time-variable, outside the time-range for which the system is known to be deterministic, the functions may become meaningless or have no application.[3] Whether *anything* in the Actual world corresponds to this ideal scheme, is a question; but on the approximation to it, of relatively isolable systems for a limited stretch of time, and that only in respect of a limited set of relations, depends the success of conceptual and predictive science, of which more than one partially effective variety has been forthcoming. The principle of determination is thus expressed by Mr Bertrand Russell: given certain data $e_1, e_2 \dots e_n$, at times $t_1, t_2 \dots t_n$ respectively, and that there is, in a system whose state E_t at the time t, a functional relation of the form $E_t = f(e_1 t_1, e_2 t_2 \dots e_n t_n, t)$, the system will be deterministic throughout a given period, if t be within the period; while, outside that period, the formula may be no longer true.

In causality, as thus interpreted (functionality), there is no reference to efficiency; nor to Actual determination in any sense: that is merely left aside. But it is not metaphysically dispensed with; indeed science does not *deny* even efficiency. There is also no reference to likeness between cause and effect: sameness of differential equations is alone involved. It is only within a deterministic system, whatever be the metaphysical ground of determination, that strictly logical inference from cause to effect is possible; but that our world, or even any finite part of it, is a deterministic scheme, is unproved and unprovable. As Prof. Hobson observes, in his already cited work, all that science has established, is that tracts of phenomena can be found which are sufficiently represented, for certain purposes, by deterministic schemes. Mr Russell also remarks that it would be fallacious to argue, from the state of more advanced sciences, to future arrival at the same state by less advanced sciences; for it may be that the former sciences are advanced, because the

---

[1] See on this and other points here alluded to, Prof. Hobson's *The Domain of Nat. Science*, ch. IV.
[2] Jourdain, *Mind*, N.S. No. 110, pp. 172–3.
[3] Hobson, *loc. cit.*

matter with which they are concerned has obeyed simple and easily ascertainable laws, while the subject-matter of other sciences has not. The same exponent points out that a system, with one set of determinants, may perhaps have other sets, of quite different kind: thus a mechanically determined system [if there be such a thing] may also be teleologically or volitionally determined.

If the form of the functions in a deterministic system be known, we can calculate and categorically predict: the system is also determin*able*. In an ideal system, the functions may be determined by postulation of the laws of the system. But whether the laws, so postulated, hold of Nature, is only ascertainable by induction. Hence, there is *no* strictly logical inference from cause to effect in the Actual realm; there is no knowledge that any Actual system is deterministic. And if we drop logical necessity, and speak in terms of probability, there is no probability, amenable to logical treatment, that does not involve uniformity: which, in turn, involves alogical 'probability' and can only be precisely formulated in terms of the concept of permanent substances—as we shall find later on. Causal laws, however refined the definition of cause, presuppose the inductive principle: this presupposes substance and cause, or Actual determination, and so involves anthropic subjectivity. The deterministic system belongs to the realm of pure science; and there we may leave it, in possession of a clarity and a logical necessitation which natural science may covet, but never appropriate. Mechanical laws exhibit acceleration as a function of configuration, not of configuration and time conjointly; hence the laws of the purer kinds of physics can be expressed in timeless formulae. But irreversible, or hitherto unreversed, Nature cannot so be described, without a further special concept. In being made abstract and logical, the causal concept has been rendered non-significant and irrelevant to Actuality: it ignores the essential.

Whatever causation be, it is something of narrower generality than connexion according to law. Cause determines effect, effect does not determine cause. Implication faces both ways; causation, only one way. Causality differs from a logical relation, in that it involves reference to time-order, though independent of time-position. In strictly immanent causation, precedence of effect by cause is obvious; in transeunt causation, it is hardly less obvious: so long as cause and effect are taken to be finite stretches of process in time, the cause-process beginning earlier and ending contemporaneously with the beginning of the effect-process. Identification of the actual with the logical, involves reduction of time to the 'unreal' or to illusion; but as Höffding has said, if time be illusion, "it is another illusion of the second power if we imagine that we can lightly rid ourselves of it".[1] Existence can never be absorbed into thought without remainder.

[1] *The Problems of Philosophy*, 1905, p. 107.

But though temporal order belongs to the essence of causation, it is not the whole of it. *Post hoc* is not identifiable with *propter hoc*, nor antecedent with *conditio sine qua non*. Geometrical and kinematical laws are laws of space and time, not of causation which is concerned with what occupies space and time. Temporal sequence and simultaneity, and even principles of equivalence or conservation, do not suffice for formulation of causal laws as to coexisting properties and changing states of things. Continuance—whether of particle or of soul—efficiency and potentiality, occurrence or occasion, are all factors involved in explanation of determination. And there is no need to stop at determination, as the last 'ultimate', as does logistic and 'descriptive' science, if explanation yet more ultimate can be found.

6. SUBSTANCE-CAUSE.

It remains to suggest that such explanation can be afforded by the concept of substance (continuant), when fused with that of cause. It has been argued in Chap. v, that determination between psychoses at different times, *e.g.* of disappointment by wish, is only comprehensible, and not merely mysterious fortuity, if both psychoses inhere in one permanent soul. Then alone is mental change other than groundless substitution. The continuant abides, as do its properties or potencies of functioning; and, as modified by one fleeting psychosis, it is ground or immanent cause of another, of a later time. Change is then substitution of one manifestation of soul for another; not substitution of one soul for another. Substance and immanent cause are thus mutually involved; neither can be without the other, if either is to have any applicability to Actuality. The occasional manifestations, in time, of a simple continuant, are due to immanent causation within it, the one bond of connexion between states and manifestations of properties. Otherwise there is no way of accounting for the stability of nexus, whether between psychoses in time, or physical events in time and space. A 'real' category over and above formal categories, and an *a priori* or mind-derived element over and above empirical data, are requisite for the adequate expression of determination. But the *a priori* element is anthropic interpretation; and its justification in respect of validity is not to be obtained logically, but only pragmatically. Nor is it a precondition of individual experience, but of common or Objective science. Determination, we have seen, is as much a fact, established by observation and induction, as regular succession; and if it can only be expounded in terms of substance-cause, it follows that laws concerning Actuality are causal laws, in the literal sense of involving a 'real' category. Space, time and likeness, the only relations which Hume would recognise, are insufficient to yield Actual determination; and the further factor of causation can only be conceived in terms of substance or continuant, and of inherence or immanence of states in a substantial ground. Here is the last residuum of mystery, ultimate because further irresolvable; but we must not stop our analysis and conceptual interpretation before we have pursued it as far as is possible. We must credit souls with activity such as expresses itself in both immanent and transeunt action; indeed, it is from the manifestations of such activity, that we derive our notions of substance and cause: but how determination in the physical realm is mediated, it is useless to inquire, until we have obtained an ontological translation for 'things', physical Objects and their elementary constituents, comparable to that which we may claim to have achieved in the psychical realm. If the mass-particle of theoretical physics be taken as the physical ultimate, there is no immanent causation, in the stricter sense of determination of varying states by identical continuant; for though the particle should be a continuant, it has no states, and its changes are but in spatial relations. Transeunt action there must be, if there be Actual determination; but mass-particles, however concretely imagined at any stage of ever-changing physical theory, are not to be taken for metaphysical ultimates, so much as for conceptual and abstract *Hülfsmittel* employed in non-explanatory 'description'. Their ontological equivalents may well be spiritual, in which case the notion of cause, as used of psychic beings such as ourselves, may, with necessary qualifications, be applied to them; while if dualism be embraced, they must at least be credited with activity requisite for *rapport* with us, in our constitution (out of them) of the phenomenal world.

7. To sum up: causation is an ejective and interpretative concept. In that respect, it is on a par not only with the concept of things or of other selves, but also with that of law, which is likewise of anthropic and ejective origin. It is in other selves that we have the best assurance, through intercourse, of numerical identity and persistence of agents; and of them, causation, both immanent and transeunt, can be predicated without transcending facts, save by inevitable explanation-process. Causality is also a necessary conception for the understanding of Nature, as distinguished from the exposition of analytical thought about it, though the Actual determination and *rapport*, which we attribute to things, cannot be affirmed with equal assurance to be analogous to that attributed to conative spiritual beings. Comte's three stages of human mentality, the theological, the metaphysical and the positive, do not represent accurately the truth: agriculture, involving crude science, presumably preceded incantations, etc.; and positive science, deanthropomorphised of real categories, does not exist. When we pass from pure dynamics to physics, ejection of causation or determination according to law, is reinstated: the activity that must be posited may be ultimate, indefinable, indescribable, empirically inapprehensible; and uniform sequence must be a frequent, though not a universal, manifestation or sign of its Actuality. If sequence were the only category used, science would be but registration of bare fact and empiric rules. Energy is but 'power' over again, and the concept of law involves that of Actual necessitation, which Hume

tried to dispel. Ejection is thus essential for constructive science and philosophy.

Note K. *Locke's usage of 'Reason'.*

Among philosophers of historical importance, Locke stands perhaps nearest to what we call common sense, in his use of the term 'reason'. Like Kant, he emphasises relating, as a primary essential in cognitive processes. He speaks of knowledge as perception of relations between ideas, ideas including for him simple percepts as well as concepts. He does not confine reason to intuition of the self-evident, which is its paramount function according to rationalists; he concentrates rather on its mediary aspect, *i.e.* on reason as consisting in the steps necessary to exhibit or explicate relations. It is the office of reason to discover, not only truth, but also the means of finding it. In doing so, reason proceeds by comparing, by establishing relations of agreement or difference between ideas (judgements), and so comprises the apprehension of implication, of inclusion or exclusion, and is concerned with logical framework or form and ratiocination. So far he is largely in agreement with rationalism; and it is this element, in his conception of reason, that was almost exclusively taken over from Locke by the deists, who surpassed their professed master in his rationalistic propensity, and forsook him in so far as he was empiricist. But Locke broke altogether with rationalism when he further included, among the functions of reason, the sagacity or shrewdness which detects significant connexions between facts, the use of the inductive method, the establishment of knowledge or belief that applies to the probable, as distinguished from the formally demonstrable or the self-evident. That he then proceeded to rule out opinion and faith (as merely *fiducia*) from the sphere of reason, is but inconsistent. Moreover he here vacillates. Faith, he teaches, is not wholly without rational grounds; it is not sheer credulity or caprice; it is assent involving credit (not necessarily blind) in the proposer or the authority, and moral allegiance. In this connexion, Locke is not clear; he is hazy as to what should, and what should not, be included in reason, once he has found room within it for both formal logic, which recognises no 'matter of thought' or differences of category, and the empirical method of science. Indeed, at an earlier stage than this, in the logical order of his thinking, he presents what might be called "a view before dawn", when he pertinently and sagely, if vaguely, remarks, *à propos* of ideas of relation, that "were we attentively to consider them, they might lead us further than at first, perhaps, we could have imagined" (*Essay*, etc., II. xii. § 8). Locke was sound but unclear; an inconsistent Lockean, on the theological side of his philosophy, he nevertheless prepared the way for Butler, with his pregnant saying "probability is the guide of life", which can now be broadened into 'probability is the foundation of science'.

Note L.   *A priori, necessary, self-evident, contingent, possible.*

A PRIORI.

It has been argued already that, if *a priori* mean 'contributed by the mind itself', and denote subjective functions other than reception of impressions, while knowledge means thought valid of Actuality, there is no *a priori* knowledge. There are but *a priori* functionings involved in knowing: factors of knowledge that are not of themselves knowledge. The antithesis between *a priori* and empirical knowledge, when *a priori* refers exclusively to the source and origination of knowledge, is fictitious. There is no more empirical knowledge without the *a priori* factors, than there is purely *a priori* knowledge without (originally) the sensory factor. Knowledge—even of universals —is evoked by sensa, though not procured by bare sensatio. If there be any necessity characterising our empirical knowledge, it is but that of the psychological inevitableness, for us men, of the synthetic forms, etc., which our minds supply, when constituting Objects and judging about them.

But there is another usage of the phrase *a priori*, in which, not psychological causation, but logical ground of truth, becomes the central reference. Kant sometimes speaks of *a priori* knowledge as concerned, not with what merely is, but with what must be; whose universality is not the generality ensured by the like functioning of human minds, but absolute universality, bespeaking necessity. Thus the *a priori* truth is the necessary truth, or the truth whose necessity we can discern; and *a priori* now stands in antithesis to the contingent. Its necessity is a logical or an intrinsic characteristic, and thus differs entirely from the psychological necessitation, involved in the *a priori* in its first signification. There the forms and categories, to which the matter of sense must conform in order to yield knowledge, supply an experience-organisation that is but anthropically inevitable. The Kantian epistemology is just saved, by its invocation of the shadowy thing *per se*, from being "a wider solipsism": synthetic judgements *a priori* are valid, because our minds cannot but give certain forms to what they apprehend. But when *a priori* means logically prior, the necessity, with which it is correlated, will be logical or implicational; and when *a priori* is said to denote a characteristic of an un-derived proposition, the necessity in question is said to be intrinsic. Here, indeed, are two new senses of *a priori*, not one. The former of them refers not to truth, but to logical connexion with other propositions, which, so far as logic knows or cares, may be either true or false. Logic may reveal the consequents or the presuppositions of a proposition; but neither of these will be proved to be truths, or validities, unless the initial proposition be true. Just as in inductive logic, as we shall see, two disparate kinds of probability are involved: the one, a characteristic of the assumed first principles, and the other, a logical relation of laws, etc., to these principles; so in deductive logic and what is called *a priori* reasoning—if it is to yield knowledge—two disparate kinds of necessity are involved. The one of these pertains to the implication-relations between a proposition and its presuppositions or consequents: the other characterises the proposition on which logic, such as should yield truth, operates, in order to reveal its implications. It is to this underived or intrinsic necessity, attributed to certain propositions, that the phrase *a priori* most commonly refers.

We need, then, to inquire what this necessity is, how it is discerned, and what classes of propositions are endowed with it: an investigation which is pursued in the next section of this Note, as well as in the discussion of rationalism, in Chap. IX. Meanwhile it is to be observed that '*a priori*' is ambiguous; and that, by confusion of its several meanings, rationalism stands to gain. We have found that the phrase is applied to functionings original to the mind, to propositions, to the ground and to the truth of propositions, to kinds of reasoning-process. Correspondingly, its several connotations can be identified with those of mind-contributed, original or innate, genetically independent of sense, functionally independent of the perceptual (once the conceptual has been distilled out of it), psychologically inevitable; logically implied or presupposed; self-evident; deductive.

NECESSARY.

The notion of the *a priori* has been observed to be connected with that of the necessary, and the uses of the latter term now need to be distinguished.

A. *As applied to Actuality.*

1. The necessity with which an effect follows on a cause, the Actual determination of events, etc., has already been shewn to be indescribable in terms of logical necessity, and to be independent of it. Immanent and transeunt causation are activity of substances; and determination has been found to be, in the last resort, a matter of the ultimate determin*ateness* of substances, an irrational surd.

2. Necessitation in Nature being the outcome of what the constituents of Reality happen to be, there is sense in saying that one event is necessitated by others: none in saying that original determinateness is necessary, or that the existence and nature of any substance are inherently necessary. Anything that can be conceived as existent, can equally be conceived as non-existent: essence, or idea, does not involve existence. This rule was believed to have one exception—God. Accordingly, God has been called a necessary Being; and this is perhaps implied in the curious phrase, *causa sui*. But to say that God necessarily exists, adds nothing to the assertion that He is self-subsistent. Necessity *per se*, so to speak, or unnecessitated and intrinsic necessity of being, is a non-significant notion, perhaps now obsolete. When necessity is further called absolute, a contradiction in terms arises; because the neces-

sary, as necessitated, is *ipso facto* dependent on something else. The All, or God, is "the last irrationality", or the ultimate inexplicability, rather than the logically necessary being.

3. When means are said to be necessary to ends, 'necessary' plainly means needful.

B. *As applied to sense-data and apprehension of them.*

Necessity is not usually predicated of the perception-judgement of individual experience. Yet there is a kind of necessitation in sensatio, or apprehension of the primarily posited, in which psychological certitude is at its maximum. The willy-nilly nature of involuntary sense-perception should find mention among the various sorts of necessity discussed by epistemologists, if only to point its difference from psychological determination. Sensa are not psychologically determined, as are images. For psychology proper, they are the most 'brute' of all facts: positings or irruptions that are inexplicable. Sensatio is a matter of the original determinateness of the pure ego, as an ultimate substance; but the sensatio of any one moment is not determined by the sensatio or the sensum of a previous experience, as is an image or (in part) a conation. In sensing, we cannot but apprehend what we do apprehend; we encounter the objective that is the basis of knowable Actuality: the peculiarity of our world, as distinct from other 'possible' worlds. Here, then, is necessitation of a kind that pertains to the empirical, that seems to have some resemblance to physical compulsion, and has nothing to do with the logically *a priori* and necessary.

C. *The necessary as the psychologically inevitable or determined.*

This kind of necessity has already been mentioned in connexion with one of the meanings of '*a priori*'. It is alogical, concerned with causes rather than grounds. It characterises all cognitive functioning: from belief that is groundless, though accompanied by psychological certitude, to universal knowledge, as described by Kant. The necessary, in this sense, is what the mind cannot help believing, entertaining or constituting, in virtue of its intrinsic capacities evoked by the objective.

D. *Necessity in the logical sense.*

Turning now from necessitation of the actual, and from psychological determination, to necessitation of the logical order, we may distinguish further senses in which 'necessity' is used, and types of propositions asserted to be necessary.

1. A necessary proposition has been described as one that is formally certified; and such propositions, may be derived or underived. The necessity of the derived proposition is mediated by the relation of implication. The first denotation of necessary to be distinguished, a logical sense of the term

being solely in view, is this relation of implication, in virtue of which one proposition necessarily follows from another or others.

2. But such necessary relation will not confer necessary truth upon a consequent, unless the premiss, from which it follows, be true. Consistency is not truth or validity; thought is not necessarily knowledge; the necessary consequent is not necessarily true. There must be premisses characterised by underived or intrinsic necessity, if there are to be necessarily true conclusions, however coercive their derivation-process. The second denotation of 'necessary' is, therefore, propositions characterised by an intrinsic quality of necessity. Several kinds of proposition have been adduced, as possessing this quality, and several criteria of necessity have been alleged.

(a) The analytical judgement, in which the predicate affirms nothing that is not already contained implicitly in the subject, is a clear case of the necessary. Formal certification is here at its maximum. But whether any such judgements are significant, or valid of Actuality, will depend on whether there are such Actual things as the conventionally defined subjects of analytical propositions. Some rationalists have made necessary truth co-extensive with analytical judgements; but whether such judgements are exhaustive of necessary truth, and whether existential judgements are ever purely analytical, are as yet open questions for us.

(b) Intuitive Inductions have better claim, than any other judgements, to be called necessary truths of reason or, at least, of understanding. The compulsion to accept them, is not psychological conditioning, but more akin to that enforcing the sense-judgement. It is in such inductions that the formal categories alone, as distinct from 'real' categories, are involved; and they seem to be as (ps) immediate and certain as is apprehension of the simplest relations, or objects of higher order. These intuitive inductions are instanced by the judgement, based on a single case, that red differs from yellow, and differs from yellow more than from orange: they involve explicit intuition of universals. This example is evidently experiential, or presupposes sense-experience; for the sensory is, in the first instance, the occasion of the intuition. In later experience the sensory objects need not be present, and the judgements then become formal. Formal intuitive induction occurs in judging that $3a + 3b = 3(a + b)$, or that 'some Mongols are Europeans' would imply 'some Europeans are Mongols'. As Mr Johnson has pointed out, these formal intuitions are not authoritatively or externally imposed imperatives [save in the sense of objective control] nor assumed rules. It is by them that we establish the fundamental principles of inference, and the "self-evident axioms" which form the major premisses of pure sciences, such as logic and mathematics. They would seem to be a unique class of propositions, in that they are as objectively compelled as are the simplest judgements of sense: are self-evident, in the sense of evident yet underived: and are different from all other so-called axioms, in not being conventional rules, prescribed by conation rather than by cognition. If so, they will be the whole stock in trade of rationalism. The sole criterion of the necessity we attribute to them, is that of 'self-evidence', which can only mean evidence such as we have no reason to believe to be (*ps*) *mediated*. And they are not analytical, but synthetic judgements. They would seem to be the only class of synthetic and existential judgements that are formally certified; whose truth or validity "shines by its own light" to certain subjects; and whose necessity is 'intrinsic', because not mediated *per aliud*, save in the sense that they cannot be intuited without, in the first instance, impressional occasioning.

(c) Other kinds of propositions than intuitive inductions and analytical propositions, have been alleged to possess intrinsic necessity and self-evidence: *e.g.* the so-called axioms of physics, etc. But this claim is discussed and refuted in Chap IX. Axioms, it was there found, are evolved products, the fittest of postulates that have survived, or that have become familiar and indispensable: their necessity is their needfulness *ad hoc*.

(d) Also other criteria of necessity than that of self-evidence, have sometimes been assigned. One such is 'impossibility of the opposite'. Hume once and for all dismissed this criterion, in so far as existential judgements are concerned. But, that the opposite of a pure or non-existential proposition contains a contradiction, is only knowable when the proposition in question is seen to be certain; the notions of contradiction and of impossibility ('inconceivability' is too vague a term to be worth including in this connexion) presuppose the notions of certainty and necessity.

A necessary proposition has sometimes been described as one that is true in all circumstances. But that quality, we are told, characterises propositional functions, rather than propositions. Lastly, necessary truths have been identified with timeless truths, though 'timeless' or 'eternal' is not a synonym for 'necessary', however coextensive may be their denotations.

It would seem then, to sum up, that necessity is applicable to implication, but this does not necessarily confer necessary truth on an implied proposition. In so far as synthetic propositions are necessary, in respect of truth, they must either be, or be implied by, intuitive inductions, and not be conventions or verbal definitions; for these are no more either true or false, than the rules we lay down for a game. The one manifest criterion of the certainty and necessity of these inductions, or apprehensions of the universal in the particular, is that of self-evidence: of objective control, akin to that of the individual sense-judgement. A sense-judgement is as certain and necessary as that, assuming the theory of number, $2 + 2 = 4$; while to the certainty and necessity of that judgement, is due the impossibility that $2 + 2 = 5$. Whether such self-evidence is all that can be meant by intrinsic or underived necessity, or whether self-evidence is but a mark or criterion of a necessity that is strictly indefinable, is a question better discussed during examination of the notion of self-evidence.

SELF-EVIDENT.

A proposition is not appropriately called evident, unless it be evident to some subject or subjects; for that is what evidence is. If subjects are abstracted, and evidence is conceived, not as a relation between a proposition and thinkers, but as an adjective intrinsically charácterising a proposition in itself, it is obvious that a wrong word is used to indicate what is meant; or a self-contradictory concept, like that of the phenomenon *per se*, is being sought. Aquinas observed[1] that "a thing can be self-evident in either of two ways; on the one hand, self-evident in itself, though not to us; on the other hand, self-evident in itself, and to us". In the former case, which Aquinas illustrates by the analytical judgement, what is really meant, by 'self-evidence', is logical necessity of the unmediated kind: which may subsist, whether recognised or not, and which *would be* evident to anyone understanding the terms of the proposition. But it is an abuse of language to call this self-*evidence*, if the truth appears evident to no one.[2] More important than the question of verbal propriety, however, is what the phrase, which does not mean what it says, is intended to connote. This is not difficult to ascertain; it has already been indicated. What gives the so-called self-evidence, or 'evidence in itself', to a truth, is its underivedness (by us) from other truth. Underivedness or non-inferability, however, is as much a psychological matter as evidentness, and so should be beside the question: indeed evidence to us, is said, by those who speak of 'self-evidence in itself', to be but a *cause* of our believ*ing*—of our certitude, not of the certainty of the proposition. If a logical ground for this certainty were assignable, the truth would not be *self*-evident. What is called self-evidence in itself, must therefore be that 'intrinsic' characteristic, in virtue of which the judgement is true and formally certified, not *per aliud* but *per se*. But here there is a reading, into propositions, of what is conditioned by *our* mentality, a mere contingency. What is *per aliud*, for us, need not be so, for God. Now the intuitive induction is only certified by its evidence, properly so called: there remains, therefore, as truth possessing the alleged self-evidence in itself, only the analytical judgement, concerned with the definition of concepts and words. For existential judgements, or rather judgements referring to Actuality, are based on sensory intuition and are synthetic. The logical self-coherence of the concept 'man', if it is to be significant of Actuality, cannot be established without knowledge of men; and if it denote beings 'born of woman', the analytical judgement 'man is a rational being' is not universally true. As for analytical judgements belonging to the pure sciences, it may be questioned whether they are so immediate, so destitute of the *per aliud* element, so true *per se*, so independent of thinkers,

[1] *Summa Theologica*, Part I, Q. ii (E.T., Fathers of the Eng. Dominican Province, I. p. 20).
[2] The self-evident is then the invisibly obvious!

as is assumed. They depend on nominal convention or definition of their subject: this convention withdrawn, they and their 'truth' also vanish. No system of geometry is more true than another; for truth, as predicated of such a system, is but logical relatedness to prescribed conventions. Validity of the Actual is quite another affair, determined ultimately by sense-experience; and there we are concerned with evidence, not with the so-called self-evidence that has nothing to do with evidentness. To say that the difference between two tunes is self-evident, while there are persons who cannot tell the one from the other, is but a roundabout and paradoxical way of asserting that the tunes are different; while knowledge that they are different, involves acquaintance with them. Thus in self-evidence of the supposedly logical kind, the 'evidence' is dismissed by abstraction; the element of 'self' alone is retained: and that, in pure analytical judgements, is matter of verbal convention.

If, in using the phrase 'self-evident', we do not intend to be in earnest with its latter half, we are but uselessly misappropriating a term to a purpose for which it is superfluous; if we intend to take 'evident' seriously, we pass from logical to psychological conditions. The self-evident is then what coerces believing, or acceptance as true, without mediation of inference, etc., in so far as reflective analysis can see. The (ψ) standpoint alone is relevant, and the (ps) standpoint must be abandoned, else confusion is inevitable. What is self-evident, is then seen to be contingent on the thinker's level of experience-organisation, his knowledge, prejudices, discrimination and so forth. Self-evidence is now no longer a criterion of [Objective] truth. Much that is (ps) false, has been accepted as (ψ) self-evident; and inductively established propositions have sometimes turned out to be 'necessary', if not self-evident. To omniscience, truth would be necessary that to us is contingent; and self-evident, that to us is undiscovered. Much that we commonly call self-evident, is but evident to reason, at the stage of developement to which ours has attained. The deists of the eighteenth century took many propositions, now convicted of falsity, to be self-evident to all mankind. The realist commonly takes what is but evident to socialised experience, to be over-social and absolute, because it happens to be mediated over-individually. Then 'necessity', of the psychological kind, is regarded as necessity of the logical order, as intrinsic to the Object or the proposition, because it has been mentally abstracted from connexion with subjects. Removed from the context in which it has originated, the abstraction becomes one of the growing number of 'indefinables' which happen, for no reason assigned, to manifest themselves in extraneous criteria. Abstractionism avoided, the criterion becomes the essence, while definability or intelligibility is preserved.

CONTINGENT.

This term, like 'necessary', has been bestowed on both being and thought, on Actuality and truth of propositions.

(A) As applied to Actuality, contingency has been predicated of it as a whole, and also of events within the whole.

(1) If nothingness cannot be the *prius* or the fount of being, if there be no derivation of the Actual out of the possible, and if 'absolutely necessary being' be a non-significant phrase, there is no more sense in calling the universe, with its determinateness, contingent, than in calling it necessary. These terms are applicable only to things or happenings within the whole; and then, until more precise definition is given, they are synonyms. That *y* is contingent on *x*, means that *y* is determined by *x*. But when contingency has been affirmed of the world and of its foundation, what appears to be meant, is that the empiric or Actual, with its determinate 'matter', is not deducible from, or conditioned by, a *prius* of logical law or of 'form'. We are then carried no further than the statement that Actuality exists. In a more particular and meaningful sense, the theist uses 'contingency' to connote the world's dependence on God, as contrasted with self-subsistence. But in the old argument *e contingentia mundi*, the false supposition was involved, that the contingent world logically implies, as its correlative, an 'absolutely necessary' Being.

(2) More commonly, contingency is asserted of things or events within the whole of Actuality. In its broadest sense it then denotes the alogical: the posited content which cannot be condensed out of the 'possible', or be derived from the pure concept, the logical axiom. The "contingent facts of history" were disparaged by Lessing, in respect of evidential value for theology, in comparison with eternal truths of reason.

A second sense is imported into 'contingent', when it denotes the event, the opposite of which is possible: *i.e.* conceivable, without involving such contradiction as is involved in the round square. It then stands in antithesis to the necessary: *i.e.* that whose opposite is impossible. In such usage there is apt to be confusion of logical with Actual determination: some overlooking of the truth, that any particular happening is determined by the course of Nature, so that its nature and occurrence are Actually necessitated and could not, in the circumstances, be other than they are. Conceivability of the opposite, or of any other happening, abstracts altogether from the conditioning circumstances; and bare 'possibility', so arrived at, is irrelevant, if it be anything at all.

'Contingent' has a third sense, when applied to an event, the happening or the nature of which we cannot, by means of known laws, connect with its determinants. Lightning 'necessarily' follows the path of least resistance, but the wind "bloweth where it listeth". The possibility of other happenings, in place of the event, is only supposable through our ignorance of the conditions. Could we read off all the causal connexions involved, there would be no games of chance.

In these several meanings, the contingent is the alogical that is not deducible from pure or formal concept and laws. But though not *so* determined, it *is* determined or necessitated, if there be any validity in causal postulates and laws.

The last meaning to be mentioned turns on distinction between kinds of causal determination. Ward's phrase, "contingency at the heart of things", signifies that the world is not a mechanism; that its course is shaped by spontaneous or self-determined creativeness, directed by interest, desire, final cause, rather than by *vis a tergo* alone. The contingent, in this special sense, must baffle prediction in some cases, because its conditioning is partly beyond human ken; it cannot wholly be formulated in laws, because the unique and historic, or once-occurring, cannot be absorbed into the repetitions and uniformities which alone can be described by laws.

(B) Further meanings of contingency emerge when we consider its application to truths and propositions—its logical usage.

The sense-given being contingent, in the sense of alogical, the simplest perception-judgements or existential propositions will be a class of contingent truths. These are not governed by the principle of contradiction nor characterised by formal necessity; their certification is experimental. Hence Leibniz placed them in antithesis to analytical judgements, and distinguished truths of fact from necessary and eternal verities.

But within the empirically certified, a distinction has been drawn between contingent judgements, and others characterised by nomic necessity. Laws, of course, do not compel happenings. They state how things determine one another. But laws of Nature have been diversely conceived. Some take them to be but descriptions of hitherto unvarying relations; 'universals' of observed fact, established by enumeration, or (more commonly and more tentatively) by problematic induction: statements of what has been, and what we may expect. Others have seen in them statements about the 'possible', as well as the observed Actual: expressing, not unvaryingness, but unconditional invariability. Laws, according to this view, express what always has been and will be, because it must be: not merely that all observed x's are y's, but that any x would be a y. This is what is meant by nomic necessity. The 'universal of law', to borrow Mr Johnson's language while presenting his teaching, is wider than the 'universal of fact'—*i.e.* of recorded observation—and implies it. But the implication does not exist in the converse direction: a fact, describable as a '*pqr* which is an x', may represent a contingency; and room be left for the turning up of a *pqr* that is not an x. Science always hopes to bring any fact, that is in this sense contingent, to its place in a deterministic scheme, and so to shew its nomic necessity. But, short of full knowledge as to the ultimate constituents of the world and their relations, such as would need to be forthcoming for inductive methods to yield categorical rather than problematic generalisations, this nomic necessity attaches to laws, as descriptions: it is not certainly known to attach to the facts described. The contingency that may beset the fact described as 'a *pqr* which is an *x*', it would appear, would be removed, if the fact could theoretically be described more adequately as 'a *pqruvw* which is necessarily an *x*'. The contingency then becomes a necessity. Yet the conditions *uvw* have been added to *pqr*, because *pqr* does not nomically necessitate *uvw*, or because the relation of *uvw* to *pqr* is nomically contingent. Whether the character *x*, of the given event, is necessary or contingent, is unanswerable. It is contingent, relatively to the incomplete description *pqr*; necessary, relatively to the description *pqruvw*, if that be complete: in other words, if the character *x* be dependent on an enumerable set of characters, finite in number. Till that admits of demonstration, there cannot be talk of known necessitation in Nature, expressible in necessary law.

'Contingent truths', to sum up, is a phrase denoting (1) truths of fact which, in virtue of their Actual content (ultimately impressional) over and above their form, are not derivable from propositions relating empty concepts, and which have been (as a matter of fact) derived from percepts or fact-judgements; (2) truths of fact such as, in the stage of scientific theory attained at a given time, are not reducible to nomic expression, presuming to state ontological and necessary connexions between the characteristics of Actual things.

POSSIBLE.

It may be well, in approaching consideration of possibility, to remind ourselves of how the general notion of the possible emerges from our original knowledge of the actual, which is actually prior. The human mind has the mysterious capacity to apprehend the imaginal; but, so far as knowledge or experience warrants us to believe, only *after* perceptual cognition involving the impressional. We have the further capacity of attending to the form of a percept or image, as distinct, and abstracted from, its impressional or its sense-bound content: in other words, the capacity of ideation. There is no psychological reason to believe that ideas, as forms dissociated from matter, or as essences lacking impressional positing, are Actualities, or 'exist' as Objects when not attended to; though they are then objective, not subjective acts or states. But, doubtless owing to their instrumentality in thought and reasoning, they have, from the early days of philosophy, been assumed to have such existence, independent of our thinking or attention. Now the idea is a frame which fits other perceptual objects, like in kind to that from which it was abstracted by subjective activity; or it is an essence, or totality of conceived qualities, that conceivably might be encountered in a future percept.

Detachable, by thought, from one percept, and capable of turning up again in another, it is an object of possible experience—experience that we *may* have. Such is the primary signification of the 'possible': the essence or the form, that by itself or as abstracted from concrete fact, does not exist, in the same sense as does the actuality.

Developed thought, after acquaintance with a large diversity of percepts, can abstract particular qualities and recombine them into ideas or 'possible' —*i.e.* imaginable or conceivable—essences, with indefinite variety. Knowing space of three dimensions, we can conceive other spaces: so, without assignable limits, we can accurately trace, as in pure mathematics, relations between non-existent essences or forms; and we can suppose, or vaguely conceive, an indefinite number of possible worlds. In its primordial and most general sense, then, we may say that whatever can be imagined or ideated or conceived, is possible. The primary antithesis to the possible will accordingly be the actual. Presumably, in this widest sense, the round square is to be counted among the possibilities.

When such self-incompatibilities are ruled out, we meet with the first more restricted sense of 'possibility': and one that is historically important. Obedience to the law of contradiction then becomes the one criterion of the possible. In other words, the possible is the ideational that is devoid of internal inconsistency. Leibniz, with whom 'possibility' is a shibboleth, in one typical passage[1] writes: "I call *possible* everything which is perfectly conceivable and which has consequently an essence, an idea, without considering whether the remainder of things allows it to become existent". The opposite to the axiom 'things equal to the same thing are equal', is impossible: the opposite to 'I am now sitting here' is possible, in the sense that there is no contradiction in the proposition itself, however invalid it be of present fact. Hence Leibniz taught that the truth of judgements of fact, or of contingent things, is not grounded in their possibility. They cannot, it follows, be derived from the law of contradiction. They must be grounded on another principle, the law of sufficient reason: and ultimately, on the selective and (logically) arbitrary will of God. Leibniz here follows Descartes and Duns Scotus: human reason, in the sense of logical *ratio*, is inadequate to read the world, because the nature of the world depends ultimately on what, for reason *quâ ratio*, is fortuitous. Spinoza, as if shocked at the Cartesian theology, which indeed subverts the Cartesian epistemology, makes reason all-sufficient by cancelling will or logical arbitrariness in God, and maintaining that everything possible is realised in the world; so that the contingent becomes the necessary or, rather, contingency is excluded.

The logically possible, according to Leibniz, may be Actually impossible. It is logically possible that I be now sitting there, whereas I am sitting here.

[1] *Lettre à Bourguet*, quoted by Latta, *Leibniz, The Monadology, etc.*, p. 63.

Either proposition is logically self-consistent; the two are not consistent
with each other, and but one is consistent with certain other truths. In
order to be Actual, the possible must be *compossible*, *i.e.* in conformity, with
other truth or with the Actual system. The axiologist, by the way, who
regards 'oughtness-to-be' as an intrinsic quality independent of everything
else whatever, overlooks this requisite of compossibility with some universe
of Actuality. Thus the opposites of contingent truths, *i.e.* of truths of fact,
though logically possible, are impossible, in the sense of non-compossible.
Only the possible that is compossible, can have existence.

Compossibility, however, is not enough, of itself, to confer existence or
Actuality on the possible. Even a possible, in the sense of an ideational,
world must have general laws, in order to be a world: there is method in the
madness of the pure mathematician. What this further element is, we have
seen already. Existence, as Kant affirmed, is the absolute positing of a thing,
distinguishing it from any and every predicate, or from mere essence.
'Posited' means, in the first instance, given in experience as actual or as
matter of fact, as distinct from possible in thought; and nothing else, we
may add, can be known to be Actual, but what such data involve or presuppose. Obviously, in *ordine cognoscendi*, the possible presupposes, and is
derived from, the actual. Remove the actual, *i.e.* think it away, and there
remains no basis for discussion of what is possible. To deny all existence and
to affirm any possibility, itself involves real incompatibility, if no logical
contradiction. *In ordine essendi*, also, the possible cannot be prior; since no
concept involves existence, and therefore none can yield it. Timeless universals
are vestal virgins. We can get from the actual to the possible; but not back.
Actuality is not the *complementum possibilitatis*, but the *condition sine qua non*
of the ideal 'existence' of possibility. Leibniz partially saw that this is so.
His systematiser, Wolff, endeavoured to deduce the principle of sufficient
reason from the principle of contradiction, and to derive the actual from the
possible: and so, after receding in Leibniz's system, the tide of rationalism
rose again to its highest.

In keeping with the Wolffian endeavour, is one side of Leibniz's own
teaching, which serves to introduce another, if now an obsolete, sense of
'possibility'. In his essay *On the ultimate origination of things* (1697) he
would derive contingent truth from eternal, essential or metaphysical truth;
and in the attempt he affirms that "in possibility or essence itself, there is a
certain need of existence or, so to speak, a claim to exist": that "essence of
itself tends to existence". This explicit assumption of the logical and Actual
priority of the possible, underlies also some of the teaching of *The Monadology*. Thus (§ 54) Leibniz speaks of each possible thing as having the right
to aspire to existence, in proportion to the amount of perfection it contains
in germ. Possibility is now potentiality, implying some potency: and the
possible has already Real existence, of some sort intermediate between ideal

'existence' (non-existence) and Actuality. There is sense in applying potentiality to Actualities, as yet only on the way to becoming what they shall be,
e.g. to the acorn as potential oak-tree; but none in applying it to the non-
Actual, the 'possible' in the senses previously discussed. In whatever way
the possible is contrasted with the Actual, it presupposes the actual, as does
the conceivable: for all concepts are derived from actuality, in the first
instance. Similarly, when the possible is contrasted with the necessary, it
presupposes necessity. That $3 + 2 = 6$, is impossible, because the identification
of the sum of 3 and 2 with 5, is necessary. A proposition that does not conflict with a necessary proposition, is formally possible; one which is not
included in a nomic description, is nomically possible; and, lastly, one which
is not known to be false, though it must be either true or false, is said to
be possible in yet another sense—*i.e.* in Mr Johnson's terminology, epis-
temically. The possibility of the proposition is then but another name for
the fact that we are ignorant of decisive *pros* and *cons*.

Note M. *The Principle of Uniformity: Uniformity of Nature.*

The principle of uniformity, or what has here been called the causal law,
which asserts that like causes produce like effects, is only precise when cause
and effect are both cross-sections of the world-course, including all contemporaneous events. In this precise form, the principle is of no use to working
science which, in order to be predictive, presupposes a nexus between events,
as particular and isolable parts of the whole universe; or between states
constituent of whole states: otherwise no particular laws could be found
or stated. Science, in short, needs to speak of particular causes; and likeness
or sameness, in order to attain the ideal limit of identity, in all respects save
position in space and time, involves negligibility of other differences: which,
in turn, presupposes uniformity of causal determination, and parsimony as to
kinds of substances. Induction, as used in science, is sometimes said to involve
only particular uniformities, not universal uniformity throughout Nature;
but this only appears to be so at first sight. To isolate particular causes and
uniformities, involves ascertaining the negligibility of others; and this negligibility, or irrelevance, depends in turn on isolability. It involves the separate
activities of constituent elements, substances or determinants, throughout
Nature; it implies that the world has what may be called fibrous structure.
In making these conditions or presuppositions of the rationality of induction
explicit, the recent logicians, whose work is described in Chap. xi, may be
said to have disentangled the independent principles that were but implicit
in the old vague principle of uniformity, confusedly amalgamated and undefined. Similarly, in emphasising that these ultimate presuppositions of
induction are in some sense 'probable', they have made more precise what
had with indefiniteness been realised before: witness W. James' statement,

that uniformity has to be sought in spite of the most rebellious appearances, and that our conviction of its truth is far more like a religious faith than assent to demonstration. We have lately become enabled to see, what precisely are the conditions of the world being rational, in the sense in which science seeks rationality: the assumptions that are logically inevitable, *if* we are to persist in belief that the world *is* rational through and through.

'Uniformity of Nature' is an ambiguous phrase, until we have specified exactly what is to be understood by 'Nature'. 'Nature' may conceivably mean 'the perceptual proper', the worlds of individual percipients; though perhaps the word never bears this sense. It may, again, mean the ontal, the world *per se*, or as independent of the knowing-processes of all subjects; and it doubtless is occasionally used with this reference. Most generally, however, by 'Nature' is understood the common, yet so-called phenomenal, world: the ontal as phenomenally apprehended, a common world conceptually elaborated out of the individually perceptual, *i.e.* the only truly phenomenal. And then we have to reckon with all the varying degrees of abstractness, from that of unscientific common sense to that of theoretical physics. Thus a particular theory of knowledge is presupposed, in any specific definition we may assign to 'Nature'. This word may have several precise meanings, whereas in common speech we assume there is but one.

In discussing uniformity, as predicated of Nature, we may confine ourselves to the last-mentioned meaning, or rather class of meanings, that 'Nature' has been said to be conceivably capable of bearing. Uniformity is irrelevant to the first, and will perhaps be deemed out of place in connexion with the second: for as to Nature, independent of the 'knowledge' of knowing subjects, we know but little, according to some philosophers, and can know nothing, according to others. As for the uniformity with which science deals, it may be said that it is the uniformity of a conceptual framework, skeleton, or diagram of the Nature that is concretely perceived by individuals. The Objects and events between which laws and uniformities subsist, are always more or less abstract and ideal; types rather than concrete particulars: and their abstractness varies between wide limits. Assertions purporting to be of sameness or identity, are really only assertions of indiscernibility of diversity; and it is conceivable that much uniformity could be found in such a world, even if Nature's elements were indefinitely diverse. Again, we have no scientific knowledge as to the world as a whole, or as to the totality of things. But more important than these reservations is the fact that, even in science, we are not dealing with the ontal world directly, or with the world as independent of experients, but with a world which experients 'make out of' the ontal. The correct phrase, therefore, is 'uniformity of Experience', or 'uniformity of Nature as Experienced'—'Experience' denoting common, so-called universal, conceptualised, experience. And since the Subjective factor in Experience is as uneliminable as the Objective (and objective), it is a question, whether uniformity is constituted by the Objective alone, or the Subjective alone, or whether it is 'emergent' from the cooperation of the two. It is obvious that the Subjective element cannot be ignored altogether. We can cause uniformity to emerge, to some extent, out of 'chaos'. Events, diverse in themselves, might be found alike, in respect of being helpful or hurtful to conative percipients; and selective attention, seeking the helpful, avoiding the hurtful, and ignoring the indifferent, could not only bring about the more frequent experiencing of the helpful, or the more frequent occurrence of it for the experient, but could thus secure for itself some orderliness of environment. The oneness of the thing, of which we predicate likeness to other things, or recurrence at intervals, is also relative to our *tempo*, etc. Within these limits the experience that organises, but does not originate, 'Nature' may set up uniformities in experience so that uniformity, in Nature as experienced, may be the outcome of interest and selection. Furthermore, uniformity does not necessarily imply mechanicalness: there are uniformities in the affairs of human beings, whose acts are characterised by uniqueness and spontaneity. Nature's uniformity may conceivably be of the same kind: a matter of approximately unvarying statistical averages, in which uniqueness or irreducible diversity is eliminated, but not annihilated.

Nevertheless, salutary as these cautions may be, the subjective origination of uniformity in Nature or in Experience, does not seem capable of carrying us so far as Dr Ward, to whom the suggestion is due, would seem to have supposed; nor can his assertion, unduly agnostic for him, that as to ontal Nature we know nothing and can predicate nothing, save with futility, be accepted without question. Besides the likenesses, etc., that we can constitute by our interest and valuation, there are likenesses, etc.—as Ward abundantly recognises elsewhere—that are simply read off from the data and are entirely independent, as to their subsistence, of any subjective interest. And further, the abstractions which science discusses, so long as they are regarded as *in rebus*, enter into the constitution of Actuality. The relations that subsist between objects must have their analogues in the things *per se*, of which objects are appearances. In other words, if phenomenal Nature be characterised by uniformity, there must be a corresponding degree of uniformity in ontal Nature. It need not, however, be absolutely rigid, exact, or the outcome of mechanical causation. The statistical method does not enable us to discover absolute uniformities; still less does it enable us to predict individual behaviour or concrete particular cases, save with, at most, approximate truth. There may be individual divergences from type, even if so slight as to be, for the purposes of science, negligible. The negligible is not necessarily the non-existent, and rigid or exact conformity of Nature's processes to law may be but apparent. Differences may cancel one another in the statistical average. Science, then, does not warrant the conclusion, that any one process of a given kind is absolutely uniform with others of the same class; room is left for endless variety of individual behaviour in natural objects, of which science takes no account, either because such variety is of no significance for science such as would but calculate and control, or because measurement is insufficiently delicate to detect it. It is in accordance with the scientific spirit, to believe in uniformity just so far as we can trace it, and no further: beyond the empirical limit, we have as much right to plant one belief as another, or else no right to plant any belief at all.

INDEX